Johannes · De · montevilla ·

The Travels
of
Sir John Mandeville

with three narratives in illustration of it:

The Voyage of Johannes de Plano Carpini

The Journal of Friar William de Rubruquis

The Journal of Friar Odoric

New York
Dover Publications, Inc.

Published in the United Kingdom by Constable
and Company, Limited, 10 Orange Street, London
W.C.2.

This Dover edition, first published in 1964, is an
unabridged and unaltered republication of the
edition first published by Macmillan and Co., Limited, London, in 1900. The publisher is grateful to
the Library of the University of Cincinnati for
furnishing a copy of the work for purposes of re-
production.

To the present edition have been added all 119
woodcut illustrations from Anton Sorg's second
Augsburg edition of Mandeville, 1481, as reproduced in Volume 4 of *Der Bilderschmuck der Früh-
drucke,* by Albert Schramm, Deutsches Museum für
Buch und Schrift, Verlag von Karl W. Hiersemann,
Leipzig, 1921.

This edition is published by special arrangement
with Macmillan and Co., Limited, London.

Library of Congress Catalog Card Number 64-18859

Manufactured in the United States of America

Dover Publications, Inc.
180 Varick Street
New York 14, N.Y.

BIBLIOGRAPHICAL NOTE

THE Travels of Sir John Mandeville were edited anonymously in 1725, in the version for which a 'Cotton' manuscript in the British Museum is our only extant authority. From 1499, when they were first printed by Wynkyn de Worde, the *Travels* had enjoyed great popularity in England, as in the rest of Europe; but the printed editions before 1725 had all followed an inferior translation (with an unperceived gap in the middle of it), which had already gained the upper hand before printing was invented. Another manuscript in the British Museum, belonging to the 'Egerton' collection, preserves yet a third version, and this was printed for the first time by Mr. G. F. Warner, for the Roxburghe Club, in 1889, together with the original French text, and an introduction, and notes, which it would be difficult to over-praise. In editing the Egerton version, Mr. Warner made constant reference to the Cotton manuscript, which he quoted in many of his critical notes. But with this exception, no one appears to have looked at the manuscript since it was first printed, and subsequent writers have been content to take the correctness of the 1725 text for granted, priding themselves, apparently, on the care with which they reproduced all the superfluous eighteenth century capitals with which every line is dotted. Unluckily, the introduction of needless capitals was the least of the original editor's crimes, for he omits words and phrases, and sometimes (a common trick with careless copyists) a whole sentence or clause which happens to end with the same word as its predecessor. He was also a deliberate as well as a careless criminal, for the paragraph about the Arabic alphabet at the end of Chapter XV. being difficult to reproduce, he omitted it altogether, and not only this, but the last sentence of Chapter XVI. as well, because it contained a reference to it.

That it has been left to the editor (who has hitherto rather avoided that name) of a series of popular reprints to restore whole phrases and sentences to the text of a famous book is not very creditable to English scholarship, and amounts, indeed, to a personal grievance; for to produce an easily readable text of an old book without a good critical edition to work on must always be difficult, while in the case of a work with the peculiar reputation of 'Mandeville' the difficulty is greatly increased. Had a critical edition existed, it would have been permissible for a popular text to botch the few sentences in which the tail does not agree with the beginning, and to correct obvious mistranslation without special note. But 'Mandeville' has an old reputation as the 'Father of English Prose,' and when no trustworthy text is available, even a popular editor must be careful lest he bear false witness. The Cotton version is, therefore, here reproduced, 'warts and all,' save in less than a dozen instances, where a dagger indicates that, to avoid printing nonsense, an obvious flaw has been corrected either from the 'Egerton' manuscript or the French text. When a word still survives, the modern form is adopted: thus 'Armenia' and 'soldiers' are here printed instead of 'Ermony' and 'soudiours.' But a new word is never substituted for an old one, and the reader who is unfamiliar with obsolete words, such as 'Almayne' (Germany) or 'dere' (harm),— there are surprisingly few for a book written five centuries ago,—must consult the unpretentious glossary. Of previous editions, that of 1725 and the reprints of it, including those of Halliwell-Phillipps, profess, though they do not do so, to reproduce the manuscript exactly. Thomas Wright's edition is really a translation, and that issued in 1895 by Mr. Arthur Layard often comes near to being one, though the artist-editor has shown far more feeling for the old text than his too whimsical illustrations might lead one to expect. It is hoped that the plan here adopted preserves as much as possible of the fourteenth century flavour, with the minimum of disturbance to the modern reader's enjoyment.

The plan of this series forbids the introduction of critical disquisitions, and I am thus absolved from attempting any theory as to how the tangled web of the authorship of the book should be unravelled. The simple faith of our childhood in a Sir John Mandeville, really born at St. Albans, who travelled, and told in an English book what he saw and heard, is shattered to pieces. We now know that our Mandeville is a compilation, as clever and artistic as Malory's 'Morte d'Arthur,' from the works of earlier writers, with few, if any, touches added from personal experience; that it was written in French, and rendered into Latin before it attracted the notice of a series of English translators (whose own accounts of the work they were translating are not to be trusted), and that the name Sir John Mandeville was a *nom de guerre* borrowed from a real knight of this name who lived in the reign of Edward II. Beyond this it is difficult to unravel the knot, despite the ends which lie temptingly loose. A Liège chronicler, Jean d'Outremeuse, tells a story of a certain Jean de Bourgogne revealing on his deathbed that his real name was Sir John Mandeville ; and in accordance with this story there is authentic record of a funeral inscription to a Sir John Mandeville in a church at Liège. Jean de Bourgogne had written other books and had been in England, which he had left in 1322 (the year in which "Mandeville" began his travels), being then implicated in killing a nobleman, just, as the real Sir John Mandeville had been implicated ten years before in the death of the Earl of Cornwall. We think for a moment that we have an explanation of the whole mystery in imagining that Jean de Bourgogne (he was also called Jean à la Barbe, Joannes Barbatus) had chosen to father his compilation on Mandeville, and eventually merged his own identity in that of his pseudonym. But Jean d'Outremeuse, the recipient of his deathbed confidence, is a tricky witness, who may have had a hand in the authorship himself, and there is no clear story as yet forthcoming. But the book remains, and is none the less delightful for the mystery which attaches to it, and little less important in the history of English literature as a translation than as an original work. For though a translation it stands as the first, or almost the first, attempt to bring secular subjects within the domain of English prose, and that is enough to make it mark an epoch.

Mandeville is here reprinted rather as a source of literary pleasure than as a medieval contribution to geography, and it is therefore no part of our duty to follow Mr. Warner in tracking out the authorities to whom the compiler had recourse in successive chapters. But as there was some space in this volume to spare, and a very pleasant method of filling it suggested itself, a threefold supplement is here printed, which may be of some use even to serious students, and is certainly very good literature. When Richard Hakluyt, at the end of the sixteenth century, was compiling his admirable work, ' The Principall Navigations, Voiages, and Discoveries of the English Nation, made by sea or over land, within the compasse of these 1500 yeeres,' he boldly overstepped the limits set forth on his title-page, and printed in the original Latin, with translations into good Elizabethan English, the narratives of three of the earlier travellers, all of them foreigners, from whom the compiler of Mandeville had drawn most freely. "And because," he tells us, " these north-eastern regions beyond Volga, by reason of the huge deserts, the cold climate, and the barbarous incivilitie of the people there inhabiting, were never yet thoroughly traveiled by any of our Nation, nor sufficiently known unto us; I have here annexed unto the said Englishman's [1] traveils the rare and memorable journals of two friers who were some of the first Christians that travailed farthest that way, and brought home most particular intelligence of all things which they had seen." These two friars were John de Plano Carpini, sent on an embassy to the great Chan by Pope Innocent IV. in 1246, and William de Rubruquis, who travelled in the interests of Louis IX. of France in 1253. In the same way in his Second Part, Hakluyt adds ' The Voyage of Frier Beatus Odoricus to Asia Minor, Armenia, Chaldaea, Persia, India, China, and other remote parts,' Odoric being a Franciscan of Pordenone in North Italy, who dictated an account of his travels in 1330. Anyone who

---

[1] Not Mandeville, but an anonymous sojourner among the Tartars, whose story fills a page and a half in Hakluyt.

compares these three narratives (more particularly Odoric's) with Mandeville's Travels will see how the compiler used his materials, and they have also very considerable interest of their own.

As this volume of the Library of English Classics has brought with it an unusual editorial responsibility, I may be permitted an editor's privilege in making two acknowledgments. The first, to my friend Mr. G. F. Warner, my readers must share with me, for without the help of his splendid edition of the 'Egerton' version and the French text, the popular 'Mandeville' could not have been attempted. My second acknowledgment is of a more personal nature. Roxburghe Club books are never easy to obtain, and the few copies of the Mandeville allowed to be sold were priced at £20 each. In noticing Mr. Warner's edition in the 'Academy' (from a borrowed copy), I remarked rather ruefully that the gratitude which students of moderate means could feel towards the Club for printing so valuable a work was somewhat tempered by this little matter of the price. I was then helping Mr. Charles Elton with the catalogue of his library, and on reading my review, he wrote me a pretty letter to say that by the rules of the Club he was the possessor of a second copy, and that he thought I was the best person to give it to. Students who have to think a good many times before they spend £20 on a book do not often receive such a present from wealthy book-lovers ; and at the risk of obtruding more of my own concerns than my rough-and-ready editing entitles me to do, I cannot send out this 'Mandeville,' within a few weeks of Mr. Elton's too early death, without telling this little story of his kindness.

A. W. POLLARD.

CONTENTS

CONTENTS

CONTENTS

THE TRAVELS OF
SIR JOHN MANDEVILLE

THE TRAVELS OF
SIR JOHN MANDEVILLE

THE PROLOGUE

FOR as much as the land beyond the sea, that is to say the Holy Land, that men call the Land of Promission or of Behest, passing all other lands, is the most worthy land, most excellent, and lady and sovereign of all other lands, and is blessed and hallowed of the precious body and blood of our Lord Jesu Christ ; in the which land it liked him to take flesh and blood of the Virgin Mary, to environ that holy land with his blessed feet ; and there he would of his blessedness enombre him in the said blessed and glorious Virgin Mary, and become man, and work many miracles, and preach and teach the faith and the law of Christian men unto his children ; and there it liked him to suffer many reprovings and scorns for us ; and he that was king of heaven, of air, of earth, of sea and of all things that be contained in them, would all only be clept king of that land, when he said, *Rex sum Judeorum*, that is to say, ' I am King of Jews ' ; and that land he chose before all other lands, as the best and most worthy land, and the most virtuous land of all the world : for it is the heart and the midst of all the world, witnessing the philosopher, that saith thus, *Virtus rerum in medio consistit*, that is to say, ' The virtue of things is in the midst ' ; and in that land he would lead his life, and suffer passion and death of Jews, for us, to buy and to deliver us from

3

pains of hell, and from death without end ; the which was
ordained for us, for the sin of our forme-father Adam,
and for our own sins also ; for as for himself, he had no
evil deserved : for he thought never evil ne did evil : and
he that was king of glory and of joy, might best in that
place suffer death ; because he chose in that land rather
than in any other, there to suffer his passion and his death.
For he that will publish anything to make it openly known,
he will make it to be cried and pronounced in the middle
place of a town ; so that the thing that is proclaimed and
pronounced, may evenly stretch to all parts : right so, he
that was former of all the world, would suffer for us at
Jerusalem, that is the midst of the world ; to that end and
intent, that his passion and his death, that was published
there, might be known evenly to all parts of the world.

See now, how dear he bought man, that he made after
his own image, and how dear he again-bought us, for the
great love that he had to us, and we never deserved it to
him.   For more precious chattel ne greater ransom ne
might he put for us, than his blessed body, his precious
blood, and his holy life, that he thralled for us ; and all he
offered for us that never did sin.

Ah dear God !   What love had he to us his subjects,
when he that never trespassed, would for trespassers
suffer death !   Right well ought us for to love and worship,
to dread and serve such a Lord ; and to worship and
praise such an holy land, that brought forth such fruit,
through the which every man is saved, but it be his own
default.   Well may that land be called delectable and
a fructuous land, that was be-bled and moisted with the
precious blood of our Lord Jesu Christ ; the which is the
same land that our Lord behight us in heritage.   And in
that land he would die, as seised, to leave it to us, his
children.

Wherefore every good Christian man, that is of power,
and hath whereof, should pain him with all his strength for to
conquer our right heritage, and chase out all the misbelieving men.   For we be clept Christian men, after Christ our
Father.   And if we be right children of Christ, we ought

for to challenge the heritage, that our Father left us, and do it out of heathen men's hands. But now pride, covetise, and envy have so inflamed the hearts of lords of the world, that they are more busy for to dis-herit their neighbours, more than for to challenge or to conquer their right heritage before-said. And the common people, that would put their bodies and their chattels, to conquer our heritage, they may not do it without the lords. For a sembly of people without a chieftain, or a chief lord, is as a flock of sheep without a shepherd; the which departeth and disperpleth and wit never whither to go. But would God, that the temporal lords and all worldly lords were at good accord, and with the common people would take this holy voyage over the sea! Then I trow well, that within a little time, our right heritage before-said should be reconciled and put in the hands of the right heirs of Jesu Christ.

And, for as much as it is long time passed, that there was no general passage ne voyage over the sea; and many men desire for to hear speak of the Holy Land, and have thereof great solace and comfort; I, John Mandeville, Knight, albeit I be not worthy, that was born in England, in the town of St. Albans, and passed the sea in the year of our Lord Jesu Christ, 1322, in the day of St. Michael; and hitherto have been long time over the sea, and have seen and gone through many diverse lands, and many provinces and kingdoms and isles and have passed throughout Turkey, Armenia the little and the great; through Tartary, Persia, Syria, Arabia, Egypt the high and the low; through Lybia, Chaldea, and a great part of Ethiopia; through Amazonia, Ind the less and the more, a great part; and throughout many other Isles, that be about Ind; where dwell many diverse folks, and of diverse manners and laws, and of diverse shapes of men. Of which lands and isles I shall speak more plainly hereafter; and I shall devise you of some part of things that there be, when time shall be, after it may best come to my mind; and specially for them, that will and are in purpose for to visit the Holy City of Jerusalem and the holy places that are thereabout. And

I shall tell the way that they shall hold thither. For I have often times passed and ridden that way, with good company of many lords. God be thanked!

And ye shall understand, that I have put this book out of Latin into French, and translated it again out of French into English, that every man of my nation may understand it. But lords and knights and other noble and worthy men that con Latin but little, and have been beyond the sea, know and understand, if I say truth or no, and if I err in devising, for forgetting or else, that they may redress it and amend it. For things passed out of long time from a man's mind or from his sight, turn soon into forgetting; because that mind of man ne may not be comprehended ne withholden, for the frailty of mankind.

CHAPTER I

To teach you the Way out of England to Constantinople

IN the name of God, Glorious and Almighty!

He that will pass over the sea and come to land [to go to the city of Jerusalem, he may wend many ways, both on sea and land], after the country that he cometh from; [for] many of them come to one end. But troweth not that I will tell you all the towns, and cities and castles that men shall go by; for then should I make too long a tale; but all only some countries and most principal steads that men shall go through to go the right way.

First, if a man come from the west side of the world, as England, Ireland, Wales, Scotland, or Norway, he may, if that he will, go through Almayne and through the kingdom of Hungary, that marcheth to the land of Polayne, and to the land of Pannonia, and so to Silesia.

And the King of Hungary is a great lord and a mighty, and holdeth great lordships and much land in his hand.

For he holdeth the kingdom of Hungary, Sclavonia, and of Comania a great part, and of Bulgaria that men call the land of Bougiers, and of the realm of Russia a great part, whereof he hath made a duchy, that lasteth unto the land of Nyfland, and marcheth to Prussia. And men go through the land of this lord, through a city that is clept Cypron, and by the castle of Neasburghe, and by the evil town, that sit toward the end of Hungary. And there pass men the river of Danube. This river of Danube is a full great river, and it goeth into Almayne, under the hills of Lombardy, and it receiveth into him forty other rivers, and it runneth through Hungary and through Greece and through Thrace, and it entereth into the sea, toward the east so rudely and so sharply, that the water of the sea is fresh and holdeth his sweetness twenty mile within the sea.

And after, go men to Belgrade, and enter into the land of Bougiers; and there pass men a bridge of stone that is upon the river of Marrok. And men pass through the land of Pyncemartz and come to Greece to the city of Nye, and to the city of Fynepape, and after to the city of Dandrenoble, and after to Constantinople, that was wont to be clept Bezanzon. And there dwelleth commonly the Emperor of Greece. And there is the most fair church and the most noble of all the world; and it is of Saint Sophie. And before that church is the image of Justinian the emperor, covered with gold, and he sitteth upon an horse y-crowned. And he was wont to hold a round apple of gold in his hand: but it is fallen out thereof. And men say there, that it is a token that the emperor hath lost a great part of his lands and of his lordships; for he was wont to be Emperor of Roumania and of Greece, of all Asia the less, and of the land of Syria, of the land of Judea in the which is Jerusalem, and of the land of Egypt, of Persia, and of Arabia. But he hath lost all but Greece; and that land he holds all only. And men would many times put the apple into the image's hand again, but it will not hold it. This apple betokeneth the lordship that he had over all the world, that is round. And the tother hand he lifteth up against the East, in token to menace the misdoers. This image stands upon a pillar of marble at Constantinople.

CHAPTER II

Of the Cross and the Crown of our Lord Jesu Christ

At Constantinople is the cross of our Lord Jesu Christ, and his coat without seams, that is clept *Tunica inconsutilis*, and the sponge, and the reed, of the which the Jews gave our Lord eysell and gall, in the cross. And there is one of the nails, that Christ was nailed with on the cross.

And some men trow that half the cross, that Christ was done on, be in Cyprus, in an abbey of monks, that men call the Hill of the Holy Cross; but it is not so. For that cross that is in Cyprus, is the cross, in the which Dismas the good thief was hanged on. But all men know not that; and that is evil y-done. For for profit of the offering, they say that it is the cross of our Lord Jesu Christ.

And ye shall understand that the cross of our Lord was made of four manner of trees, as it is contained in this verse,—*In cruce fit palma, cedrus, cypressus, oliva.* For that piece that went upright from the earth to the head was of cypress ; and the piece that went overthwart, to the which his hands were nailed, was of palm ; and the stock, that stood within the earth, in the which was made the mortise, was of cedar ; and the table above his head, that was a foot and an half long, on the which the title was written in Hebrew, Greek and Latin, that was of olive.

And the Jews made the cross of these four manner of trees ; for they trowed that our Lord Jesu Christ should have hanged on the cross, as long as the cross might last. And therefore made they the foot of the cross of cedar ; for cedar may not, in earth nor water, rot, and therefore they would that it should have lasted long. For they trowed that the body of Christ should have stunken, they

made that piece, that went from the earth upwards of cypress, for it is well-smelling, so that the smell of his body should not grieve men that went forby. And the overthwart piece was of palm, for in the Old Testament it was ordained, that when one was overcome he should be crowned with palm; and for they trowed that they had the victory of Christ Jesus, therefore made they the overthwart piece of palm. And the table of the title they made of olive ; for olive betokeneth peace, as the story of Noe witnesseth ; when that the culver brought the branch of olive, that betokened peace made between God and man. And so trowed the Jews for to have peace, when Christ was dead ; for they said that he made discord and strife amongst them. And ye shall understand that our Lord was y-nailed on the cross lying, and therefore he suffered the more pain.

And the Christian men, that dwell beyond the sea, in Greece, say that the tree of the cross, that we call cypress, was of that tree that Adam ate the apple off ; and that find they written. And they say also, that their scripture saith, that Adam was sick, and said to his son Seth, that he should go to the angel that kept Paradise, that he would send him oil of mercy, for to anoint with his members, that he might have health. And Seth went. But the angel would not let him come in ; but said to him, that he might not have of the oil of mercy. But he took him three grains of the same tree, that his father ate the apple off ; and bade him, as soon as his father was dead, that he should put these three grains under his tongue, and grave him so : and so he did. And of these three grains sprang a tree, as the angel said that it should, and bare a fruit, through the which fruit Adam should be saved. And when Seth came again, he found his father near dead. And when he was dead, he did with the grains as the angel bade him ; of the which sprung three trees, of the which the cross was made, that bare good fruit and blessed, our Lord Jesu Christ ; through whom, Adam and all that come of him, should be saved and delivered from dread of death without end, but it be their own default.

This holy cross had the Jews hid in the earth, under a rock of the mount of Calvary; and it lay there two hundred year and more, into the time that St. Helen, that was mother to Constantine the Emperor of Rome. And she was daughter of King Coel, born in Colchester, that was King of England, that was clept then Britain the more; the which the Emperor Constance wedded to his wife, for her beauty, and gat upon her Constantine, that was after Emperor of Rome, and King of England.

And ye shall understand, that the cross of our Lord was eight cubits long, and the overthwart piece was of length three cubits and a half. And one part of the crown of our Lord, wherewith he was crowned, and one of the nails, and the spear head, and many other relics be in France, in the king's chapel. And the crown lieth in a vessel of crystal richly dight. For a king of France bought these relics some time of the Jews, to whom the emperor had laid them in wed for a great sum of silver.

And if all it be so, that men say, that this crown is of thorns, ye shall understand, that it was of jonkes of the sea, that is to say, rushes of the sea, that prick as sharply as thorns. For I have seen and beholden many times that of Paris and that of Constantinople; for they were both one, made of rushes of the sea. But men have departed them in two parts: of the which, one part is at Paris, and the other part is at Constantinople. And I have one of those precious thorns, that seemeth like a white thorn; and that was given to me for great specialty. For there are many of them broken and fallen into the vessel that the crown lieth in; for they break for dryness when men move them to show them to great lords that come thither.

And ye shall understand, that our Lord Jesu, in that night that he was taken, he was led into a garden; and there he was first examined right sharply; and there the Jews scorned him, and made him a crown of the branches of albespine, that is white thorn, that grew in that same garden, and set it on his head, so fast and so sore, that the blood ran down by many places of his visage, and of his neck, and of his shoulders. And therefore hath the white thorn many virtues, for he that beareth a branch on him thereof, no thunder ne no manner of tempest may dere him; nor in the house, that it is in, may no evil ghost enter nor come unto the place that it is in. And in that same garden, Saint Peter denied our Lord thrice.

Afterward was our Lord led forth before the bishops and the masters of the law, into another garden of Annas; and there also he was examined, reproved, and scorned, and crowned eft with a sweet thorn, that men clepeth barbarines, that grew in that garden, and that hath also many virtues.

And afterward he was led into a garden of Caiphas, and there he was crowned with eglantine.

And after he was led into the chamber of Pilate, and there he was examined and crowned. And the Jews set him in a chair, and clad him in a mantle; and there made they the crown of jonkes of the sea; and there they kneeled to him, and scorned him, saying, *Ave, Rex Judeorum!* that is to say, ' Hail, King of Jews!' And of this crown, half is at Paris, and the other half at Constantinople. And this crown had Christ on his head, when he was done upon the cross; and therefore ought men to worship it and hold it more worthy than any of the others.

And the spear shaft hath the Emperor of Almayne; but the head is at Paris. And natheles the Emperor of Constantinople saith that he hath the spear head; and I have often time seen it, but it is greater than that at Paris.

CHAPTER III

Of the City of Constantinople, and of the Faith of Greeks

AT Constantinople lieth Saint Anne, our Lady's mother, whom Saint Helen let bring from Jerusalem. And there

lieth also the body of John Chrisostome, that was Archbishop of Constantinople.   And there lieth also Saint Luke
the Evangelist: for his bones were brought from Bethany,
where he was buried.   And many other relics be there.
And there is the vessel of stone, as it were of marble, that
men clepe enydros, that evermore droppeth water, and
filleth himself every year, till that it go over above, without that that men take from within.

Constantinople is a full fair city, and a good, and well
walled; and it is three-cornered.   And there is an arm of
the sea Hellespont: and some men call it the Mouth
of Constantinople; and some men call it the Brace of
Saint George: and that arm closeth the two parts of the
city.   And upward to the sea, upon the water, was wont
to be the great city of Troy, in a full fair plain: but that
city was destroyed by them of Greece, and little appeareth
thereof, because it is so long sith it was destroyed.

About Greece there be many isles, as Calliste, Calcas,
Oertige, Tesbria, Mynia, Flaxon, Melo, Carpate, and
Lemnos.   And in this isle is the mount Athos, that
passeth the clouds.   And there be many diverse languages
and many countries, that be obedient to the emperor; that
is to say, Turcople, Pyncynard, Comange, and many other,
as Thrace and Macedonia, of the which Alexander was
king.   In this country was Aristotle born, in a city that
men clepe Stagyra, a little from the city of Thrace.   And
at Stagyra lieth Aristotle; and there is an altar
upon his tomb.   And there make men great feasts for
him every year, as though he were a saint.   And at his
altar they holden their great councils and their assemblies,
and they hope, that through inspiration of God and of him,
they shall have the better council.

In this country be right high hills, toward the end of
Macedonia.   And there is a great hill, that men clepe
Olympus, that departeth Macedonia and Thrace.   And it
is so high, that it passeth the clouds.   And there is another
hill, that is clept Athos, that is so high, that the shadow of
him reacheth to Lemne, that is an isle; and it is seventy-
six mile between.   And above at the cop of the hill is

the air so clear, that men may find no wind there, and therefore may no beast live there, so is the air dry.

And men say in these countries, that philosophers some time went upon these hills, and held to their nose a sponge moisted with water, for to have air; for the air above was so dry. And above, in the dust and in the powder of those hills, they wrote letters and figures with their fingers. And at the year's end they came again, and found the same letters and figures, the which they had written the year before, without any default. And therefore it seemeth well, that these hills pass the clouds and join to the pure air.

At Constantinople is the palace of the emperor, right fair and well-dight: and therein is a fair place for joustings, or for other plays and desports. And it is made with stages, and hath degrees about, that every man may well see, and none grieve other. And under these stages be stables well vaulted for the emperor's horses; and all the pillars be of marble.

And within the Church of Saint Sophia, an emperor sometime would have buried the body of his father, when he was dead. And, as they made the grave, they found a body in the earth, and upon the body lay a fine plate of gold; and thereon was written, in Hebrew, Greek, and Latin, letters that said thus; *Jesu Christus nascetur de Virgine Maria, et ego credo in eum*; that is to say, 'Jesu Christ shall be born of the Virgin Mary, and I trow in him.' And the date when it was laid in the earth, was two thousand year before our Lord was born. And yet is the plate of gold in the treasury of the church. And men say, that it was Hermogenes the wise man.

And if all it so be, that men of Greece be Christian yet they vary from our faith. For they say, that the Holy Ghost may not come of the Son; but all only of the Father. And they are not obedient to the Church of Rome, ne to the Pope. And they say that their Patriarch hath as much power over the sea, as the Pope hath on this side the sea. And therefore Pope John xxii. sent letters to them, how Christian faith should be all one; and that they should be obedient to the Pope, that is God's Vicar on earth, to whom

God gave his plein power for to bind and to assoil, and therefore they should be obedient to him.

And they sent again diverse answers; and among others they said thus: *Potentiam tuam summam circa tuos subjectos, firmiter credimus. Superbiam tuam summam tolerare non possumus. Avaritiam tuam summam satiare non intendimus. Dominus tecum; quia Dominus nobiscum est.* That is to say: 'We trow well, that thy power is great upon thy subjects. We may not suffer thine high pride. We be not in purpose to fulfil thy great covetise. Lord be with thee; for our Lord is with us. Farewell.' And other answer might he not have of them.

And also they make their sacrament of the altar of Therf bread, for our Lord made it of such bread, when he made his Maundy. And on the Shere-Thursday make they their Therf bread, in token of the Maundy, and dry it at the sun, and keep it all the year, and give it to sick men, instead of God's body. And they make but one unction, when they christen children. And they anoint not the sick men. And they say that there is no Purgatory, and that souls shall not have neither joy ne pain till the day of doom. And they say that fornication is no sin deadly, but a thing that is kindly, and that men and women should not wed but once, and whoso weddeth oftener than once, their children be bastards and gotten in sin. And their priests also be wedded.

And they say also that usury is no deadly sin. And they sell benefices of Holy Church. And so do men in other places: God amend it when his will is! And that is great sclaundre, for now is simony king crowned in Holy Church: God amend it for his mercy!

And they say, that in Lent, men shall not fast, ne sing Mass, but on the Saturday and on the Sunday. And they fast not on the Saturday, no time of the year, but it be Christmas Even or Easter Even. And they suffer not the Latins to sing at their altars; and if they do, by any adventure, anon they wash the altar with holy water. And they say that there should be but one Mass said at one altar upon one day.

And they say also that our Lord ne ate never meat; but he made token of eating.   And also they say, that we sin deadly in shaving our beards, for the beard is token of a man, and gift of our Lord.   And they say that we sin deadly in eating of beasts that were forbidden in the Old Testament, and of the old Law, as swine, hares and other beasts, that chew not their cud.   And they say that we sin, when we eat flesh on the days before Ash Wednesday, and of that that we eat flesh the Wednesday, and eggs and cheese upon the Fridays.   And they accurse all those that abstain them to eat flesh the Saturday.

Also the Emperor of Constantinople maketh the patriarch, the archbishops and the bishops ; and giveth the dignities and the benefices of churches and depriveth them that be unworthy, when he findeth any cause.   And so is he lord both temporal and spiritual in his country.

And if ye will wit of their A.B.C. what letters they be, here ye may see them, with the names that they clepe them there amongst them : Alpha, Betha, Gama, Deltha, ε longe, ε brevis, Epilmon, Thetha, Iota, Kapda, Lapda, Mi, Ni, Xi, o brevis, Pi, Coph, Ro, Summa, Tau, Vi, Fy, Chi, Psi, Othomega, Diacosyn.[1]

And all be it that these things touch not to one way, nevertheless they touch to that, that I have hight you, to shew you a part of customs and manners, and diversities of countries.   And for this is the first country that is discordant in faith and in belief, and varieth from our faith, on this half the sea, therefore I have set it here, that ye may know the diversity that is between our faith and theirs. For many men have great liking, to hear speak of strange things of diverse countries.

[1] The letters themselves in clumsy forms, as well as the names, are written in the manuscript, but the scribe has inserted " an A.B.C. of another manner " in the midst of them.   The passage can be adequately represented only by a facsimile.

CHAPTER IV

*[Of the Way from Constantinople to Jerusalem.] Of Saint
John the Evangelist. And of the Ypocras Daughter,
transformed from a Woman to a Dragon*

Now return I again, for to teach you the way from Constantinople to Jerusalem. He that will through Turkey,
he goeth toward the city of Nyke, and passeth through the
gate of Chienetout, and always men see before them the
hill of Chienetout, that is right high ; and it is a mile and
an half from Nyke.

And whoso will go by water, by the brace of St. George,
and by the sea where St. Nicholas lieth, and toward many
other places—first men go to an isle that is clept Sylo. In
that isle groweth mastick on small trees, and out of them
cometh gum, as it were of plum-trees or of cherry-trees.

And after go men through the isle of Patmos ; and
there wrote St. John the Evangelist the Apocalypse. And
ye shall understand, that St. John was of age thirty-two
year, when our Lord suffered his passion ; and after his
passion, he lived sixty-seven year, and in the hundredth
year of his age he died.

From Patmos men go unto Ephesus, a fair city and
nigh to the sea. And there died St. John, and was buried
behind the high altar in a tomb. And there is a fair
church ; for Christian men were wont to holden that place
always. And in the tomb of St. John is nought but manna,
that is clept angels' meat ; for his body was translated into
Paradise. And Turks hold now all that place, and the city
and the church ; and all Asia the less is y-clept Turkey. And
ye shall understand, that St. John let make his grave there
in his life, and laid himself therein all quick ; and therefore
some men say, that he died not, but that he resteth there till
the day of doom. And, forsooth, there is a great marvel ;
for men may see there the earth of the tomb apertly many
times stir and move, as there were quick things under.

And from Ephesus men go through many isles in the sea, unto the city of Patera, where St. Nicholas was born, and so to Martha, where he was chosen to be bishop; and there groweth right good wine and strong, and that men call wine of Martha. And from thence go men to the isle of Crete, that the emperor gave sometime to [the] Genoese.

And then pass men through the isles of Colcos and of Lango, of the which isles Ypocras was lord of. And some men say, that in the isle of Lango is yet the daughter of Ypocras, in form and likeness of a great dragon, that is a hundred fathom of length, as men say, for I have not seen her. And they of the isles call her Lady of the Land. And she lieth in an old castle, in a cave, and sheweth twice or thrice in the year, and she doth no harm to no man, but if men do her harm. And she was thus changed and transformed, from a fair damosel, into likeness of a dragon, by a goddess that was clept Diana. And men say, that she shall so endure in that form of a dragon, unto [the] time that a knight come, that is so hardy, that dare come to her and kiss her on the mouth; and then shall she turn again to her own kind, and be a woman again, but after that she shall not live long.

And it is not long sithen, that a knight of Rhodes, that was hardy and doughty in arms, said that he would kiss her. And when he was upon his courser, and went to the castle, and entered into the cave, the dragon lift up her head against him. And when the knight saw her in that form so hideous and so horrible he fled away. And the dragon bare the knight upon a rock, maugre his head; and from that rock, she cast him into the sea. And so was lost both horse and man.

And also a young man, that wist not of the dragon, went out of a ship, and went through the isle till that he came to the castle, and came into the cave, and went so long, till that he found a chamber; and there he saw a damosel that combed her head and looked in a mirror; and she had much treasure about her. And he trowed that she had been a common woman, that dwelled there to receive men to folly. And he abode, till the damosel saw the shadow of him in the mirror. And she turned her toward him, and asked him what he would ? And he said, he would be her leman or paramour. And she asked him, if that he were a knight ? And he said, nay. And then she said, that he might not be her leman ; but she bade him go again unto his fellows, and make him knight, and come again upon the morrow, and she should come out of the cave before him, and then come and kiss her on the mouth and have no dread,—for I shall do thee no manner of harm, albeit that thou see me in likeness of a dragon ; for though thou see me hideous and horrible to look on, I do thee to wit that it is made by enchantment ; for without doubt, I am none other than thou seest now, a woman, and therefore dread thee nought. And if thou kiss me, thou shalt have all this treasure, and be my lord, and lord also of all the isle.

And he departed from her and went to his fellows to ship, and let make him knight and came again upon the morrow for to kiss this damosel. And when he saw her come out of the cave in form of a dragon, so hideous and so horrible, he had so great dread, that he fled again to the ship, and she followed him. And when she saw that he turned not again, she began to cry, as a thing that had much sorrow ; and then she turned again into her cave. And anon the knight died. And sithen hitherward might no knight see her, but that he died anon. But when a knight cometh, that is so hardy to kiss her, he shall not die ; but he shall turn the damosel into her right form and kindly shape, and he shall be lord of all the countries and isles abovesaid.

And from thence men come to the isle of Rhodes, the which isle Hospitallers holden and govern ; and that took they some-time from the emperor. And it was wont to be clept Collos ; and so call it the Turks yet. And Saint Paul in his epistle writeth to them of that isle *ad Colossenses*. This isle is nigh eight hundred mile long from Constantinople.

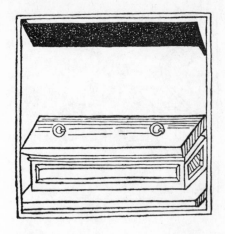

CHAPTER V

*[Of diversities in Cyprus; of the Road from Cyprus to Jeru-
salem, and of the Marvel of a Fosse full of Sand]*[1]

AND from this isle of Rhodes men go to Cyprus, where
be many vines, that first be red and after one year they
become white; and those wines that be most white, be
most clear and best of smell.

And men pass by that way, by a place that was wont to
be a great city, and a great land; and the city was clept
Cathailye, the which city and land was lost through
folly of a young man. For he had a fair damosel, that he
loved well to his paramour; and she died suddenly, and
was done in a tomb of marble. And for the great lust
that he had to her, he went in the night unto her tomb and
opened it, and went in and lay by her, and went his way.
And when it came to the end of nine months, there came
a voice to him and said, Go to the tomb of that woman,
and open it and behold what thou hast begotten on her;
and if thou let to go, thou shalt have a great harm. And
he yede and opened the tomb, and there flew out an adder
right hideous to see; the which as swithe flew about the
city and the country, and soon after the city sank down.
And there be many perilous passages without fail.

From Rhodes to Cyprus be five hundred mile and
more. But men may go to Cyprus, and come not at
Rhodes. Cyprus is right a good isle, and a fair and a
great, and it hath four principal cities within him. And
there is an Archbishop at Nicosea, and four other bishops
in that land. And at Famagost is one of the principal
havens of the sea that is in the world; and there arrive
Christian men and Saracens and men of all nations. In
Cyprus is the Hill of the Holy Cross; and there is an
abbey of monks black, and there is the cross of Dismas the
good thief, as I have said before. And some men trow,

1 This rubric is omitted in the manuscript.

that there is half the cross of our Lord ; but it is not so, and they do evil that make men to believe so.

In Cyprus lieth Saint Zenonimus, of whom men of that country make great solemnity. And in the castle of Amours lieth the body of Saint Hilarion, and men keep it right worshipfully. And beside Famagost was Saint Barnabas the apostle born.

In Cyprus men hunt with papyonns, that be like leopards, and they take wild beasts right well, and they be somewhat more than lions ; and they take more sharply the beasts, and more deliver than do hounds.

In Cyprus is the manner of lords and all other men all to eat on the earth. For they make ditches in the earth all about in the hall, deep to the knee, and they do pave them ; and when they will eat, they go therein and sit there. And the skill is for they may be the more fresh ; for that land is much more hotter than it is here. And at great feasts, and for strangers, they set forms and tables, as men do in this country, but they had lever sit in the earth.

From Cyprus, men go to the land of Jerusalem by the sea : and in a day and in a night, he that hath good wind may come to the haven of Tyre, that is now clept Surrye. There was some-time a great city and a good of Christian men, but Saracens have destroyed it a great part ; and they keep that haven right well, for dread of Christian men. Men might go more right to that haven, and come not in Cyprus, but they go gladly to Cyprus to rest them on the land, or else to buy things, that they have need to their living. On the sea-side men may find many rubies. And there is the well of the which holy writ speaketh of, and saith, *Fons ortorum, et puteus aquarum viventium* : that is to say, ' the well of gardens, and the ditch of living waters.'

In this city of Tyre, said the woman to our Lord, *Beatus venter qui te portavit, et ubera que succisti* : that is to say, ' Blessed be the body that thee bare, and the paps that thou suckedst.' And there our Lord forgave the woman of Canaan her sins. And before Tyre was wont to be the stone, on the which our Lord sat and preached, and on that stone was founded the Church of Saint Saviour.

And eight mile from Tyre, toward the east, upon the sea, is the city of Sarphen, in Sarepta of Sidonians. And there was wont for to dwell Elijah the prophet ; and there raised he Jonas, the widow's son, from death to life. And five mile from Sarphen is the city of Sidon ; of the which city, Dido was lady, that was Aeneas' wife, after the destruction of Troy, and that founded the city of Carthage in Africa, and now is clept Sidonsayete. And in the city of Tyre, reigned Agenor, the father of Dido. And sixteen mile from Sidon is Beirout. And from Beirout to Sardenare is three journeys and from Sardenare is five mile to Damascus.

And whoso will go long time on the sea, and come nearer to Jerusalem, he shall go from Cyprus by sea to port Jaffa. For that is the next haven to Jerusalem ; for from that haven is not but one day journey and a half to Jerusalem. And the town is called Jaffa ; for one of the sons of Noah that hight Japhet founded it, and now it is clept Joppa. And ye shall understand, that it is one of the oldest towns of the world, for it was founded before Noah's flood. And yet there sheweth in the rock, there as the iron chains were fastened, that Andromeda, a great giant, was bounden with, and put in prison before Noah's flood, of the which giant, is a rib of his side that is forty foot long.

And whoso will arrive at the port of Tyre or of Surrye, that I have spoken of before, may go by land, if he will, to Jerusalem. And men go from Surrye unto the city of Akon in a day. And it was clept some-time Ptolemaïs. And it was some-time a city of Christian men, full fair, but it is now destroyed ; and it stands upon the sea. And from Venice to Akon, by sea, is two thousand and four score miles of Lombardy ; and from Calabria, or from Sicily to Akon, by sea, is a 1300 miles of Lombardy ; and the isle of Crete is right in the midway.

And beside the city of Akon, toward the sea, six score furlongs on the right side, toward the south, is the Hill of Carmel, where Elijah the prophet dwelled, and there was first the Order of Friars Carmelites founded. This hill is not right great, nor full high. And at the foot of this hill was some-time a good city of Christian men, that men clept Caiffa, for Caiaphas first founded it; but it is now all wasted. And on the left side of the Hill of Carmel is a town, that men clepe Saffre, and that is set on another hill. There Saint James and Saint John were born; and, in worship of them there is a fair church. And from Ptolemaïs, that men clepe now Akon, unto a great hill, that is clept Scale of Tyre, is one hundred furlongs. And beside the city of Akon runneth a little river, that is clept Belon.

And there nigh is the Foss of Mennon that is all round; and it is one hundred cubits of largeness, and it is all full of gravel, shining bright, of the which men make fair verres and clear. And men come from far, by water in ships, and by land with carts, for to fetch of that gravel. And though there be never so much taken away thereof in the day, at morrow it is as full again as ever it was; and that is a great marvel. And there is evermore great wind in that foss, that stirreth evermore the gravel, and maketh it trouble. And if any man do therein any manner metal, it turneth anon to glass. And the glass, that is made of that gravel, if it be done again into the gravel, it turneth anon into gravel as it was first. And therefore some men say, that it is a swallow of the gravelly sea.

Also from Akon, above-said, go men forth four journeys to the city of Palestine, that was of the Philistines, that now is clept Gaza, that is a gay city and a rich; and it is right fair and full of folk, and it is a little from the sea. And from this city brought Samson the strong the gates upon an high land, when he was taken in that city, and there he slew in a palace the king and himself, and great number of the best of the Philistines, the which had put out his eyen and shaved his head, and imprisoned him by treason of Dalida his paramour. And therefore he made fall upon them a great hall, when they were at meat.

And from thence go men to the city of Cesarea, and so to the Castle of Pilgrims, and so to Ascalon; and then to Jaffa, and so to Jerusalem.

And whoso will go by land through the land of Babylon, where the soldan dwelleth commonly, he must get grace of him and leave to go more siker through those lands and countries.

And for to go to the Mount of Sinai, before that men go to Jerusalem, they shall go from Gaza to the Castle of Daire. And after that, men come out of Syria, and enter into wilderness, and there the way is full sandy; and that wilderness and desert lasteth eight journeys, but always men find good inns, and all that they need of victuals. And men clepe that wilderness Achelleke. And when a man cometh out of that desert, he entereth into Egypt, that men clepe Egypt-Canopac, and after other language, men clepe it Morsyn. And there first men find a good town, that is clept Belethe; and it is at the end of the kingdom of Aleppo. And from thence men go to Babylon and to Cairo.

CHAPTER VI

Of many Names of Soldans, and of the Tower of Babylon

AT Babylon there is a fair church of our Lady, where she dwelled seven year, when she fled out of the land of Judea for dread of King Herod. And there lieth the body of Saint Barbara the virgin and martyr. And there dwelled Joseph, when he was sold of his brethren. And there made Nebuchadnezzar the king put three children into the furnace of fire, for they were in the right truth of belief, the which children men clept Anania, Azariah, Mishael, as the Psalm of *Benedicite* saith : but Nebuchadnezzar clept them otherwise, Shadrach, Meshach, and Abednego, that is to say, God glorious, God victorious, and God over all things and realms : and that was for the miracle, that he saw God's Son go with the children through the fire, as he said.

There dwelleth the soldan in his Calahelyke (for there

is commonly his seat) in a fair castle, strong and great, and well set upon a rock. In that castle dwell alway, to keep it and to serve the soldan, more then 6000 persons, that take all their necessaries off the soldan's court. I ought right well to know it; for I dwelled with him as soldier in his wars a great while against the Bedouins. And he would have married me full highly to a great prince's daughter, if I would have forsaken my law and my belief; but I thank God, I had no will to do it, for nothing that he behight me.

And ye shall understand that the soldan is lord of five kingdoms, that he hath conquered and appropred to him by strength. And these be the names: the kingdom of Canapac, that is Egypt; and the kingdom of Jerusalem, where that David and Solomon were kings; and the kingdom of Syria, of the which the city of Damascus was chief; and the kingdom of Aleppo in the land of Mathe; and the kingdom of Arabia, that was to one of the three kings, that made offering to our Lord, when he was born. And many other lands he holdeth in his hand. And therewithal he holdeth caliphs, that is a full great thing in their language, and it is as much to say as king.

And there were wont to be five soldans; but now there is no more but he of Egypt. And the first soldan was Zarocon, that was of Media, as was father to Saladin that took the Caliph of Egypt and slew him, and was made soldan by strength. After that was Soldan Saladin, in whose time the King of England, Richard the First, with many other, kept the passage, that Saladin ne might not pass. After Saladin reigned his son Boradin, and after him his nephew. After that, the Comanians that were in servage in Egypt, felt themselves that they were of great power, they chose them a soldan amongst them, the which made him to be clept Melechsalan. And in his time entered into the country of the kings of France Saint Louis, and fought with him; and [the soldan] took him and imprisoned him; and this [soldan] was slain by his own servants. , And after, they chose another to be soldan, that they clept Tympieman; and he let deliver Saint Louis out of prison

for a certain ransom. And after, one of these Comanians reigned, that hight Cachas, and slew Tympieman, for to be soldan; and made him be clept Melechmenes. And after another that had to name Bendochdare, that slew Melechmenes, for to be sultan, and clept himself Melechdare. In his time entered the good King Edward of England into Syria, and did great harm to the Saracens. And after, was this soldan empoisoned at Damascus, and his son thought to reign after him by heritage, and made him to be clept Melechsache; but another that had to name Elphy, chased him out of the country and made him soldan. This man took the city of Tripoli and destroyed many of the Christian men, the year of grace 1289, and after was he imprisoned of another that would be soldan, but he was anon slain. After that was the son of Elphy chosen to be soldan, and clept him Melechasseraff, and he took the city of Akon and chased out the Christian men; and this was also empoisoned, and then was his brother made soldan, and was clept Melechnasser. And after, one that was clept Guytoga took him and put him in prison in the castle of Mountroyal, and made him soldan by strength, and clept him Melechadel; and he was of Tartary. But the Comanians chased him out of the country, and did him much sorrow, and made one of themself soldan, that had to name Lachin. And he made him to be clept Melechmanser, the which on a day played at the chess, and his sword lay beside him; and so befell, that one wrathed him, and with his own proper sword he was slain. And after that, they were at great discord, for to make a soldan; and finally they accorded to Melechnasser, that Guytoga had put in prison at Mountroyal. And this reigned long and governed wisely, so that his eldest son was chosen after him, Melechmader, the which his brother let slay privily for to have the lordship, and made him to be clept Melechmadabron, and he was soldan when I departed from those countries.

And wit ye well that the soldan may lead out of Egypt more than 20,000 men of arms, and out of Syria, and out of Turkey and out of other countries that he holds, he may arrere more than 50,000. And all those be at his wages, and they be always at him, without the folk of his country, that is without number. And every each of them hath by year the mountance of six score florins; but it behoveth, that every of them hold three horses and a camel. And by the cities and by towns be admirals, that have the governance of the people; one hath to govern four, and another hath to govern five, another more, and another well more. And as many taketh the admiral by him alone, as all the other soldiers have under him; and therefore, when the soldan will advance any worthy knight, he maketh him an admiral. And when it is any dearth, the knights be right poor, and then they sell both their horse and their harness.

And the soldan hath four wives, one Christian and three Saracens, of the which one dwelleth at Jerusalem, and another at Damascus, and another at Ascalon ; and when them list, they remove to other cities, and when the soldan will he may go to visit them. And he hath as many paramours as him liketh. For he maketh to come before him the fairest and the noblest of birth, and the gentlest damosels of his country, and he maketh them to be kept and served full honourably. And when he will have one to lie with him, he maketh them all to come before him, and he beholdeth in all, which of them is most to his pleasure, and to her anon he sendeth or casteth a ring from his finger. And then anon she shall be bathed and richly attired, and anointed with delicate things of sweet smell, and then led to the soldan's chamber; and thus he doth as often as him list, when he will have any of them.

And before the soldan cometh no stranger, but if he be clothed in cloth of gold, or of Tartary or of Camaka, in the Saracens' guise, and as the Saracens use. And it behoveth, that anon at the first sight that men see the soldan, be it in window or in what place else, that men kneel to him and kiss the earth, for that is the manner to do reverence to the soldan of them that speak with him. And when that messengers of strange countries come before him, the meinie of the soldan, when the strangers speak to him, they be about the soldan with swords drawn and gisarmes and axes, their arms lifted up in high with those weapons for to smite upon them, if they say any word that is displeasance to the soldan. And also, no stranger cometh before him, but that he maketh him some promise and grant of that the [stranger] asketh reasonably ; by so it be not against his law. And so do other princes beyond, for they say that no man shall come before no prince, but that [he be] better, and shall be more gladder in departing from his presence than he was at the coming before him.

And understandeth, that that Babylon that I have spoken of, where that the sultan dwelleth, is not that great Babylon where the diversity of languages was first made for vengeance by the miracle of God, when the great Tower of Babel was begun to be made ; of the which the walls were sixty-four furlongs of height ; that is in the great desert of Arabia, upon the way as men go toward the kingdom of Chaldea. But it is full long since that any man durst nigh to the tower ; for it is all desert and full of dragons and great serpents, and full of diverse venomous beasts all about. That tower, with the city, was of twenty-five mile in circuit of the walls, as they of the country say, and as men may deem by estimation, after that men tell of the country.

And though it be clept the Tower of Babylon, yet nevertheless there were ordained within many mansions and many great dwelling-places, in length and breadth. And that tower contained great country in circuit, for the tower alone contained ten mile square. That tower founded King Nimrod that was king of that country; and he was the first king of the world. And he let make an image in the likeness of his father, and constrained all his subjects for to worship it ; and anon began other lords to do the same, and so began the idols and the simulacres first.

The town and the city were full well set in a fair country and a plain that men clepe the country of Samar, of the which the walls of the city were two hundred cubits in height, and fifty cubits of deepness ; and the river of Euphrates ran throughout the city and about the tower also. But Cyrus the King of Persia took from them the river, and destroyed all the city and the tower also ; for he departed that river in 360 small rivers, because that he had sworn, that he should put the river in such point, that a woman might well pass there, without casting off of her clothes, forasmuch as he had lost many worthy men that trowed to pass that river by swimming.

And from Babylon where the soldan dwelleth, to go right between the Orient and the Septentrion toward the great Babylon, is forty journeys to pass by desert. But it is not the great Babylon in the land and in the power of the said soldan, but it is in the power and the lordship of Persia, but he holdeth it of the great Chan, that is the greatest emperor and the most sovereign lord of all the parts beyond, and he is lord of the isles of Cathay and of many other isles and of a great part of Ind, and his land marcheth unto Prester John's Land, and he holdeth so much land, that he knoweth not the end : and he is more mighty and greater lord without comparison than is the soldan : of his royal estate and of his might I shall speak more plenerly, when I shall speak of the land and of the country of Ind.

Also the city of Mecca where Mohammet lieth is of the great deserts of Arabia ; and there lieth [the] body of him full honourably in their temple, that the Saracens clepen Musketh. And it is from Babylon the less, where the soldan dwelleth, unto Mecca above-said, into a thirty-two journeys.

And wit well, that the realm of Arabia is a full great country, but therein is over-much desert. And no man may dwell there in that desert for default of water, for that land is all gravelly and full of sand. And it is dry and no thing fruitful, because that it hath no moisture ; and therefore is there so much desert. And if it had rivers and wells, and the land also were as it is in other parts, it should be as full of people and as full inhabited with folk as in other places ; for there is full great multitude of people, whereas the land is inhabited. Arabia dureth from the ends of the realm of Chaldea unto the last end of Africa, and marcheth to the land of Idumea toward the end of Botron. And in Chaldea the chief city is Bagdad. And of Africa the chief city is Carthage, that Dido, that

was Eneas's wife, founded; the which Eneas was of the
city of Troy, and after was King of Italy.

Mesopotamia stretcheth also unto the deserts of Arabia,
and it is a great country.   In this country is the city of
Haran, where Abraham's father dwelled, and from whence
Abraham departed by commandment of the angel.   And
of that city was Ephraim, that was a great clerk and a
great doctor.   And Theophilus was of that city also, that
our lady saved from our enemy.   And Mesopotamia
dureth from the river of Euphrates, unto the river of
Tigris, for it is between those two rivers.

And beyond the river of Tigris is Chaldea, that is a full
great kingdom.   In that realm, at Bagdad above-said, was
wont to dwell the caliph, that was wont to be both as
Emperor and Pope of the Arabians, so that he was lord
spiritual and temporal; and he was successor to Mahommet,
and of his generation.   That city of Bagdad was wont to
be clept Sutis, and Nebuchadnezzar founded it; and there
dwelled the holy prophet Daniel, and there he saw visions
of heaven, and there he made the exposition of dreams.

And in old time there were wont to be three caliphs,
he of Arabia and †of Chaldea dwelt in the city of Bagdad
above-said; and at Cairo beside Babylon dwelt the Caliph
of Egypt; and at Morocco, upon the West Sea, dwelt the
Caliph of the people of Barbary and of Africans.   And
now is there none of the caliphs, nor nought have been
since the time of the Soldan Saladin; for from that time
hither the soldan clepeth himself caliph, and so have the
caliphs lost their name.

Also witeth well, that Babylon the less, where the
soldan dwelleth, and at the city of Cairo that is nigh beside
it, be great huge cities many and fair; and that one sitteth
nigh that other.   Babylon sitteth upon the river of Gyson,
sometimes clept Nile, that cometh out of Paradise
terrestrial.

That river of Nile, all the year, when the sun entereth
into the sign of Cancer, it beginneth to wax, and it waxeth
always, as long as the sun is in Cancer and in the sign of
the Lion; and it waxeth in such manner, that it is some-

times so great, that it is twenty cubits or more of deepness, and then it doth great harm to the goods that be upon the land.   For then may no man travail to plough the lands for the great moisture, and therefore is there dear time in that country.   And also, when it waxeth little, it is dear time in that country, for default of moisture.   And when the sun is in the sign of Virgo, then beginneth the river for to wane and to decrease little and little, so that when the sun is entered into the sign of Libra, then they enter between these rivers.   This river cometh, running from Paradise terrestrial, between the deserts of Ind, and after it smiteth unto land, and runneth long time many great countries under earth.   And after it goeth out under an high hill, that men clepe Alothe, that is between Ind and Ethiopia the mountance of five months' journeys from the entry of Ethiopia ; and after it environeth all Ethiopia and Mauritania, and goeth all along from the land of Egypt unto the city of Alexandria to the end of Egypt, and there it falleth into the sea.   About this river be many birds and fowls, as sikonies, that they clepen ibes.

CHAPTER VII

Of the Country of Egypt; of the Bird Phoenix of Arabia; of the City of Cairo; of the Cunning to know Balm and to prove it; and of the Garners of Joseph

EGYPT is a long country, but it is straight, that is to say narrow, for they may not enlarge it toward the desert for default of water.   And the country is set along upon the river of Nile, by as much as that river may serve by floods or otherwise, that when it floweth it may spread abroad through the country ; so is the country large of length. For there it raineth not but little in that country, and for that cause they have no water, but if it be of that flood of that river.   And forasmuch as it ne raineth not in that

country, but the air is alway pure and clear, therefore in that country be the good astronomers, for they find there no clouds to letten them. Also the city of Cairo is right great and more huge than that of Babylon the less, and it sitteth above toward the desert of Syria, a little above the river above-said.

In Egypt there be two parts : the height, that is toward Ethiopia, and the lower, that is toward Arabia. In Egypt is the land of Rameses and the land of Goshen. Egypt is a strong country, for it hath many shrewd havens because of the great rocks that be strong and dangerous to pass by. And at Egypt, toward the east, is the Red Sea, that dureth unto the city of Coston ; and toward the west is the †country of Lybia, that is a full dry land and little of fruit, for it is overmuch plenty of heat, and that land is clept Fusthe. And toward the part meridional is Ethiopia. And toward the north is the desert, that dureth unto Syria, and so is the country strong on all sides. And it is well a fifteen journeys of length, and more than two so much of desert, and it is but two journeys in largeness. And between Egypt and Nubia it hath well a twelve journeys of desert. And men of Nubia be Christian, but they be black as the Moors for great heat of the sun.

In Egypt there be five provinces : that one is Sahythe ; that other Demeseer ; another Resith, that is an isle in the Nile ; another Alexandria ; and another the land of Damietta. That city was wont to be right strong, but it was twice won of the Christian men, and therefore after that the Saracens beat down the walls ; and with the walls and the tower thereof, the Saracens made another city more far from the sea, and clept it the new Damietta ; so that now no man dwelleth at the rather town of Damietta. At that city of Damietta is one of the havens of Egypt ; and at Alexandria is that other. That is a full strong city, but there is no water to drink, but if it come by conduit from Nile, that entereth into their cisterns ; and whoso stopped that water from them, they might not endure there. In Egypt there be but few forcelets or castles, because that the country is so strong of himself.

At the deserts of Egypt was a worthy man, that was an holy hermit, and there met with him a monster (that is to say, a monster is a thing deformed against kind both of man or of beast or of anything else, and that is clept a monster). And this monster, that met with this holy hermit, was as it had been a man, that had two horns trenchant on his forehead ; and he had a body like a man unto the navel, and beneath he had the body like a goat. And the hermit asked him what he was. And the monster answered him, and said he was a deadly creature, such as God had formed, and dwelt in those deserts in purchasing his sustenance. And [he] besought the hermit, that he would pray God for him, the which that came from heaven for to save all mankind, and was born of a maiden and suffered passion and death (as we well know) and by whom we live and be. And yet is the head with the two horns of that monster at Alexandria for a marvel.

In Egypt is the city of Heliopolis, that is to say, the city of the Sun. In that city there is a temple, made round after the shape of the Temple of Jerusalem. The priests of that temple have all their writings, under the date of the fowl that is clept phoenix ; and there is none but one in all the world. And he cometh to burn himself upon the altar of that temple at the end of five hundred year; for so long he liveth. And at the five hundred years' end, the priests array their altar honestly, and put thereupon spices and sulphur vif and other things that will burn lightly ; and then the bird phoenix cometh and burneth himself to ashes. And the first day next after, men find in the ashes a worm ; and the second day next after, men find a bird quick and perfect ; and the third day next after, he flieth his way. And so there is no more birds of that kind in all the world, but it alone, and truly that is a great miracle of God. And men may well liken that bird unto God, because that there ne is no God but one ; and also, that our Lord arose from death to life the third day. This bird men see often-time fly in those countries ; and he is not mickle more than an eagle. And he hath a crest of feathers upon his head more great than the peacock hath ; and is neck his yellow after colour of an oriel that is a stone well shining ; and his beak is coloured blue as ind ; and his wings be of purple colour, and his tail is † barred overthwart with green and yellow and red. And he is a full fair bird to look upon, against the sun, for he shineth full gloriously and nobly.

Also in Egypt be gardens, that have trees and herbs, the which bear fruits seven times in the year. And in that land men find many fair emeralds and enough ; and therefore they be greater cheap. Also when it raineth once in the summer in the land of Egypt, then is all the country full of great mires. Also at Cairo, that I spake of before, sell men commonly both men and women of other laws as we do here beasts in the market. And there is a common house in that city that is all full of small furnaces, and thither bring women of the town their eyren of hens, of geese, and of ducks for to be put into those furnaces. And they that keep that house cover them with heat of horse dung, without hen, goose or duck or any other fowl. And at the end of three weeks or of a month they come again and take their chickens and nourish them and bring them forth, so that all the country is full of them. And so men do there both winter and summer.

Also in that country and in others also, men find long apples to sell, in their season, and men clepe them apples of Paradise ; and they be right sweet and of good savour. And though ye cut them in never so many gobbets or parts, overthwart or endlong, evermore ye shall find in the midst the figure of the Holy Cross of our Lord Jesu. But they will rot within eight days, and for that cause men may not carry of those apples to no far countries ; of them men find the mountance of a hundred in a basket, and they have great leaves of a foot and a half of length, and they be convenably large. And men find there also the apple tree of Adam, that have a bite at one of the sides ; and there be also fig trees that bear no leaves, but figs upon the small branches ; and men clepe them figs of Pharaoh.

Also beside Cairo, without that city, is the field where

balm groweth; and it cometh out on small trees, that be none higher than to a man's breeks' girdle, and they seem as wood that is of the wild vine. And in that field be seven wells, that our Lord Jesu Christ made with one of his feet, when he went to play with other children. That field is not so well closed, but that men may enter at their own list; but in that season that the balm is growing, men put thereto good keeping, that no man dare be hardy to enter.

This balm groweth in no place, but only there. And though that men bring of the plants, for to plant in other countries, they grow well and fair; but they bring forth no fructuous thing, and the leaves of balm fall not. And men cut the branches with a sharp flintstone, or with a sharp bone, when men will go to cut them; for whoso cut them with iron, it would destroy his virtue and his nature.

And the Saracens clepe the wood *Enonch-balse*, and the fruit, the which is as cubebs, they clepe *Abebissam*, and the liquor that droppeth from the branches they clepe *Guybalse*. And men make always that balm to be tilled of the Christian men, or else it would not fructify; as the Saracens say themselves, for it hath been often-time proved. Men say also, that the balm groweth in Ind the more, in that desert where Alexander spake to the trees of the sun and of the moon, but I have not seen it; for I have not been so far above upward, because that there be too many perilous passages.

And wit ye well, that a man ought to take good keep for to buy balm, but if he con know it right well, for he may right lightly be deceived. For men sell a gum, that men clepe turpentine, instead of balm, and they put thereto a little balm for to give good odour. And some put wax in oil of the wood of the fruit of balm, and say that it is balm. And some distil cloves of gilofre and of spikenard of Spain and of other spices, that be well smelling; and the liquor that goeth out thereof they clepe it balm, and they think that they have balm, and they have none. For the Saracens counterfeit it by subtlety of craft for to deceive the Christian men, as I have seen full many a time; and after them the merchants and the apothecaries counterfeit it eft sones, and then it is less worth, and a great deal worse.

But if it like you, I shall shew how ye shall know and prove, to the end that ye shall not be deceived. First ye shall well know, that the natural balm is full clear, and of citron colour and strongly smelling; and if it be thick, or red or black, it is sophisticate, that is to say, counterfeited and made like it for deceit. And understand, that if ye will put a little balm in the palm of your hand against the sun, if it be fine and good, ye ne shall not suffer your hand against the heat of the sun. Also take a little balm with the point of a knife, and touch it to the fire, and if it burn it is a good sign. After take also a drop of balm, and put it into a dish, or in a cup with milk of a goat, and if it be natural balm anon it will take and beclippe the milk. Or put a drop of balm in clear water in a cup of silver or in a clear basin, and stir it well with the clear water; and if the balm be fine and of his own kind, the water shall never trouble; and if the balm be sophisticate, that is to say counterfeited, the water shall become anon trouble; and also if the balm be fine it shall fall to the bottom of the vessel, as though it were quicksilver, for the fine balm is more heavy twice than is the balm that is sophisticate and counterfeited. Now I have spoken of balm.

And now also I shall speak of another thing that is beyond Babylon, above the flood of the Nile, toward the desert between Africa and Egypt; that is to say, of the garners of Joseph, that he let make for to keep the grains for the peril of the dear years. And they be made of stone, full well made of masons' craft; of the which two be marvellously great and high, and the tother ne be not so great. And every garner hath a gate for to enter within, a little high from the earth; for the land is wasted and fallen since the garners were made. And within they be all full of serpents. And above the garners without be many scriptures of diverse languages. And some men say, that they be sepultures of great lords, that were sometime, but that is not true, for all the common rumour and speech is of all the people there, both far and near, that they be the garners of Joseph; and so find they in their scriptures, and in their chronicles. On the other part, if they were sepultures, they should not be void within, ne they should have no gates for to enter within; for ye may well know, that tombs and sepultures be not made of such greatness, nor of such highness; wherefore it is not to believe, that they be tombs or sepultures.

In Egypt also there be diverse languages and diverse letters, and of other manner and condition than there be in other parts. As I shall devise you, such as they be, and the names how they clepe them, to such intent, that ye may know the difference of them and of others,—Athoimis, Bimchi, Chinok, Duram, Eni, Fin, Gomor, Heket, Janny, Karacta, Luzanin, Miche, Naryn, Oldach, Pilon, Qyn, Yron, Sichen, Thola, Urmron, Yph and Zarm, Thoit.

CHAPTER VIII

Of the Isle of Sicily; of the way from Babylon to the Mount Sinai; of the Church of Saint Katherine and of all the marvels there

Now will I return again, ere I proceed any further, for to declare to you the other ways, that draw toward Babylon, where the sultan himself dwelleth, that is at the entry of Egypt; for as much as many folk go thither first and after that to the Mount Sinai, and after return to Jerusalem, as I have said you here before. For they fulfil first the more long pilgrimage, and after return again by the next ways, because that the more nigh way is the more worthy, and that is Jerusalem; for no other pilgrimage is not like in comparison to it. But for to fulfil their pilgrimages more easily and more sikerly, men go first the longer way rather than the nearer way.

But whoso will go to Babylon by another way, more short from the countries of the west that I have rehearsed before, or from other countries next to them—then men go by France, by Burgundy and by Lombardy. It needeth not to tell you the names of the cities, nor of the towns that be in that way, for the way is common, and it is known of many nations. And there be many havens [where] men take the sea. Some men take the sea at Genoa, some at Venice, and pass by the sea Adriatic, that is clept the Gulf of Venice, that departeth Italy and Greece on that side; and some go to Naples, some to Rome, and from Rome to Brindisi and there they take the sea, and in many other places where that havens be. And men go by Tuscany, by Campania, by Calabria, by Apulia, and by the hills of Italy, by Corsica, by Sardinia, and by Sicily, that is a great isle and a good.

In that isle of Sicily there is a manner of a garden, in the which be many diverse fruits; and the garden is always green and flourishing, all the seasons of the year as well in winter as in summer. That isle holds in compass about 350 French miles. And between Sicily and Italy there is not but a little arm of the sea, that men clepe the Farde of Messina. And Sicily is between the sea Adriatic and the sea of Lombardy. And from Sicily into Calabria is but eight miles of Lombardy.

And in Sicily there is a manner of serpent, by the which men assay and prove, whether their children be bastards or no, or of lawful marriage : for if they be born in right marriage, the serpents go about them, and do them no harm, and if they be born in avoutry, the serpents bite them and envenom them. And thus many wedded men prove if the children be their own.

Also in that isle is the Mount Etna, that men clepe Mount Gybelle, and the volcanoes that be evermore burning. And there be seven places that burn and that cast out diverse flames and diverse colour : and by the changing of those flames, men of that country know when it shall be dearth or good time, or cold or hot or moist or dry, or in all other manners how the time shall be governed. And from Italy unto the volcanoes ne is but twenty-five mile. And men say, that the volcanoes be ways of hell.

And whoso goeth by Pisa, if that men list to go that way, there is an arm of the sea, where that men go to other havens in those marches. And then men pass by the isle of Greaf that is at Genoa. And after arrive men in Greece at the haven of the city of Myrok, or at the haven of Valone, or at the city of Duras; and there is a Duke at Duras, or at other havens in those marches; and so men go to Constantinople. And after go men by water to the isle of Crete and to the isle of Rhodes, and so to Cyprus, and so to Athens, and from thence to Constantinople. To hold the more right way by sea, it is well a thousand eight hundred and four score mile of Lombardy. And after from Cyprus men go by sea, and leave Jerusalem and all the country on the left hand, unto Egypt, and arrive at the city of Damietta, that was wont to be full strong, and it sits at the entry of Egypt. And from Damietta go men to the city of Alexandria, that sits also upon the sea. In that city was Saint Catherine beheaded: and there was Saint Mark the evangelist martyred and buried, but the Emperor Leo made his bones to be brought to Venice.

And yet there is at Alexandria a fair church, all white without paintures; and so be all the other churches that were of the Christian men, all white within, for the Paynims and the Saracens made them white for to fordo the images of saints that were painted on the walls. That city of Alexandria is well thirty furlongs in length, but it is but ten on largeness; and it is a full noble city and a fair. At that city entereth the river of Nile into the sea, as I to you have said before. In that river men find many precious stones, and much also of lignum aloes; and it is a manner of wood, that cometh out of Paradise terrestrial, the which is good for many diverse medicines, and it is right dear-worth. And from Alexandria men go to Babylon, where the sultan dwelleth; that sits also upon the river of Nile: and this way is the most short, for to go straight unto Babylon.

Now shall I say you also the way, that goeth from Babylon to the Mount of Sinai, where Saint Catherine lieth. He must pass by the deserts of Arabia, by the which deserts Moses led the people of Israel. And then

pass men by the well that Moses made with his hand in
the deserts, when the people grucched; for they found
nothing to drink.   And then pass men by the Well of
Marah, of the which the water was first bitter; but the
children of Israel put therein a tree, and anon the water
was sweet and good for to drink.   And then go men by
desert unto the vale of Elim, in the which vale be twelve
wells; and there be seventy-two trees of palm, that bear
the dates the which Moses found with the children of
Israel.   And from that valley is but a good journey to the
Mount of Sinai.

And whoso will go by another way from Babylon, then
men go by the Red Sea, that is an arm of the sea Ocean.
And there passed Moses with the children of Israel, overthwart the sea all dry, when Pharaoh the King of Egypt
chased them.   And that sea is well a six mile of largeness in
length; and in that sea was Pharaoh drowned and all his
host that he led.   That sea is not more red than another
sea; but in some place thereof is the gravel red, and therefore men clepen it the Red Sea.   That sea runneth to the
ends of Arabia and of Palestine.

That sea lasteth more than a four journeys, and then go
men by desert unto the Vale of Elim, and from thence to
the Mount of Sinai.   And ye may well understand, that
by this desert no man may go on horseback, because that
there ne is neither meat for horse ne water to drink; and for
that cause men pass that desert with camels.   For the camel
finds alway meat in trees and on bushes, that he feedeth
him with: and he may well fast from drink two days or
three.   And that may no horse do.

And wit well that from Babylon to the Mount Sinai is
well a twelve good journeys, and some men make them
more.   And some men hasten them and pain them, and
therefore they make them less.   And always men find
latiners to go with them in the countries, and further
beyond, into time that men con the language: and it
behoveth men to bear victuals with them, that shall dure
them in those deserts, and other necessaries for to
live by.

And the Mount of Sinai is clept the Desert of Sin, that is for to say, the bush burning ; because there Moses saw our Lord God many times in the form of fire burning upon that hill, and also in a bush burning, and spake to him.   And that was at the foot of the hill.   There is an abbey of monks, well builded and well closed with gates of iron for dread of the wild beasts ; and the monks be Arabians or men of Greece.   And there [is] a great convent, and all they be as hermits, and they drink no wine, but if it be on principal feasts ; and they be full devout men, and live poorly and simply with joutes and with dates, and they do great abstinence and penances.

There is the Church of Saint Catherine, in the which be many lamps burning ; for they have of oil of olives enough, both for to burn in their lamps and to eat also. And that plenty have they by the miracle of God ; for the ravens and the crows and the choughs and other fowls of the country assemble them there every year once, and fly thither as in pilgrimage ; and everych of them bringeth a branch of the bays or of olive in their beaks instead of offering, and leave them there ; of the which the monks make great plenty of oil.   And this is a great marvel.   And sith that fowls that have no kindly wit or reason go thither to seek that glorious Virgin, well more ought men then to seek her, and to worship her.

Also behind the altar of that church is the place where Moses saw our Lord God in a burning bush.   And when the monks enter into that place, they do off both hosen and shoon or boots always, because that our Lord said to Moses, Do off thy hosen and thy shoon, for the place that thou standest on is land holy and blessed.   And the monks clepe that place Dozoleel, that is to say, the shadow of God.   And beside the high altar, three degrees of height is the fertre of alabaster, where the bones of Saint Catherine lie.   And the prelate of the monks sheweth the relics to the pilgrims, and with an instrument of silver he froteth the bones ; and then there goeth out a little oil, as though it were a manner sweating, that is neither like to oil ne to balm, but it is full sweet of smell ;

and of that they give a little to the pilgrims, for there goeth out but little quantity of the liquor. And after that they shew the head of Saint Catherine, and the cloth that she was wrapped in, that is yet all bloody ; and in that same cloth so wrapped, the angels bare her body to the Mount Sinai, and there they buried her with it. And then they shew the bush, that burned and wasted nought, in the which our Lord spake to Moses, and other relics enough.

Also, when the prelate of the abbey is dead, I have understood, by information, that his lamp quencheth. And when they choose another prelate, if he be a good man and worthy to be prelate, his lamp shall light with the grace of God without touching of any man. For everych of them hath a lamp by himself, and by their lamps they know well when any of them shall die. For when any shall die, the light beginneth to change and to wax dim ; and if he be chosen to be prelate, and is not worthy, his lamp quencheth anon. And other men have told me, that he that singeth the mass for the prelate that is dead—he shall find upon the altar the name written of him that shall be prelate chosen. And so upon a day, I asked of the monks, both one and other, how this befell. But they would not tell me nothing, into the time that I said that they should not hide the grace that God did them, but that they should publish it to make the people have the more devotion, and that they did sin to hide God's miracle, as me seemed. For the miracles that God hath done and yet doth every day, be the witness of his might and of his marvels, as David saith in the Psalter : *Mirabilia testimonia tua, Domine*, that is to say, 'Lord thy marvels be thy witness.' And then they told me, both one and other, how it befell full many a time, but more I might not have of them.

In that abbey ne entereth not no fly, ne toads ne newts, ne such foul venomous beasts, ne lice ne fleas, by the miracle of God, and of our Lady. For there were wont to be so many such manner of filths, that the monks were in will to leave the place and the abbey, and were gone from thence upon the mountain above to eschew that place ; and our Lady came to them and bade them turn again, and from thence forwards never entered such filth in that place amongst them, ne never shall enter hereafter. Also, before the gate is the well, where Moses smote the stone, of the which the water came out plenteously.

From that abbey men go up the mountain of Moses, by many degrees. And there men find first a church of our Lady, where that she met the monks, when they fled away for the vermin above-said. And more high upon that mountain is the chapel of Elijah the prophet ; and that place they clepe Horeb, whereof holy writ speaketh, *Et ambulavit in fortitudine cibi illius usque, ad montem Oreb* ; that is to say, 'And he went in strength of that meat unto the hill of God, Horeb.' And there nigh is the vine that Saint John the Evangelist planted that men clepe raisins of Staphis. And a little above is the chapel of Moses, and the rock where Moses fled to for dread when he saw our Lord face to face. And in that rock is printed the form of his body, for he smote so strongly and so hard himself in that rock, that all his body was dolven within through the miracle of God. And there beside is the place where our Lord took to Moses the Ten Commandments of the Law. And there is the cave under the rock where Moses dwelt, when he fasted forty days and forty nights. But he died in the Land of Promission, and no man knoweth where he was buried. And from that mountain men pass a great valley for to go to another mountain, where Saint Catherine was buried of the angels of the Lord. And in that valley is a church of forty martyrs, and there sing the monks of the abbey, often-time : and that valley is right cold. And after men go up the mountain of Saint Catherine, that is more high than the mount of Moses ; and there, where Saint Catherine was buried, is neither church nor chapel, nor other dwelling place, but there is an heap of stones about the place, where body of her, was put of the angels. There was wont to be a chapel, but it was cast down, and yet lie the stones there. And albeit that the Collect of Saint Catherine says, that it is the place where our Lord betaught the Ten Commandments to Moses, and there, where the blessed Virgin Saint Catherine was buried, that is to understand in one country, or in one place bearing one name; for both that one and that other is clept the mount of Sinai. But it is a great way from that one to that other, and a great deep valley between them.

CHAPTER IX

Of the Desert between the Church of Saint Catherine and Jerusalem. Of the Dry Tree; and how Roses came first into the World

Now, after that men have visited those holy places, then will they turn toward Jerusalem. And then will they take leave of the monks, and recommend themselves to their prayers. And then they give the pilgrims of their victuals for to pass with the deserts toward Syria. And those deserts dure well a thirteen journeys.

In that desert dwell many of Arabians, that men clepe Bedouins and Ascopards, and they be folk full of all evil conditions. And they have none houses, but tents, that they make of skins of beasts, as of camels and of other beasts that they eat; and there beneath these they couch them and dwell in place where they may find water, as on the Red Sea or elsewhere: for in that desert is full great default of water, and often-time it falleth that where men find water at one time in a place it faileth another time; and for that skill they make none habitations there. These folk that I speak of, they till not the land, and they labour nought; for they eat no bread, but if it be any that dwell nigh a good town, that go thither and eat bread sometime. And they roast their flesh and their fish upon the hot stones against the sun. And they be strong men and well-fighting; and there so is much multitude of that folk, that they be without number. And they ne reck of nothing, ne do not but chase after beasts to eat

suggests observation, not fable.

many facts about Bedouins are still relevant today and therefore are probably based on factual observation.

them. And they reck nothing of their life, and therefore they fear not the sultan, ne no other prince; but they dare well war with them, if they do anything that is grievance to them. And they have often-times war with the sultan, and, namely, that time that I was with him. And they bear but one shield and one spear, without other arms; and they wrap their heads and their necks with a great quantity of white linen cloth; and they be right felonous and foul, and of cursed kind.

And when men pass this desert, in coming toward Jerusalem, they come to Bersabe (Beersheba), that was wont to be a full fair town and a delectable of Christian men; and yet there be some of their churches. In that town dwelled Abraham the patriarch, a long time. That town of Bersabe founded Bersabe (Bathsheba), the wife of Sir Uriah the Knight, on the which King David gat Solomon the Wise, that was king after David upon the twelve kindreds of Jerusalem and reigned forty year.

And from thence go men to the city of Hebron, that is the mountance of twelve good mile. And it was clept sometime the Vale of Mamre, and some-time it was clept the Vale of Tears, because that Adam wept there an hundred year for the death of Abel his son, that Cain slew. Hebron was wont to be the principal city of the Philistines, and there dwelled some time the giants. And that city was also sacerdotal, that is to say, sanctuary of the tribe of Judah; and it was so free, that men received there all manner of fugitives of other places for their evil deeds. In Hebron Joshua, Caleb and their company came first to aspy, how they might win the land of Behest. In Hebron reigned first king David seven year and a half; and in Jerusalem he reigned thirty-three year and a half.

And in Hebron be all the sepultures of the patriarchs, Adam, Abraham, Isaac, and of Jacob; and of their wives, Eve, Sarah and Rebecca, and of Leah; the which sepultures the Saracens keep full curiously, and have the place in great reverence for the holy fathers, the patriarchs that lie there. And they suffer no Christian man to enter into that place, but if it be of special grace of the sultan; for they hold

Christian men and Jews as dogs, and they say, that they should not enter into so holy place. And men clepe that place, where they lie, Double Spelunk, or Double Cave, or Double Ditch, forasmuch as that one lieth above that other. And the Saracens clepe that place in their language, *Karicarba*, that is to say, 'The Place of Patriarchs.' And the Jews clepe that place *Arboth*. And in that same place was Abraham's house, and there he sat and saw three persons, and worshipped but one; as holy writ saith, *Tres vidit et unum adoravit*, that is to say, 'He saw three and worshipped one': and of those same received Abraham the angels into his house.

And right fast by that place is a cave in the rock, where Adam and Eve dwelled when they were put out of Paradise; and there got they their children. And in that same place was Adam formed and made, after that some men say: (for men were wont for to clepe that place the field of Damascus, because that it was in the lordship of Damascus), and from thence was he translated into Paradise of delights, as they say; and after that he was driven out of Paradise he was there left. And the same day that he was put in Paradise, the same day he was put out, for anon he sinned. There beginneth the Vale of Hebron, that dureth nigh to Jerusalem. There the angel commanded Adam that he should dwell with his wife Eve, of the which he gat Seth; of which tribe, that is to say kindred, Jesu Christ was born.

In that valley is a field, where men draw out of the earth a thing that men clepe cambile, and they eat it instead of spices, and they bear it to sell. And men may not make the hole or the cave, where it is taken out of the earth, so deep or so wide, but that it is, at the year's end, full again up to the sides, through the grace of God.

And two mile from Hebron is the grave of Lot, that was Abraham's brother.

And a little from Hebron is the mount of Mamre, of the which the valley taketh his name. And there is a tree of oak, that the Saracens clepe *Dirpe*, that is of Abraham's time: the which men clepe the Dry Tree. And they say that it hath been there since the beginning of the world, and was some-time green and bare leaves, unto the time that our Lord died on the cross, and then it dried: and so did all the trees that were then in the world. And some say, by their prophecies, that a lord, a prince of the west side of the world, shall win the Land of Promission that is the Holy Land with help of Christian men, and he shall do sing a mass under that dry tree; and then the tree shall wax green and bear both fruit and leaves, and through that miracle many Saracens and Jews shall be turned to Christian faith: and, therefore, they do great worship thereto, and keep it full busily. And, albeit so, that it be dry, natheles yet he beareth great virtue, for certainly he that hath a little thereof upon him, it healeth him of the falling evil, and his horse shall not be a-foundered: and many other virtues it hath; wherefore men hold it full precious.

From Hebron men go to Bethlehem in half a day, for it is but five mile; and it is full fair way, by plains and woods full delectable. Bethlehem is a little city, long and narrow and well walled, and in each side enclosed with good ditches: and it was wont to be clept Ephrata, as holy writ saith, *Ecce, audivimus eum in Ephrata*, that is to say, 'Lo, we heard him in Ephrata.' And toward the east end of the city is a full fair church and a gracious, and it hath many towers, pinacles and corners, full strong and curiously made; and within that church be forty-four pillars of marble, great and fair.

And between the city and the church is the field *Floridus*, that is to say, the 'field flourished.' For as much as a fair maiden was blamed with wrong, and slandered that she had done fornication; for which cause she was demned to death, and to be burnt in that place, to the which she was led. And, as the fire began to burn about her, she made her prayers to our Lord, that as wisely as she was not guilty of that sin, that he would help her and make it to be known to all men, of his merciful grace. And when she had thus said, she entered into the fire, and anon was the fire quenched and out; and the brands that were

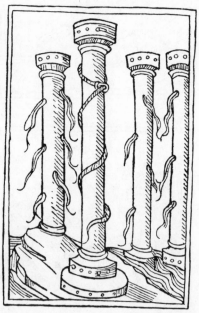

burning became red rose-trees, and the brands that were not kindled became white rose-trees, full of roses. And these were the first rose-trees and roses, both white and red, that ever any man saw ; and thus was this maiden saved by the grace of God. And therefore is that field clept the field of God flourished, for it was full of roses.

Also beside the choir of the church, at the right side, as men come downward sixteen degrees, is the place where our Lord was born, that is full well dight of marble, and full richly painted with gold, silver, azure and other colours. And three paces beside is the crib of the ox and the ass. And beside that is the place where the star fell, that led the three kings, Jaspar, Melchior and Balthazar : but men of Greece clepe them thus, *Galgalath*, *Malgalath*, and *Seraphie*, and the Jews clepe them, in this manner, in Hebrew, *Appelius*, *Amerrius*, and *Damasus*. These three kings offered to our Lord, gold, incense and myrrh, and they met together through miracle of God ; for they met together in a city in Ind, that men clepe Cassak, that is a fifty-three journeys from Bethlehem ; and they were at Bethlehem the thirteenth day ; and that was the fourth day after that they had seen the star, when they met in that city, and thus they were in nine days from that city at Bethlehem, and that was great miracle.

Also, under the cloister of the church, by eighteen degrees at the right side, is the charnel of the Innocents, where their bones lie. And before the place where our Lord was born is the tomb of Saint Jerome, that was a priest and a cardinal, that translated the Bible and the Psalter from Hebrew into Latin : and without the minster is the chair that he sat in when he translated it. And fast beside that church, a sixty fathom, is a church of Saint Nicholas, where our Lady rested her after she was lighted of our Lord ; and forasmuch as she had too much milk in her paps, that grieved her, she milked them on the red stones of marble, so that the traces may yet be seen, in the stones, all white.

And ye shall understand, that all that dwell in Bethlehem be Christian men.

And there be fair vines about the city, and great plenty of wine, that the Christian men have do let make. But the Saracens ne till not no vines, ne they drink no wine: for their books of their law, that Mahomet betoke them, which they clepe their *Al Koran*, and some clepe it *Mesaph*, and in another language it is clept *Harme*, and the same book forbiddeth them to drink wine. For in that book, Mahomet cursed all those that drink wine and all them that sell it: for some men say, that he slew once an hermit in his drunkenness, that he loved full well; and therefore he cursed wine and them that drink it. But his curse be turned on to his own head, as holy writ saith, *Et in verticem ipsius iniquitas ejus descendet*, that is for to say, 'His wickedness shall turn and fall in his own head.'

And also the Saracens bring forth no pigs, nor they eat no swine's flesh, for they say it is brother to man, and it was forbidden by the old law; and they hold him all accursed that eat thereof. Also in the land of Palestine and in the land of Egypt, they eat but little or none of flesh of veal or of beef, but if be so old, that he may no more travel for old; for it is forbidden, and for because they have but few of them; therefore they nourish them for to ere their lands.

In this city of Bethlehem was David the king born; and he had sixty wives, and the first wife was called Michal; and also he had three hundred lemans. *MISTRESSES*

And from Bethlehem unto Jerusalem is but two mile; and in the way to Jerusalem half a mile from Bethlehem is a church, where the angel said to the shepherds of the birth of Christ. And in that way is the tomb of Rachel, that was Joseph's mother, the patriarch; and she died anon after that she was delivered of her son Benjamin. And there she was buried of Jacob her husband, and he let set twelve great stones on her, in token that she had born twelve children. In the same way, half mile from Jerusalem, appeared the star to the three kings. In that way also be many churches of Christian men, by the which men go towards the city of Jerusalem.

CHAPTER X

Of the Pilgrimages in Jerusalem, and of the Holy Places thereabout

AFTER, for to speak of Jerusalem the holy city : ye shall understand, that it stands full fair between hills, and there be no rivers ne wells, but water cometh by conduit from Hebron. And ye shall understand, that Jerusalem of old time, unto the time of Melchisadech, was clept Jebus ; and after it was clept Salem, unto the time of King David, that put these two names together, and clept it Jebusalem ; and after that, King Solomon clept it Jerosolomye ; and after that, men clept it Jerusalem, and so it is clept yet.

And about Jerusalem is the kingdom of Syria. And there beside is the land of Palestine, and beside it is Ascalon, and beside that is the land of Maritaine. But Jerusalem is in the land of Judea, and it is clept Judea, for that Judas Maccabeus was king of that country ; and it marcheth eastward to the kingdom of Arabia ; on the south side to the land of Egypt ; and on the west side to the Great Sea ; on the north side, towards the kingdom of Syria and to the sea of Cyprus. In Jerusalem was wont to be a patriarch ; and archbishops and bishops about in the country. About Jerusalem be these cities : Hebron, at seven mile ; Jericho, at six mile ; Beersheba, at eight mile ; Ascalon, at seventeen mile ; Jaffa, at sixteen mile ; Ramath, at three mile ; and Bethlehem, at two mile. And a two mile from Bethlehem, toward the south, is the Church of St. Karitot, that was abbot there, for whom they made much dole amongst the monks when he should die ; and yet they be in mourning in the wise that they made their lamentation for him the first time ; and it is full great pity to behold.

This country and land of Jerusalem hath been in many divers nations' hands, and often, therefore, hath the country suffered much tribulation for the sin of the people that dwell there. For that country hath been in the hands of all nations; that is to say, of Jews, of Canaanites, Assyrians, Persians, Medes, Macedonians, of Greeks, Romans, of Christian men, of Saracens, Barbarians, Turks, Tartars, and of many other divers nations; for God will not that it be long in the hands of traitors ne of sinners, be they Christian or other. And now have the heathen men held that land in their hands forty year and more; but they shall not hold it long, if God will.

And ye shall understand, that when men come to Jerusalem, their first pilgrimage is to the Church of the Holy Sepulchre, where our Lord was buried, that is without the city on the north side; but it is now enclosed in with the town wall. And there is a full fair church, all round, and open above, and covered with lead; and on the west side is a fair tower and an high for bells, strongly made.

And in the midst of the church is a tabernacle, as it were a little house, made with a low little door, and that tabernacle is made in manner of half a compass, right curiously and richly made of gold and azure and other rich colours full nobly made. And in the right side of that tabernacle is the sepulchre of our Lord; and the tabernacle is eight foot long, and five foot wide, and eleven foot in height. And it is not long sith the sepulchre was all open, that men might kiss it and touch it; but for pilgrims that came thither pained them to break the stone in pieces or in powder, therefore the soldan hath do make a wall about the sepulchre that no man may touch it: but in the left side of the wall of the tabernacle is, well the height of a man, a great stone to the quantity of a man's head, that was of the holy sepulchre; and that stone kiss the pilgrims that come thither. In that tabernacle be no windows, but it is all made light with lamps that hang before the sepulchre. And there is a lamp that hangeth before the sepulchre, that burneth light; and on the Good Friday it goeth out by himself, [and lighteth again by him self] at that hour that our Lord rose from death to life.

Also within the church, at the right side, beside the choir of the church, is the mount of Calvary, where our Lord was put on the cross; and it is a rock of white colour and a little medled with red. And the cross was set in a mortise in the same rock. And on that rock dropped the wounds of our Lord when he was pined on the cross. And that is clept Golgotha.

And men go up to that Golgotha by degrees; and in the place of that mortise was Adam's head found after Noah's flood, in token that the sins of Adam should be bought in that same place. And upon that rock made Abraham sacrifice to our Lord. And there is an altar; and before that altar lie Godefray de Bouillon and Baldwin, and other Christian kings of Jerusalem.

And there, nigh where our Lord was crucified, is this written in Greek:

✝ Ὁ θεὸς Βασιλεῦς ἡμῶν πρὸ αἰώνων εἰργάσατο σωτηρίαν ἐν μέσῳ τῆς γῆς;

that is to say, in Latin,—

Deus Rex noster ante secula operatus est salutem, in medio terrae;

that is to say,—

This God our King, before the worlds, hath wrought health in midst of the earth.

And also on that rock, where the cross was set, is written within the rock these words:

✝ Ὁ εἴδεις, ἐστί βάσις τῆς πίστεως ὅλης τοῦ κόσμου τούτου;

that is to say, in Latin,—

Quod vides, est fundamentum totius fidei mundi hujus;

that is to say,—

✝ *That thou seest, is the ground of all the faith of this world.*

And ye shall understand, that when our Lord was done upon the cross, he was thirty-three year and three months of old. And the prophecy of David saith thus: *Quadraginta annis proximus fui generationi huic;* that is to say,

' Forty year was I neighbour to this kindred.' And thus should it seem that the prophecies were not true. But they be both true; for in old time men made a year of ten months, of the which March was the first and December was the last. But Gaius, that was Emperor of Rome, put these two months thereto, January and February, and ordained the year of twelve months; that is to say, 365 days, without leap year, after the proper course of the sun. And therefore, after counting of ten months of the year, he died in the fortieth year, as the prophet said. And after the year of twelve months, he was of age thirty-three year and three months.

Also, within the mount of Calvary, on the right side, is an altar, where the pillar lieth that our Lord Jesu was bounden to when he was scourged. And there beside be four pillars of stone, that always drop water; and some men say that they weep for our Lord's death. And nigh that altar is a place under earth forty-two degrees of deepness, where the holy cross was found, by the wit of Saint Helen, under a rock where the Jews had hid it. And that was the very cross assayed; for they found three crosses, one of our Lord, and two of the two thieves; and Saint Helen proved them by a dead body that arose from death to life, when that it was laid on it, that our Lord died on. And thereby in the wall is the place where the four nails of our Lord were hid: for he had two in his hands and two in his feet. And, of one of these, the Emperor of Constantinople made a bridle to his horse to bear him in battle; and, through virtue thereof, he overcame his enemies, and won all the land of Asia the less, that is to say, Turkey, Armenia the less and the more, and from Syria to Jerusalem, from Arabia to Persia, from Mesopotamia to the kingdom of Aleppo, from Egypt the high and the low and all the other kingdoms unto the depth of Ethiopia, and into Ind the less that then was Christian.

And there were in that time many good holy men and holy hermits, of whom the book of Fathers' lives speaketh, and they be now in Paynims' and Saracens' hands: but when God Almighty will, right as the lands were lost through sin of Christian men, so shall they be won again by Christian men through help of God.

And in midst of that church is a compass, in the which Joseph of Arimathea laid the body of our Lord when he had taken him down off the cross; and there he washed the wounds of our Lord. And that compass, say men, is the midst of the world.

And in the church of the sepulchre, on the north side, is the place where our Lord was put in prison (for he was in prison in many places); and there is a part of the chain that he was bounden with; and there he appeared first to Mary Magdalene when he was risen, and she wend that he had been a gardener.

In the church of Saint Sepulchre was wont to be canons of the order of Saint Augustine, and had a prior, but the patriarch was their sovereign.

And without the doors of the church, on the right side as men go upward eighteen grees, said our Lord to his mother, *Mulier, ecce Filius tuus*; that is to say, Woman, lo! thy Son! And after that he said to John, his disciple, *Ecce mater tua*; that is to say, Lo! behold thy mother! And these words he said on the cross. And on these grees went our Lord when he bare the cross on his shoulder. And under these grees is a chapel, and in that chapel sing priests, Indians, that is to say, priests of Ind, not after our law, but after theirs; and alway they make their sacrament of the altar, saying, *Pater Noster* and other prayers therewith; with the which prayers they say the words that the sacrament is made of, for they ne know not the additions that many popes have made; but they sing with good devotion. And there near, is the place where that our Lord rested him when he was weary for bearing of the cross.

And ye shall understand that before the church of the sepulchre is the city more feeble than in any other part, for the great plain that is between the church and the city. And toward the east side, without the walls of the city, is the vale of Jehosaphat that toucheth to the walls as though it were a large ditch. And above that vale of Jehosaphat, out of the city, is the church of Saint Stephen where he was stoned to death. And there beside, is the Golden Gate, that may not be opened, by the which gate our Lord entered on Palm-Sunday upon an ass: and the gate opened against him when he would go unto the temple; and yet appear the steps of the ass's feet in three places of the degrees that be of full hard stone.

And before the church of Saint Sepulchre, toward the south, at 200 paces, is the great hospital of Saint John, of which the hospitallers had their foundation. And within the palace of the sick men of that hospital be 124 pillars of stone. And in the walls of the house, without the number above-said, there be fifty-four pillars that bear up the house. And from that hospital to go toward the east is a full fair church, that is clept *Nôtre Dame la Grande*. And then is there another church right nigh, that is clept *Nôtre Dame de Latine*. And there were Mary Cleophas and Mary Magdalene, and tore their hair when our Lord was pained in the cross.

CHAPTER XI

Of the Temple of our Lord. Of the Cruelty of King Herod.
Of the Mount Sion. Of Probatica Piscina; and of
Natatorium Siloe

AND from the church of the sepulchre, toward the east, at eight score paces, is *Templum Domini*. It is right a fair house, and it is all round and high, and covered with lead. And it is well paved with white marble. But the Saracens will not suffer no Christian man ne Jews to come therein, for they say that none so foul sinful men should not come in so holy place: but I came in there and in other places there I would, for I had letters of the soldan with his great seal, and commonly other men have but his signet. In the which letters he commanded, of his special grace, to all his subjects, to let me see all the places, and to inform me pleinly all the mysteries of every place, and to con-

duct me from city to city, if it were need, and buxomly to receive me and my company, and for to obey to all my requests reasonable if they were not greatly against the royal power and dignity of the soldan or of his law. And to others, that ask him grace, such as have served him, he ne giveth not but his signet, the which they make to be borne before them hanging on a spear. And the folk of the country do great worship and reverence to his signet or seal, and kneel thereto as lowly as we do to *Corpus Domini*. And yet men do full greater reverence to his letters; for the admiral and all other lords that they be shewed to, before or they receive them, they kneel down ; and then they take them and put them on their heads ; and after, they kiss them and then they read them, kneeling with great reverence ; and then they offer them to do all that the bearer asketh.

And in this *Templum Domini* were some-time canons regulars, and they had an abbot to whom they were obedient ; and in this temple was Charlemagne when that the angel brought him the prepuce of our Lord Jesus Christ of his circumcision ; and after, King Charles let bring it to Paris into his chapel, and after that he let bring it to Peyteres, and after that to Chartres.

And ye shall understand, that this is not the temple that Solomon made, for that temple dured not but 1102 year. For Titus, Vespasian's son, Emperor of Rome, had laid siege about Jerusalem for to discomfit the Jews ; for they put our Lord to death, without leave of the emperor. And, when he had won the city, he burnt the temple and beat it down, and all the city, and took the Jews and did them to death—1,100,000 ; and the others he put in prison and sold them to servage,—thirty for one penny ; for they said they bought Jesu for thirty pennies, and he made of them better cheap when he gave thirty for one penny.

And after that time, Julian Apostate, that was emperor, gave leave to the Jews to make the temple of Jerusalem, for he hated Christian men. And yet he was christened, but he forsook his law, and became a renegade. And when the Jews had made the temple, came an earthquaking, and cast it down (as God would) and destroyed all that they had made.

And after that, Adrian, that was Emperor of Rome, and of the lineage of Troy, made Jerusalem again and the temple in the same manner as Solomon made it. And he would not suffer no Jews to dwell there, but only Christian men. For although it were so that he was not christened, yet he loved Christian men more than any other nation save his own. This emperor let enclose the church of Saint Sepulchre, and walled it within the city; that, before, was without the city, long time before. And he would have changed the name of Jerusalem, and have clept it Aelia; but that name lasted not long.

Also, ye shall understand, that the Saracens do much reverence to that temple, and they say, that that place is right holy. And when they go in they go bare-foot, and kneel many times. And when my fellows and I saw that, when we came in we did off our shoes and came in bare-foot, and thought that we should do as much worship and reverence thereto, as any of the misbelieving men should, and as great compunction in heart to have.

This temple is sixty-four cubits of wideness, and as many in length; and of height it is six score cubits. And it is within, all about, made with pillars of marble. And in the middle place of the temple be many high stages, of fourteen degrees of height, made with good pillars all about: and this place the Jews call *Sancta Sanctorum*; that is to say, 'Holy of Hallows.' And, in that place, cometh no man save only their prelate, that maketh their sacrifice. And the folk stand all about, in diverse stages, after they be of dignity or of worship, so that they all may see the sacrifice. And in that temple be four entries, and the gates be of cypress, well made and curiously dight: and within the east gate our Lord said, 'Here is Jerusalem.' And in the north side of that temple, within the gate, there is a well, but it runneth nought, of the which holy writ speaketh of and saith, *Vidi aquam egredientem de templo*; that is to say, 'I saw water come out of the temple.'

And on that other side of the temple there is a rock that men clepe Moriach, but after it was clept Bethel, where the ark of God with relics of Jews were wont to be put. That ark or hutch with the relics Titus led with him to Rome, when he had discomfited all the Jews. In that ark were the Ten Commandments, and of Aaron's yard, and Moses' yard with the which he made the Red Sea depart, as it had been a wall, on the right side and on the left side, whiles that the people of Israel passed the sea dry-foot : and with that yard he smote the rock, and the water came out of it : and with that yard he did many wonders. And therein was a vessel of gold full of manna, and clothing and ornaments and the tabernacle of Aaron, and a tabernacle square of gold with twelve precious stones, and a box of jasper green with four figures and eight names of our Lord, and seven candlesticks of gold, and twelve pots of gold, and four censers of gold, and an altar of gold, and four lions of gold upon the which they bare cherubin of gold twelve spans long, and the circle of swans of heaven with a tabernacle of gold and a table of silver, and two trumps of silver, and seven barley loaves and all the other relics that were before the birth of our Lord Jesu Christ.

And upon that rock was Jacob sleeping when he saw the angels go up and down by a ladder, and he said, *Vere locus iste sanctus est, et ego ignorabam* ; that is to say, ' Forsooth this place is holy, and I wist it nought.' And there an angel held Jacob still, and turned his name, and clept him Israel. And in that same place David saw the angel that smote the folk with a sword, and put it up bloody in the sheath. And in that same rock was Saint Simeon when he received our Lord into the temple. And in this rock he set him when the Jews would have stoned him ; and a star came down and gave him light. And upon that rock preached our Lord often-time to the people. And out that said temple our Lord drove out the buyers and the sellers. And upon that rock our Lord set him when the Jews would have stoned him ; and the rock clave in two, and in that cleaving was our Lord hid, and there came down a

star and gave light and served him with clarity.   And
upon that rock sat our Lady, and learned her psalter.
And there our Lord forgave the woman her sins, that was
found in avowtry.   And there was our Lord circumcised.
And there the angels shewed tidings to Zacharias of the
birth of Saint Baptist his son.   And there offered first
Melchisadech bread and wine to our Lord, in token of the
sacrament that was to come.   And there fell David praying
to our Lord and to the angel that smote the people, that
he would have mercy on him and on the people : and our
Lord heard his prayer, and therefore would he make the
temple in that place, but our Lord forbade him by an
angel ; for he had done treason when he let slay Uriah the
worthy knight, for to have Bathsheba his wife.   And
therefore, all the purveyance that he had ordained to make
the temple with he took it Solomon his son, and he made it.
And he prayed our Lord, that all those that prayed to him
in that place with good heart—that he would hear their
prayer and grant it them if they asked it rightfully : and
our Lord granted it him, and therefore Solomon clept that
temple the Temple of Counsel and of Help of God.

And without the gate of that temple is an altar where
Jews were in wont to offer doves and turtles.   And
between the temple and that altar was Zacharias slain.
And upon the pinnacle of that temple was our Lord
brought for to be tempted of the enemy, the fiend.   And
on the height of that pinnacle the Jews set Saint James, and
cast him down to the earth, that first was Bishop of
Jerusalem.   And at the entry of that temple, toward the
west, is the gate that is clept *Porta Speciosa*.   And nigh
beside that temple, upon the right side, is a church, covered
with lead, that is clept Solomon's School.

And from that temple towards the south, right nigh, is
the temple of Solomon, that is right fair and well polished.
And in that temple dwell the Knights of the Temple that
were wont to be clept Templars ; and that was the foundation of their order, so that there dwelled knights and in
Templo Domini canons regulars.

From that temple toward the east, a six score paces, in

the corner of the city, is the bath of our Lord; and in that bath was wont to come water from Paradise, and yet it droppeth. And there beside is our Lady's bed. And fast by is the temple of Saint Simeon, and without the cloister of the temple, toward the north, is a full fair church of Saint Anne, our Lady's mother; and there was our Lady conceived; and before that church is a great tree that began to grow the same night. And under that church, in going down by twenty-two degrees, lieth Joachim, our Lady's father, in a fair tomb of stone; and there beside lay some-time Saint Anne, his wife; but Saint Helen let translate her to Constantinople. And in that church is a well, in manner of a cistern, that is clept *Probatica Piscina*, that hath five entries. Into that well angels were wont to come from heaven and bathe them within. And what man, that first bathed him after the moving of the water, was made whole of what manner of sickness that he had. And there our Lord healed a man of the palsy that lay thirty-eight year, and our Lord said to him, *Tolle grabatum tuum et ambula*, that is to say, 'Take thy bed and go.' And there beside was Pilate's house.

And fast by is King Herod's house, that let slay the innocents. This Herod was over-much cursed and cruel. For first he let slay his wife that he loved right well; and for the passing love that he had to her when he saw her dead, he fell in a rage and out of his wit a great while; and sithen he came again to his wit. And after he let slay his two sons that he had of that wife. And after that he let slay another of his wives, and a son that he had with her. And after that he let slay his own mother; and he would have slain his brother also, but he died suddenly. And after that he did all the harm that he could or might. And after he fell into sickness; and when he felt that he should die, he sent after his sister and after all the lords of his land; and when they were come he let command them to prison. And then he said to his sister, he wist well that men of the country would make no sorrow for his death; and therefore he made his sister swear that she should let smite off all the heads of the lords when he were dead;

and then should all the land make sorrow for his death, and else, nought ; and thus he made his testament. But his sister fulfilled not his will. For, as soon as he was dead, she delivered all the lords out of prison and let them go, each lord to his own, and told them all the purpose of her brother's ordinance. And so was this cursed king never made sorrow for, as he supposed for to have been. And ye shall understand, that in that time there were three Herods, of great name and fame for their cruelty. This Herod, of which I have spoken of was Herod Ascalonite ; and he that let behead Saint John the Baptist was Herod Antipas ; and he that let smite off Saint James's head was Herod Agrippa, and he put Saint Peter in prison.

Also, furthermore, in the city is the church of Saint Saviour ; and there is the left arm of John Chrisostome, and the more part of the head of Saint Stephen. And on that other side in the street, toward the south as men go to Mount Sion, is a church of Saint James, where he was beheaded.

And from that church, a six score paces, is the Mount Sion. And there is a fair church of our Lady, where she dwelled ; and there she died. And there was wont to be an abbot of canons regulars. And from thence was she borne of the apostles unto the vale of Jehosaphat. And there is the stone that the angel brought to our Lord from the mount of Sinai, and it is of that colour that the rock is of Saint Catherine. And there beside is the gate where through our Lady went, when she was with child, when she went to Bethlehem. Also at the entry of the Mount Sion is a chapel. And in that chapel is the stone, great and large, with the which the sepulchre was covered with, when Joseph of Arimathea had put our Lord therein ; the which stone the three Marys saw turn upward when they came to the sepulchre the day of his resurrection, and there found an angel that told them of our Lord's uprising from death to life. And there also is a stone in the wall, beside the gate, of the pillar that our Lord was scourged at. And there was Annas's house, that was bishop of the Jews in that time. And there was our Lord examined in the night, and scourged and smitten and villainous entreated. And in that same place Saint Peter forsook our Lord thrice or the cock crew. And there is a part of the table that he made his supper on, when he made his maundy with his disciples, when he gave them his flesh and his blood in form of bread and wine.

And under that chapel, thirty-two degrees, is the place where our Lord washed his disciples' feet, and yet is the vessel where the water was. And there beside that same vessel was Saint Stephen buried. And there is the altar where our Lady heard the angels sing mass. And there appeared first our Lord to his disciples after his resurrection, the gates enclosed, and said to them, *Pax vobis!* that is to say, 'Peace to you!' And on that mount appeared Christ to Saint Thomas the apostle and bade him assay his wounds; and then believed he first, and said, *Dominus meus et Deus meus!* that is to say 'My Lord and my God!' In the same church, beside the altar, were all the apostles on Whitsunday, when the Holy Ghost descended on them in likeness of fire. And there made our Lord his pasque with his disciples. And there slept Saint John the evangelist upon the breast of our Lord Jesu Christ, and saw sleeping many heavenly privities.

Mount Sion is within the city, and it is a little higher than the other side of the city; and the city is stronger on that side than on that other side. For at the foot of the Mount Sion is a fair castle and a strong that the soldan let make. In the Mount Sion were buried King David and King Solomon, and many other kings, Jews of Jerusalem. And there is the place where the Jews would have cast up the body of our Lady when the apostles bare the body to be buried in the vale of Jehosaphat. And there is the place where Saint Peter wept full tenderly after that he had forsaken our Lord. And a stone's cast from that chapel is another chapel, where our Lord was judged, for that time was there Caiaphas's house. From that chapel, to go toward the east, at seven score paces, is a deep cave under the rock, that is clept the Galilee of our Lord, where Saint Peter hid him when he had forsaken our Lord. *Item,* between the Mount Sion and the Temple of Solomon is the place where our Lord raised the maiden in her father's house.

Under the Mount Sion, toward the vale of Jehosaphat, is a well that is clept *Natatorium Siloe*. And there was our Lord washed after his baptism ; and there made our Lord the blind man to see. And there was y-buried Isaiah the prophet. Also, straight from *Natatorium Siloe*, is an image, of stone and of old ancient work, that Absalom let make, and because thereof men clepe it the hand of Absalom. And fast by is yet the tree of elder that Judas hanged himself upon, for despair that he had, when he sold and betrayed our Lord. And there beside was the synagogue, where the bishops of Jews and the †Pharisees came together and held their council ; and there cast Judas the thirty pence before them, and said that he had sinned betraying our Lord. And there nigh was the house of the apostles Philip and Jacob Alphei. And on that other side of Mount Sion, toward the south, beyond the vale a stone's cast, is Aceldama ; that is to say, the field of blood, that was bought for the thirty pence, that our Lord was sold for. And in that field be many tombs of Christian men, for there be many pilgrims graven. And there be many oratories, chapels and hermitages, where hermits were wont to dwell. And toward the east, an hundred paces, is the charnel of the hospital of Saint John, where men were wont to put the bones of dead men.

Also from Jerusalem, toward the west, is a fair church, where the tree of the cross grew. And two mile from thence is a fair church, where our Lady met with Elizabeth, when they were both with child ; and Saint John stirred in his mother's womb, and made reverence to his Creator that he saw not. And under the altar of that church is the place where Saint John was born. And from that church is a mile to the castle of Emmaus : and there also our Lord shewed him to two of his disciples after his resurrection. Also on that other side, 200 paces from Jerusalem, is a church, where was wont to be the cave

of the lion.   And under that church, at thirty degrees of
deepness, were interred 12,000 martyrs, in the time of
King Cosdroe that the lion met with, all in a night, by
the will of God.

Also from Jerusalem, two mile, is the Mount Joy, a
full fair place and a delicious ; and there lieth Samuel the
prophet in a fair tomb.   And men clepe it Mount Joy, for
it giveth joy to pilgrims' hearts, because that there men
see first Jerusalem.

Also between Jerusalem and the mount of Olivet is the
vale of Jehosaphat, under the walls of the city, as I have
said before.   And in the midst of the vale is a little river
that men clepe *Torrens Cedron*, and above it, overthwart,
lay a tree (that the cross was made of) that men yede over
on.   And fast by it is a little pit in the earth, where the
foot of the pillar is yet interred ; and there was our Lord
first scourged, for he was scourged and villainously entreated in many places.   Also in the middle place of the
vale of Jehosaphat is the church of our Lady : and it is of
forty-three degrees under the earth unto the sepulchre of
our Lady.   And our Lady was of age, when she died,
seventy-two year.   And beside the sepulchre of our Lady is
an altar, where our Lord forgave Saint Peter all his sins.
And from thence, toward the west, under an altar, is a
well that cometh out of the river of Paradise.   And wit
well, that that church is full low in the earth, and some is
all within the earth.   But I suppose well, that it was not
so founded.   But for because that Jerusalem hath often-
time been destroyed and the walls abated and beten down
and tumbled into the vale, and that they have been so
filled again and the ground enhanced ; and for that skill is
the church so low within the earth.   And, natheles,
men say there commonly, that the earth hath so been
cloven sith the time that our Lady was there buried ; and
yet men say there, that it waxeth and groweth every day,
without doubt.   In that church were wont to be monks
black, that had their abbot.

And beside that church is a chapel, beside the rock that
hight Gethsemane.   And there was our Lord kissed of

Judas; and there was he taken of the Jews. And there left our Lord his disciples, when he went to pray before his passion, when he prayed and said, *Pater, si fieri potest, transeat a me calix iste*; that is to say, ' Father, if it may be, do let this chalice go from me ' : and, when he came again to his disciples, he found them sleeping. And in the rock within the chapel yet appear the fingers of our Lord's hand, when he put them in the rock, when the Jews would have taken him.

And from thence, a stone's cast towards the south, is another chapel, where our Lord sweat drops of blood. And there, right nigh, is the tomb of King Jehosaphat, of whom the vale beareth the name. This Jehosaphat was king of that country, and was converted by an hermit, that was a worthy man and did much good. And from thence, a bow draught towards the south, is the church, where Saint James and Zachariah the prophet were buried.

And above the vale is the mount of Olivet; and it is clept so for the plenty of olives that grow there. That mount is more high than the city of Jerusalem is; and, therefore, may men upon that mount see many of the streets of the city. And between that mount and the city is not but the vale of Jehosaphat that is not full large. And from that mount styed our Lord Jesu Christ to heaven upon Ascension Day; and yet there sheweth the shape of his left foot in the stone. And there is a church where was wont to be an abbot and canons regulars. And a little thence, twenty-eight paces, is a chapel; and therein is the stone on the which our Lord sat, when he preached the eight blessings and said thus : *Beati pauperes spiritu :* and there he taught his disciples the *Pater Noster*; and wrote with his finger in a stone. And there nigh is a church of Saint Mary Egyptian, and there she lieth in a tomb. And from thence toward the east, a three bow shot, is Bethphage, to the which our Lord sent Saint Peter and Saint James for to seek the ass upon Palm-Sunday, and rode upon that ass to Jerusalem.

And in coming down from the mount of Olivet, toward the east, is a castle that is clept Bethany. And there dwelt

Simon leprous, and there harboured our Lord: and after
he was baptised of the apostles and was clept Julian, and
was made bishop; and this is the same Julian that men
clepe to for good harbourage, for our Lord harboured with
him in his house. And in that house our Lord forgave
Mary Magdalene her sins: there she washed his feet
with her tears, and wiped them with her hair. And there
served Saint Martha our Lord. There our Lord raised
Lazarus from death to life, that was dead four days and
stank, that was brother to Mary Magdalene and to Martha.
And there dwelt also Mary Cleophas. That castle is well
a mile long from Jerusalem. Also in coming down from
the mount of Olivet is the place where our Lord wept
upon Jerusalem. And there beside is the place where our
Lady appeared to Saint Thomas the apostle after her
assumption, and gave him her girdle. And right nigh is
the stone where our Lord often-time sat upon when he
preached; and upon that same he shall sit at the day of
doom, right as himself said.

Also after the mount of Olivet is the mount of Galilee.
There assembled the apostles when Mary Magdalene came
and told them of Christ's uprising. And there, between
the Mount Olivet and the Mount Galilee, is a church, where
the angel said to our Lady of her death.

Also from Bethany to Jericho was sometime a little city,
but it is now all destroyed, and now is there but a little
village. That city took Joshua by miracle of God and
commandment of the angel, and destroyed it, and cursed it
and all them that bigged it again. Of that city was Zaccheus
the dwarf that clomb up into the sycamore tree for to see
our Lord, because he was so little he might not see him
for the people. And of that city was Rahab the common
woman that escaped alone with them of her lineage: and
she often-time refreshed and fed the messengers of Israel,
and kept them from many great perils of death; and,
therefore, she had good reward, as holy writ saith: *Qui
accipit prophetam in nomine meo, mercedem prophetae accipiet*;
that is to say, 'He that taketh a prophet in my name, he
shall take meed of the prophet.' And so had she. For

she prophesied to the messengers, saying, *Novi quod Dominus tradet vobis terram hanc*; that is to say, ' I wot well, that our Lord shall betake you this land ' : and so he did. And after, Salomon, Naasson's son, wedded her, and from that time was she a worthy woman, and served God well.

Also from Bethany go men to flom Jordan by a mountain and through desert. And it is nigh a day journey from Bethany, toward the east, to a great hill, where our Lord fasted forty days. Upon that hill the enemy of hell bare our Lord and tempted him, and said, *Dic ut lapides isti panes fiant*; that is to say, ' Say, that these stones be made loaves.' In that place, upon the hill, was wont to be a fair church ; but it is all destroyed, so that there is now but an hermitage, that a manner of Christian men hold, that be clept Georgians, for Saint George converted them. Upon that hill dwelt Abraham a great while, and therefore men clepe it Abraham's Garden. And between the hill and this garden runneth a little brook of water that was wont to be bitter ; but, by the blessing of Elisha the prophet, it became sweet and good to drink. And at the foot of this hill, toward the plain, is a great well, that entereth into flom Jordan.

From that hill to Jericho, that I spake of before, is but a mile in going toward flom Jordan. Also as men go to Jericho sat the blind man crying, *Jesu, Fili David, miserere mei* ; that is to say, ' Jesu, David's Son, have mercy on me.' And anon he had his sight. Also, two mile from Jericho, is flome Jordan. And, an half mile more nigh, is a fair church of Saint John the Baptist, where he baptised our Lord. And there beside is the house of Jeremiah the prophet.

CHAPTER XII

*Of the Dead Sea; and of the Flome Jordan.   Of the Head
    of Saint John the Baptist; and of the Usages of the
    Samaritans*

AND from Jericho, a three mile, is the Dead Sea.   About
that sea groweth much alum and of alkatran.   Between
Jericho and that sea is the land of Engeddi.   And there
was wont to grow the balm; but men make draw the
branches thereof and bear them to be grafted at Babylon;
and yet men clepe them vines of Geddi.   At a coast of
that sea, as men go from Arabia, is the mount of the
Moabites, where there is a cave, that men clepe Karua.
Upon that hill led Balak, the son of Beor, Balaam the
priest for to curse the people of Israel.

That Dead Sea parteth the land of Ind and of Arabia,
and that sea lasteth from Soara unto Arabia.   The water
of that sea is full bitter and salt, and, if the earth were
made moist and wet with that water, it would never bear
fruit.   And the earth and the land changeth often his
colour.   And it casteth out of the water a thing that men
clepe asphalt, also great pieces, as the greatness of an
horse, every day and on all sides.   And from Jerusalem
to that sea is 200 furlongs.   That sea is in length
five hundred and four score furlongs, and in breadth
an hundred and fifty furlongs; and it is clept the Dead
Sea, for it runneth nought, but is ever un-movable.
And neither man, ne beast, ne nothing that beareth
life in him ne may not die in that sea.   And that hath
been proved many times, by men that have deserved to
be dead that have been cast therein and left therein three
days or four, and they ne might never die therein; for
it receiveth no thing within him that beareth life.   And no
man may drink of the water for bitterness.   And if a man
cast iron therein, it will float above.   And if men cast a

feather therein, it will sink to the bottom, and these be
things against kind.

And also, the cities there were lost because of sin. And
there beside grow trees that bear full fair apples, and fair
of colour to behold; but whoso breaketh them or cutteth
them in two, he shall find within them coals and cinders,
in token that by wrath of God the cities and the land were
burnt and sunken into hell. Some men clepe that sea the
lake Dalfetidee; some, the flome of Devils; and some
the flome that is ever stinking. And into that sea sunk
the five cities by wrath of God; that is to say, Sodom,
Gomorrah, Aldama, Zeboim, and Zoar, for the abominable
sin of sodomy that reigned in them. But Zoar, by the
prayer of Lot, was saved and kept a great while, for it was
set upon a hill; and yet sheweth thereof some part above
the water, and men may see the walls when it is fair
weather and clear. In that city Lot dwelt a little while;
and there was he made drunk of his daughters, and lay with
them, and engendered of them Moab and Ammon. And
the cause why his daughters made him drunk and for to
lie by him was this: because they saw no man about them,
but only their father, and therefore they trowed that God
had destroyed all the world as he had done the cities, as
he had done before by Noah's flood. And therefore they
would lie by with their father for to have issue, and for to
replenish the world again with people to restore the world
again by them; for they trowed that there had been no
more men in all the world; and if their father had not
been drunk, he had not lain with them.

And the hill above Zoar men cleped it then Edom and
after men cleped it Seir, and after Idumea. Also at the
right side of that Dead Sea, dwelleth yet the wife of Lot in
likeness of a salt stone; for that she looked behind her
when the cities sunk into hell. This Lot was Haran's
son, that was brother to Abraham; and Sarah, Abraham's
wife, and Milcah, Nahor's wife, were sisters to the said
Lot. And the same Sarah was of eld four score and
ten year when Isaac her son was gotten on her. And
Abraham had another son Ishmael that he gat upon Hagar

his chamberer. And when Isaac his son was eight days old, Abraham his father let him be circumcised, and Ishmael with him that was fourteen year old: wherefore the Jews that come of Isaac's line be circumcised the eighth day, and the Saracens that come of Ishmael's line be circumcised when they be fourteen year of age.

And ye shall understand, that within the Dead Sea, runneth the flom Jordan, and there it dieth, for it runneth no further more, and that is a place that is a mile from the church of Saint John the Baptist toward the west, a little beneath the place where that Christian men bathe them commonly. And a mile from flom Jordan is the river of Jabbok, the which Jacob passed over when he came from Mesopotamia. This flom Jordan is no great river, but it is plenteous of good fish; and it cometh out of the hill of Lebanon by two wells that be clept Jor and Dan, and of the two wells hath it the name. And it passeth by a lake that is clept Maron. And after it passeth by the sea of Tiberias, and passeth under the hills of Gilboa; and there is a full fair vale, both on that one side and on that other of the same river. And men go [on] the hills of Lebanon, all in length unto the desert of Pharan; and those hills part the kingdom of Syria and the country of Phoenicia; and upon those hills grow trees of cedar that be full high, and they bear long apples, and as great as a man's head.

And also this flom Jordan departeth the land of Galilee and the land of Idumea and the land of Betron, and that runneth under earth a great way unto a fair plain and a great that is clept Meldan in Sarmois; that is to say, Fair or market in their language, because that there is often fairs in that plain. And there becometh the water great and large. In that plain is the tomb of Job.

And in that flom Jordan above-said was our Lord baptised of Saint John, and the voice of God the Father was heard saying: *Hic est Filius meus dilectus, etc.*; that is to say, 'This is my beloved Son, in the which I am well pleased; hear him!' and the Holy Ghost alighted upon him in likeness of a culver; and so at his baptising was all the whole Trinity.

And through that flome passed the children of Israel, all dry feet; and they put stones there in the middle place, in token of the miracle that the water withdrew him so. Also in that flome Jordan Naaman of Syria bathed him, that was full rich, but he was mesell; and there anon he took his health.

About the flome Jordan be many churches where that many Christian men dwelled. And nigh thereto is the city of Ai that Joshua assailed and took. Also beyond the flome Jordan is the vale of Mamre, and that is a full fair vale. Also upon the hill that I spake of before, where our Lord fasted forty days, a two mile long from Galilee, is a fair hill and an high, where the enemy the fiend bare our Lord the third time to tempt him, and shewed him all the regions of the world and said, *Hec omnia tibi dabo, si cadens adoraveris me*; that is to say, 'All this shall I give thee, if thou fall and worship me.'

Also from the Dead Sea to go eastward, out of the marches of the Holy Land that is clept the Land of Promission, is a strong castle and a fair, in an hill that is clept Carak in Sarmois; that is to say, Royally. That castle let make King Baldwin, that was King of France, when he had conquered that land, and put it into Christian men's hands for to keep that country; and for that cause was it clept the Mount Royal. And under it there is a town that hight Sobach, and there, all about, dwell Christian men, under tribute.

From thence go men to Nazareth, of the which our Lord beareth the surname. And from thence there is three journeys to Jerusalem : and men go by the province of Galilee by Ramath, by Sothim and by the high hill of Ephraim, where Elkanah and Hannah the mother of Samuel the prophet dwelled. There was born this prophet; and, after his death, he was buried at Mount Joy, as I have said you before.

And then go men to Shiloh, where the Ark of God with the relics were kept long time under Eli the prophet. There made the people of Hebron sacrifice to our Lord, and they yielded up their vows. And there spake

God first to Samuel, and shewed him the mutation of Order of Priesthood, and the mystery of the Sacrament. And right nigh, on the left side, is Gibeon and Ramah and Benjamin, of the which holy writ speaketh of.

And after men go to Sichem, some-time clept Sichar ; and that is in the province of Samaritans. And there is a full fair vale and a fructuous ; and there is a fair city and a good that men clepe Neople. And from thence is a journey to Jerusalem. And there is the well, where our Lord spake to the woman of Samaritan. And there was wont to be a church, but it is beaten down. Beside that well King Rehoboam let make two calves of gold and made them to be worshipped, and put that one at Dan and that other at Bethel. And a mile from Sichar is the city of Luz ; and in that city dwelt Abraham a certain time. Sichem is a ten mile from Jerusalem, and it is clept Neople ; that is for to say, the New City. And nigh beside is the tomb of Joseph the son of Jacob that governed Egypt : for the Jews bare his bones from Egypt and buried them there, and thither go the Jews often-time in pilgrimage with great devotion. In that city was Dinah, Jacob's daughter, ravished, for whom her brethren slew many persons and did many harms to the city. And there beside is the hill of Gerizim, where the Samaritans make their sacrifice : in that hill would Abraham have sacrificed his son Isaac. And there beside is the vale of Dotaim, and there is the cistern, where Joseph, was cast in of his brethren, which they sold ; and that is two mile from Sichar.

From thence go men to Samaria that men clepe now Sebast ; and that is the chief city of that country, and it sits between the hill of Aygnes[1] as Jerusalem doth. In that city was the sittings of the twelve tribes of Israel; but the city is not now so great as it was wont to be. There was buried Saint John the Baptist between two prophets, Elisha and Abdon ; but he was beheaded in the castle of Macharim beside the Dead Sea, and after he was translated of his disciples, and buried at Samaria. And there let Julianus Apostata dig him up and let burn his bones (for

[1] French: *entre montaignes.*

he was at that time emperor) and let winnow the ashes in
the wind.   But the finger that shewed our Lord, saying,
Ecce Agnus Dei ; that is to say, ' Lo ! the Lamb of God,'
that would never burn, but is all whole ;—that finger let
Saint Thecla, the holy virgin, be born into the hill of
Sebast ; and there make men great feast.

In that place was wont to be a fair church ; and many
other there were ; but they be all beaten down.   There
was wont to be the head of Saint John Baptist, enclosed in
the wall.   But the Emperor Theodosius let draw it out,
and found it wrapped in a little cloth, all bloody ; and so
he let it to be born to Constantinople.   And yet at Constantinople is the hinder part of the head, and the fore
part of the head, till under the chin, is at Rome under the
church of Saint Silvester, where be nuns of an hundred
orders [1]: and it is yet all broilly, as though it were half-
burnt, for the Emperor Julianus above-said, of his cursedness and malice, let burn that part with the other bones,
and yet it sheweth ; and this thing hath been proved both
by popes and by emperors.   And the jaws beneath, that
hold to the chin, and a part of the ashes and the platter
that the head was laid in, when it was smitten off, is at
Genoa ; and the Genoese make of it great feast, and so do
the Saracens also.   And some men say that the head of
Saint John is at Amiens in Picardy ; and other men say that
it is the head of Saint John the Bishop.   I wot never, but
God knoweth ; but in what wise that men worship it, the
blessed Saint John holds him a-paid.

From this city of Sebast unto Jerusalem is twelve mile.
And between the hills of that country there is a well that
four sithes in the year changeth his colour, sometime green,
sometime red, sometime clear and sometime trouble ; and
men clepe that well, Job.   And the folk of that country,
that men clepe Samaritans, were converted and baptized by
the apostles ; but they hold not well their doctrine, and
always they hold laws by themselves, varying from Christian men, from Saracens, Jews and Paynims.   And the
Samaritans lieve well in one God, and they say well that

[1] The translator mistakes *cordelers* for *c. ordres.*

there is but only one God, that all formed, and all shall
doom ; and they hold the Bible after the letter, and they
use the Psalter as the Jews do. And they say that they be
the right sons of God. And among all other folk, they say
that they be best beloved of God, and that to them
belongeth the heritage that God behight to his beloved
children. And they have also diverse clothing and
shape to look on than other folk have ; for they wrap
their heads in red linen cloth, in difference from others.
And the Saracens wrap their heads in white linen cloth ;
and the Christian men, that dwell in the country, wrap
them in blue of Ind ; and the Jews in yellow cloth. In
that country dwell many of the Jews, paying tribute as
Christian men do. And if ye will know the letters that
the Jews use they be such, and the names be as they clepe
them written above, in manner of their A. B. C.

†Aleph	Beth	Gymel	Deleth	He	Vau	Zay
א	ב	ג	ד	ה	ו	ז
Heth	Thet	Joht	Kapho	Lampd	Mem	Num
ח	ט	י	כ	ל	מ	נ
Sameth	Ey	Fhee	Sade	Coph	Resch	Son	Tau
ס	ע	פ	צ	ק	ר	ש	ת

CHAPTER XIII

*Of the Province of Galilee, and where Antichrist shall be
born. Of Nazareth. Of the age of Our Lady. Of the
Day of Doom. And of the customs of Jacobites, Syrians;
and of the usages of Georgians*

FROM this country of the Samaritans that I have spoken of
before go men to the plains of Galilee, and men leave the
hills on that one part.

And Galilee is one of the provinces of the Holy Land,
and in that province is the city of Nain—and Capernaum,
and Chorazin and Bethsaida. In this Bethsaida was Saint

Peter and Saint Andrew born.   And thence, a four mile, is Chorazin.   And five mile from Chorazin is the city of Kedar whereof the Psalter speaketh : *Et habitavi cum habitantibus Kedar;* that is for to say, ' And I have dwelled with the dwelling men in Kedar.'   In Chorazin shall Antichrist be born, as some men say.   And other men say he shall be born in Babylon ; for the prophet saith : *De Babilonia coluber exiet, qui totum mundum devorabit;* that is to say, ' Out of Babylon shall come a worm that shall devour all the world.'   This Antichrist shall be nourished in Bethsaida, and he shall reign in Capernaum : and therefore saith holy writ; *Vae tibi, Chorazin!   Vae tibi, Bethsaida!   Vae tibi, Capernaum!* that is to say, ' Woe be to thee, Chorazin ! Woe to thee, Bethsaida !   Woe to thee, Capernaum.' And all these towns be in the land of Galilee.   And also the Cana of Galilee is four mile from Nazareth : of that city was Simon Chananeus and his wife Canee, of the which the holy evangelist speaketh of.   There did our Lord the first miracle at the wedding, when he turned water into wine.

And in the end of Galilee, at the hills, was the Ark of God taken ; and on that other side is the Mount Endor or Hermon.   And, thereabout, goeth the Brook of Torrens Kishon ; and there beside, Barak, that was Abimelech's son with Deborah the prophetess overcame the host of Idumea, when Sisera the king was slain of Jael the wife of Heber, and chased beyond the flome Jordan, by strength of sword, Zeeb and Zebah and Zalmunna, and there he slew them. Also a five mile from Nain is the city of Jezreel that sometime was clept Zarim, of the which city Jezabel, the cursed queen, was lady and queen, that took away the vine of Naboth by her strength.   Fast by that city is the field Megiddo, in the which the King Joram was slain of the King of Samaria and after was translated and buried in the Mount Sion.

And a mile from Jezreel be the hills of Gilboa, where Saul and Jonathan, that were so fair, died ; wherefore David cursed them, as holy writ saith : *Montes Gilboae, nec ros nec pluvia, etc.;* that is to say, ' Ye hills of Gilboa, neither dew ne rain come upon you.' And a mile from the hills of Gilboa toward the east is the city of Cyropolis, that was clept before Bethshan ; and upon the walls of that city was the head of Saul hanged.

After go men by the hill beside the plains of Galilee unto Nazareth, where was wont to be a great city and a fair ; but now there is not but a little village, and houses abroad here and there. And it is not walled. And it sits in a little valley, and there be hills all about. There was our Lady born, but she was gotten at Jerusalem. And because that our Lady was born at Nazareth, therefore bare our Lord his surname of that town. There took Joseph our Lady to wife, when she was fourteen year of age. And there Gabriel greeted our Lady, saying, *Ave gratia plena, Dominus tecum!* that is to say, ' Hail, full of grace, our Lord is with thee !' And this salutation was done in a place of a great altar of a fair church that was wont to be sometime, but it is now all down, and men have made a little receipt, beside a pillar of that church, to receive the offerings of pilgrims. And the Saracens keep that place full dearly, for the profit that they have thereof. And they be full wicked Saracens and cruel, and more despiteful than in any other place, and have destroyed all the churches. There nigh is Gabriel's Well, where our Lord was wont to bathe him, when he was young, and from that well bare he water often-time to his mother. And in that well she washed often-time the clouts of her Son Jesu Christ. And from Jerusalem unto thither is three journeys. At Nazareth was our Lord nourished. Nazareth is as much to say as, ' Flower of the garden' ; and by good skill may it be clept flower, for there was nourished the flower of life that was Christ Jesu.

And two mile from Nazareth is the city of Sephor, by the way that goeth from Nazareth to Akon. And an half mile from Nazareth is the Leap of our Lord. For the Jews led him upon an high rock for to make him leap down, and have slain him; but Jesu passed amongst them, and leapt upon another rock, and yet be the steps of his feet seen in the rock, where he alighted. And therefore say some men, when they dread them of thieves in any way, or of enemies; *Jesus autem transiens per medium illorum ibat;* that is to say, ' Jesus, forsooth, passing by the midst of them, he went' : in token and mind, that our Lord passed through, out the Jews' cruelty, and scaped safely from them, so surely may men pass the peril of thieves. And then say men two verses of the Psalter three sithes : *Irruat super eos formido & pavor, in magnitudine brachii tui, Domine. Fiant immobiles, quasi lapis, donec pertranseat populus tuus, Domine; donec pertranseat populus tuus iste, quem possedisti;* and then may men pass without peril.

And ye shall understand, that our Lady had child when she was fifteen year old. And she was conversant with her son thirty-three year and three months. And after the passion of our Lord she lived twenty-four year.

Also from Nazareth men go to the Mount Tabor; and that is a four mile. And it is a full fair hill and well high, where was wont to be a town and many churches; but they be all destroyed. But yet there is a place that men clepe the school of God, where he was wont to teach his disciples, and told them the privities of heaven. And, at the foot of that hill, Melchisedech that was King of Salem, in the turning of that hill met Abraham in coming again from the battle, when he had slain Abimelech. And this Melchisedech was both king and priest of Salem that now is clept Jerusalem. In that hill Tabor our Lord transfigured him before Saint Peter, Saint John and Saint Jame; and there they saw, ghostly, Moses and Elias the prophets beside them. And therefore said Saint Peter; *Domine, bonum est nos hic esse; faciamus hic tria tabernacula;* that is to say, 'Lord, it is good for us to be here; make we here three dwelling-places.' And there heard they a voice of the Father that say; *Hic est Filius meus dilectus, in quo mihi bene complacui.* And our Lord defended them that they should not tell that avision till that he were risen from death to life.

In that hill and in that same place, at the day of doom, four angels with four trumpets shall blow and raise all men that had suffered death, sith that the world was

formed, from death to life ; and shall come in body and soul in judgment, before the face of our Lord in the Vale of Jehosaphat. And the doom shall be on Easter Day, such time as our Lord arose. And the doom shall begin, such hour as our Lord descended to hell and despoiled it. For at such hour shall he despoil the world and lead his chosen to bliss ; and the other shall he condemn to perpetual pains. And then shall every man have after his desert, either good or evil, but if the mercy of God pass his righteousness.

Also a mile from Mount Tabor is the Mount Hermon ; and there was the city of Nain. Before the gate of that city raised our Lord the widow's son, that had no more children. Also three miles from Nazareth is the Castle Safra, of the which the sons of Zebedee and the sons of Alpheus were. Also a seven mile from Nazareth is the Mount Cain, and under that is a well ; and beside that well Lamech, Noah's father, slew Cain with an arrow. For this Cain went through briars and bushes as a wild beast ; and he had lived from the time of Adam his father unto the time of Noah, and so he lived nigh to 2000 year. And this Lamech was all blind for eld.

From Safra men go to the sea of Galilee and to the city of Tiberias, that sits upon the same sea. And albeit that men clepe it a sea, yet is it neither sea ne arm of the sea. For it is but a stank of fresh water that is in length one hundred furlongs, and of breadth forty furlongs, and hath within him great plenty of good fish, and runneth into flom Jordan. The city is not full great, but it hath good baths within him.

And there, as the flome Jordan parteth from the sea of Galilee, is a great bridge, where men pass from the Land of Promission to the land of King Bashan and the land of Gennesaret, that be about the flom Jordan and the beginning of the sea of Tiberias. And from thence may men go to Damascus, in three days, by the kingdom of Traconitis, the which kingdom lasteth from Mount Hermon to the sea of Galilee, or to the sea of Tiberias, or to the sea of Gennesaret ; and all is one sea, and this the tank that I have told you, but it changeth thus the name for the names of the cities that sit beside him.

Upon that sea went our Lord dry feet ; and there he took up Saint Peter, when he began to drench within the sea, and said to him, *Modice fidei, quare dubitasti ?* And after his resurrection our Lord appeared on that sea to his disciples and bade them fish, and filled all the net full of great fishes. In that sea rowed our Lord often-time ; and there he called to him Saint Peter, Saint Andrew, Saint James and Saint John, the sons of Zebedee.

In that city of Tiberias is the table upon the which our Lord ate upon with his disciples after his resurrection ; and they knew him in breaking of bread, as the gospel saith : *Et cognoverunt eum in fractione panis.* And nigh that city of Tiberias is the hill, where our Lord fed 5000 persons with five barley loaves and two fishes.

In that city a man cast a burning dart in wrath after our Lord. And the head smote into the earth and waxed green ; and it growed to a great tree. And yet it groweth and the bark thereof is all like coals.

Also in the head of that sea of Galilee, toward the septentrion is a strong castle and an high that hight Saphor. And fast beside it is Capernaum. Within the Land of Promission is not so strong a castle. And there is a good town beneath that is clept also Saphor. In that castle Saint Anne our Lady's mother was born. And there beneath, was Centurio's house. That country is clept the Galilee of Folk that were taken to tribute of Zebulon and Napthali.

And in again coming from that castle, a thirty mile, is the city of Dan, that sometime was clept Belinas or Cesarea Philippi ; that sits at the foot of the Mount of Lebanon, where the flome Jordan beginneth. There beginneth the Land of Promission and dureth unto Beersheba in length, in going toward the north into the south, and it containeth well a nine score miles ; and of †breadth, that is to say, from Jericho unto Jaffa, and that containeth a forty mile of Lombardy, or of our country, that be also little miles ; these be not miles of Gascony ne of the province of Almayne, where be great miles.   And wit ye well, that the Land of Promission is in Syria.   For the realm of Syria dureth from the deserts of Arabia unto Cilicia, and that is Armenia the great ;   that is to say, from the south to the north.   And, from the east to the west, it dureth from the great deserts of Arabia unto the West Sea.   But in that realm of Syria is the kingdom of Judea and many other provinces, as Palestine, Galilee, Little Cilicia, and many other.

In that country and other countries beyond they have a custom, when they shall use war, and when men hold siege about city or castle, and they within dare not send out messengers with letters from lord to lord for to ask succour, they make their letters and bind them to the neck of a culver, and let the culver flee.   And the culvers be so taught, that they flee with those letters to the very place that men would send them to.   For the culvers be nourished in those places where they be sent to, and they send them thus, for to bear their letters.   And the culvers return again whereas they be nourished ; and so they do commonly.

And ye shall understand that amongst the Saracens, one part and other, dwell many Christian men of many manners and diverse names.   And all be baptized and have diverse laws and diverse customs.   But all believe in God the Father and the Son and the Holy Ghost ; but always fail they in some articles of our faith.   Some of these be clept Jacobites, for Saint James converted them and Saint John baptized them.   They say that a man shall make his confession only to God, and not to a man ; for only to him should man yield him guilty of all that he hath misdone.   Ne God ordained not, ne never devised, ne the prophet neither, that a man should shrive him to another (as they say), but only to God.   As Moses writeth in the Bible, and as David saith in the Psalter Book; *Confitebor tibi, Domine, in toto corde meo,* and *Delictum meum tibi cognitum feci,* and *Deus meus es tu, & confitebor tibi,* and *Quoniam cogitatio hominis confitebitur tibi,* etc.   For they know all the Bible and the Psalter.   And therefore allege they so the letter.   But they allege not the authorities thus in Latin, but in their language full apertly, and say well, that David and other prophets say it.

Natheles, Saint Augustine and Saint Gregory say thus :—Augustinus : *Qui scelera sua cogitat, & conversus fuerit, veniam sibi credat.* Gregorius : *Dominus potius mentem quam verba respicit.* And Saint Hilary saith : *Longorum temporum crimina, in ictu oculi pereunt, si cordis nata fuerit compunctio.* And for such authorities they say, that only to God shall a man knowledge his defaults, yielding himself guilty and crying him mercy, and behoting to him to amend himself. And therefore, when they will shrive them, they take fire and set it beside them, and cast therein powder of frankincense ; and in the smoke thereof they shrive them to God, and cry him mercy. But sooth it is, that this confession was first and kindly. But Saint Peter the apostle, and they that came after him, have ordained to make their confession to man, and by good reason ; for they perceived well that no sickness was curable, [ne] good medicine to lay thereto, but if men knew the nature of the malady ; and also no man may give convenable medicine, but if he know the quality of the deed. For one sin may be greater in one man than in another, and in one place and in one time than in another ; and therefore it behoveth him that he know the kind of the deed, and thereupon to give him penance.

There be other, that be clept Syrians ; and they hold the belief amongst us, and of them of Greece. And they use all beards, as men of Greece do. And they make the sacrament of therf bread. And in their language they use letters of Saracens. But after the mystery of Holy Church they use letters of Greece. And they make their confession, right as the Jacobites do.

There be other, that men clepe Georgians, that Saint George converted ; and him they worship more than any other saint, and to him they cry for help. And they came out of the realm of Georgia. These folk use crowns shaven. The clerks have round crowns, and the lewd men have crowns all square. And they hold Christian law, as do they of Greece ; of whom I have spoken of before.

Other there be that men clepe Christian men of Girding, for they be all girt above. And there be other that men clepe Nestorians. And some Arians, some Nubians, some of Greece, some of Ind, and some of Prester John's Land. And all these have many articles of our faith, and to other they be variant. And of their variance were too long to tell, and so I will leave, as for the time, without more speaking of them.

CHAPTER XIV

Of the City of Damascus. Of three ways to Jerusalem; one, by land and by sea; another, more by land than by sea; and the third way to Jerusalem, all by land

Now after that I have told you some part of folk in the countries before, now will I turn again to my way, for to turn again on this half. Then whoso will go from the land of Galilee, of that that I have spoke for, to come again on this half, men come again by Damascus, that is a full fair city and full noble, and full of all merchandises, and a three journeys long from the sea, and a five journeys from Jerusalem. But upon camels, mules, horses, dromedaries and other beasts, men carry their merchandise thither. And thither come the merchants with merchandise by sea from India, Persia, Chaldea, Armenia, and of many other kingdoms.

This city founded Eliezer Damascus, that was yeoman and dispenser of Abraham before that Isaac was born. For he thought for to have been Abraham's heir, and he named the town after his surname Damascus. And in that place, where Damascus was founded, Cain slew Abel his brother. And beside Damascus is the Mount Seir. In that city of Damascus there is great plenty of wells. And within the city and without be many fair gardens and of diverse fruits. None other city is not like in comparison to it of fair gardens, and of fair disports.

The city is great and full of people, and well walled with double walls. And there be many physicians. And Saint Paul himself was there a physician for to keep men's bodies in health, before he was converted. And after that he was physician of souls. And Saint Luke the evangelist was disciple of Saint Paul for to learn physic, and many other ; for Saint Paul held then school of physic. And near beside Damascus was he converted. And after his conversion ne dwelt in that city three days, without sight and without meat or drink ; and in those three days he was ravished to heaven, and there he saw many privities of our Lord.

And fast beside Damascus is the castle of Arkes that is both fair and strong.

From Damascus men come again by our Lady of Sardenak, that is a five mile on this half Damascus. And it sitteth upon a rock, and it is a full fair place ; and it seemeth a castle, for there was wont to be a castle, but it is now a full fair church. And there within be monks and nuns Christian. And there is a vault under the church, where that Christian men dwell also. And they have many good vines. And in the church, behind the high altar, in the wall, is a table of black wood, on the which sometime was depainted an image of our Lady that turneth into flesh : but now the image sheweth but little, but alway, by the grace of God,[1] that table evermore drops oil, as it were of olive ; and there is a vessel of marble under the table to receive the oil. Thereof they give to pilgrims, for it heals of many sicknesses ; and men say that, if it be kept well seven year, afterwards it turns into flesh and blood. From Sardenak men come through the vale of Bochar, the which is a fair vale and a plenteous of all manner of fruit ; and it is amongst hills. And there are therein fair rivers and great meadows and noble pasture for beasts. And men go by the mounts of Libanus, which lasts from Armenia the more towards the north unto Dan, the which is the end of the Land of Repromission toward the north, as I said before. Their hills are right fruitful, and there are many fair wells and cedars and cypresses, and many other trees

[1] From here to page 87 l. 8 is supplied from the Egerton MS.

of divers kinds. There are also many good towns toward the head of their hills, full of folk.

Between the city of Arkez and the city of Raphane is a river, that is called Sabatory; for on the Saturday it runs fast, and all the week else it stand still and runs not, or else but fairly. Between the foresaid hills also is another water that on nights freezes hard and on days is no frost seen thereon. And, as men come again from those hills, is a hill higher than any of the other, and they call it there the High Hill. There is a great city and a fair, the which is called Tripoli, in the which are many good Christian men, yemand the same rites and customs that we use. From thence men come by a city that is called Beyrout, where Saint George slew the dragon ; and it is a good town, and a fair castle therein, and it is three journeys from the foresaid city of Sardenak. At the one side of Beyrout sixteen mile, to come hitherward, is the city of Sydon. At Beyrout enters pilgrims into the sea that will come to Cyprus, and they arrive at the port of Surry or of Tyre, and so they come to Cyprus in a little space. Or men may come from the port of Tyre and come not at Cyprus, and arrive at some haven of Greece, and so come to these parts, as I said before.

I have told you now of the way by which men go farrest and longest to Jerusalem, as by Babylon and Mount Sinai and many other places which ye heard me tell of; and also by which ways men shall turn again to the Land of Repromission. Now will I tell you the rightest way and the shortest to Jerusalem. For some men will not go the other; some for they have not spending enough, some for they have no good company, and some for they may not endure the long travel, some for they dread them of many perils of deserts, some for they will haste them homeward, desiring to see their wives and their children, or for some other reasonable cause that they have to turn soon home. And therefore I will shew how men may pass tittest and in shortest time make their pilgrimage to Jerusalem. A man that comes from the lands of the west, he goes through France, Burgoyne, and Lumbardy. And so to Venice or Genoa, or some other haven, and ships there and wends by sea to the isle of Greff, the which pertains to the Genoans.

And syne he arrives in Greece at Port Mirrok, or at Valoun, or at Duras, or at some other haven of that country, and rests him there and buys him victuals and ships again and sails to Cyprus and arrives there at Famagost and comes not at the isle of Rhodes. Famagost is the chief haven of Cyprus; and there he refreshes him and purveys him of victuals, and then he goes to ship and comes no more on land, if he will, before he comes at Port Jaffa, that is the next haven to Jerusalem, for it is but a day journey and a half from Jerusalem, that is to say thirty-six mile. From the Port Jaffa men go to the city of Rames, the which is but a little thence; and it is a fair city and a good and mickle folk therein. And without that city toward the south is a kirk of our Lady, where our Lord shewed him to her in three clouds, the which betokened the Trinity. And a little thence is another city, that men call Dispolis, but it hight some time Lidda, a fair city and a well inhabited: there is a kirk of Saint George, where he was headed. From thence men go to the castle of Emmaus, and so to the Mount Joy; there may pilgrims first see Jerusalem. At Mount Joy lies Samuel the prophet. From thence men go to Jerusalem. Beside their ways is the city of Ramatha and the Mount Modyn; and thereof was Matathias, Judas Machabeus father, and there are the graves of the Machabees. Beyond Ramatha is the town of Tekoa, whereof Amos the prophet was; and there is his grave.

I have told you before of the holy places that are at Jerusalem and about it, and therefore I will speak no more of them at this time. But I will turn again and shew you other ways a man may pass more by land, and namely for them that may not suffer the savour of the sea, but is liefer to go by land, if all it be the more pain. From a man be entered into the sea he shall pass till one of the havens of Lumbardy, for there is the best making of purveyance of victuals; or he may pass to Genoa or Venice

or some other.   And he shall pass by sea in to Greece to
the Port Mirrok, or to Valoun or to Duras, or some
other haven of that country.   And from thence he shall
go by land to Constantinople, and he shall pass the water
that is called Brace Saint George, the which is one arm of
the sea.   And from thence he shall by land go to Ruffynell, where a good castle is and a strong; and from
therein he shall go to Puluual, and syne to the castle of
Sinope, and from thence to Cappadocia, that is a great
country, where are many great hills.   And he shall go
through Turkey to the port of Chiutok and to the city of
Nicæa, which is but seven miles thence.   That city won the
Turks from the Emperor of Constantinople; and it is a
fair city and well walled on the one side, and on the other
side is a great lake and a great river, the which is called Lay.
From thence men go by the hills of Nairmount and by the
vales of Mailbrins and strait fells and by the town of
Ormanx or by the towns that are on Riclay and Stancon,
the which are great rivers and noble, and so to Antioch
the less, which is set on the river of Riclay.   And there
abouts are many good hills and fair, and many fair woods
and great plenty of wild beasts for to hunt at.

And he that will go another way, he shall go by the
plains of Romany coasting the Roman Sea.   On that coast
is a fair castle that men call Florach, and it is right a
strong place.   And uppermore amongst the mountains
is a fair city, that is called Tarsus, and the city of
Longemaath, and the city of Assere, and the city of
Marmistre.   And when a man is passed those mountains
and those fells, he goes by the city of Marioch and by
Artoise, where is a great bridge upon the river of Ferne,
that is called Farfar, and it is a great river bearing ships
and it runs right fast out of the mountains to the city of
Damascus.   And beside the city of Damascus is another great
river that comes from the hills of Liban, which men call
Abbana.   At the passing of this river Saint Eustace, that
some-time was called Placidas, lost his wife and his two
children.   This river runs through the plain of Archades,
and so to the Red Sea.   From thence men go to the city

of Phenice, where are hot wells and hot baths. And then
men go to the city of Ferne; and between Phenice and
Ferne are ten mile. And there are many fair woods.
And then men come to Antioch, which is ten mile thence.
And it is a fair city and well walled about with many
fair towers; and it is a great city, but it was some-time
greater than it is now. For it was some-time two mile
on length and on breadth other half mile. And through
the midst of that city ran the water of Farphar and a
great bridge over it; and there was some-time in the walls
about this city three hundred and fifty towers, and at each
pillar of the bridge was a stone. This is the chief city of
the kingdom of Syria. And ten mile from this city is the
port of Saint Symeon; and there goes the water of Farphar
into the sea. From Antioch men go to a city that is
called Lacuth, and then to Gebel, and then to Tortouse.
And there near is the land of Channel; and there is a
strong castle that is called Maubek. From Tortouse pass
men to Tripoli by sea, or else by land through the straits
of mountains and fells. And there is a city that is called
Gibilet. From Tripoli go men to Acres; and from thence
are two ways to Jerusalem, the one on the left half and the
other on the right half. By the left way men go by
Damascus and by the flum Jordan. By the right way men
go by Maryn and by the land of Flagramy and near the
mountains into the city of Cayphas, that some men call
the castle of Pilgrims. And from thence to Jerusalem are
three day journey, in the which men shall go through
Caesarea Philippi, and so to Jaffa and Rames and the castle
of Emmaus, and so to Jerusalem.

Now have I told you some ways by land and by water
that men may go by to the Holy Land after the countries
that they come from. Nevertheless they come all to one
end. Yet is there another way to Jerusalem all by land,
and pass not the sea, from France or Flanders; but that
way is full long and perilous and of great travel, and
therefore few go that way. He that shall go that way, he
shall go through Almayne and Prussia and so to Tartary.
This Tartary is holden of the great Caan of Cathay, of

whom I think to speak afterward.   This is a full ill land
and sandy and little fruit bearing.   For there grows no
corn, ne wine, ne beans, ne peas, ne none other fruit convenable to man for to live with.   But there are beasts in
great plenty: and therefore they eat but flesh without
bread and sup the broth and they drink milk of all manner
of beasts.   They eat hounds, cats, ratons, and all other
wild beasts.   And they have no wood, or else little; and
therefore they warm and seethe their meat with horse-dung
and cow-dung and of other beasts, dried against the sun.
And princes and other eat not but once in the day, and
that but little.   And they be right foul folk and of evil
kind.   And in summer, by all the countries, fall many
tempests and many hideous thunders and leits and
slay much people and beasts also full often-time.   And
suddenly is there passing heat, and suddenly also passing
cold; and it is the foulest country and the most cursed
and the poorest that men know.   And their prince, that
governeth that country, that they clepe Batho, dwelleth at
the city of Orda.   And truly no good man should not
dwell in that country, for the land and the country is not
worthy hounds to dwell in.   It were a good country to
sow in thistle and briars and broom and thorns and briars;
and for no other thing is it not good.   Natheles, there is
good land in some place, but it is pure little, as men say.

I have not been in that country, nor by those ways.
But I have been at other lands that march to those
countries, as in the land of Russia, as in the land of
Nyflan, and in the realm of Cracow and of Letto, and in
the realm of Daristan, and in many other places that march
to the coasts.   But I went never by that way to Jerusalem,
wherefore I may not well tell you the manner.

But, if this matter please to any worthy man that hath
gone by that way, he may tell it if him like, to that intent,
that those, that will go by that way and make their voyage
by those coasts, may know what way is there.   For no
man may pass by that way goodly, but in time of winter,
for the perilous waters and wicked mareys, that be in
those countries, that no man may pass but if it be strong

frost and snow above.   For if the snow ne were not, men might not go upon the ice, ne horse ne car neither.

And it is well a three journeys of such way to pass from Prussia to the land of Saracens habitable.   And it behoveth to the Christian men, that shall war against them every year, to bear their victuals with them ; for they shall find there no good.   And then must they let carry their victual upon the ice with cars that have no wheels, that they clepe sleighs.   And as long as their victuals last they may abide there, but no longer ; for there shall they find no wight that will sell them any victual or anything.   And when the spies see any Christian men come upon them, they run to the towns, and cry with a loud voice ; *Kerra, Kerra, Kerra.*   And then anon they arm them and assemble them together.

And ye shall understand that it freezeth more strongly in those countries than on this half.   And therefore hath every man stews in his house, and in those stews they eat and do their occupations all that they may.   For that is at the north parts that men clepe the Septentrional where it is all only cold.   For the sun is but little or none toward those countries.   And therefore in the Septentrion, that is very north, is the land so cold, that no man may dwell there.   And, in the contrary, toward the south it is so hot, that no man ne may dwell there, because that the sun, when he is upon the south, casteth his beams all straight upon that part.

CHAPTER XV

Of the Customs of Saracens, and of their Law.   And how the Soldan reasoned me, Author of this Book; and of the beginning of Mohammet

Now, because that I have spoken of Saracens and of their country—now, if ye will know a part of their law and of their belief, I shall tell you after that their book that is

clept *Alkaron* telleth.   And some men clepe that book
Meshaf.   And some men clepe it *Harme*, after the diverse
languages of the country.   The which book Mohammet
took them.   In the which book, among other things, is
written, as I have often-time seen and read, that the good
shall go to paradise, and the evil to hell ; and that believe
all Saracens.   And if a man ask them what paradise they
mean, they say, to paradise that is a place of delights where
men shall find all manner of fruits in all seasons, and
rivers running of milk and honey, and of wine and of
sweet water ; and that they shall have fair houses and
noble, every man after his desert, made of precious stones
and of gold and of silver ; and that every man shall have
four score wives all maidens, and he shall have ado every
day with them, and yet he shall find them always maidens.

Also they believe and speak gladly of the Virgin Mary
and of the Incarnation.   And they say that Mary was
taught of the angel ; and that Gabriel said to her, that she
was for-chosen from the beginning of the world ; and that
he shewed to her the Incarnation of Jesu Christ ; and that
she conceived and bare child maiden ; and that witnesseth
their book.

And they say also, that Jesu Christ spake as soon as he
was born ; and that he was an holy prophet and a true in
word and deed, and meek and piteous and rightful and
without any vice.

And they say also, that when the angel shewed the
Incarnation of Christ unto Mary, she was young and had
great dread.   For there was then an enchanter in the
country that dealt with witchcraft, that men clept Taknia,
that by his enchantments could make him in likeness of an
angel, and went often-times and lay with maidens.   And
therefore Mary dreaded lest it had been Taknia, that came
for to deceive the maidens.   And therefore she conjured
the angel, that he should tell her if it were he or no.   And
the angel answered and said that she should have no dread
of him, for he was very messenger of Jesu Christ.   Also
their book saith, that when that she had childed under a
palm tree she had great shame, that she had a child ; and

she greet and said that she would that she had been dead. And anon the child spake to her and comforted her, and said, "Mother, ne dismay thee nought, for God hath hid in thee his privities for the salvation of the world." And in other many places saith their *Alkaron*, that Jesu Christ spake as soon as he was born. And that book saith also that Jesu was sent from God Almighty for to be mirror and example and token to all men.

And the *Alkaron* saith also of the day of doom how God shall come to doom all manner of folk. And the good he shall draw on his side and put them into bliss, and the wicked he shall condemn to the pains of hell. And among all prophets Jesu was the most excellent and the most worthy next God, and that he made the gospels in the which is good doctrine and healthful, full of clarity and soothfastness and true preaching to them that believe in God. And that he was a very prophet and more than a prophet, and lived without sin, and gave sight to the blind, and healed the lepers, and raised dead men, and styed to heaven.

And when they may hold the Book of the Gospels of our Lord written and namely *Missus est Angelus Gabriel*, that gospel they say, those that be lettered, often-times in their orisons, and they kiss it and worship it with great devotion.

They fast an whole month in the year and eat nought but by night. And they keep them from their wives all that month. But the sick men be not constrained to that fast.

Also this book speaketh of Jews and saith that they be cursed; for they would not believe that Jesu Christ was come of God. And that they lied falsely on Mary and on her son Jesu Christ, saying that they had crucified Jesu the son of Mary; for he was never crucified, as they say, but that God made him to sty up to him without death and without annoy. But he transfigured his likeness into Judas Iscariot, and him crucified the Jews, and weened that it had been Jesus. But Jesus styed to heavens all quick. And therefore they say, that the Christian men err and have no good knowledge of this, and that they believe folily and falsely that Jesu Christ was crucified.

And they say yet, that and he had been crucified, that God had done against his righteousness for to suffer Jesu Christ, that was innocent, to be put upon the cross without guilt. And in this article they say that we fail and that the great righteousness of God might not suffer so great a wrong: and in this faileth their faith. For they knowledge well, that the works of Jesu Christ be good, and his words and his deeds and his doctrine by his gospels were true, and his miracles also true; and the blessed Virgin Mary is good, and holy maiden before and after the birth of Jesu Christ; and that all those that believe perfectly in God shall be saved. And because that they go so nigh our faith, they be lightly converted to Christian law when men preach them and shew them distinctly the law of Jesu Christ, and when they tell them of the prophecies.

And also they say, that they know well by the prophecies that the law of Mahomet shall fail, as the law of the Jews did; and that the law of Christian people shall last to the day of doom. And if any man ask them what is their belief, they answer thus, and in this form: "We believe God, former of heaven and of earth, and of all other things that he made. And without him is nothing made. And we believe of the day of doom, and that every man shall have his merit, after he hath deserved. And, we believe it for sooth, all that God hath said by the mouths of his prophets."

Also Mahomet commanded in his *Alkaron*, that every man should have two wives, or three or four; but now they take unto nine, and of lemans as many as he may sustain. And if any of their wives mis-bear them against their husband, he may cast her out of his house, and depart from her and take another; but he shall depart with her his goods.

Also, when men speak to them of the Father and of the Son and of the Holy Ghost, they say, that they be three persons, but not one God; for their *Alkaron* speaketh not of the Trinity. But they say well, that God hath speech, and else were he dumb. And God hath also a spirit they know well, for else they say, he were not alive. And when men speak to them of the Incarnation how that by the word of the angel God sent his wisdom in to earth and enombred him in the Virgin Mary, and by the word of God shall the dead be raised at the day of doom, they say, that it is sooth and that the word of God hath great strength. And they say that whoso knew not the word of God he should not know God. And they say also that Jesu Christ is the word of God : and so saith their *Alkaron*, where it saith that the angel spake to Mary and said : "Mary, God shall preach thee the gospel by the word of his mouth and his name shall be clept Jesu Christ."

And they say also, that Abraham was friend to God, and that Moses was familiar speaker with God, and Jesu Christ was the word and the spirit of God, and that Mohammet was right messenger of God. And they say, that of these four, Jesu was the most worthy and the most excellent and the most great. So that they have many good articles of our faith, albeit that they have no perfect law and faith as Christian men have ; and therefore be they lightly converted, and namely those that understand the scriptures and the prophecies. For they have the gospels and the prophecies and the Bible written in their language ; wherefore they ken much of holy writ, but they understand it not but after the letter. And so do the Jews, for they understand not the letter ghostly, but bodily ; and therefore be they reproved of the wise, that ghostly understand it. And therefore saith Saint Paul : *Litera occidit; spiritus autem vivificat.* Also the Saracens say, that the Jews be cursed ; for they have befouled the law that God sent them by Moses : and the Christian be cursed also, as they say ; for they keep not the commandments and the precepts of the gospel that Jesu Christ taught them.

And, therefore, I shall tell you what the soldan told me upon a day in his chamber. He let void out of his chamber all manner of men, lords and others, for he would speak with me in counsel. And there he asked me how the Christian men governed them in our country. And I said him, " Right well, thanked be God ! "

And he said me, " Truly nay ! For ye Christian men

ne reck right nought, how untruly to serve God! Ye should give ensample to the lewd people for to do well, and ye give them ensample to do evil. For the commons, upon festival days, when they should go to church to serve God, then go they to taverns, and be there in gluttony all the day and all night, and eat and drink as beasts that have no reason, and wit not when they have enough. And also the Christian men enforce themselves in all manners that they may, for to fight and for to deceive that one that other. And therewithal they be so proud, that they know not how to be clothed; now long, now short, now strait, now large, now sworded, now daggered, and in all manner guises. They should be simple, meek and true, and full of alms-deeds, as Jesu was, in whom they trow; but they be all the contrary, and ever inclined to the evil, and to do evil. And they be so covetous, that, for a little silver, they sell their daughters, their sisters and their own wives to put them to lechery. And one withdraweth the wife of another, and none of them holdeth faith to another; but they defoul their law that Jesu Christ betook them to keep for their salvation. And thus, for their sins, have they lost all this land that we hold. For, for their sins, their God hath taken them into our hands, not only by strength of ourself, but for their sins. For we know well, in very sooth, that when ye serve God, God will help you; and when he is with you, no man may be against you. And that know we well by our prophecies, that Christian men shall win again this land out of our hands, when they serve God more devoutly; but as long as they be of foul and of unclean living (as they be now) we have no dread of them in no kind, for their God will not help them in no wise."

And then I asked him, how he knew the state of Christian men. And he answered me, that he knew all the state of all courts of Christian kings and princes and the state of the commons also by his messengers that he sent to all lands, in manner as they were merchants of precious stones, of cloths of gold and of other things, for to know the manner of every country amongst Christian men. And then he let clepe in all the lords that he made void first out of his chamber, and there he shewed me four that were great lords in the country, that told me of my country and of many other Christian countries, as well as they had been of the same country; and they spake French right well, and the soldan also; whereof I had great marvel.

Alas! that it is great slander to our faith and to our law, when folk that be without law shall reprove us and undernim us of our sins, and they that should be converted to Christ and to the law of Jesu by our good ensamples and by our acceptable life to God, and so converted to the law of Jesu Christ, be, through our wickedness and evil living, far from us and strangers from the holy and very belief, shall thus appeal us and hold us for wicked livers and cursed. And truly they say sooth, for the Saracens be good and faithful; for they keep entirely the commandment of the holy book *Alkaron* that God sent them by his messenger Mahomet, to the which, as they say, Saint Gabriel the angel oftentime told the will of God.

And ye shall understand, that Mahomet was born in Arabia, that was first a poor knave that kept camels, that went with merchants for merchandise. And so befell, that he went with the merchants into Egypt; and they were then Christian in those parts. And at the deserts of Arabia, he went into a chapel where a hermit dwelt. And when he entered into the chapel that was but a little and a low thing and had but a little door and a low, then the entry began to wax so great, and so large and so high as though it had been of a great minster or the gate of a palace. And this was the first miracle, the Saracens say, that Mahomet did in his youth.

After began he for to wax wise and rich. And he was a great astronomer. And after, he was governor and prince of the land of Cozrodane; and he governed it full wisely, in such manner, that when the prince was dead, he took the lady to wife that hight Gadrige. And Mahomet fell often in the great sickness that men call the falling evil; wherefore the lady was full sorry that ever she took him to husband. But Mahomet made her to believe, that all times, when he fell so, Gabriel the angel came for to speak with him, and for the great light and brightness of the angel he might not sustain him from falling ; and therefore the Saracens say, that Gabriel came often to speak with him.

This Mahomet reigned in Arabia, the year of our Lord Jesu Christ 610, and was of the generation of Ishmael that was Abraham's son, that he gat upon Hagar his chamberer. And therefore there be Saracens that be clept Ishmaelites ; and some Hagarenes, of Hagar. And the other properly be clept Saracens, of Sarah. And some be clept Moabites and some Ammonites, for the two sons of Lot, Moab and Ammon, that he begat on his daughters, that were afterward great earthly princes.

And also Mahomet loved well a good hermit that dwelled in the deserts a mile from Mount Sinai, in the way that men go from Arabia toward Chaldea and toward Ind, one day's journey from the sea, where the merchants of Venice come often for merchandise. And so often went Mahomet to this hermit, that all his men were wroth ; for he would gladly hear this hermit preach and make his men wake all night. And therefore his men thought to put the hermit to death. And so it befell upon a night, that Mahomet was drunken of good wine, and he fell on sleep. And his men took Mahomet's sword out of his sheath, whiles he slept, and therewith they slew this hermit, and put his sword all bloody in his sheath again. And at morrow, when he found the hermit dead, he was full sorry and wroth, and would have done his men to death. But they all, with one accord, said that he himself had slain him, when he was drunken, and shewed him his sword all bloody. And he trowed that they had said sooth. And then he cursed the wine and all those that drink it. And therefore Saracens that be devout drink never no wine. But some drink it privily ; for if they drunk it openly, they should be reproved. But they drink good beverage and sweet and nourishing that is made of gallamelle and that is that men make sugar of, that is of right good savour, and it is good for the breast.

Also it befalleth some-time, that Christian men become

Saracens, either for poverty or for simpleness, or else for their own wickedness. And therefore the archflamen or the flamen, as our archbishop or bishop, when he receiveth them saith thus: *La ellec olla Sila, Machomete rores alla*; that is to say, 'There is no God but one, and Mahomet his messenger.'

Now I have told you a part of their law and of their customs, I shall say you of their letters that they have, with their names and the manner of their figures what they be: Almoy, Bethath, Cathi, Ephoti, Delphoi, Fothi, Garothi, Hechum, Iotty, Kaythi, Lothum, Malach, Nabaloth, Orthi, Chesiri, 30ch, Ruth, Holath, Routhi, Salathi, Thatimus, Yrthom, A3a3oth, Arrocchi, 30tipyn, Ichetus. And these be the names of their a. b. c. Now shall ye know the figures. . . . And four letters they have more than other for diversity of their language and speech, forasmuch as they speak in their throats; and we in England have in our language and speech two letters more than they have in their a. b. c.; and that is þ and 3, which be clept thorn and 30gh.

CHAPTER XVI

Of the lands of Albania and of Libia. Of the wishings for watching of the Sparrow-hawk; and of Noah's ship

Now, sith I have told you before of the Holy Land and of that country about, and of many ways for to go to that land and to the Mount Sinai, and of Babylon the more and the less, and to other places that I have spoken before, now is time, if it like you, for to tell you of the marches and isles and diverse beasts, and of diverse folk beyond these marches.

For in those countries beyond be many diverse countries and many great kingdoms, that be departed by the four floods that come from paradise terrestrial. For Mesopotamia and the kingdom of Chaldea and Arabia be between the two

rivers of Tigris and of Euphrates ; and the kingdom of
Media and of Persia be between the rivers of Nile and of
Tigris ; and the kingdom of Syria, whereof I have spoken
before, and Palestine and Phoenicia be between Euphrates
and the sea Mediterranean, the which sea dureth in length
from Morocco, upon the sea of Spain, unto the Great Sea,
so that it lasteth beyond Constantinople 3040 miles of
Lombardy.

And toward the sea Ocean in Ind is the kingdom of
Scythia, that is all closed with hills. And after, under
Scythia, and from the sea of Caspian unto the flom of
Thainy, is Amazonia, that is the land of feminye, where
that no man is, but only all women. And after is Albania,
a full great realm ; and it is clept Albania, because that
the folk be whiter there than in other marches there-about:
and in that country be so great hounds and so strong,
that they assail lions and slay them. And then after is
Hircania, Bactria, Hiberia and many other kingdoms.

And between the Red Sea and the sea Ocean, toward the
south is the kingdom of Ethiopia and of Lybia the higher,
the which land of Lybia (that is to say, Lybia the low) that
beginneth at the sea of Spain from thence where the pillars
of Hercules be, and endureth unto anent Egypt and toward
Ethiopia. In that country of Lybia is the sea more high
than the land, and it seemeth that it would cover the earth,
and natheles yet it passeth not his marks. And men
see in that country a mountain to the which no man cometh.
In this land of Lybia whoso turneth toward the east, the
shadow of himself is on the right side ; and here, in our
country, the shadow is on the left side. In that sea of
Lybia is no fish ; for they may not live ne dure for the
great heat of the sun, because that the water is evermore
boiling for the great heat. And many other lands there be
that it were too long to tell or to number. But of some
parts I shall speak more plainly hereafter.

Whoso will then go toward Tartary, toward Persia,
toward Chaldea and toward Ind, he must enter the sea at
Genoa or at Venice or at some other haven that I have told
you before. And then pass men the sea and arrive at

Trebizond that is a good city; and it was wont to be the haven of Pontus. There is the haven of Persians and of Medians and of the marches there beyond. In that city lieth Saint Athanasius that was bishop of Alexandria, that made the psalm *Quicunque vult*.

This Athanasius was a great doctor of divinity. And, because that he preached and spake so deeply of divinity and of the Godhead, he was accused to the Pope of Rome that he was an heretic. Wherefore the Pope sent after him and put him in prison. And whiles he was in prison he made that psalm and sent it to the Pope, and said, that if he were an heretic, then was that heresy, for that, he said, was his belief. And when the Pope saw it, and had examined it that it was perfect and good, and verily our faith and our belief, he made him to be delivered out of prison, and commanded that psalm to be said every day at prime; and so he held Athanasius a good man. But he would never go to his bishopric again, because that they accused him of heresy.

Trebizond was wont to be holden of the Emperor of Constantinople; but a great man, that he sent for to keep the country against the Turks, usurped the land and held it to himself, and cleped him Emperor of Trebizond.

And from thence men go through Little Armenia. And in that country is an old castle that stands upon a rock; the which is clept the castle of the Sparrow-hawk, that is beyond the city of Layays beside the town of Pharsipee, that belongeth to the lordship of Cruk, that is a rich lord and a good Christian man; where men find a sparrow-hawk upon a perch right fair and right well made, and a fair lady of faerie that keepeth it. And who that will watch that sparrow-hawk seven days and seven nights, and, as some men say, three days and three nights, without company and without sleep, that fair lady shall give him, when he hath done, the first wish that he will wish of earthly things; and that hath been proved often-times.

And one time befell, that a King of Armenia, that was a worthy knight and doughty man, and a noble prince, watched that hawk some time. And at the end of seven days and seven nights the lady came to him and bade him wish, for he had well deserved it. And he answered that he was great lord enough, and well in peace, and had enough of worldly riches; and therefore he would wish none other thing, but the body of that fair lady, to have it at his will. And she answered him, that he knew not what he asked, and said that he was a fool to desire that he might not have; for she said that he should not ask but earthly thing, for she was none earthly thing, but a ghostly thing. And the king said that he ne would ask none other thing. And the lady answered; "Sith that I may not withdraw you from your lewd corage, I shall give you without wishing, and to all them that shall come of you. Sir king! ye shall have war without peace, and always to the nine degree, ye shall be in subjection of your enemies, and ye shall be needy of all goods." And never since, neither the King of Armenia nor the country were never in peace; ne they had never sith plenty of goods; and they have been sithen always under tribute of the Saracens.

Also the son of a poor man watched that hawk and wished that he might chieve well, and to be happy to merchandise. And the lady granted him. And he became the most rich and the most famous merchant that might be on sea or on earth. And he became so rich that he knew not the thousand part of that he had. And he was wiser in wishing than was the king.

Also a knight of the Temple watched there, and wished a purse evermore full of gold. And the lady granted him. But she said him that he had asked the destruction of their order for the trust and the affiance of that purse, and for the great pride that they should have. And so it was. And therefore look he keep him well, that shall wake. For if he sleep he is lost, that never man shall see him more.

This is not the right way for to go to the parts that I have named before, but for to see the marvel that I have spoken of. And therefore whoso will go right way, men go from Trebizond toward Armenia the Great unto a city that is clept Erzeroum, that was wont to be a good city and a plenteous; but the Turks have greatly wasted it. There-about groweth no wine nor fruit, but little or else none. In this land is the earth more high than in any other, and that maketh great cold. And there be many good waters and good wells that come under earth from the flom of Paradise, that is clept Euphrates, that is a journey beside that city ; and that river cometh towards Ind under earth, and resorteth into the land of Altazar. And so pass men by this Armenia and enter the sea of Persia.

From that city of Erzeroum go men to an hill that is clept Sabissocolle. And there beside is another hill that men clepe Ararat, but the Jews clepe it Taneez, where Noah's ship rested, and yet is upon that mountain. And men may see it afar in clear weather. And that mountain is well a seven mile high. And some men say that they have seen and touched the ship, and put their fingers in the parts where the fiend went out, when that Noah said, *Benedicite*. But they that say such words, say their will. For a man may not go up the mountain, for great plenty of snow that is always on that mountain, neither summer nor winter. So that no man may go up there, ne never man did, since the time of Noah, save a monk that, by the grace of God, brought one of the planks down, that yet is in the minster at the foot of the mountain.

And beside is the city of Dain that Noah founded. And fast by is the city of Any in the which were wont to be a thousand churches.

But upon that mountain to go up, this monk had great desire. And so upon a day, he went up. And when he was upward the three part of the mountain he was so weary that he might no further, and so he rested him, and fell asleep. And when he awoke he found himself lying at the foot of the mountain. And then he prayed devoutly to God that he would vouchsafe to suffer him go up. And an angel came to him, and said that he should go up. And so he did. And sith that time never none. Wherefore men should not believe such words.

From that mountain go men to the city of Thauriso that was wont to be clept Taxis, that is a full fair city and a great, and one of the best that is in the world for merchandise ; thither come all merchants for to buy avoirdupois, and it is in the land of the Emperor of Persia. And men say that the emperor taketh more good in that city for custom of merchandise than doth the richest Christian king of all his realm that liveth. For the toll and the custom of his merchants is without estimation to be numbered. Beside that city is a hill of salt, and of that salt every man taketh what he will for to salt with, to his need. There dwell many Christian men under tribute of Saracens. And from that city, men pass by many towns and castles in going toward Ind unto the city of Sadonia, that is a ten journeys from Thauriso, and it is a full noble city and a great. And there dwelleth the Emperor of Persia in summer ; for the country is cold enough. And there be good rivers bearing ships.

After go men the way toward Ind by many journeys, and by many countries, unto the city that is clept Cassak, and that is a full noble city, and a plenteous of corns and wines and of all other goods. This is the city where the three kings met together when they went to seek our Lord in Bethlehem to worship him and to present him with gold, incense, and myrrh. And it is from that city to Bethlehem fifty-three journeys. From that city men go to another city that is clept Gethe, that is a journey from the sea that men clepe the Gravelly Sea. That is the best city that the Emperor of Persia hath in all his land. And they clepe flesh there Dabago and the wine Vapa. And the Paynims say that no Christian man may not long dwell ne endure with the life in that city, but die within short time ; and no man knoweth not the cause.

After go men by many cities and towns and great countries that it were too long to tell unto the city of Cornaa that was wont to be so great that the walls about hold twenty-five mile about. The walls shew yet, but it is not all inhabited. From Cornaa go men by many lands and many cities and towns unto the land of Job. And there endeth the land of the Emperor of Persia. And if ye will know the letters of Persians and what names they have, they be such as I last devised you, but not in sounding of their words.

CHAPTER XVII

Of the land of Job; and of his age.   Of the array of
men of Chaldea.   Of the land where women dwell
without company of men.   Of the knowledge and virtues
of the very diamond

AFTER the departing from Cornaa, men enter into the
land of Job that is a full fair country and a plenteous
of all goods.   And men clepe that land the Land of Susiana.
In that land is the city of Theman.

Job was a paynim, and he was Aram of Gosre, his son,
and held that land as prince of that country.   And he was
so rich that he knew not the hundred part of his goods.
And although he were a paynim, nevertheless he served
well God after his law.   And our Lord took his service to
his pleasane.   And when he fell in poverty he was seventy-
eight year of age.   And after, when God had proved his
patience and that it was so great, he brought him again to
riches and to higher estate than he was before.   And after
that he was King of Idumea after King Esau, and when he
was king he was clept Jobab.   And in that kingdom he
lived after 170 year.   And so he was of age, when he died,
248 year.

In that land of Job there ne is no default of no thing
that is needful to man's body.   There be hills, where men
get great plenty of manna in greater abundance than in any
other country.   This manna is clept bread of angels.   And
it is a white thing that is full sweet and right delicious,
and more sweet than honey or sugar.   And it cometh of
the dew of heaven that falleth upon the herbs in that
country.   And it congealeth and becometh all white and
sweet.   And men put it in medicines for rich men to
make the womb lax, and to purge evil blood.   For it
cleanseth the blood and putteth out melancholy.   This
land of Job marcheth to the kingdom of Chaldea.

This land of Chaldea is full great.   And the language

of that country is more great in sounding than it is in
other parts beyond the sea.   Men pass to go beyond by
the Tower of Babylon the Great, of the which I have told
you before, where that all the languages were first changed.
And that is a four journeys from Chaldea.   In that realm be
fair men, and they go full nobly arrayed in clothes of gold,
orfrayed and apparelled with great pearls and precious
stones full nobly.   And the women be right foul and evil
arrayed.   And they go all bare-foot and clothed in evil
garments large and wide, but they be short to the knees,
and long sleeves down to the feet like a monk's frock,
and their sleeves be hanging about their shoulders.   And
they be black women foul and hideous, and truly as foul
as they be, as evil they be.

In that kingdom of Chaldea, in a city that is clept Ur,
dwelled Terah, Abraham's father.   And there was Abraham
born.   And that was in that time that Ninus was king of
Babylon, of Arabia and of Egypt.   This Ninus made
the city of Nineveh, the which that Noah had begun
before.   And because that Ninus performed it, he cleped
it Nineveh after his own name.   There lieth Tobit the
prophet, of whom Holy Writ speaketh of.   And from that
city of Ur Abraham departed, by the commandment of
God, from thence, after the death of his father, and led
with him Sarah his wife and Lot his brother's son, because
that he had no child.   And they went to dwell in the land
of Canaan in a place that is clept Shechem.   And this Lot
was he that was saved, when Sodom and Gomorrah and
the other cities were burnt and sunken down to hell, where
that the Dead Sea is now, as I have told you before.   In
that land of Chaldea they have their proper languages and
their proper letters, such as ye may see hereafter.

Beside the land of Chaldea is the land of Amazonia,
that is the land of Feminye.   And in that realm is all
women and no man ; not, as some men say, that men may
not live there, but for because that the women will not
suffer no men amongst them to be their sovereigns.

For sometime there was a king in that country.   And
men married, as in other countries.   And so befell

that the king had war with them of Scythia, the which king hight Colopeus, that was slain in battle, and all the good blood of his realm. And when the queen and all the other noble ladies saw that they were all widows, and that all the royal blood was lost, they armed them and, as creatures out of wit, they slew all the men of the country that were left; for they would that all the women were widows as the queen and they were. And from that time hitherwards they never would suffer man to dwell amongst them longer than seven days and seven nights; ne that no child that were male should dwell amongst them longer than he were nourished; and then sent to his father. And when they will have any company of man then they draw them towards the lands marching next to them. And then they have loves that use them; and they dwell with them an eight days or ten, and then go home again. And if they have any knave child they keep it a certain time, and then send it to the father when he can go alone and eat by himself; or else they slay it. And if it be a female they do away that one pap with an hot iron. And if it be a woman of great lineage they do away the left pap that they may the better bear a shield. And if it be a woman on foot they do away the right pap, for to shoot with bow turkeys: for they shoot well with bows.

In that land they have a queen that governeth all that land, and all they be obeissant to her. And always they make her queen by election that is most worthy in arms; for they be right good warriors and orped, and wise, noble and worthy. And they go oftentime in solde to help of other kings in their wars, for gold and silver as other soldiers do; and they maintain themselves right vigourously. This land of Amazonia is an isle, all environed with the sea save in two places, where be two entries. And beyond that water dwell the men that be their paramours and their loves, where they go to solace them when they will.

Beside Amazonia is the land of Tarmegyte that is a great country and a full delectable. And for the goodness of the country King Alexander let first make there the city of Alexandria, and yet he made twelve cities of the same name ; but that city is now clept Celsite.

And from that other coast of Chaldea, toward the south, is Ethiopia, a great country that stretcheth to the end of Egypt. Ethiopia is departed in two parts principal, and that is in the east part and in the meridional part ; the which part meridional is clept Mauritania ; and the folk of that country be black enough and more black than in the tother part, and they be clept Moors. In that part is a well, that in the day it is so cold, that no man may drink thereof ; and in the night it is so hot, that no man may suffer his hand therein. And beyond that part, toward the south, to pass by the sea Ocean, is a great land and a great country ; but men may not dwell there for the fervent burning of the sun, so is it passing hot in that country.

In Ethiopia all the rivers and all the waters be trouble, and they be somedeal salt for the great heat that is there. And the folk of that country be lightly drunken and have but little appetite to meat. And they have commonly the flux of the womb. And they live not long. In Ethiopia be many diverse folk ; and Ethiope is clept Cusis. In that country be folk that have but one foot, and they go so blyve that it is marvel. And the foot is so large, that it shadoweth all the body against the sun, when they will lie and rest them. In Ethiopia, when the children be young and little, they be all yellow ; and, when that they wax of age, that yellowness turneth to be all black. In Ethiopia is the city of Saba, and the land of the which one of the three kings that presented our Lord in Bethlehem, was king of.

From Ethiopia men go into Ind by many diverse countries. And men clepe the high Ind, Emlak. And Ind is divided in three principal parts ; that is, the more that is a full hot country ; and Ind the less, that is a full attempre country, that stretcheth to the land of Media ; and the three part toward the septentrion is full cold, so that, for pure cold and continual frost, the water becometh crystal. And upon those rocks of crystal grow the good diamonds that be of trouble colour. Yellow crystal draweth colour like oil. And they be so hard, that no man may polish them. And men clepe them diamonds in that country, and *Hamese* in another country. Other diamonds men find in Arabia that be not so good, and they be more brown and more tender. And other diamonds also men find in the isle of Cyprus, that be yet more tender, and them men may well polish. And in the land of Macedonia men find diamonds also. But the best and the most precious be in Ind.

And men find many times hard diamonds in a mass that cometh out of gold, when men pure it and refine it out of the mine; when men break that mass in small pieces, and sometime it happens that men find some as great as a peas and some less, and they be as hard as those of Ind.

And albeit that men find good diamonds in Ind, yet nevertheless men find them more commonly upon the rocks in the sea and upon hills where the mine of gold is. And they grow many together, one little, another great. And there be some of the greatness of a bean and some as great as an hazel nut. And they be square and pointed of their own kind, both above and beneath, without working of man's hand. And they grow together, male and female. And they be nourished with the dew of heaven. And they engender commonly and bring forth small children, that multiply and grow all the year. I have often-times assayed, that if a man keep them with a little of the rock and wet them with May-dew oft-sithes, they shall grow every year, and the small will wax great. For right as the fine pearl congealeth and waxeth great of the dew of heaven, right so doth the very diamond; and right as the pearl of his own kind taketh roundness, right so the diamond, by virtue of God, taketh squareness. And men shall bear the diamond on his left side, for it is of greater virtue then, than on the right side; for the strength of their growing is toward the north, that is the left side of the world, and the left part of man is when he turneth his face toward the east.

And if you like to know the virtues of the diamond, (as men may find in *The Lapidary* that many men know not),

I shall tell you, as they beyond the sea say and affirm, of whom all science and all philosophy cometh from. He that beareth the diamond upon him, it giveth him hardiness and manhood, and it keepeth the limbs of his body whole. It giveth him victory of his enemies in plea and in war, if his cause be rightful. And it keepeth him that beareth it in good wit. And it keepeth him from strife and riot, from evil swevens from sorrows and from enchantments, and from fantasies and illusions of wicked spirits. And if any cursed witch or enchanter would bewitch him that beareth the diamond, all that sorrow and mischance shall turn to himself through virtue of that stone. And also no wild beast dare assail the man that beareth it on him. Also the diamond should be given freely, without coveting and without buying, and then it is of greater virtue. And it maketh a man more strong and more sad against his enemies. And it healeth him that is lunatic, and them that the fiend pursueth or travaileth. And if venom or poison be brought in presence of the diamond, anon it beginneth to wax moist and for to sweat.

There be also diamonds in Ind that be clept violastres, (for their colour is like violet, or more brown than the violets), that be full hard and full precious. But yet some men love not them so well as the other; but, in sooth, to me, I would love them as much as the other, for I have seen them assayed.

Also there is another manner of diamonds that be as white as crystal, but they be a little more trouble. And they be good and of great virtue, and all they be square and pointed of their own kind. And some be six squared, some four squared, and some three as nature shapeth them. And therefore when great lords and knights go to seek worship in arms, they bear gladly the diamond upon them.

I shall speak a little more of the diamonds, although I tarry my matter for a time, to the end, that they that know them not, be not deceived by gabbers that go by the country, that sell them. For whoso will buy the diamond it is needful to him that he know them. Because that men counterfeit them often of crystal that is yellow and of sapphires of citron colour that is yellow also, and of the sapphire loupe and of many other stones. But I tell you these counterfeits be not so hard ; and also the points will break lightly, and men may easily polish them. But some workmen, for malice, will not polish them ; to that intent, to make men believe that they may not be polished. But men may assay them in this manner. First shear with them or write with them in sapphires, in crystal or in other precious stones. After that, men take the adamant, that is the shipman's stone, that draweth the needle to him, and men lay the diamond upon the adamant, and lay the needle before the adamant; and, if the diamond be good and virtuous, the adamant draweth not the needle to him whiles the diamond is there present. And this is the proof that they beyond the sea make.

Natheles it befalleth often-time, that the good diamond loseth his virtue by sin, and for incontinence of him that beareth it. And then it is needful to make it to recover his virtue again, or else it is of little value.

CHAPTER XVIII

Of the customs of Isles about Ind. Of the difference betwixt Idols and Simulacres. Of three manner growing of Pepper upon one tree. Of the Well that changeth his odour every hour of the day; and that is marvel

IN Ind be full many diverse countries. And it is clept Ind, for a flom that runneth throughout the country that is clept Ind. In that flom men find eels of thirty foot long and more. And the folk that dwell nigh that water be of evil colour, green and yellow.

In Ind and about Ind be more than 5000 isles good and great that men dwell in, without those that be inhabitable, and without other small isles. In every isle is great plenty of cities, and of towns, and of folk without number. For men of Ind have this condition of kind, that they never go out of their own country, and therefore is there great multitude of people. But they be not stirring ne movable, because that they be in the first climate, that is of Saturn; and Saturn is slow and little moving, for he tarryeth to make his turn by the twelve signs thirty year. And the moon passeth through the twelve signs in one month. And for because that Saturn is of so late stirring, therefore the folk of that country that be under his climate have of kind no will for to move ne stir to seek strange places. And in our country is all the contrary; for we be in the seventh climate, that is of the moon. And the moon is of lightly moving, and the moon is planet of way; and for that skill it giveth us will of kind for to move lightly and for to go divers ways, and to seek strange things and other diversities of the world; for the moon environeth the earth more hastily than any other planet.

Also men go through Ind by many diverse countries to the great sea Ocean. And after, men find there an isle that is clept Crues. And thither come merchants of Venice and Genoa, and of other marches, for to buy merchandises. But there is so great heat in those marches, and namely in that isle, that, for the great distress of the heat, men's ballocks hang down to their knees for the great dissolution of the body. And men of that country, that know the manner, let bind them up, or else might they not live, and anoint them with ointments made therefore, to hold them up.

In that country and in Ethiopia, and in many other countries, the folk lie all naked in rivers and waters, men and women together, from undern of the day till it be past the noon. And they lie all in the water, save the visage, for the great heat that there is. And the women have no shame of the men, but lie all together, side to side, till the heat be past. There may men see many foul figure assembled, and namely nigh the good towns.

In that isle be ships without nails of iron or bonds, for the rocks of the adamants, for they be all full thereabout in that sea, that it is marvel to speak of. And if a ship

passed by those marches that had either iron bonds or iron
nails, anon he should be perished ; for the adamant of his
kind draweth the iron to him.   And so would it draw to
him the ship because of the iron, that he should never
depart from it, ne never go thence.

From that isle men go by sea to another isle that is
clept Chana, where is great plenty of corn and wine.   And
it was wont to be a great isle, and a great haven and a
good ; but the sea hath greatly wasted it and overcome it.
The king of that country was wont to be so strong and so
mighty that he held war against King Alexander.

The folk of that country have a diverse law.   For some
of them worship the sun, some the moon, some the fire,
some trees, some serpents, or the first thing that they meet
at morrow.   And some worship simulacres and some
idols.   But between simulacres and idols is a great difference.   For simulacres be images made after likeness of
men or of women, or of the sun, or of the moon, or of
any beast, or of any kindly thing.   And idols is an image
made of lewd will of man, that man may not find among
kindly things, as an image that hath four heads, one of a
man, another of an horse or of an ox, or of some other
beast, that no man hath seen after kindly disposition.

And they that worship simulacres, they worship them
for some worthy man that was sometime, as Hercules, and
many other that did many marvels in their time.   For
they say well that they be not gods ; for they know well
that there is a God of kind that made all things, the which
is in heaven.   But they know well that this may not do the
marvels that he made, but if it had been by the special gift
of God ; and therefore they say that he was well with God,
and for because that he was so well with God, therefore they
worship him.   And so say they of the sun, because that he
changeth the time, and giveth heat, and nourisheth all
things upon earth ; and for it is of so great profit, they
know well that that might not be, but that God loveth it
more than any other thing, and, for that skill, God hath
given it more great virtue in the world.   Therefore, it is
good reason, as they say, to do it worship and reverence.

And so say they, and make their reasons, of other planets, and of the fire also, because it is so profitable.

And of idols they say also that the ox is the most holy beast that is in earth and most patient, and more profitable than any other.   For he doth good enough and he doth no evil ; and they know well that it may not be without special grace of God.   And therefore make they their god of an ox the one part, and the other half of a man. Because that man is the most noble creature in earth, and also for he hath lordship above all beasts, therefore make they the halvendel of idol of a man upwards ; and the tother half of an ox downwards, and of serpents, and of other beasts and diverse things, that they worship, that they meet first at morrow.

And they worship also specially all those that they have good meeting of ; and when they speed well in their journey, after their meeting, and namely such as they have proved and assayed by experience of long time ; for they say that thilk good meeting ne may not come but of the grace of God. And therefore they make images like to those things that they have belief in, for to behold them and worship them first at morning, or they meet any contrarious things.   And there be also some Christian men that say, that some beasts have good meeting, that is to say for to meet with them first at morrow, and some beasts wicked meeting ; and that they have proved oft-time that the hare hath full evil meeting, and swine and many other beasts.   And the sparrow-hawk or other fowls of ravine, when they fly after their prey and take it before men of arms, it is a good sign ; and if he fail of taking his prey, it is an evil sign. And also to such folk, it is an evil meeting of ravens.

In these things and in such other, there be many folk that believe ; because it happeneth so often-time to fall after their fantasies.   And also there be men enough that have no belief in them.   And, sith that Christian men have such belief, that be informed and taught all day by holy doctrine, wherein they should believe, it is no marvel then, that the paynims, that have no good doctrine but only of their nature, believe more largely for their simplesse.

And truly I have seen of paynims and Saracens that men clepe Augurs, that, when we ride in arms in divers countries upon our enemies, by the flying of fowls they would tell us the prognostications of things that fell after; and so they did full oftentimes, and proffered their heads to-wedde, but if it would fall as they said. But natheles, therefore should not a man put his belief in such things, but always have full trust and belief in God our sovereign Lord.

This isle of Chana the Saracens have won and hold. In that isle be many lions and many other wild beasts. And there be rats in that isle as great as hounds here; and men take them with great mastiffs, for cats may not take them. In this isle and many other men bury not no dead men, for the heat is there so great, that in a little time the flesh will consume from the bones.

From thence men go by sea toward Ind the more to a city, that men clepe Sarche, that is a fair city and a good. And there dwell many Christian men of good faith. And there be many religious men, and namely of mendicants.

After go men by sea to the land of Lomb. In that land groweth the pepper in the forest that men clepe Combar. And it groweth nowhere else in all the world, but in that forest, and that endureth well an eighteen journeys in length. In the forest be two good cities; that one hight Fladrine and that other Zinglantz, and in every of them dwell Christian men and Jews, great plenty. For it is a good country and a plentiful, but there is overmuch passing heat.

And ye shall understand, that the pepper groweth in manner as doth a wild vine that is planted fast by the trees of that wood for to sustain it by, as doth the vine. And the fruit thereof hangeth in manner as raisins. And the tree is so thick charged, that it seemeth that it would break. And when it is ripe it is all green, as it were ivy berries. And then men cut them, as men do the vines, and then they put it upon an oven, and there it waxeth black and crisp. And there is three manner of pepper all upon one tree; long pepper, black pepper and white pepper. The long pepper men clepe *Sorbotin*, and the black pepper is clept *Fulfulle*, and the white pepper is clept *Bano*. The long pepper cometh first when the leaf beginneth to come, and it is like the cats of hazel that cometh before the leaf, and it hangeth low. And after cometh the black with the leaf, in manner of clusters of raisins, all green. And when men have gathered it, then cometh the white that is somedeal less than the black. And of that men bring but little into this country ; for they beyond withhold it for themselves, because it is better and more attempre in kind than the black. And therefore is there not so great plenty as of the black.

In that country be many manner of serpents and of other vermin for the great heat of the country and of the pepper. And some men say, that when they will gather the pepper, they make fire, and burn about to make the serpents and the cockodrills to flee. But save their grace of all that say so. For if they burnt about the trees that bear, the pepper should be burnt, and it would dry up all the virtue, as of any other thing ; and then they did themselves much harm, and they should never quench the fire. But thus they do : they anoint their hands and their feet [with a juice] made of snails and of other things made therefore, of the which the serpents and the venomous beasts hate and dread the savour ; and that maketh them flee before them, because of the smell, and then they gather it surely enough.

Also toward the head of that forest is the city of Polombe. And above the city is a great mountain that also is clept Polombe. And of that mount the city hath his name.

And at the foot of that mount is a fair well and a great, that hath odour and savour of all spices. And at every hour of the day he changeth his odour and his savour diversely. And whoso drinketh three times fasting of that water of that well he is whole of all manner sickness that he hath. And they that dwell there and drink often of that well they never have sickness ; and they seem always young. I have drunken thereof three or four sithes, and yet, methinketh, I fare the better. Some men

clepe it the well of youth.   For they that often drink
thereof seem always young-like, and live without sickness.
And men say, that that well cometh out of Paradise, and
therefore it is so virtuous.

By all that country groweth good ginger, and therefore
thither go the merchants for spicery.

In that land men worship the ox for his simpleness and
for his meekness, and for the profit that cometh of him.
And they say, that he is the holiest beast in earth.   For
them seemeth, that whosoever be meek and patient, he is
holy and profitable; for then, they say, he hath all virtues
in him.   They make the ox to labour six year or seven,
and then they eat him.   And the king of the country hath
alway an ox with him.   And he that keepeth him hath
every day great fees, and keepeth every day his dung
and his urine in two vessels of gold, and bring it before
their prelate that they clepe Archi-protopapaton.   And he
beareth it before the king and maketh there over a great
blessing.   And then the king wetteth his hands there, in
that they clepe gall, and anointeth his front and his breast.
And after, he froteth him with the dung and with the
urine with great reverence, for to be fullfilled of virtues
of the ox and made holy by the virtue of that holy thing
that nought is worth.   And when the king hath done,
then do the lords ; and after them their ministers and
other men, if they may have any remenant.

In that country they make idols, half man half ox.
And in those idols evil spirits speak and give answer to
men of what is asked them.   Before these idols men slay
their children many times, and spring the blood upon the
idols ; and so they make their sacrifice.

And when any man dieth in the country they burn his
body in name of penance ; to that intent, that he suffer no
pain in earth to be eaten of worms.   And if his wife have
no child they burn her with him, and say, that it is reason,
that she make him company in that other world as she did
in this.   But and she have children with him, they let her
live with them, to bring them up if she will.   And if that
she love more to live with her children than for to die

with her husband, men hold her for false and cursed; ne she shall never be loved ne trusted of the people. And if the woman die before the husband, men burn him with her, if that he will; and if he will not, no man constraineth him thereto, but he may wed another time without blame or reproof.

In that country grow many strong vines. And the women drink wine, and men not. And the women shave their beards, and the men not.

CHAPTER XIX

Of the Dooms made by St. Thomas's hand. Of devotion and sacrifice made to Idols there, in the city of Calamye; and of the Procession in going about the city

FROM that country men pass by many marches toward a country, a ten journeys thence, that is clept Mabaron; and it is a great kingdom, and it hath many fair cities and towns.

In that kingdom lieth the body of Saint Thomas the apostle in flesh and bone, in a fair tomb in the city of Calamye; for there he was martyred and buried. And men of Assyria bare his body into Mesopotamia into the city of Edessa, and after, he was brought thither again. And the arm and the hand that he put in our Lord's side, when he appeared to him after his resurrection and said to him, *Noli esse incredulus, sed fidelis*, is yet lying in a vessel without the tomb. And by that hand they make all their judgments in the country, whoso hath right or wrong. For when there is any dissension between two parties, and every of them maintaineth his cause, and saith that his cause is rightful, and that other saith the contrary, then both parties write their causes in two bills and put them in the hand of Saint Thomas. And anon he casteth away the bill of the wrong cause and holdeth still the bill with the right cause. And therefore men come from far countries to have judgment of doubtable causes. And other judgment use they none there.

Also the church, where Saint Thomas lieth, is both great and fair, and all full of great simulacres, and those be great images that they clepe their gods, of the which the least is as great as two men.

And, amongst these other, there is a great image more than any of the other, that is all covered with fine gold and precious stones and rich pearls; and that idol is the god of false Christians that have reneyed their faith. And it sitteth in a chair of gold, full nobly arrayed, and he hath about his neck large girdles wrought of gold and precious stones and pearls. And this church is full richly wrought and, all overgilt within. And to that idol go men on pilgrimage, as commonly and with as great devotion as Christian men go to Saint James, or other holy pilgrimages. And many folk that come from far lands to seek that idol for the great devotion that they have, they look never upward, but evermore down to the earth, for dread to see anything about them that should let them of their devotion. And some there be that go on pilgrimage to this idol, that bear knives in their hands, that be made full keen and sharp; and always as they go, they smite themselves in their arms and in their legs and in their thighs with many hideous wounds; and so they shed their blood for love of that idol. And they say, that he is blessed and holy, that dieth so for love of his god. And other there be that lead their children for to slay, to make sacrifice to that idol; and after they have slain them they spring the blood upon the idol. And some there be that come from far; and in going toward this idol, at every third pace that they go from their house, they kneel; and so continue till they come thither: and when they come there, they take incense and other aromatic things of noble smell, and cense the idol, as we would do here God's precious body. And so come folk to worship this idol, some from an hundred mile, and some from many more.

And before the minster of this idol, is a vivary, in manner of a great lake, full of water. And therein pilgrims cast gold and silver, pearls and precious stones without number, instead of offerings. And when the ministers of that church need to make any reparation of the church or of any of the idols, they take gold and silver, pearls and precious stones out of the vivary, to quit the costage of such thing as they make or repair; so that nothing is faulty, but anon it shall be amended. And ye shall understand, that when [there be] great feasts and solemnities of that idol, as the dedication of the church and the throning of the idol, all the country about meet there together. And they set this idol upon a car with great reverence, well arrayed with cloths of gold, of rich cloths of Tartary, of Camaka, and other precious cloths. And they lead him about the city with great solemnity. And before the car go first in procession all the maidens of the country, two and two together full ordinatly. And after those maidens go the pilgrims. And some of them fall down under the wheels of the car, and let the car go over them, so that they be dead anon. And some have their arms or their limbs all to-broken, and some the sides. And all this do they for love of their god, in great devotion. And them thinketh that the more pain, and the more tribulation that they suffer for love of their god, the more joy they shall have in another world. And, shortly to say you, they suffer so great pains, and so hard martyr-doms for love of their idol, that a Christian man, I trow, durst not take upon him the tenth part the pain for love of our Lord Jesu Christ. And after, I say you, before the car, go all the minstrels of the country without number, with diverse instruments, and they make all the melody that they can.

And when they have gone all about the city, then they return again to the minster, and put the idol again into his place. And then for the love and in worship of that idol, and for the reverence of the feast, they slay themselves, a wo hundred or three hundred persons, with sharp knives, of the which they bring the bodies before the idol. And then they say that those be saints, because that they slew themselves of their own good will for love of their idol. And as men here that had an holy saint of his kin would think that it were to them an high worship, right so them thinketh there.   And as men here devoutly would write holy saints' lives and their miracles, and sue for their canonizations, right so do they there for them that slay themselves wilfully for love of their idol, and say, that they be glorious martyrs and saints, and put them in their writings and in their litanies, and avaunt them greatly, one to another, of their holy kinsmen that so become saints, and say, I have more holy saints in my kindred, than thou in thine !

And the custom also there is this, that when they that have such devotion and intent for to slay himself for love of his god, they send for all their friends, and have great plenty of minstrels ; and they go before the idol leading him that will slay himself for such devotion between them, with great reverence.   And he, all naked, hath a full sharp knife in his hand, and he cutteth a great piece of his flesh, and casteth it in the face of his idol, saying his orisons, recommending him to his god.   And then he smiteth himself and maketh great wounds and deep, here and there, till he fall down dead.   And then his friends present his body to the idol.   And then they say, singing, Holy god ! behold what thy true servant hath done for thee.   He hath forsaken his wife and his children and his riches, and all the goods of the world and his own life for the love of thee, and to make thee sacrifice of his flesh and of his blood.   Wherefore, holy god, put him among thy best beloved saints in thy bliss of paradise, for he hath well deserved it.   And then they make a great fire, and burn the body.   And then everych of his friends take a quantity of the ashes, and keep them instead of relics, and say that it is holy thing.   And they have no dread of no peril whiles they have those holy ashes upon them.   And [they] put his name in their litanies as a saint.

CHAPTER XX

Of the evil customs used in the Isle of Lamary. And how the earth and the sea be of round form and shape, by proof of the star that is clept Antarctic, that is fixed in the south

From that country go men by the sea ocean, and by many divers isles and by many countries that were too long for to tell of. And a fifty-two journeys from this land that I have spoken of, there is another land, that is full great, that men clepe Lamary. In that land is full great heat. And the custom there is such, that men and women go all naked. And they scorn when they see any strange folk going clothed. And they say, that God made Adam and Eve all naked, and that no man should shame him to shew him such as God made him, for nothing is foul that is of kindly nature. And they say, that they that be clothed be folk of another world, or they be folk that trow not in God. And they say, that they believe in God that formed the world, and that made Adam and Eve and all other things. And they wed there no wives, for all the women there be common and they forsake no man. And they say they sin if they refuse any man; and so God commanded to Adam and Eve and to all that come of him, when he said, *Crescite et multiplicamini et replete terram.* And therefore may no man in that country say, This is my wife; ne no woman may say, This my husband. And when they have children, they may give them to what man they will that hath companied with them. And also all the land is common; for all that a man holdeth one year, another man hath it another year; and every man taketh what part that him liketh. And also all the goods of the land be common, corns and all other things: for nothing there is kept in close, ne nothing there is under lock, and every man there taketh what he will without any contradiction, and as rich is one man there as is another.

But in that country there is a cursed custom, for they eat more gladly man's flesh than any other flesh; and yet is that country abundant of flesh, of fish, of corns, of gold and silver, and of all other goods. Thither go merchants and bring with them children to sell to them of the country, and they buy them. And if they be fat they eat them anon. And if they be lean they feed them till they be fat, and then they eat them. And they say, that it is the best flesh and the sweetest of all the world.

In that land, ne in many other beyond that, no man may see the Star Transmontane, that is clept the Star of the Sea, that is unmovable and that is toward the north, that we clepe the Lode-star. But men see another star, the contrary to him, that is toward the south, that is clept Antartic. And right as the ship-men take their advice here and govern them by the Lode-star, right so do ship-men beyond those parts by the star of the south, the which star appeareth not to us. And this star that is toward the north, that we clepe the Lode-star, ne appeareth not to them. For which cause men may well perceive, that the land and the sea be of round shape and form; for the part of the firmament sheweth in one country that sheweth not in another country. And men may well prove by experience and subtle compassment of wit, that if a man found passages by ships that would go to search the world, men might go by ship all about the world and above and beneath.

The which thing I prove thus after that I have seen. For I have been toward the parts of Brabant, and beholden the Astrolabe that the star that is clept the Transmontane is fifty-three degrees high; and more further in Almayne and Bohemia it hath fifty-eight degrees; and more further toward the parts septentrional it is sixty-two degrees of height and certain minutes; for I myself have measured it by the Astrolabe. Now shall ye know, that against the Transmontane is the tother star that is clept Antarctic, as I have said before. And those two stars ne move never, and by them turneth all the firmament right as doth a wheel that turneth by his axle-tree. So that those stars bear the firmament in two equal parts, so that it hath as much

above as it hath beneath. After this, I have gone toward the parts meridional, that is, toward the south, and I have found that in Lybia men see first the star Antarctic. And so far I have gone more further in those countries, that I have found that star more high ; so that toward the High Lybia it is eighteen degrees of height and certain minutes (of the which sixty minutes make a degree). After going by sea and by land toward this country of that I have spoken, and to other isles and lands beyond that country, I have found the Star Antarctic of thirty-three degrees of height and more minutes. And if I had had company and shipping for to go more beyond, I trow well, in certain, that we should have seen all the roundness of the firmament all about. For, as I have said to you before, the half of the firmament is between those two stars, the which halvendel I have seen. And of the tother halvendel I have seen, toward the north under the Transmontane, sixty-two degrees and ten minutes, and toward the part meridional I have seen under the Antarctic, thirty-three degrees and sixteen minutes. And then, the halvendel of the firmament in all holdeth not but nine score degrees. And of those nine score, I have seen sixty-two on that one part and thirty-three on that other part ; that be, ninety-five degrees and nigh the halvendel of a degree. And so, there ne faileth but that I have seen all the firmament, save four score and four degrees and the halvendel of a degree, and that is not the fourth part of the firmament ; for the fourth part of the roundness of the firmament holds four score and ten degrees, so there faileth but five degrees and an half of the fourth part. And also I have seen the three parts of all the roundness of the firmament and more yet five degrees and a half. By the which I say you certainly that men may environ all the earth of all the world, as well under as above, and turn again to his country, that had company and shipping and conduct. And always he should find men, lands and isles, as well as in this country. For ye wit well, that they that be toward the Antarctic, they be straight, feet against feet, of them that dwell under the Transmontane ; also well as we and

they that dwell under us be feet against feet.   For all the
parts of sea and of land have their opposites, habitable or
trepassable, and they of this half and beyond half.

And wit well, that, after that that I may perceive and
comprehend, the lands of Prester John, Emperor of Ind,
be under us.   For in going from Scotland or from England toward Jerusalem men go upward always.   For our
land is in the low part of the earth toward the west, and
the land of Prester John is in the low part of the earth
toward the east.   And [they] have there the day when we
have the night ; and also, high to the contrary, they have
the night when we have the day.   For the earth and
the sea be of round form and shape, as I have said before ;
and that that men go upward to one coast, men go downward to another coast.

Also ye have heard me say that Jerusalem is in the
midst of the world.   And that may men prove, and shew
there by a spear, that is pight into the earth, upon the hour
of midday, when it is equinox, that sheweth no shadow
on no side.   And that it should be in the midst of the
world, David witnesseth it in the Psalter, where he saith,
Deus operatus est salutem in medio terrae.   Then, they, that
part from those parts of the west for to go toward Jerusalem, as many journeys as they go upward for to go
thither, in as many journeys may they go from Jerusalem
unto other confines of the superficiality of the earth beyond.   And when men go beyond those journeys toward
Ind and to the foreign isles, all is environing the roundness of the earth and of the sea under our countries on
this half.

And therefore hath it befallen many times of one thing
that I have heard counted when I was young, how a worthy
man departed some-time from our countries for to go
search the world.   And so he passed Ind and the isles
beyond Ind, where be more than 5000 isles.   And so
long he went by sea and land, and so environed the world
by many seasons, that he found an isle where he heard
speak his own language, calling on oxen in the plough,
such words as men speak to beasts in his own country ;

whereof he had great marvel, for he knew not how it might be. But I say, that he had gone so long by land and by sea, that he had environed all the earth; that he was come again environing, that is to say, going about, unto his own marches, and if he would have passed further, till he had found his country and his own knowledge. But he turned again from thence, from whence he was come from. And so he lost much painful labour, as himself said a great while after that he was come home. For it befell after, that he went into Norway. And there tempest of the sea took him, and he arrived in an isle. And, when he was in that isle, he knew well that it was the isle, where he had heard speak his own language before and the calling of oxen at the plough; and that was possible thing.

But how it seemeth to simple men unlearned, that men ne may not go under the earth, and also that men should fall toward the heaven from under. But that may not be, upon less than we may fall toward heaven from the earth where we be. For from what part of the earth that men dwell, either above or beneath, it seemeth always to them that dwell that they go more right than any other folk. And right as it seemeth to us that they be under us, right so it seemeth to them that we be under them. For if a man might fall from the earth unto the firmament, by greater reason the earth and the sea that be so great and so heavy should fall to the firmament: but that may not be, and therefore saith our Lord God, *Non timeas me, qui suspendi terram ex nihilo?*

And albeit that it be possible thing that men may so environ all the world, natheles, of a thousand persons, one ne might not happen to return into his country. For, for the greatness of the earth and of the sea, men may go by a thousand and a thousand other ways, that no man could ready him perfectly toward the parts that he came from, but if it were by adventure and hap, or by the grace of God. For the earth is full large and full great, and holds in roundness and about environ, by above and by beneath, 20425 miles, after the opinion of old wise astronomers; and their sayings I reprove nought. But, after my little wit, it seemeth me, saving their reverence, that it is more.

And for to have better understanding I say thus. Be there imagined a figure that hath a great compass. And, about the point of the great compass that is clept the centre, be made another little compass. Then after, be the great compass devised by lines in many parts, and that all the lines meet at the centre. So, that in as many parts as the great compass shall be departed, in as many shall be departed the little, that is about the centre, albeit that the spaces be less. Now then, be the great compass represented for the firmament, and the little compass represented for the earth. Now then, the firmament is devised by astronomers in twelve signs, and every sign is devised in thirty degrees; that is, 360 degrees that the firmament hath above. Also, be the earth devised in as many parts as the firmament, and let every part answer to a degree of the firmament. And wit it well, that, after the authors of astronomy, 700 furlongs of earth answer to a degree of the firmament, and those be eighty-seven miles and four furlongs. Now be that here multiplied by 360 sithes, and then they be 31,500 miles every of eight furlongs, after miles of our country. So much hath the earth in roundness and of height environ, after mine opinion and mine understanding.

And ye shall understand, that after the opinion of old wise philosophers and astronomers, our country ne Ireland ne Wales ne Scotland ne Norway ne the other isles coasting to them ne be not in the superficiality counted above the earth, as it sheweth by all the books of astronomy. For the superficiality of the earth is parted in seven parts for the seven planets, and those parts be clept climates. And our parts be not of the seven climates, for they be descending toward the west †[drawing] towards the roundness of the world. †And also these isles of Ind which be even against us be not reckoned in the climates. For they be against us that be in the low country. And the seven climates stretch them environing the world.

CHAPTER XXI

Of the Palace of the King of the Isle of Java. Of the Trees that bear meal, honey, wine, and venom; and of other marvels and customs used in the Isles marching thereabout

BESIDE that isle that I have spoken of, there is another isle that is clept Sumobor. That is a great isle, and the king thereof is right mighty. The folk of that isle make them always to be marked in the visage with an hot iron, both men and women, for great noblesse, for to be known from other folk; for they hold themselves most noble and most worthy of all the world. And they have war always with the folk that go all naked.

And fast beside is another isle, that is clept Betemga, that is a good isle and a plenteous. And many other isles be thereabout, where there be many of diverse folk, of the which it were too long to speak of all.

But fast beside that isle, for to pass by sea, is a great isle and a great country that men clepe Java. And it is nigh two thousand mile in circuit. And the king of that country is a full great lord and a rich and a mighty, and hath under him seven other kings of seven other isles about him. This isle is full well inhabited, and full well manned. There grow all manner of spicery, more plenteously than in any other country, as of ginger, cloves-gilofre, canell, seedwall, nutmegs and maces. And wit well, that the nutmeg beareth the maces; for right as the nut of the hazel hath an husk without, that the nut is closed in till it be ripe and that after falleth out, right so it is of the nutmeg and of the maces. Many other spices and many other goods grow in that isle. For of all things is there plenty, save only of wine. But there is gold and silver, great plenty.

And the king of that country hath a palace full noble and full marvellous, and more rich than any in the world. For all the degrees to go up into halls and chambers be, one of gold, another of silver. And also, the pavements of halls and chambers be all square, of gold one, and another of silver. And all the walls within be covered with gold and silver in fine plates, and in those plates be stories and battles of knights enleved, and the crowns and the circles about their heads be made of precious stones and rich pearls and great. And the halls and the chambers of the palace be all covered within with gold and silver, so that no man would trow the riches of that palace but he had seen it. And wit well, that the king of that isle is so mighty, that he hath many times overcome the great Chan of Cathay in battle, that is the most great emperor that is under the firmament either beyond the sea or on this half. For they have had often-time war between them, because that the great Chan would constrain him to hold his land of him; but that other at all times defendeth him well against him.

After that isle, in going by sea, men find another isle, good and great, that men clepe Pathen, that is a great kingdom full of fair cities and full of towns. In that land grow trees that bear meal, whereof men make good bread and white and of good savour; and it seemeth as it were of wheat, but it is not allinges of such savour. And there be other trees that bear honey good and sweet, and other trees that bear venom, against the which there is no medicine but [one]; and that is to take their proper leaves and stamp them and temper them with water and then drink it, and else he shall die; for triacle will not avail, ne none other medicine. Of this venom the Jews had let seek of one of their friends for to empoison all Christianity, as I have heard them say in their confession before their dying: but thanked be Almighty God! they failed of their purpose; but always they make great mortality of people. And other trees there be also that bear wine of noble sentiment. And if you like to hear how the meal cometh out of the trees I shall say you. Men hew the trees with an hatchet, all about the foot of the tree, till that the bark be parted in many parts, and then cometh out thereof a thick liquor, the which they receive in vessels, and dry it at the heat of the sun; and then they have it to a mill to grind and it becometh fair meal and white.   And the honey and the wine and the venom be drawn out of other trees in the same manner, and put in vessels for to keep.

In that isle is a dead sea, that is a lake that hath no ground; and if anything fall into that lake it shall never come up again.   In that lake grow reeds, that be canes, that they clepe Thaby, that be thirty fathoms long; and of these canes men make fair houses.   And there be other canes that be not so long, that grow near the land and have so long roots that endure well a four quarters of a furlong or more; and at the knots of those roots men find precious stones that have great virtues.   And he that beareth any of them upon him, iron ne steel may not hurt him, ne draw no blood upon him; and therefore, they that have those stones upon them fight full hardily both on sea and land, for men may not harm [them] on no part. And therefore, they that know the manner, and shall fight with them, they shoot to them arrows and quarrels without iron or steel, and so they hurt them and slay them.   And also of those canes they make houses and ships and other things, as we have here, making houses and ships of oak or of any other trees.   And deem no man that I say it but for a trifle, for I have seen of the canes with mine own eyes, full many times, lying upon the river of that lake, of the which twenty of our fellows ne might not lift up ne bear one to the earth.

After this isle men go by sea to another isle that is clept Calonak.   And it is a fair land and a plenteous of goods. And the king of that country hath as many wives as he will. For he maketh search all the country to get him the fairest maidens that may be found, and maketh them to be brought before him.   And he taketh one one night, and another another night, and so forth continually suing; so that he hath a thousand wives or more.   And he lieth never but one night with one of them, and another night with another; but if that one happen to be more lusty to his pleasance than another.   And therefore the king getteth full many children, some-time an hundred, some-time a two-

hundred, and some-time more.   And he hath also into a
14,000 elephants or more that he maketh for to be brought
up amongst his villains by all his towns.   For in case that
he had any war against any other king about him, then [he]
maketh certain men of arms for to go up into the castles
of tree made for the war, that craftily be set upon the
elephants' backs, for to fight against their enemies.   And
so do other kings there-about.   For the manner of war is
not there as it is here or in other countries, ne the ordinance of war neither.   And men clepe the elephants
Warkes.

And in that isle there is a great marvel, more to speak
of than in any other part of the world.   For all manner of
fishes, that be there in the sea about them, come once in
the year—each manner of diverse fishes, one manner of
kind after other.   And they cast themselves to the sea
bank of that isle so great plenty and multitude, that no
man may unnethe see but fish.   And there they abide
three days.   And every man of the country taketh of
them as many as him liketh.   And after, that manner of
fish after the third day departeth and goeth into the sea.
And after them come another multitude of fish of another
kind and do in the same manner as the first did, other
three days.   And after them another, till all the diverse
manner of fishes have been there, and that men have taken
of them that them liketh.   And no man knoweth the cause
wherefore it may be.   But they of the country say that it
is for to do reverence to their king, that is the most worthy
king that is in the world as they say ; because that he
fulfilleth the commandment that God bade to Adam and
Eve, when God said, *Crescite et multiplicamini et replete
terram*.   And for because that he multiplieth so the world
with children, therefore God sendeth him so the fishes of
diverse kinds of all that be in the sea, to take at his will
for him and all his people.   And therefore all the fishes of
the sea come to make him homage as the most noble and
excellent king of the world, and that is best beloved with
God, as they say.   I know not the reason, why it is,
but God knoweth ; but this, me-seemeth, is the most

marvel that ever I saw. For this marvel is against kind and not with kind, that the fishes that have freedom to environ all the coasts of the sea at their own list, come of their own will to proffer them to the death, without constraining of man. And therefore, I am siker that this may not be, without a great token.

There be also in that country a kind of snails that be so great, that many persons may lodge them in their shells, as men would do in a little house. And other snails there be that be full great but not so huge as the other. And of these snails, and of great white worms that have black heads that be as great as a man's thigh, and some less as great worms that men find there in woods, men make viand royal for the king and for other great lords. And if a man that is married die in that country, men bury his wife with him all quick; for men say there, that it is reason that she make him company in that other world as she did in this.

From that country men go by the sea ocean by an isle that is clept Caffolos. Men of that country when their friends be sick they hang them upon trees, and say that it is better that birds, that be angels of God, eat them, than the foul worms of the earth.

From that isle men go to another isle, where the folk be of full cursed kind. For they nourish great dogs and teach them to strangle their friends when they be sick. For they will not that they die of kindly death. For they say, that they should suffer too great pain if they abide to die by themselves, as nature would. And, when they be thus enstrangled, they eat their flesh instead of venison.

Afterward men go by many isles by sea unto an isle that men clepe Milke. And there is a full cursed people. For they delight in nothing more than for to fight and to slay men. And they drink gladliest man's blood, the which they clepe Dieu. And the more men that a man may slay, the more worship he hath amongst them. And if two persons be at debate and, peradventure, be accorded by their friends or by some of their alliance, it behoveth that every of them that shall be accorded drink of other's blood: and else the accord ne the alliance is nought worth: ne it shall not be no reproof to him to break the alliance and the accord, but if every of them drink of others' blood.

And from that isle men go by sea, from isle to isle, unto an isle that is clept Tracoda, where the folk of that country be as beasts, and unreasonable, and dwell in caves that they make in the earth; for they have no wit to make them houses. And when they see any man passing through their countries they hide them in their caves. And they eat flesh of serpents, and they eat but little. And they speak nought, but they hiss as serpents do. And they set no price by no avoir ne riches, but only of a precious stone, that is amongst them, that is of sixty colours. And for the name of the isle, they clepe it Tracodon. And they love more that stone than anything else; and yet they know not the virtue thereof, but they covet it and love it only for the beauty.

After that isle men go by the sea ocean, by many isles, unto an isle that is clept Nacumera, that is a great isle and good and fair. And it is in compass about, more than a thousand mile. And all the men and women of that isle have hounds' heads, and they be clept Cynocephales. And they be full reasonable and of good understanding, save that they worship an ox for their God. And also every one of them beareth an ox of gold or of silver in his forehead, in token that they love well their God. And they go all naked save a little clout, that they cover with their knees and their members. They be great folk and well-fighting. And they have a great targe that covereth all the body, and a spear in their hand to fight with. And if they take any man in battle, anon they eat him.

The king of that isle is full rich and full mighty and right devout after his law. And he hath about his neck 300 pearls orient, good and great and knotted, as paternosters here of amber. And in manner as we say our *Pater Noster* and our *Ave Maria*, counting the *Pater Nosters*, right so this king saith every day devoutly 300

prayers to his God, or that he eat.   And he beareth also
about his neck a ruby orient, noble and fine, that is a foot
of length and five fingers large.   And, when they choose
their king, they take him that ruby to bear in his hand;
and so they lead him, riding all about the city.   And from
thence-fromward they be all obeissant to him.   And that
ruby he shall bear always about his neck, for if he had not
that ruby upon him men would not hold him for king.
The great Chan of Cathay hath greatly coveted that ruby,
but he might never have it for war, ne for no manner of
goods.   This king is so rightful and of equity in his
dooms, that men may go sikerly throughout all his country
and bear with them what them list; that no man shall be
hardy to rob them, and if he were, the king would justified
anon.

From this land men go to another isle that is clept Silha.
And it is well a 800 miles about.   In that land is full much
waste, for it is full of serpents, of dragons and of cockodrills, that no man dare dwell there.   These cockodrills be
serpents, yellow and rayed above, and have four feet and
short thighs, and great nails as claws or talons.   And there
be some that have five fathoms in length, and some of six
and of eight and of ten.   And when they go by places that
be gravelly, it seemeth as though men had drawn a great
tree through the gravelly place.   And there be also many
wild beasts, and namely of elephants.

In that isle is a great mountain.   And in mid place of
the mount is a great lake in a full fair plain; and there is
great plenty of water.   And they of the country say, that
Adam and Eve wept upon that mount an hundred year,
when they were driven out of Paradise, and that water,
they say, is of their tears; for so much water they wept,
that made the foresaid lake.   And in the bottom of that
lake men find many precious stones and great pearls.   In
that lake grow many reeds and great canes; and there
within be many cocodrills and serpents and great water-
leeches.   And the king of that country, once every year,
giveth leave to poor men to go into the lake to gather
them precious stones and pearls, by way of alms, for the

love of God that made Adam.   And all the year men find enough.   And for the vermin that is within, they anoint their arms and their thighs and legs with an ointment made of a thing that is clept lemons, that is a manner of fruit like small pease ; and then have they no dread of no cockodrills, ne of none other venomous vermin.   This water runneth, flowing and ebbing, by a side of the mountain, and in that river men find precious stones and pearls, great plenty.   And men of that isle say commonly, that the serpents and the wild beasts of that country will not do no harm ne touch with evil no strange man that entereth into that country, but only to men that be born of the same country.

In that country and others thereabout there be wild geese that have two heads.   And there be lions, all white and as great as oxen, and many other diverse beasts and fowls also that be not seen amongst us.

And wit well, that in that country and in other isles thereabout, the sea is so high, that it seemeth as though it hung at the clouds, and that it would cover all the world. And that is great marvel that it might be so, save only the will of God, that the air sustaineth it.   And therefore saith David in the Psalter, *Mirabiles elationes maris.*

CHAPTER XXII

How men know by the Idol, if the sick shall die or not.   Of Folk of diverse shape and marvellously disfigured.   And of the Monks that gave their relief to baboons, apes, and marmosets, and to other beasts

FROM that isle, in going by sea toward the south, is another great isle that is clept Dondun.   In that isle be folk of diverse kinds, so that the father eateth the son, the son the father, the husband the wife, and the wife the husband.   And if it so befall, that the father or mother or any of their friends be sick, anon the son goeth to the priest of their law and prayeth him to ask the idol if his father or mother or friend shall die on that evil or not. And then the priest and the son go together before the idol and kneel full devoutly and ask of the idol their demand. And if the devil that is within answer that he shall live, they keep him well ; and if he say that he shall die, then the priest goeth with the son, with the wife of him that is sick, and they put their hands upon his mouth and stop his breath, and so they slay him. And after that, they chop all the body in small pieces, and pray all his friends to come and eat of him that is dead. And they send for all the minstrels of the country and make a solemn feast. And when they have eaten the flesh, they take the bones and bury them, and sing and make great melody. And all those that be of his kin or pretend them to be his friends, an they come not to that feast, they be reproved for evermore and shamed, and make great dole, for never after shall they be holden as friends. And they say also, that men eat their flesh for to deliver them out of pain ; for if the worms of the earth eat them the soul should suffer great pain, as they say. And namely when the flesh is tender and meagre, then say their friends, that they do great sin to let them have so long languor to suffer so much pain without reason. And when they find the flesh fat, then they say, that it is well done to send them soon to Paradise, and that they have not suffered him too long to endure in pain.

The king of this isle is a full great lord and a mighty, and hath under him fifty-four great isles that give tribute to him. And in everych of these isles is a king crowned; and all be obeissant to that king. And he hath in those isles many diverse folk.

In one of these isles be folk of great stature, as giants. And they be hideous for to look upon. And they have but one eye, and that is in the middle of the front. And they eat nothing but raw flesh and raw fish.

And in another isle toward the south dwell folk of foul

stature and of cursed kind that have no heads.   And their eyen be in their shoulders.

And in another isle be folk that have the face all flat, all plain, without nose and without mouth.   But they have two small holes, all round, instead of their eyes, and their mouth is plat also without lips.

And in another isle be folk of foul fashion and shape that have the lip above the mouth so great, that when they sleep in the sun they cover all the face with that lip.

And in another isle there be little folk, as dwarfs.   And they be two so much as the pigmies.   And they have no mouth ; but instead of their mouth they have a little round hole, and when they shall eat or drink, they take through a pipe or a pen or such a thing, and suck it in, for they have no tongue ; and therefore they speak not, but they make a manner of hissing as an adder doth, and they make signs one to another as monks do, by the which every of them understandeth other.

And in another isle be folk that have great ears and long, that hang down to their knees.

And in another isle be folk that have horses' feet.   And they be strong and mighty, and swift runners ; for they take wild beasts with running, and eat them.

And in another isle be folk that go upon their hands and their feet as beasts.   And they be all skinned and feathered, and they will leap as lightly into trees, and from tree to tree, as it were squirrels or apes.

And in another isle be folk that be both man and woman, and they have kind of that one and of that other. And they have but one pap on the one side, and on that other none.   And they have members of generation of man and woman, and they use both when they list, once that one, and another time that other.   And they get children, when they use the member of man ; and they bear children, when they use the member of woman.

And in another isle be folk that go always upon their knees full marvellously.   And at every pace that they go, it seemeth that they would fall.   And they have in every foot eight toes.

Many other diverse folk of diverse natures be there in other isles about, of the which it were too long to tell, and therefore I pass over shortly.

From these isles, in passing by the sea ocean toward the east by many journeys, men find a great country and a great kingdom that men clepe Mancy. And that is in Ind the more. And it is the best land and one the fairest that may be in all the world, and the most delectable and the most plenteous of all goods that is in power of man. In that land dwell many Christian men and Saracens, for it is a good country and a great. And there be therein more than 2000 great cities and rich, without other great towns. And there is more plenty of people there than in any other part of Ind, for the bounty of the country. In that country is no needy man, ne none that goeth on begging. And they be full fair folk, but they be all pale. And the men have thin beards and few hairs, but they be long ; but unnethe hath any man passing fifty hairs in his beard, and one hair sits here, another there, as the beard of a leopard or of a cat. In that land be many fairer women than in any other country beyond the sea, and therefore men clepe that land Albany, because that the folk be white.

And the chief city of that country is clept Latorin, and it is a journey from the sea, and it is much more than Paris. In that city is a great river bearing ships that go to all the coasts in the sea. No city of the world is so well stored of ships as is that. And all those of the city and of the country worship idols. In that country be double sithes more birds than be here. There be white geese, red about the neck, and they have a great crest as a cock's comb upon their heads ; and they be much more there than they be here, and men buy them there all quick, right great cheap. And there is great plenty of adders of whom men make great feasts and eat them at great solemnities ; and he that maketh there a feast be it never so costly, an he have no adders he hath no thank for his travail.

Many good cities there be in that country and men have great plenty and great cheap of all wines and victuals. In that country be many churches of religious men, and of their law. And in those churches be idols as great as giants; and to these idols they give to eat at great festival days in this manner. They bring before them meat all sodden, as hot as they come from the fire, and they let the smoke go up towards the idols; and then they say that the idols have eaten; and then the religious men eat the meat afterwards.

In that country be white hens without feathers, but they bear white wool as sheep do here. In that country women that be unmarried, they have tokens on their heads like coronals to be known for unmarried. Also in that country there be beasts taught of men to go into waters, into rivers and into deep stanks for to take fish; the which beast is but little, and men clepe them loirs. And when men cast them into the water, anon they bring up great fishes, as many as men will. And if men will have more, they cast them in again, and they bring up as many as men list to have.

And from that city, passing many journeys is another city, one the greatest of the world, that men clepe Cassay; that is to say, the 'City of heaven.' That city is well a fifty mile about, and it is strongly inhabited with people, insomuch that in one house men make ten households. In that city be twelve principal gates; and before every gate, a three mile or a four mile in length, is a great town or a great city. That city sits upon a great lake on the sea as doth Venice. And in that city be more than 12,000 bridges. And upon every bridge be strong towers and good, in the which dwell the wardens for to keep the city from the great Chan. And on that one part of the city runneth a great river all along the city. And there dwell Christian men and many merchants and other folk of diverse nations, because that the land is so good and so plenteous. And there groweth full good wine that men clepe Bigon, that is full mighty, and gentle in drinking. This is a city royal where the King of Mancy was wont to dwell. And there dwell many religious men, as it were of the Order of Friars, for they be mendicants.

From that city men go by water, solacing and disporting them, till they come to an abbey of monks that

is fast by, that be good religious men after their faith and law. In that abbey is a great garden and a fair, where be many trees of diverse manner of fruits. And in this garden is a little hill full of delectable trees. In that hill and in that garden be many diverse beasts, as of apes, marmosets, baboons and many other diverse beasts. And every day, when the convent of this abbey hath eaten, the almoner let bear the relief to the garden, and he smiteth on the garden gate with a clicket of silver that he holdeth in his hand; and anon all the beasts of the hill and of diverse places of the garden come out a 3000, or a 4000; and they come in guise of poor men, and men give them the relief in fair vessels of silver, clean over-gilt. And when they have eaten, the monk smiteth eftsoons on the garden gate with the clicket, and then anon all the beasts return again to their places that they come from. And they say that these beasts be souls of worthy men that resemble in likeness of those beasts that be fair, and therefore they give them meat for the love of God; and the other beasts that be foul, they say be souls of poor men and of rude commons. And thus they believe, and no man may put them out of this opinion. These beasts above-said they let take when they be young, and nourish them so with alms, as many as they may find. And I asked them if it had not been better to have given that relief to poor men, rather than to those beasts. And they answered me and said, that they had no poor men amongst them in that country; and though it had been so that poor men had been among them, yet were it greater alms to give it to those souls that do there their penance. Many other marvels be in that city and in the country thereabout, that were too long to tell you.

From that city go men by the country a six journeys to another city that men clepe Chilenfo, of the which city the walls be twenty mile about. In that city be sixty bridges of stone, so fair that no man may see fairer. In that city was the first siege of the King of Mancy, for it is a fair city and plenteous of all goods.

After, pass men overthwart a great river that men clepe

Dalay. And that is the greatest river of fresh water that is in the world. For there, as it is most narrow, it is more than four mile of breadth. And then enter men again into the land of the great Chan.

That river goeth through the land of Pigmies, where that the folk be of little stature, that be but three span long, and they be right fair and gentle, after their quantities, both the men and the women. And they marry them when they be half year of age and get children. And they live not but six year or seven at the most; and he that liveth eight year, men hold him there right passing old. These men be the best workers of gold, silver, cotton, silk and of all such things, of any other that be in the world. And they have oftentimes war with the birds of the country that they take and eat. This little folk neither labour in lands ne in vines; but they have great men amongst them of our stature that till the land and labour amongst the vines for them. And of those men of our stature have they as great scorn and wonder as we would have among us of giants, if they were amongst us. There is a good city, amongst others, where there is dwelling great plenty of those little folk, and it is a great city and a fair. And the men be great that dwell amongst them, but when they get any children they be as little as the pigmies. And therefore they be, all for the most part, all pigmies; for the nature of the land is such. The great Chan let keep this city full well, for it is his. And albeit, that the pigmies be little, yet they be full reasonable after their age, and can both wit and good and malice enough.

From that city go men by the country by many cities and many towns unto a city that men clepe Jamchay; and it is a noble city and a rich and of great profit to the Lord, and thither go men to seek merchandise of all manner of thing. That city is full much worth yearly to the lord of the country. For he hath every year to rent of that city (as they of the city say) 50,000 cumants of florins of gold: for they count there all by cumants, and every cumant is 10,000 †florins of gold. Now may men well reckon how much that it amounteth. The king of that country is full mighty, and yet he is under the great Chan. And the great Chan hath under him twelve such provinces. In that country in the good towns is a good custom: for whoso will make a feast to any of his friends, there be certain inns in every good town, and he that will make the feast will say to the hosteler, array for me to-morrow a good dinner for so many folk, and telleth him the number, and deviseth him the viands; and he saith also, thus much I will dispend and no more. And anon the hosteler arrayeth for him so fair and so well and so honestly, that there shall lack nothing; and it shall be done sooner and with less cost than an a man made it in his own house.

And a five mile from that city, toward the head of the river of Dalay, is another city that men clepe Menke. In that city is strong navy of ships. And all be white as snow of the kind of the trees that they be made of. And they be full great ships and fair, and well ordained, and made with halls and chambers and other easements, as though it were on the land.

From thence go men, by many towns and many cities, through the country, unto a city that men clepe Lanterine. And it is an eight journeys from the city above-said. This city sits upon a fair river, great and broad, that men clepe Caramaron. This river passeth throughout Cathay. And it doth often-time harm, and that full great, when it is over great.

CHAPTER XXIII

Of the great Chan of Cathay. Of the royalty of his palace, and how he sits at meat; and of the great number of officers that serve him

CATHAY is a great country and a fair, noble and rich, and full of merchants. Thither go merchants all years for to seek spices and all manner of merchandises, more commonly than in any other part.   And ye shall understand, that merchants that come from Genoa or from Venice or from Romania or other parts of Lombardy, they go by sea and by land eleven months or twelve, or more sometime, ere they may come to the isle of Cathay that is the principal region of all parts beyond; and it is of the great Chan.

From Cathay go men toward the east by many journeys. And then men find a good city between these others, that men clepe Sugarmago.   That city is one of the best stored of silk and other merchandises that is in the world.

After go men yet to another old city toward the east. And it is in the province of Cathay.   And beside that city the men of Tartary have let make another city that is clept Caydon.   And it hath twelve gates, and between the two gates there is always a great mile; so that the two cities, that is to say, the old and the new, have in circuit more than twenty mile.

In this city is the siege of the great Chan in a full great palace and the most passing fair in all the world, of the which the walls be in circuit more than two mile.   And within the walls it is all full of other palaces.   And in the garden of the great palace there is a great hill, upon the which there is another palace; and it is the most fair and the most rich that any man may devise.   And all about the palace and the hill be many trees bearing many diverse fruits.   And all about that hill be ditches great and deep, and beside them be great vivaries on that one part and on that other.   And there is a full fair bridge to pass over the ditches.   And in these vivaries be so many wild geese and ganders and wild ducks and swans and herons that it is without number.   And all about these ditches and vivaries is the great garden full of wild beasts.   So that when the great Chan will have any disport on that, to take any of the wild beasts or of the fowls, he will let chase them and take them at the windows without going out of his chamber.

This palace, where his siege is, is both great and passing

fair. And within the palace, in the hall, there be twenty-four pillars of fine gold. And all the walls be covered within of red skins of beasts that men clepe panthers, that be fair beasts and well smelling; so that for the sweet odour of those skins no evil air may enter into the palace. Those skins be as red as blood, and they shine so bright against the sun, that unnethe no man may behold them. And many folk worship those beasts, when they meet them first at morning, for their great virtue and for the good smell that they have. And those skins they prize more than though they were plate of fine gold.

And in the midst of this palace is the mountour for the great Chan, that is all wrought of gold and of precious stones and great pearls. And at four corners of the mountour be four serpents of gold. And all about there is y-made large nets of silk and gold and great pearls hanging all about the mountour. And under the mountour be conduits of beverage that they drink in the emperor's court. And beside the conduits be many vessels of gold, by the which they that be of household drink at the conduit.

And the hall of the palace is full nobly arrayed, and full marvellously attired on all parts in all things that men apparel with any hall. And first, at the chief of the hall is the emperor's throne, full high, where he sitteth at the meat. And that is of fine precious stones, bordered all about with pured gold and precious stones, and great pearls. And the grees that he goeth up to the table be of precious stones mingled with gold.

And at the left side of the emperor's siege is the siege of his first wife, one degree lower than the emperor; and it is of jasper, bordered with gold and precious stones. And the siege of his second wife is also another siege, more lower than his first wife; and it is also of jasper, bordered with gold, as that other is. And the siege of the third wife is also more low, by a degree, than the second wife. For he hath always three wives with him, where that ever he be.

And after his wives, on the same side, sit the ladies of

his lineage yet lower, after that they be of estate. And all those that be married have a counterfeit made like a man's foot upon their heads, a cubit long, all wrought with great pearls, fine and orient, and above made with peacocks' feathers and of other shining feathers; and that stands upon their heads like a crest, in token that they be under man's foot and under subjection of man. And they that be unmarried have none such.

And after at the right side of the emperor first sitteth his eldest son that shall reign after him. And he sitteth also one degree lower than the emperor, in such manner of sieges as do the empresses. And after him sit other great lords of his lineage, every of them a degree lower than the other, as they be of estate.

And the emperor hath his table alone by himself, that is of gold and of precious stones, or of crystal bordered with gold, and full of precious stones or of amethysts, or of lignum aloes that cometh out of paradise, or of ivory bound or bordered with gold. And every one of his wives hath also her table by herself. And his eldest son and the other lords also, and the ladies, and all that sit with the emperor have tables alone by themselves, full rich. And there ne is no table but that it is worth an huge treasure of goods.

And under the emperor's table sit four clerks that write all that the emperor saith, be it good, be it evil; for all that he saith must be holden, for he may not change his word, ne revoke it.

And [at] great solemn feasts before the emperor's table men bring great tables of gold, and thereon be peacocks of gold and many other manner of diverse fowls, all of gold and richly wrought and enamelled. And men make them dance and sing, clapping their wings together, and make great noise. And whether it be by craft or by necromancy I wot never; but it is a good sight to behold, and a fair; and it is great marvel how it may be. But I have the less marvel, because that they be the most subtle men in all sciences and in all crafts that be in the world; for of subtlety and of malice and of farcasting they pass all men under heaven. And therefore they say themselves, that they see with two eyes and the Christian men see but with one, because that they be more subtle than they. For all other nations, they say, be but blind in cunning and working in comparison to them. I did great business for to have learned that craft, but the master told me that he had made avow to his god to teach it to no creature, but only to his eldest son.

Also above the emperor's table and the other tables, and above a great part in the hall, is a vine made of fine gold. And it spreadeth all about the hall. And it hath many clusters of grapes, some white, some green, some yellow and some red and some black, all of precious stones. The white be of crystal and of beryl and of iris; the yellow be of topazes; the red be of rubies and of grenaz and of alabrandines; the green be of emeralds, of perydoz and of chrysolites; and the black be of onyx and garantez. And they be all so properly made that it seemeth a very vine bearing kindly grapes.

And before the emperor's table stand great lords and rich barons and other that serve the emperor at the meat. And no man is so hardy to speak a word, but if the emperor speak to him; but if it be minstrels that sing songs and tell jests or other disports, to solace with the emperor. And all the vessels that men be served with in the hall or in chambers be of precious stones, and specially at great tables either of jasper or of crystal or of amethysts or of fine gold. And the cups be of emeralds and of sapphires, or of topazes, of perydoz, and of many other precious stones. Vessels of silver is there none, for they tell no price thereof to make no vessels of: but they make thereof grecings and pillars and pavements to halls and chambers. And before the hall door stand many barons and knights clean armed to keep that no man enter, but if it be the will or the commandment of the emperor, or but if they be servants or minstrels of the household; and other none is not so hardy to neighen nigh the hall door.

And ye shall understand, that my fellows and I with our yeomen, we served this emperor, and were his soldiers fifteen months against the King of Mancy, that held war against him. And the cause was for we had great lust to see his noblesse and the estate of his court and all his governance, to wit if it were such as we heard say that it was. And truly we found it more noble and more excellent, and richer and more marvellous, than ever we heard speak of, insomuch that we would never have lieved it had we not seen it. For I trow, that no man would believe the noblesse, the riches ne the multitude of folk that be in his court, but he had seen it; for it is not there as it is here. For the lords here have folk of certain number as they may suffice; but the great Chan hath every day folk at his costage and expense as without number. But the ordinance, ne the expenses in meat and drink, ne the honesty, ne the cleanness, is not so arrayed there as it is here; for all the commons there eat without cloth upon their knees, and they eat all manner of flesh and little of bread, and after meat they wipe their hands upon their skirts, and they eat not but once a day. But the estate of lords is full great, and rich and noble.

And albeit that some men will not trow me, but hold it for fable to tell them the noblesse of his person and of his estate and of his court and of the great multitude of folk that he holds, natheles I shall say you a part of him and of his folk, after that I have seen the manner and the ordinance full many a time. And whoso that will may lieve me if he will, and whoso will not, may leave also. For I wot well, if any man hath been in those countries beyond, though he have not been in the place where the great Chan dwelleth, he shall hear speak of him so much marvellous thing, that he shall not trow it lightly. And truly, no more did I myself, till I saw it. And those that have been in those countries and in the great Chan's household know well that I say sooth. And therefore I will not spare for them, that know not ne believe not but that that they see, for to tell you a part of him and of his estate that he holdeth, when he goeth from country to country, and when he maketh solemn feasts.

CHAPTER XXIV.

Wherefore he is clept the great Chan. Of the Style of his Letters: and of the Superscription about his great Seal and his Privy Seal

First I shall say you why he was clept the great Chan.

Ye shall understand, that all the world was destroyed by Noah's flood, save only Noah and his wife and his children. Noah had three sons, Shem, Cham, and Japhet. This Cham was he that saw his father's privy members naked when he slept, and scorned them, and shewed them with his finger to his brethren in scorning wise. And therefore he was cursed of God. And Japhet turned his face away and covered them.

These three brethren had seisin in all the land. And this Cham, for his cruelty, took the greater and the best part, toward the east, that is clept Asia, and Shem took Africa, and Japhet took Europe. And therefore is all the earth parted in these three parts by these three brethren. Cham was the greatest and the most mighty, and of him came more generations than of the other. And of his son Chuse was engendered Nimrod the giant, that was the first king that ever was in the world; and he began the foundation of the tower of Babylon. And that time, the fiends of hell came many times and lay with the women of his generation and engendered on them diverse folk, as monsters and folk disfigured, some without heads, some with great ears, some with one eye, some giants, some with horses' feet, and many other diverse shape against kind. And of that generation of Cham be come the Paynims and divers folk that be in isles of the sea by all Ind. And forasmuch as he was the most mighty, and no man might withstand him, he cleped himself the Son of God and sovereign of all the world. And for this Cham, this emperor clepeth him Cham, and sovereign of all the world.

And of the generation of Shem be come the Saracens.
And of the generation of Japhet is come the people of
Israel.   And though that we dwell in Europe, this is the
opinion, that the Syrians and the Samaritans have amongst
them.   And that they told me, before that I went toward
Ind, but I found it otherwise.   Natheles, the sooth is
this ; that Tartars and they that dwell in the great Asia,
they came of Cham ; but the Emperor of Cathay clepeth
him not Cham, but Can, and I shall tell you how.

It is but little more but eight score year that all Tartary
was in subjection and in servage to other nations about.
For they were but bestial folk and did nothing but kept
beasts and led them to pastures.   But among them they
had seven principal nations that were sovereigns of them all.
Of the which, the first nation or lineage was clept Tartar,
and that is the most noble and the most prized.   The
second lineage is clept Tanghot, the third Eurache, the
fourth Valair, the fifth Semoche, the sixth Megly, the
seventh Coboghe.

Now befell it so that of the first lineage succeeded an
old worthy man that was not rich, that had to name
Changuys.   This man lay upon a night in his bed.   And
he saw in avision, that there came before him a knight
armed all in white.   And he sat upon a white horse, and
said to him, Can, sleepest thou ?   The Immortal God hath
sent me to thee, and it is his will, that thou go to the
seven lineages and say to them that thou shalt be their
emperor.   For thou shalt conquer the lands and the
countries that be about, and they that march upon you
shall be under your subjection, as ye have been under
theirs, for that is God's will immortal.

And when he came at morrow, Changuys rose, and
went to seven lineages, and told them how the white
knight had said.   And they scorned him, and said that he
was a fool.   And so he departed from them all ashamed.
And the night ensuing, this white knight came to the seven
lineages, and commanded them on God's behalf immortal,
that they should make this Changuys their emperor, and
they should be out of subjection, and they should hold all

other regions about them in their servage as they had
been to them before. And on the morrow, they chose
him to be their emperor. And they set him upon a black
fertre, and after that they lift him up with great solemnity.
And they set him in a chair of gold and did him all
manner of reverence, and they cleped him Chan, as the white
knight called him.

And when he was thus chosen, he would assay if he
might trust in them or no, and whether they would be
obeissant to him or no. And then he made many
statutes and ordinances that they clepe *Ysya Chan*. The
first statute was, that they should believe and obey in
God Immortal, that is Almighty, that would cast them out
of servage, and at all times clepe to him for help in time
of need. The tother statute was, that all manner of men
that might bare arms should be numbered, and to every
ten should be a master, and to every hundred a master,
and to every thousand a master, and to every ten thousand
a master. After he commanded to the principals of the
seven lineages, that they should leave and forsake all that
they had in goods and heritage, and from thenceforth to
hold them paid of that that he would give them of his
grace. And they did so anon. After he commanded to
the principals of the seven lineages, that every of them
should bring his eldest son before him, and with their own
hands smite off their heads without tarrying. And anon
his commandment was performed.

And when the Chan saw that they made none obstacle
to perform his commandment, then he thought well that
he might trust in them, and commanded them anon to
make them ready and to sue his banner. And after this,
Chan put in subjection all the lands about him.

Afterward it befell upon a day, that the Can rode with
a few meinie for to behold the strength of the country
that he had won. And so befell, that a great multitude of
his enemies met with him. And for to give good example
of hardiness to his people, he was the first that fought, and
in the midst of his enemies encountered, and there he was
cast from his horse, and his horse slain. And when his

folk saw him at the earth, they were all abashed, and weened he had been dead, and flew every one, and their enemies after and chased them, but they wist not that the emperor was there. And when the enemies were far pursuing the chase, the emperor hid him in a thick wood. And when they were come again from the chase, they went and sought the woods if any of them had been hid in the thick of the woods; and many they found and slew them anon. So it happened that as they went searching toward the place that the emperor was, they saw an owl sitting upon a tree above him; and then they said amongst them, that there was no man because that they saw that bird there, and so they went their way; and thus escaped the emperor from death. And then he went privily all by night, till he came to his folk that were full glad of his coming, and made great thankings to God Immortal, and to that bird by whom their lord was saved. And therefore principally above all fowls of world they worship the owl; and when they have any of their feathers, they keep them full preciously instead of relics, and bear them upon their heads with great reverence; and they hold themselves blessed and safe from all perils while that they have them upon them, and therefore they bear their feathers upon their heads.

After all this the Chan ordained him, and assembled his people, and went upon them that had assailed him before, and destroyed them, and put them in subjection and servage. And when he had won and put all the lands and countries on this half the Mount Belian in subjection, the white knight came to him again in his sleep, and said to him, Chan! the will of God Immortal is that thou pass the Mount Belian. And thou shalt win the land and thou shalt put many nations in subjection. And for thou shalt find no good passage for to go toward that country, go [to] the Mount Belian that is upon the sea, and kneel there nine times toward the east in the worship of God Immortal, and he shall shew the way to pass by. And the Chan did so. And anon the sea that touched and was fast to the mount began to withdraw him, and shewed fair way of nine foot breadth large; and so he passed with his folk, and won the land of Cathay that is the greatest kingdom of the world.

And for the nine kneelings and for the nine foot of way the Chan and all the men of Tartary have the number of nine in great reverence. And therefore who that will make the Chan any present, be it of horses, be it of birds, or of arrows or bows, or of fruit, or of any other thing, always he must make it of the number of nine. And so then be the presents of greater pleasure to him; and more benignly he will receive them than though he were presented with an hundred or two hundred. For him seemeth the number of nine so holy, because the messenger of God Immortal devised it.

Also, when the Chan of Cathay had won the country of Cathay, and put in subjection and under foot many countries about, he fell sick. And when he felt well that he should die, he said to his twelve sons, that everych of them should bring him one of his arrows. And so they did anon. And then he commanded that men should bind them together in three places. And then he took them to his eldest son, and bade him break them all together. And he enforced him with all his might to break them, but he ne might not. And then the Chan bade his second son to break them; and so, shortly, to all, each after other; but none of them might break them. And then he bade the youngest son dissever every one from other, and break everych by himself. And so he did. And then said the Chan to his eldest son and to all the others, Wherefore might ye not break them? And they answered that they might not, because that they were bound together. And wherefore, quoth he, hath your little youngest brother broken them? Because, quoth they, that they were parted each from other. And then said the Chan, My sons, quoth he, truly thus will it fare by you. For as long as ye be bound together in three places, that is to say, in love, in truth and in good accord, no man shall be of power to grieve you. But and ye be dissevered from these three places, that your one help not your other, ye shall be destroyed and brought to nought. And if each of you love other and help other, ye shall be lords and sovereigns of all others. And when he had made his ordinances, he died.

And then after him reigned Ecchecha Cane, his eldest son. And his other brethren went to win them many countries and kingdoms, unto the land of Prussia and of Russia, and made themselves to be clept Chane; but they were all obeissant to their elder brother, and therefore was he clept the great Chan.

After Ecchecha reigned Guyo Chan.

And after him Mango Chan that was a good Christian man and baptized, and gave letters of perpetual peace to all Christian men, and sent his brother Halaon with great multitude of folk for to win the Holy Land and for to put it into Christian men's hands, and for to destroy Mahomet's law, and for to take the Caliph of Bagdad that was emperor and lord of all the Saracens. And when this caliph was taken, men found him of so high worship, that in all the remnant of the world, ne might a man find a more reverend man, ne higher in worship. And then Halaon made him come before him, and said to him, Why, quoth he, haddest thou not taken with thee more soldiers and men enough, for a little quantity of treasure, for to defend thee and thy country, that art so abundant of treasure and so high in all worship? And the caliph answered him, For he well trowed that he had enough of his own proper men. And then said Halaon, Thou wert as a god of the Saracens. And it is convenient to a god to eat no meat that is mortal. And therefore, thou shall not eat but precious stones, rich pearls and treasure, that thou lovest so much. And then he commanded him to prison, and all his treasure about him. And so he died for hunger and thirst. And then after this, Halaon won all the Land of Promission, and put it into Christian men's hands. But the great Chan, his brother, died; and that was great sorrow and loss to all Christian men.

After Mango Chan reigned Cobyla Chan that was also a Christian man. And he reigned forty-two year. He founded the great city Izonge in Cathay, that is a great deal more than Rome.

The tother great Chan that came after him became a Paynim, and all the others after him.

The kingdom of Cathay is the greatest realm of the world. And also the great Chan is the most mighty emperor of the world and the greatest lord under the firmament. And so he clepeth him in his letters, right thus: *Chan! Filius Dei excelsi, omnium universam terram colentium summus imperator, & dominus omnium dominantium!* And the letter of his great seal, written about, is this; *Deus in coelo, Chan super terram, ejus fortitudo. Omnium hominum imperatoris sigillum.* And the superscription about his little seal is this; *Dei fortitudo, omnium hominum imperatoris sigillum.*

And albeit that they be not christened, yet nevertheless the emperor and all the Tartars believe in God Immortal. And when they will menace any man, then they say, God knoweth well that I shall do thee such a thing, and telleth his menace.

And thus have ye heard, why he is clept the great Chan.

CHAPTER XXV

Of the Governance of the great Chan's Court, and when he maketh solemn feasts. Of his Philosophers. And of his array, when he rideth by the country

Now shall I tell you the governance of the court of the great Chan, when he maketh solemn feasts; and that is principally four times in the year.

The first feast is of his birth, that other is of his presentation in their temple that they clepe their Moseache, where they make a manner of circumcision, and the tother two feasts be of his idols. The first feast of the idol is when he is first put into their temple and throned; the tother feast is when the idol beginneth first to speak, or to work miracles. More be there not of solemn feasts, but if he marry any of his children.

Now understand, that at every of these feasts he hath great multitude of people, well ordained and well arrayed, by thousands, by hundreds, and by tens. And every man knoweth well what service he shall do, and every man giveth so good heed and so good attendance to his service that no man findeth no default. And there be first ordained 4000 barons, mighty and rich, for to govern and to make ordinance for the feast, and for to serve the emperor. And these solemn feasts be made without in halls and tents made of cloths of gold and of tartaries, full nobly. And all those barons have crowns of gold upon their heads, full noble and rich, full of precious stones and great pearls orient. And they be all clothed in cloths of gold or of tartaries or of camakas, so richly and so perfectly, that no man in the world can amend it, ne better devise it. And all those robes be orfrayed all about, and dubbed full of precious stones and of great orient pearls, full richly. And they may well do so, for cloths of gold and of silk be greater cheap there a great deal than be cloths of wool. And these 4000 barons be devised in four companies, and every thousand is clothed in cloths all of one colour, and that so well arrayed and so richly, that it is marvel to behold.

The first thousand, that is of dukes, of earls, of marquises and of admirals, all clothed in cloths of gold, with tissues of green silk, and bordered with gold full of precious stones in manner as I have said before. The second thousand is all clothed in cloths diapered of red silk, all wrought with gold, and the orfrays set full of great pearl and precious stones, full nobly wrought. The third thousand is clothed in cloths of silk, of purple or of Ind. And the fourth thousand is in cloths of yellow. And all their clothes be so nobly and so richly wrought with gold and precious stones and rich pearls, that if a man of this country had but only one of their robes, he might well say that he should never be poor; for the gold and the precious stones and the great orient pearls be of greater value on this half the sea than they be beyond the sea in those countries.

And when they be thus apparelled, they go two and two together, full ordinately, before the emperor, without speech of any word, save only inclining to him. And every one of them beareth a tablet of jasper or of ivory or of crystal, and the minstrels going before them, sounding their instruments of diverse melody. And when the first thousand is thus passed and hath made his muster, he withdraweth him on that one side; and then entereth that other second thousand, and doth right so, in the same manner of array and countenance, as did the first; and after, the third; and then, the fourth; and none of them saith not one word.

And at one side of the emperor's table sit many philosophers that be proved for wise men in many diverse sciences, as of astronomy, necromancy, geomancy, pyromancy, hydromancy, of augury and of many other sciences. And everych of them have before them astrolabes of gold, some spheres, some the brain pan of a dead man, some vessels of gold full of gravel or sand, some vessels of gold full of coals burning, some vessels of gold full of water and of wine and of oil, and some horologes of gold, made full nobly and richly wrought, and many other manner of instruments after their sciences.

And at certain hours, when them thinketh time, they say to certain officers that stand before them, ordained for the time to fulfil their commandments; Make peace!

And then say the officers; Now peace! listen!

And after that, saith another of the philosophers; Every man do reverence and incline to the emperor, that is God's Son and sovereign lord of all the world! For now is time! And then every man boweth his head toward the earth.

And then commandeth the same philosopher again; Stand up! And they do so.

And at another hour, saith another philosopher; Put your little finger in your ears! And anon they do so.

And at another hour, saith another philosopher; Put your hand before your mouth! And anon they do so.

And at another hour, saith another philosopher; Put
your hand upon your head! And after that he biddeth
them to do their hand away. And they do so.

And so, from hour to hour, they command certain
things; and they say, that those things have diverse
significations. And I asked them privily what those
things betokened. And one of the masters told me,
that the bowing of the head at that hour betokened this;
that all those that bowed their heads should evermore
after be obeissant and true to the emperor, and never, for
gifts ne for promise in no kind, to be false ne traitor unto
him for good nor evil. And the putting of the little
finger in the ear betokeneth, as they say, that none of
them ne shall not hear speak no contrarious thing to the
emperor but that he shall tell it anon to his council or
discover it to some men that will make relation to the
emperor, though he were his father or brother or son.
And so forth, of all other things that is done by the
philosophers, they told me the causes of many diverse
things. And trust right well in certain, that no man doth
nothing to the emperor that belongeth unto him, neither
clothing ne bread ne wine ne bath ne none other
thing that longeth to him, but at certain hours that his
philosophers will devise. And if there fall war in any
side to the emperor, anon the philosophers come and say
their advice after their calculations, and counsel the
emperor of their advice by their sciences; so that the
emperor doth nothing without their counsel.

And when the philosophers have done and performed
their commandments, then the minstrels begin to do
their minstrelsy, everych in their instruments, each after
other, with all the melody that they can devise. And
when they have done a good while, one of the officers of
the emperor goeth up on a high stage wrought full
curiously, and crieth and saith with loud voice; Make
Peace! And then every man is still.

And then, anon after, all the lords that be of the
emperor's lineage, nobly arrayed in rich cloths of gold
and royally apparelled on white steeds, as many as may

well sue him at that time, be ready to make their presents to the emperor. And then saith the steward of the court to the lords, by name; N. of N.! and nameth first the most noble and the worthiest by name, and saith; Be ye ready with such a number of white horses, for to serve the emperor, your sovereign lord! And to another lord he saith; N. of N., be ye ready with such a number, to serve your sovereign lord! And to another, right so, and to all the lords of the emperor's lineage, each after other, as they be of estate. And when they be all cleped, they enter each after other, and present the white horses to the emperor, and then go their way. And then after, all the other barons every of them, give him presents or jewels or some other thing, after that they be of estate. And then after them, all the prelates of their law, and religious men and others; and every man giveth him something. And when that all men have thus presented the emperor, the greatest of dignity of the prelates giveth him a blessing, saying an orison of their law.

And then begin the minstrels to make their minstrelsy in divers instruments with all the melody that they can devise. And when they have done their craft, then they bring before the emperor, lions, leopards and other diverse beasts, and eagles and vultures and other divers fowls, and fishes and serpents, for to do him reverence. And then come jugglers and enchanters, that do many marvels; for they make to come in the air, by seeming, the sun and the moon to every man's sight. And after they make the night so dark that no man may see nothing. And after they make the day to come again, fair and pleasant with bright sun, to every man's sight. And then they bring in dances of the fairest damsels of the world, and richest arrayed. And after they make to come in other damsels bringing cups of gold full of milk of diverse beasts, and give drink to lords and to ladies. And then they make knights to joust in arms full lustily; and they run together a great random, and they frussch together full fiercely, and they break their spears so rudely that the truncheons fly in sprouts and pieces all about the hall. And then they make to come in hunting for the hart and for the boar, with hounds running with open mouth. And many other things they do by craft of their enchantments, that it is marvel for to see. And such plays of disport they make till the taking up of the boards. This great Chan hath full great people for to serve him, as I have told you before. For he hath of minstrels the number of thirteen cumants, but they abide not always with him. For all the minstrels that come before him, of what nation that they be of, they be withholden with him as of his household, and entered in his books as for his own men. And after that, where that ever they go, ever more they claim for minstrels of the great Chan; and under that title, all kings and lords cherish them the more with gifts and all things. And therefore he hath so great multitude of them.

And he hath of certain men as though they were yeomen, that keep birds, as ostriches, gerfalcons, sparrow-hawks, falcons gentle, lanyers, sakers, sakrets, popinjays well speaking, and birds singing, and also of wild beasts, as of elephants tame and other, baboons, apes, marmosets, and other diverse beasts; the mountance of fifteen cumants of yeomen.

And of physicians Christian he hath 200, and of leeches that be Christian he hath 210, and of leeches and physicians that be Saracens twenty, but he trusteth more in the Christian leeches than in the Saracen. And his other common household is without number, and they all have all necessaries and all that them needeth of the emperor's court. And he hath in his court many barons as servitors, that be Christian and converted to good faith by the preaching of religious Christian men that dwell with him; but there be many more, that will not that men know that they be Christian.

This emperor may dispend as much as he will without estimation; for he not dispendeth ne maketh no money but of leather imprinted or of paper. And of that money is some of greater price and some of less price, after the diversity of his statutes. And when that money hath run

so long that it beginneth to waste, then men bear it to
the emperor's treasury and then they take new money for
the old.   And that money goeth throughout all the country and throughout all his provinces, for there and beyond
them they make no money neither of gold nor of silver ;
and therefore he may dispend enough, and outrageously.
And of gold and silver that men bear in his country he
maketh cylours, pillars and pavements in his palace, and
other diverse things what him liketh.

This emperor hath in his chamber, in one of the pillars
of gold, a ruby and a carbuncle of half a foot long, that in
the night giveth so great clearness and shining, that it is
as light as day.   And he hath many other precious stones
and many other rubies and carbuncles ; but those be the
greatest and the most precious.

This emperor dwelleth in summer in a city that is
toward the north that is clept Saduz ; and there is cold
enough.   And in winter he dwelleth in a city that is clept
Camaaleche, and that is an hot country.   But the country,
where he dwelleth in most commonly, is in Gaydo or in
Jong, that is a good country and a temperate, after that
the country is there ; but to men of this country it were
too passing hot.

And when this emperor will ride from one country to
another he ordaineth four hosts of his folk, of the which
the first host goeth before him a day's journey.   For that
host shall be lodged the night where the emperor shall
lie upon the morrow.   And there shall every man have all
manner of victual and necessaries that be needful, of the
emperor's costage.   And in this first host is the number of
people fifty cumants, what of horse what of foot, of the
which every cumant amounteth 10,000, as I have told
you before.   And another host goeth in the right side of
the emperor, nigh half a journey from him.   And another
goeth on the left side of him, in the same wise.   And in
every host is as much multitude of people as in the first
host.   And then after cometh the fourth host, that is much
more than any of the others, and that goeth behind him, the
mountance of a bow draught.   And every host hath his

journeys ordained in certain places, where they shall be
lodged at night, and there they shall have all that them
needeth.   And if it befall that any of the host die, anon
they put another in his place, so that the number shall
evermore be whole.

And ye shall understand, that the emperor, in his proper
person, rideth not as other great lords do beyond, but if
he list to go privily with few men, for to be unknown.
And else, he rides in a chariot with four wheels, upon the
which is made a fair chamber, and it is made of a certain
wood, that cometh out of Paradise terrestrial, that men
clepe lignum aloes, that the floods of Paradise bring out at
divers seasons, as I have told you here before.   And this
chamber is full well smelling because of the wood that it is
made of.   And all this chamber is covered within of plate of
fine gold dubbed with precious stones and great pearls.
And four elephants and four great destriers, all white and
covered with rich covertures, leading the chariot.   And
four, or five, or six, of the greatest lords ride about this
chariot, full richly arrayed and full nobly, so that no man
shall neigh the chariot, but only those lords, but if that the
emperor call any man to him that him list to speak withal.
And above the chamber of this chariot that the emperor
sitteth in be set upon a perch four or five or six gerfalcons,
to that intent, that when the emperor seeth any wild fowl,
that he may take it at his own list, and have the disport and
the play of the flight, first with one, and after with
another ; and so he taketh his disport passing by the country.   And no man rideth before him of his company, but
all after him.   And no man dare not come nigh the
chariot, by a bow draught, but those lords only that be
about him.   And all the host cometh fairly after him in
great multitude.

And also such another chariot with such hosts ordained
and arrayed go with the empress upon another side, everych
by himself, with four hosts, right as the emperor did ;
but not with so great multitude of people.   And his
eldest son goeth by another way in another chariot, in the
same manner.   So that there is between them so great

multitude of folk that it is marvel to tell it. And no man should trow the number, but he had seen it. And sometime it happeth that when he will not go far, and that it like him to have the empress and his children with him, then they go altogether, and their folk be all mingled in fere, and divided in four parties only.

And ye shall understand, that the empire of this great Chan is divided in twelve provinces; and every province hath more than two thousand cities, and of towns without number. This country is full great, for it hath twelve principal kings in twelve provinces, and every of those kings have many kings under them, and all they be obeissant to the great Chan. And his land and his lordship dureth so far, that a man may not go from one head to another, neither by sea ne land, the space of seven year. And through the deserts of his lordship, there as men may find no towns, there be inns ordained by every journey, to receive both man and horse, in the which they shall find plenty of victual, and of all things that they need for to go by the country.

And there is a marvellous custom in that country (but it is profitable), that if any contrarious thing that should be prejudice or grievance to the emperor in any kind, anon the emperor hath tidings thereof and full knowledge in a day, though it be three or four journeys from him or more. For his ambassadors take their dromedaries or their horses, and they prick in all that ever they may toward one of the inns. And when they come there, anon they blow an horn. And anon they of the inn know well enough that there be tidings to warn the emperor of some rebellion against him. And then anon they make other men ready, in all haste that they may, to bear letters, and prick in all that ever they may, till they come to the other inns with their letters. And then they make fresh men ready, to prick forth with the letters toward the emperor, while that the last bringer rest him, and bait his dromedary or his horse. And so, from inn to inn, till it come to the emperor. And thus anon hath he hasty tidings of anything that beareth charge, by his couriers, that run so

hastily throughout all the country.   And also when the
Emperor sendeth his couriers hastily throughout his land,
every one of them hath a large thong full of small bells,
and when they neigh near to the inns of other couriers that
be also ordained by the journeys, they ring their bells, and
anon the other couriers make them ready, and run their
way unto another inn.   And thus runneth one to other,
full speedily and swiftly, till the emperor's intent be served,
in all haste.   And these couriers be clept *Chydydo*, after
their language, that is to say, a messenger.

Also when the emperor goeth from one country to
another, as I have told you here before, and he pass
through cities and towns, every man maketh a fire before
his door, and putteth therein powder of good gums that be
sweet smelling, for to make good savour to the emperor.
And all the people kneel down against him, and do him
great reverence.   And there, where religious Christian
men dwell, as they do in many cities in the land, they go
before him with procession with cross and holy water, and
they sing, *Veni creator spiritus!* with an high voice, and go
towards him.   And when he heareth them, he commandeth
to his lords to ride beside him, that the religious men may
come to him.   And when they be nigh him with the cross,
then he doth adown his galiot that sits on his head in
manner of a chaplet, that is made of gold and precious
stones and great pearls, and it is so rich, that men prize it
to the value of a realm in that country.   And then he
kneeleth to the cross.   And then the prelate of the religious
men saith before him certain orisons, and giveth him a
blessing with the cross; and he inclineth to the blessing
full devoutly.   And then the prelate giveth him some
manner fruit, to the number of nine, in a platter of
silver, with pears or apples, or other manner fruit.   And
he taketh one.   And then men give to the other lords
that be about him.   For the custom is such, that no
stranger shall come before him, but if he give him some
manner thing, after the old law that saith, *Nemo accedat in
conspectu meo vacuus*.   And then the emperor saith to the
religious men, that they withdraw them again, that they be

neither hurt nor harmed of the great multitude of horses that come behind him. And also, in the same manner, do the religious men that dwell there, to the empresses that pass by them, and to his eldest son. And to every of them they present fruit.

And ye shall understand, that the people that he hath so many hosts of, about him and about his wives and his son, they dwell not continually with him. But always, when him liketh, they be sent for. And after, when they have done, they return to their own households, save only they that be dwelling with him in household for to serve him and his wives and his sons for to govern his household. And albeit, that the others be departed from him after that they have performed their service, yet there abideth continually with him in court 50,000 men at horse and 200,000 men a foot, without minstrels and those that keep wild beasts and divers birds, of the which I have told you the number before.

Under the firmament is not so great a lord, ne so mighty, ne so rich as is the great Chan; not Prester John, that is emperor of the high Ind, ne the Soldan of Babylon, ne the Emperor of Persia. All these ne be not in comparison to the great Chan, neither of might, ne of noblesse, ne of royalty, ne of riches; for in all these he passeth all earthly princes. Wherefore it is great harm that he believeth not faithfully in God. And natheles he will gladly hear speak of God. And he suffereth well that Christian men dwell in his lordship, and that men of his faith be made Christian men if they will, throughout all his country; for he defendeth no man to hold no law other than him liketh.

In that country some men hath an hundred wives, some sixty, some more, some less. And they take the next of their kin to their wives, save only that they out-take their mothers, their daughters, and their sisters of the mother's side; but their sisters on the father's side of another woman they may well take, and their brothers' wives also after their death, and their step-mothers also in the same wise.

CHAPTER XXVI

*Of the Law and the Customs of the Tartarians dwelling in
Cathay. And how that men do when the Emperor shall
die, and how he shall be chosen*

THE folk of that country use all long clothes without furs.
And they be clothed with precious cloths of Tartary, and
of cloths of gold. And their clothes be slit at the side,
and they be fastened with laces of silk. And they clothe
them also with pilches, and the hide without; and they use
neither cape ne hood. And in the same manner as the
men go, the women go, so that no man may unneth know
the men from the women, save only those women that be
married, that bear the token upon their heads of a man's
foot, in sign that they be under man's foot and under subjection of man.

And their wives ne dwell not together, but every of them
by herself; and the husband may lie with whom of them
that him liketh. Everych hath his house, both man and
woman. And their houses be made round of staves, and
it hath a round window above that giveth them light, and
also that serveth for deliverance of smoke. And the
heling of their houses and the walls and the doors be all of
wood. And when they go to war, they lead their houses
with them upon chariots, as men do tents or pavilions.
And they make their fire in the midst of their houses.

And they have great multitude of all manner of beasts,
save only of swine, for they bring none forth. And they
believe well one God that made and formed all things.
And natheles yet have they idols of gold and silver, and of
tree and of cloth. And to those idols they offer always
their first milk of their beasts, and also of their meats and
of their drinks before they eat. And they offer often-times
horses and beasts. And they clepe the God of kind *Yroga*.

And their emperor also, what name that ever he have,
they put evermore thereto, Chan. And when I was there,

their emperor had to name Thiaut, so that he was clept
Thiaut-Chan. And his eldest son was clept Tossue; and
when he shall be emperor, he shall be clept Tossue-Chan.
And at that time the emperor had twelve sons without
him, that were named Cuncy, Ordii, Chadahay, Buryn,
† Negu, Nocab, Cadu, [Siban], Cuten, Balacy, Babylan, and
Garegan. And of his three wives, the first and principal,
that was Prester John's daughter, had to name Serioche-
Chan, and the tother Borak-Chan, and the tother Karanke-
Chan.

The folk of that country begin all their things in the
new moon, and they worship much the moon and the sun
and often-time kneel against them. And all the folk of the
country ride commonly without spurs, but they bear always
a little whip in their hands for to chace with their horses.

And they have great conscience and hold it for a great
sin to cast a knife in the fire, and for to draw flesh out of
a pot with a knife, and for to smite an horse with the
handle of a whip, or to smite an horse with a bridle, or to
break one bone with another, or for to cast milk or any
liquor that men may drink upon the earth, or for to take
and slay little children. And the most sin that any man
may do is to piss in their houses that they dwell in, and
whoso that may be found with that sin sikerly they slay
him. And of everych of these sins it behoveth them to
be shriven of their priests, and to pay great sum of silver
for their penance. And it behoveth also, that the place
that men have pissed in be hallowed again, and else dare
no man enter therein. And when they have paid their
penance, men make them pass through a fire or through
two, for to cleanse them of their sins. And also when any
messenger cometh and bringeth letters or any present to
the emperor, it behoveth him that he, with the thing that
he bringeth, pass through two burning fires for to purge
them, that he bring no poison ne venom, ne no wicked
thing that might be grievance to the Lord. And also if
any man or woman be taken in avoutry or fornication,
anon they slay him. And who that stealeth anything, anon
they slay him.

Men of that country be all good archers and shoot right well, both men and women, as well on horse-back, pricking, as on foot, running. And the women make all things and all manner mysteries and crafts, as of clothes, boots and other things ; and they drive carts, ploughs and wains and chariots ; and they make houses and all manner mysteres, out taken bows and arrows and armours that men make. And all the women wear breeches, as well as men.

All the folk of that country be full obeissant to their sovereigns ; ne they fight not, ne chide not one with another. And there be neither thieves ne robbers in that country. And every man worshippeth other ; but no man there doth no reverence to no strangers, but if they be great princes.

And they eat hounds, lions, leopards, mares and foals, asses, rats and mice and all manner of beasts, great and small, save only swine and beasts that were defended by the old law. And they eat all the beasts without and within, without casting away of anything, save only the filth. And they eat but little bread, but if it be in courts of great lords. And they have not in many places, neither pease ne beans ne none other pottages but the broth of the flesh. For little eat they anything but flesh and the broth. And when they have eaten, they wipe their hands upon their skirts ; for they use no napery ne towels, but if it be before great lords ; but the common people hath none. And when they have eaten, they put their dishes unwashen into the pot or cauldron with remnant of the flesh and of the broth till they will eat again. And the rich men drink milk of mares or of camels or of asses or of other beasts. And they will be lightly drunken of milk and of another drink that is made of honey and of water sodden together ; for in that country is neither wine ne ale. They live full wretchedly, and they eat but once in the day, and that but little, neither in courts ne in other places. And in sooth, one man alone in this country will eat more in a day than one of them will eat in three days. And if any strange messenger come there to a lord, men make him to eat but once a day, and that full little.

And when they war, they war full wisely and always do
their business, to destroy their enemies.   Every man there
beareth two bows or three, and of arrows great plenty, and
a great axe.   And the gentles have short spears and large
and full trenchant on that one side.   And they have plates
and helms made of quyrboylle, and their horses covertures of the same.   And whoso fleeth from the battle they
slay him.   And when they hold any siege about castle or
town that is walled and defensible, they behote to them
that be within to do all the profit and good, that it
is marvel to hear ; and they grant also to them that be
within all that they will ask them.   And after that they
be yielden, anon they slay them all ; and cut off their ears
and souse them in vinegar, and thereof they make great
service for lords.   All their lust and all their imagination is for to put all lands under their subjection.   And
they say that they know well by their prophecies, that they
shall be overcome by archers and by strength of them ;
but they know not of what nation ne of what law they
shall be of, that shall overcome them.   And therefore
they suffer that folk of all laws may peaceably dwell
amongst them.

Also when they will make their idols or an image of
any of their friends for to have remembrance of him, they
make always the image all naked without any manner of
clothing.   For they say that in good love should be no
covering, that man should not love for the fair clothing
ne for the rich array, but only for the body, such as God
hath made it, and for the good virtues that the body is
endowed with of Nature, not only for fair clothing that is
not of kindly Nature.

And ye shall understand that it is great dread for to
pursue the Tartars if they flee in battle.   For in fleeing
they shoot behind them and slay both men and horses.
And when they will fight they will shock them together in
a plump ; that if there be 20,000 men, men shall not
ween that there be scant 10,000.   And they can well win
land of strangers, but they cannot keep it ; for they have
greater lust to lie in tents without than for to lie in castle

or in towns. And they prize nothing the wit of other nations.

And amongst them oil of olive is full dear, for they hold it for full noble medicine. And all the Tartars have small eyen and little of beard, and not thick haired but shear. And they be false and traitors; and they last nought that they behote. They be full hardy folk, and much pain and woe may suffer and disease, more than any other folk, for they be taught thereto in their own country of youth. And therefore they spend as who saith, right nought.

And when any man shall die, men set a spear beside him. And when he draweth towards the death, every man fleeth out of the house till he be dead. And after that they bury him in the fields.

And when the emperor dieth, men set him in a chair in midst the place of his tent. And men set a table before him clean, covered with a cloth, and thereupon flesh and diverse viands and a cup full of mare's milk. And men put a mare beside him with her foal, and an horse saddled and bridled. And they lay upon the horse gold and silver, great quantity. And they put about him great plenty of straw. And then men make a great pit and a large, and with the tent and all these other things they put him in earth. And they say that when he shall come into another world, he shall not be without an house, ne without horse, ne without gold and silver; and the mare shall give him milk, and bring him forth more horses till he be well stored in the tother world. For they trow that after their death they shall be eating and drinking in that other world, and solacing them with their wives, as they did here.

And after time that the emperor is thus interred no man shall be so hardy to speak of him before his friends. And yet natheles, sometime falleth of many that they make him to be interred privily by night in wild places, and put again the grass over the pit for to grow; or else men cover the pit with gravel and sand, that no man shall perceive where, ne know where, the pit is, to that intent that never after none of his friends shall have mind ne remembrance of him. And then they say that he is ravished into another world, where he is a greater lord than he was here.

And then, after the death of the emperor, the seven lineages assemble them together, and choose his eldest son, or the next after him of his blood. And thus they say to him; we will and we pray and ordain that ye be our lord and our emperor.

And then he answereth, If ye will that I reign over you as lord, do everych of you that I shall command him, either to abide or to go; and whomsoever that I command to be slain, that anon he be slain.

And they answer all with one voice, Whatsoever ye command, it shall be done.

Then saith the emperor, Now understand well, that my word from henceforth is sharp and biting as a sword.

After, men set him upon a black steed and so men bring him to a chair full richly arrayed, and there they crown him. And then all the cities and good towns send him rich presents. So that at that journey he shall have more than sixty chariots charged with gold and silver, without jewels of gold and precious stones, that lords gave him, that be without estimation, and without horses, and cloths of gold, and of camakas, and tartarins that be without number.

CHAPTER XXVII

Of the Realm of Tharse and the Lands and Kingdoms towards the Septentrional Parts, in coming down from the land of Cathay

THIS land of Cathay is in Asia the deep; and after, on this half, is Asia the more. The kingdom of Cathay marcheth toward the west unto the kingdom of Tharse, the which was one of the kings that came to present our Lord in Bethlehem. And they that be of the lineage of that king are some Christian. In Tharse they eat no flesh, ne they drink no wine.

And on this half, toward the west, is the kingdom of Turkestan, that stretcheth him toward the west to the kingdom of Persia, and toward the septentrional to the kingdom of Khorasan. In the country of Turkestan be but few good cities ; but the best city of that land hight Octorar. There be great pastures, but few corns ; and therefore, for the most part, they be all herdsmen, and they lie in tents and they drink a manner ale made of honey.

And after, on this half, is the kingdom of Khorasan, that is a good land and a plenteous, without wine. And it hath a desert toward the east that lasteth more than an hundred journeys. And the best city of that country is clept Khorasan, and of that city beareth the country his name. The folk of that country be hardy warriors.

And on this half is the kingdom of Comania, whereof the Comanians that dwelled in Greece sometime were chased out. This is one of the greatest kingdoms of the world, but it is not all inhabited. For at one of the parts there is so great cold that no man may dwell there ; and in another part there is so great heat that no man may endure it, and also there be so many flies, that no man may know on what side he may turn him. In that country is but little arboury ne trees that bear fruit ne other. They lie in tents ; and they burn the dung of beasts for default of wood. This kingdom descendeth on this half toward us and toward Prussia and toward Russia.

And through that country runneth the river of Ethille that is one of the greatest rivers of the world. And it freezeth so strongly all years that many times men have fought upon the ice with great hosts, both parties on foot, and their horses voided for the time, and what on horse and on foot, more than 200,000 persons on every side.

And between that river and the great sea Ocean, that

they clepe the Sea Maure, lie all these realms. And toward the head, beneath, in that realm is the Mount Chotaz, that is the highest mount of the world, and it is between the Sea Maure and the Sea Caspian. There is full strait and dangerous passage for to go toward Ind. And therefore King Alexander let make there a strong city, that men clepe Alexandria, for to keep the country that no man should pass without his leave. And now men clepe that city, the Gate of Hell.

And the principal city of Comania is clept Sarak, that is one of the three ways for to go into Ind. But by that way, ne may not pass no great multitude of people, but if it be in winter. And that passage men clepe the Derbent. The tother way is for to go from the city of Turkestan by Persia, and by that way be many journeys by desert. And the third way is that cometh from Comania and then to go by the Great Sea and by the kingdom of Abchaz.

And ye shall understand, that all these kingdoms and all these lands above-said unto Prussia and to Russia be all obeissant to the great Chan of Cathay, and many other countries that march to other coasts. Wherefore his power and his lordship is full great and full mighty.

CHAPTER XXVIII

Of the Emperor of Persia, and of the Land of Darkness; and of other kingdoms that belong to the great Chan of Cathay, and other lands of his, unto the sea of Greece

Now, since I have devised you the lands and the kingdoms toward the parts Septentrionals in coming down from the land of Cathay unto the lands of the Christian, towards Prussia and Russia,—now shall I devise you of other lands and kingdoms coming down by other coasts, toward the right side, unto the sea of Greece, toward the land of Christian men. And, therefore, that after Ind and

after Cathay the Emperor of Persia is the greatest lord,
therefore, I shall tell you of the kingdom of Persia.

First, where he hath two kingdoms, the first kingdom
beginneth toward the east, toward the kingdom of
Turkestan, and it stretcheth toward the west unto
the river of Pison, that is one of the four rivers
that come out of Paradise. And on another side it
stretcheth toward the Septentrion unto the sea of Caspian ;
and also toward the south unto the desert of Ind. And
this country is good and plain and full of people. And
there be many good cities. But the two principal cities
be these, Boyturra, and Seornergant, that some men clepe
Sormagant. The tother kingdom of Persia stretcheth
toward the river of Pison and the parts of the west unto
the kingdom of Media, and from the great Armenia and
toward the Septentrion to the sea of Caspian and toward
the south to the land of Ind. That is also a good land
and a plenteous, and it hath three great principal cities
—Messabor, Saphon, and Sarmassan.

And then after is Armenia, in the which were wont to
be four kingdoms ; that is a noble country and full of
goods. And it beginneth at Persia and stretcheth toward
the west in length unto Turkey. And in largeness it
dureth to the city of Alexandria, that now is clept the
Gate of Hell, that I spake of before, under the kingdom
of Media. In this Armenia be full many good cities, but
Taurizo is most of name.

After this is the kingdom of Media, that is full long,
but it is not full large, that beginneth toward the east to
the land of Persia and to Ind the less ; and it stretcheth
toward the west, toward the kingdom of Chaldea and
toward the Septentrion, descending toward the little
Armenia. In that kingdom of Media there be many
great hills and little of plain earth. There dwell Saracens
and another manner of folk, that men clepe Cordynes.
The best two cities of that kingdom be Sarras and Karemen.

After that is the kingdom of Georgia, that beginneth
toward the east to the great mountain that is clept
Abzor, where that dwell many diverse folk of diverse

nations. And men clepe the country Alamo. This kingdom stretcheth him towards Turkey and toward the Great Sea, and toward the south it marcheth to the great Armenia. And there be two kingdoms in that country; that one is the kingdom of Georgia, and that other is the kingdom of Abchaz. And always in that country be two kings; and they be both Christian. But the king of Georgia is in subjection to the great Chan. And the king of Abchaz hath the more strong country, and he always vigorously defendeth his country against all those that assail him, so that no man may make him in subjection to no man.

In that kingdom of Abchaz is a great marvel. For a province of the country that hath well in circuit three journeys, that men clepe Hanyson, is all covered with darkness, without any brightness or light; so that no man may see ne hear, ne no man dare enter into him. And, natheles, they of the country say, that sometimes men hear voice of folk, and horses neighing, and cocks crowing. And men wit well, that men dwell there, but they know not what men. And they say, that the darkness befell by miracle of God. For a cursed emperor of Persia, that hight Saures, pursued all Christian men to destroy them and to compel them to make sacrifice to his idols, and rode with great host, in all that ever he might, for to confound the Christian men. And then in that country dwelled many good Christian men, the which that left their goods and would have fled into Greece. And when they were in a plain that hight Megon, anon this cursed emperor met with them with his host for to have slain them and hewn them to pieces. And anon the Christian men kneeled to the ground, and made their prayers to God to succour them. And anon a great thick cloud came and covered the emperor and all his host. And so they endure in that manner that they ne may not go out on no side; and so shall they evermore abide in that darkness till the day of doom, by the miracle of God. And then the Christian men went where them liked best, at their own pleasance, without letting of any creature, and their enemies enclosed and confounded in darkness, without any stroke.

Wherefore we may well say with David, *A Domino factum est istud; & est mirabile in oculis nostris.* And that was a great miracle, that God made for them. Wherefore methinketh that Christian men should be more devout to serve our Lord God than any other men of any other sect. For without any dread, ne were not cursedness and sin of Christian men, they should be lords of all the world. For the banner of Jesu Christ is always displayed, and ready on all sides to the help of his true loving servants. Insomuch, that one good Christian man in good belief should overcome and out-chase a thousand cursed misbelieving men, as David saith in the Psalter, *Quoniam persequebatur unus mille, & duo fugarent decem milia*; *et cadent a latere tuo mille, & decem milia a dextris tuis.* And how that it might be that one should chase a thousand, David himself saith following, *Quia manus Domini fecit haec omnia*, and our Lord himself saith, by the prophet's mouth, *Si in viis meis ambulaveritis, super tribulantes vos misissem manum meam.* So that we may see apertly that if we will be good men, no enemy may not endure against us.

Also ye shall understand that out of that land of darkness goeth out a great river that sheweth well that there be folk dwelling, by many ready tokens; but no man dare not enter into it.

And wit well, that in the kingdoms of Georgia, of Abchaz and of the little Armenia be good Christian men and devout. For they shrive them and housel them evermore once or twice in the week. And there be many of them that housel them every day; and so do we not on this half, albeit that Saint Paul commandeth it, saying, *Omnibus diebus dominicis ad communicandum hortor.* They keep that commandment, but we ne keep it not.

Also after, on this half, is Turkey, that marcheth to the great Armenia. And there be many provinces, as Cappadocia, Saure, Brique, Quesiton, Pytan, and Gemethe. And in everych of these be many good cities. This

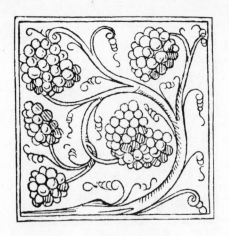

Turkey stretcheth unto the city of Sachala that sitteth upon the sea of Greece, and so it marcheth to Syria. Syria is a great country and a good, as I have told you before.   And also it hath, above toward Ind, the kingdom of Chaldea, that stretcheth from the mountains of Chaldea toward the east unto the city of Nineveh, that sitteth upon the river of Tigris; and in largeness it beginneth toward the north to the city of Maraga; and it stretcheth toward the south unto the sea Ocean.   In Chaldea is a plain country, and few hills and few rivers.

After is the kingdom of Mesopotamia, that beginneth, toward the east, to the flom of Tigris, unto a city that is clept Mosul; and it stretcheth toward the west to the flom of Euphrates unto a city that is clept Roianz; and in length it goeth to the mount of Armenia unto the desert of Ind the less.   This is a good country and a plain, but it hath few rivers.   It hath but two mountains in that country, of the which one hight Symar and that other Lyson.   And this land marcheth to the kingdom of Chaldea.

Yet there is, toward the parts Meridionals many countries and many regions, as the land of Ethiopia, that marcheth, toward the east to the great deserts, toward the west to the kingdom of Nubia, toward the south to the kingdom of Moretane, and toward the north to the Red Sea.

After is Moretane, that dureth from the mountains of Ethiopia unto Lybia the high.   And that country lieth along from the sea ocean toward the south ; and toward the north it marcheth to Nubia and to the high Lybia. (These men of Nubia be Christian.)   And it marcheth from the lands above-said to the deserts of Egypt, and that is the Egypt that I have spoken of before.

And after is Lybia the high and Lybia the low, that descendeth down low toward the great sea of Spain, in the which country be many kingdoms and many diverse folk.

Now I have devised you many countries on this half the kingdom of Cathay, of the which many be obeissant to the great Chan.

CHAPTER XXIX

Of the Countries and Isles that be beyond the Land of Cathay; and of the fruits there; and of twenty-two kings enclosed within the mountains

Now shall I say you, suingly, of countries and isles that be beyond the countries that I have spoken of.

Wherefore I say you, in passing by the land of Cathay toward the high Ind and toward Bacharia, men pass by a kingdom that men clepe Caldilhe, that is a full fair country.

And there groweth a manner of fruit, as though it were gourds. And when they be ripe, men cut them a-two, and men find within a little beast, in flesh, in bone, and blood, as though it were a little lamb without wool. And men eat both the fruit and the beast. And that is a great marvel. Of that fruit I have eaten, although it were wonderful, but that I know well that God is marvellous in his works. And, natheles, I told them of as great a marvel to them, that is amongst us, and that was of the Bernakes. For I told them that in our country were trees that bear a fruit that become birds flying, and those that fell in the water live, and they that fall on the earth die anon, and they be right good to man's meat. And hereof had they as great marvel, that some of them trowed it were an impossible thing to be.

In that country be long apples of good savour, whereof be more than an hundred in a cluster, and as many in another; and they have great long leaves and large, of two foot long or more. And in that country, and in other countries thereabout, grow many trees that bear clove-gylofres and nutmegs, and great nuts of Ind, and of Canell and of many other spices. And there be vines that bear so great grapes, that a strong man should have enough to do for to bear one cluster with all the grapes.

In that same region be the mountains of Caspian that

men clepe Uber in the country.   Between those mountains
the Jews of ten lineages be enclosed, that men clepe Goth
and Magoth and they may not go out on no side.   There
were enclosed twenty-two kings with their people, that
dwelled between the mountains of Scythia.   There King
Alexander chased them between those mountains, and
there he thought for to enclose them through work of
his men.   But when he saw that he might not do it, ne bring
it to an end, he prayed to God of nature that he would
perform that that he had begun.   And all were it so, that
he was a paynim and not worthy to be heard, yet God of
his grace closed the mountains together, so that they dwell
there all fast locked and enclosed with high mountains all
about, save only on one side, and on that side is the sea of
Caspian.

Now may some men ask, since that the sea is on that
one side, wherefore go they not out on the sea side, for to
go where that them liketh ?

But to this question, I shall answer; that sea of Caspian
goeth out by land under the mountains, and runneth by
the desert at one side of the country, and after it stretcheth
unto the ends of Persia, and although it be clept a sea, it
is no sea, ne it toucheth to none other sea, but it is a lake,
the greatest of the world ; and though they would put
them into that sea, they ne wist never where that they
should arrive ; and also they can no language but only
their own, that no man knoweth but they ; and therefore
may they not go out.

And also ye shall understand, that the Jews have no
proper land of their own for to dwell in, in all the world,
but only that land between the mountains.   And yet they
yield tribute for that land to the Queen of Amazonia, the
which that maketh them to be kept in close full diligently,
that they shall not go out on no side but by the coast of
their land ; for their land marcheth to those mountains.

And often it hath befallen, that some of the Jews have
gone up the mountains and avaled down to the valleys.   But
great number of folk ne may not do so, for the mountains
be so high and so straight up, that they must abide there,

maugre their might.   For they may not go out, but by a
little issue that was made by strength of men, and it lasteth
well a four great mile.

And after, is there yet a land all desert, where men may
find no water, neither for digging ne for none other
thing.   Wherefore men may not dwell in that place, so
is it full of dragons, of serpents and of other venomous
beasts, that no man dare not pass, but if it be strong
winter.   And that strait passage men clepe in that country
Clyron.   And that is the passage that the Queen of
Amazonia maketh to be kept.   And though it happen
some of them by fortune to go out, they can no manner
of language but Hebrew, so that they cannot speak to the
people.

And yet, natheles, men say they shall go out in the
time of anti-Christ, and that they shall make great
slaughter of Christian men.   And therefore all the Jews
that dwell in all lands learn always to speak Hebrew, in
hope, that when the other Jews shall go out, that they
may understand their speech, and to lead them into
Christendom for to destroy the Christian people.   For
the Jews say that they know well by their prophecies, that
they of Caspia shall go out, and spread throughout all the
world, and that the Christian men shall be under their
subjection, as long as they have been in subjection of them.

And if that ye will wit how that they shall find their
way, after that I have heard say I shall tell you.

In the time of anti-Christ a fox shall make there his
train, and mine an hole where King Alexander let make
the gates ; and so long he shall mine and pierce the earth,
till that he shall pass through towards that folk.   And
when they see the fox, they shall have great marvel of
him, because that they saw never such a beast.   For of
all other beasts they have enclosed amongst them, save
only the fox.   And then they shall chase him and pursue
him so strait, till that he come to the same place that he
came from.   And then they shall dig and mine so strongly,
till that they find the gates that King Alexander let make
of great stones, and passing huge, well cemented and made

strong for the mastery. And those gates they shall break, and so go out by finding of that issue.

From that land go men toward the land of Bacharia, where be full evil folk and full cruel. In that land be trees that bear wool, as though it were of sheep, whereof men make clothes and all things that may be made of wool.

In that country be many hippotaynes that dwell sometime in the water and sometime on the land. And they be half man and half horse, as I have said before. And they eat men when they may take them.

And there be rivers of waters that be full bitter, three sithes more than is the water of the sea.

In that country be many griffins, more plenty than in any other country. Some men say that they have the body upward as an eagle and beneath as a lion ; and truly they say sooth, that they be of that shape. But one griffin hath the body more great and is more strong than eight lions, of such lions as be on this half, and more great and stronger than an hundred eagles such as we have amongst us. For one griffin there will bear, flying to his nest, a great horse, if he may find him at the point, or two oxen yoked together as they go at the plough. For he hath his talons so long and so large and great upon his feet, as though they were horns of great oxen or of bugles or of kine, so that men make cups of them to drink of. And of their ribs and of the pens of their wings, men make bows, full strong, to shoot with arrows and quarrels.

From thence go men by many journeys through the land of Prester John, the great Emperor of Ind. And men clepe his realm the Isle of Pentexoire.

CHAPTER XXX

Of the Royal Estate of Prester John. And of a rich man that made a marvellous castle and cleped it Paradise; and of his subtlety

THIS emperor, Prester John, holds full great land, and hath many full noble cities and good towns in his realm, and many great diverse isles and large. For all the country of Ind is devised in isles for the great floods that come from Paradise, that depart all the land in many parts. And also in the sea he hath full many isles. And the best city in the Isle of Pentexoire is Nyse, that is a full royal city and a noble, and full rich.

This Prester John hath under him many kings and many isles and many diverse folk of diverse conditions. And this land is full good and rich, but not so rich as is the land of the great Chan. For the merchants come not thither so commonly for to buy merchandises, as they do in the land of the great Chan, for it is too far to travel to. And on that other part, in the Isle of Cathay, men find all manner thing that is need to man—cloths of gold, of silk, of spicery and all manner avoirdupois. And therefore, albeit that men have greater cheap in the Isle of Prester John, natheles, men dread the long way and the great perils in the sea in those parts.

For in many places of the sea be great rocks of stones of the adamant, that of his proper nature draweth iron to him. And therefore there pass no ships that have either bonds or nails of iron within them. And if there do, anon the rocks of the adamants draw them to them, that never they may go thence. I myself have seen afar in that sea, as though it had been a great isle full of trees and buscaylle, full of thorns and briars, great plenty. And the shipmen told us, that all that was of ships that were drawn thither by the adamants, for the iron that was in them. And of the rotten-ness, and other thing that was within the ships, grew such buscaylle, and thorns and briars and green grass, and such manner of thing ; and of the masts and the sail-yards; it seemed a great wood or a grove.   And such rocks be in many places thereabout. And therefore dare not the merchants pass there, but if they know well the passages, or else that they have good lodesmen.

And also they dread the long way.   And therefore they go to Cathay, for it is more nigh.   And yet it is not so nigh, but that men must be travelling by sea and land, eleven months or twelve, from Genoa or from Venice, or he come to Cathay.   And yet is the land of Prester John more far by many dreadful journeys.

And the merchants pass by the kingdom of Persia, and go to a city that is clept Hermes, for Hermes the philosopher founded it.   And after that they pass an arm of the sea, and then they go to another city that is clept Golbache.   And there they find merchandises, and of popinjays, as great plenty as men find here of geese.   And if they will pass further, they may go sikerly enough. In that country is but little wheat or barley, and therefore they eat rice and honey and milk and cheese and fruit.

This Emperor Prester John taketh always to his wife the daughter of the great Chan ; and the great Chan also, in the same wise, the daughter of Prester John.   For these two be the greatest lords under the firmament.

In the land of Prester John be many diverse things and many precious stones, so great and so large, that men make of them vessels, as platters, dishes and cups.   And many other marvels be there, that it were too cumbrous and too long to put it in scripture of books; but of the principal isles and of his estate and of his law, I shall tell you some part.

This Emperor Prester John is Christian, and a great part of his country also.   But yet, they have not all the articles of our faith as we have.   They believe well in the Father, in the Son and in the Holy Ghost.   And they be full devout and right true one to another.   And they set not by no barretts, ne by cautels, nor of no deceits.

And he hath under him seventy-two provinces, and in every province is a king. And these kings have kings under them, and all be tributaries to Prester John. And he hath in his lordships many great marvels.

For in his country is the sea that men clepe the Gravelly Sea, that is all gravel and sand, without any drop of water, and it ebbeth and floweth in great waves as other seas do, and it is never still ne in peace, in no manner season. And no man may pass that sea by navy, ne by no manner of craft, and therefore may no man know what land is beyond that sea. And albeit that it have no water, yet men find therein and on the banks full good fish of other manner of kind and shape, than men find in any other sea, and they be of right good taste and delicious to man's meat.

And a three journeys long from that sea be great mountains, out of the which goeth out a great flood that cometh out of Paradise. And it is full of precious stones, without any drop of water, and it runneth through the desert on that one side, so that it maketh the sea gravelly; and it beareth into that sea, and there it endeth. And that flome runneth, also, three days in the week and bringeth with him great stones and the rocks also therewith, and that great plenty. And anon, as they be entered into the Gravelly Sea, they be seen no more, but lost for evermore. And in those three days that that river runneth, no man dare enter into it; but in the other days men dare enter well enough.

Also beyond that flome, more upward to the deserts, is a great plain all gravelly, between the mountains. And in that plain, every day at the sun-rising, begin to grow small trees, and they grow till mid-day, bearing fruit; but no man dare take of that fruit, for it is a thing of faerie. And after mid-day, they decrease and enter again into the earth, so that at the going down of the sun they appear no more. And so they do, every day. And that is a great marvel.

In that desert be many wild men, that be hideous to look on; for they be horned, and they speak nought, but they grunt, as pigs. And there is also great plenty of wild hounds. And there be many popinjays, that they clepe psittakes in their language. And they speak of their proper nature, and salute men that go through the deserts, and speak to them as apertly as though it were a man. And they that speak well have a large tongue, and have five toes upon a foot. And there be also of another manner, that have but three toes upon a foot, and they speak not, or but little, for they can not but cry.

This Emperor Prester John when he goeth into battle against any other lord, he hath no banners borne before him; but he hath three crosses of gold, fine, great and high, full of precious stones, and every of those crosses be set in a chariot, full richly arrayed. And for to keep every cross, be ordained 10,000 men of arms and more than 100,000 men on foot, in manner as men would keep a standard in our countries, when that we be in land of war. And this number of folk is without the principal host and without wings ordained for the battle. And when he hath no war, but rideth with a privy meinie, then he hath borne before him but one cross of tree, without painting and without gold or silver or precious stones, in remembrance that Jesu Christ suffered death upon a cross of tree. And he hath borne before him also a platter of gold full of earth, in token that his noblesse and his might and his flesh shall turn to earth. And he hath borne before him also a vessel of silver, full of noble jewels of gold full rich and of precious stones, in token of his lordship and of his noblesse and of his might.

He dwelleth commonly in the city of Susa. And there is his principal palace, that is so rich and so noble, that no man will trow it by estimation, but he had seen it. And above the chief tower of the palace be two round pommels of gold, and in everych of them be two carbuncles great and large, that shine full bright upon the night. And the principal gates of his palace be of precious stone that men clepe sardonyx, and the border and the bars be of ivory. And the windows of the halls and chambers be of crystal. And the tables whereon men eat, some be of emeralds, some of amethyst, and some of gold, full of precious stones;

and the pillars that bear up the tables be of the same precious stones. And the degrees to go up to his throne, where he sitteth at the meat, one is of onyx, another is of crystal, and another of jasper green, another of amethyst, another of sardine, another of cornelian, and the seventh, that he setteth on his feet, is of chrysolite. And all these degrees be bordered with fine gold, with the tother precious stones, set with great pearls orient. And the sides of the siege of his throne be of emeralds, and bordered with gold full nobly, and dubbed with other precious stones and great pearls. And all the pillars in his chamber be of fine gold with precious stones, and with many carbuncles, that give great light upon the night to all people. And albeit that the carbuncles give light right enough, natheles, at all times burneth a vessel of crystal full of balm, for to give good smell and odour to the emperor, and to void away all wicked airs and corruptions. And the form of his bed is of fine sapphires, bended with gold, for to make him sleep well and to refrain him from lechery ; for he will not lie with his wives, but four sithes in the year, after the four seasons, and that is only for to engender children.

He hath also a full fair palace and a noble at the city of Nyse, where that he dwelleth, when him best liketh ; but the air is not so attempre, as it is at the city of Susa.

And ye shall understand, that in all his country nor in the countries there all about, men eat not but once in the day, †as they do in the court of the great Chan. And so they eat every day in his court, more than 30,000 persons, without goers and comers. But the 30,000 persons of his country, ne of the country of the great Chan, ne spend not so much good as do 12,000 of our country.

This Emperor Prester John hath evermore seven kings with him to serve him, and they depart their service by certain months. And with these kings serve always seventy-two dukes and three hundred and sixty earls. And all the days of the year, there eat in his household and in his court, twelve archbishops and twenty bishops. And the patriarch of Saint Thomas is there as is the pope here. And the archbishops and the bishops and the abbots in

that country be all kings.   And everych of these great
lords know well enough the attendance of their service.
The one is master of his household, another is his
chamberlain, another serveth him of a dish, another of the
cup, another is steward, another is marshal, another is
prince of his arms, and thus is he full nobly and royally
served.   And his land dureth in very breadth four
months' journeys, and in length out of measure, that is to
say, all the isles under earth that we suppose to be
under us.

Beside the isle of Pentexoire, that is the land of Prester
John, is a great isle, long and broad, that men clepe
Mistorak ; and it is in the lordship of Prester John.   In
that isle is great plenty of goods.

There was dwelling, sometime, a rich man ; and it is
not long since ; and men clept him Gatholonabes.   And he
was full of cautels and of subtle deceits.   And he had a full
fair castle and a strong in a mountain, so strong and so
noble, that no man could devise a fairer ne stronger.
And he had let mure all the mountain about with a strong
wall and a fair.   And within those walls he had the fairest
garden that any man might behold.   And therein were
trees bearing all manner of fruits, that any man could
devise.   And therein were also all manner virtuous herbs
of good smell, and all other herbs also that bear fair flowers.
And he had also in that garden many fair wells ; and
beside those wells he had let make fair halls and fair
chambers, depainted all with gold and azure ; and there
were in that place many diverse things, and many diverse
stories: and of beasts, and of birds that sung full delectably
and moved by craft, that it seemed that they were quick.
And he had also in his garden all manner of fowls and of
beasts that any man might think on, for to have play or
sport to behold them.

And he had also, in that place, the fairest damsels that
might be found, under the age of fifteen years, and the
fairest young striplings that men might get, of that same
age.   And all they were clothed in cloths of gold, full
richly.   And he said that those were angels.

And he had also let make three wells, fair and noble, and all environed with stone of jasper, of crystal, diapered with gold, and set with precious stones and great orient pearls.   And he had made a conduit under earth, so that the three wells, at his list, one should run milk, another wine and another honey.   And that place he clept Paradise.

And when that any good knight, that was hardy and noble, came to see this royalty, he would lead him into his paradise, and show him these wonderful things to his disport, and the marvellous and delicious song of diverse birds, and the fair damsels, and the fair wells of milk, of wine and of honey, plenteously running.   And he would let make divers instruments of music to sound in an high tower, so merrily, that it was joy for to hear ; and no man should see the craft thereof.   And those, he said, were angels of God, and that place was Paradise, that God had behight to his friends, saying, *Dabo vobis terram fluentem lacte et melle*.   And then would he make them to drink of certain drink, whereof anon they should be drunk.   And then would them think greater delight than they had before.   And then would he say to them, that if they would die for him and for his love, that after their death they should come to his paradise ; and they should be of the age of those damosels, and they should play with them, and yet be maidens.   And after that yet should he put them in a fairer paradise, where that they should see God of nature visibly, in his majesty and in his bliss. And then would he shew them his intent, and say them, that if they would go slay such a lord, or such a man that was his enemy or contrarious to his list, that they should not dread to do it and for to be slain therefore themselves. For after their death, he would put them into another paradise, that was an hundred-fold fairer than any of the tother ; and there should they dwell with the most fairest damosels that might be, and play with them ever-more.

And thus went many diverse lusty bachelors for to slay great lords in diverse countries, that were his enemies, and made themselves to be slain, in hope to have that paradise.

And thus, often-time, he was revenged of his enemies by his subtle deceits and false cautels.

And when the worthy men of the country had perceived this subtle falsehood of this Gatholonabes, they assembled them with force, and assailed his castle, and slew him, and destroyed all the fair places and all the nobilities of that paradise. The place of the wells and of the walls and of many other things be yet apertly seen, but the riches is voided clean. And it is not long gone, since that place was destroyed.

CHAPTER XXXI

Of the Devil's Head in the Valley Perilous. And of the Customs of Folk in diverse Isles that be about in the Lordship of Prester John

BESIDE that Isle of Mistorak upon the left side nigh to the river of Pison is a marvellous thing. There is a vale between the mountains, that dureth nigh a four mile. And some men clepe it the Vale Enchanted, some clepe it the Vale of Devils, and some clepe it the Vale Perilous. In that vale hear men often-time great tempests and thunders, and great murmurs and noises, all days and nights, and great noise, as it were sound of tabors and of nakers and of trumps, as though it were of a great feast. This vale is all full of devils, and hath been always. And men say there, that it is one of the entries of hell. In that vale is great plenty of gold and silver. Wherefore many misbelieving men, and many Christian men also, go in oftentime for to have of the treasure that there is ; but few come again, and namely of the misbelieving men, ne of the Christian men neither, for anon they be strangled of devils.

And in mid place of that vale, under a rock, is an head and the visage of a devil bodily, full horrible and dreadful to see, and it sheweth not but the head, to the shoulders.

But there is no man in the world so hardy, Christian man ne other, but that he would be adread to behold it, and that it would seem him to die for dread, so is it hideous for to behold. For he beholdeth every man so sharply with dreadful eyen, that be evermore moving and sparkling as fire, and changeth and stirreth so often in diverse manner, with so horrible countenance, that no man dare not neighen towards him. And from him cometh out smoke and stinking fire and so much abomination, that unnethe no man may there endure.

But the good Christian men, that be stable in the faith, enter well without peril. For they will first shrive them and mark them with the token of the holy cross, so that the fiends ne have no power over them. But albeit that they be without peril, yet, natheles, ne be they not without dread, when that they see the devils visibly and bodily all about them, that make full many diverse assaults and menaces, in air and in earth, and aghast them with strokes of thunder-blasts and of tempests. And the most dread is, that God will take vengeance then of that that men have misdone against his will.

And ye shall understand, that when my fellows and I were in that vale, we were in great thought, whether that we durst put our bodies in adventure, to go in or not, in the protection of God. And some of our fellows accorded to enter, and some not. So there were with us two worthy men, friars minors, that were of Lombardy, that said, that if any man would enter they would go in with us. And when they had said so, upon the gracious trust of God and of them, we let sing mass, and made every man to be shriven and houseled. And then we entered fourteen persons ; but at our going out we were but nine. And so we wist never, whether that our fellows were lost, or else turned again for dread. But we saw them never after ; and those were two men of Greece, and three of Spain. And our other fellows that would not go in with us, they went by another coast to be before us ; and so they were.

And thus we passed that perilous vale, and found therein

gold and silver, and precious stones and rich jewels, great plenty, both here and there, as us seemed. But whether that it was, as us seemed, I wot never. For I touched none, because that the devils be so subtle to make a thing to seem otherwise than it is, for to deceive mankind. And therefore I touched none, and also because that I would not be put out of my devotion; for I was more devout then, than ever I was before or after, and all for the dread of fiends that I saw in diverse figures, and also for the great multitude of dead bodies, that I saw there lying by the way, by all the vale, as though there had been a battle between two kings, and the mightiest of the country, and that the greater part had been discomfited and slain. And I trow, that unnethe should any country have so much people within him, as lay slain in that vale as us thought, the which was an hideous sight to see. And I marvelled much, that there were so many, and the bodies all whole without rotting. But I trow, that fiends made them seem to be so whole without rotting. But that might not be to mine advice that so many should have entered so newly, ne so many newly slain, without stinking and rotting. And many of them were in habit of Christian men, but I trow well, that it were of such that went in for covetise of the treasure that was there, and had overmuch feebleness in the faith; so that their hearts ne might not endure in the belief for dread. And therefore were we the more devout a great deal. And yet we were cast down, and beaten down many times to the hard earth by winds and thunders and tempests. But evermore God of his grace holp us. And so we passed that perilous vale without peril and without encumbrance, thanked be Almighty God.

After this, beyond the vale, is a great isle, where the folk be great giants of twenty-eight foot long, or of thirty foot long. And they have no clothing but of skins of beasts that they hang upon them. And they eat no bread, but all raw flesh; and they drink milk of beasts, for they have plenty of all bestial. And they have no houses to lie in. And they eat more gladly Man's flesh than any other flesh. Into that isle dare no man gladly enter. And if they see a ship and men therein, anon they enter into the sea for to take them.

And men said us, that in an isle beyond that were giants of greater stature, some of forty-five foot, or of fifty foot long, and, as some men say, some of fifty cubits long. But I saw none of those, for I had no lust to go to those parts, because that no man cometh neither into that isle ne into the other, but if he be devoured anon. And among those giants be sheep as great as oxen here, and they bear great wool and rough. Of the sheep I have seen many times. And men have seen, many times, those giants take men in the sea out of their ships, and brought them to land, two in one hand and two in another, eating them going, all raw and all quick.

Another isle is there toward the north, in the sea Ocean, where that be full cruel and full evil women of nature. And they have precious stones in their eyen. And they be of that kind, that if they behold any man with wrath, they slay him anon with the beholding, as doth the basilisk.

Another isle is there, full fair and good and great, and full of people, where the custom is such, that the first night that they be married, they make another man to lie by their wives for to have their maidenhead : and therefore they take great hire and great thank. And there be certain men in every town that serve of none other thing ; and they clepe them cadeberiz, that is to say, the fools of wanhope. For they of the country hold it so great a thing and so perilous for to have the maidenhead of a woman, that them seemeth that they that have first the maidenhead putteth him in adventure of his life. And if the husband find his wife maiden that other next night after that she should have been lain by of the man that is assigned therefore, peradventure for drunkenness or for some other cause, the husband shall plain upon him that he hath not done his devoir, in such cruel wise as though the officers would have slain him. But after the first night that they be lain by, they keep them so straitly that they be not so hardy to speak with no man. And I asked them the cause why that they held such custom : and they said me, that of old time men had been dead for deflowering of maidens, that had serpents in their bodies that stung men upon their yards, that they died anon : and therefore they held that custom, to make other men ordained therefore to lie by their wives, for dread of death, and to assay the passage by another [rather] than for to put them in that adventure.

After that is another isle where that women make great sorrow when their children be y-born. And when they die, they make great feast and great joy and revel, and then they cast them into a great fire burning. And those that love well their husbands, if their husbands be dead, they cast them also in the fire with their children, and burn them. And they say that the fire shall cleanse them of all filths and of all vices, and they shall go pured and clean into another world to their husbands, and they shall lead their children with them. And the cause why that they weep, when their children be born is this; for when they come into this world, they come to labour, sorrow and heaviness. And why they make joy and gladness at their dying is because that, as they say, then they go to Paradise where the rivers run milk and honey, where that men see them in joy and in abundance of goods, without sorrow and labour.

In that isle men make their king evermore by election, and they ne choose him not for no noblesse nor for no riches, but such one as is of good manners and of good conditions, and therewithal rightfull, and also that he be of great age, and that he have no children. In that isle men be full rightfull and they do rightfull judgments in every cause both of rich and poor, small and great, after the quantity of the trespass that is mis-done. And the king may not doom no man to death without assent of his barons and other men wise of counsel, and that all the court accord thereto. And if the king himself do any homicide or any crime, as to slay a man, or any such case, he shall die there for. But he shall not be slain as another man ; but men shall defend, in pain of death, that no man be so hardy to make him company ne to speak with him, ne that no man give him, ne sell him, ne serve him, neither of meat ne of drink ; and so shall he die in mischief. They spare no man that hath trespassed, neither for love, ne for favour ne for riches, ne for noblesse ; but that he shall have after that he hath done.

Beyond that isle is another isle, where is great multitude of folk. And they will not, for no thing, eat flesh of hares, ne of hens, ne of geese ; and yet they bring forth enough, for to see them and to behold them only ; but they eat flesh of all other beasts, and drink milk. In that country they take their daughters and their sisters to their wives, and their other kinswomen. And if there be ten men or twelve men or more dwelling in an house, the wife of everych of them shall be common to them all that dwell in that house ; so that every man may lie with whom he will of them on one night, and with another, another night. And if she have any child, she may give it to what man that she list, that hath companied with her, so that no man knoweth there whether the child be his or another's. And if any man say to them, that they nourish other men's children, they answer that so do over men theirs.

In that country and by all Ind be great plenty of cocko-drills, that is a manner of a long serpent, as I have said before. And in the night they dwell in the water, and on the day upon the land, in rocks and in caves. And they eat no meat in all the winter, but they lie as in a dream, as do the serpents. These serpents slay men, and they eat them weeping ; and when they eat they move the over jaw, and not the nether jaw, and they have no tongue.

In that country and in many other beyond that, and also in many on this half, men put in work the seed of cotton, and they sow it every year. And then groweth it in small trees, that bear cotton. And so do men every year, so that there is plenty of cotton at all times. Item ; in this isle and in many other, there is a manner of wood, hard and strong. Whoso covereth the coals of that wood under the ashes thereof, the coals will dwell and abide all quick, a year or more. And that tree hath many leaves, as the juniper hath. And there be also many trees, that of nature they will never burn, ne rot in no manner. And there be nut trees, that bear nuts as great as a man's head.

There also be many beasts, that be clept orafles. In Arabia, they be clept gerfaunts. That is a beast, pomely or spotted, that is but a little more high than is a steed, but he hath the neck a twenty cubits long; and his croup and his tail is as of an hart; and he may look over a great high house. And there be also in that country many camles; that is a little beast as a goat, that is wild, and he liveth by the air and eateth nought, ne drinketh nought, at no time. And he changeth his colour often-time, for men see him often sithes, now in one colour and now in another colour; and he may change him into all manner colours that him list, save only into red and white. There be also in that country passing great serpents, some of six score foot long, and they be of diverse colours, as rayed, red, green, and yellow, blue and black, and all speckled. And there be others that have crests upon their heads, and they go upon their feet, upright, and they be well a four fathom great, or more, and they dwell always in rocks or in mountains, and they have alway the throat open, of whence they drop venom always. And there be also wild swine of many colours, as great as be oxen in our country, and they be all spotted, as be young fawns. And there be also urchins, as great as wild swine here; we clepe them Porcz de Spine. And there be lions all white, great and mighty. And there be also of other beasts, as great and more greater than is a destrier, and men clepe them Loerancs; and some men clepe them odenthos; and they have a black head and three long horns trenchant in the front, sharp as a sword, and the body is slender; and he is a full felonious beast, and he chaseth and slayeth the elephant. There be also many other beasts, full wicked and cruel, that be not mickle more than a bear, and they have the head like a boar, and they have six feet, and on every foot two large claws, trenchant; and the body is like a bear, and the tail as a lion. And there be also mice as great as hounds, and yellow mice as great as ravens. And there be geese, all red, three sithes more great than ours here, and they have the head, the neck and the breast all black.

And many other diverse beasts be in those countries, and elsewhere there-about, and many diverse birds also, of the which it were too long for to tell you. And therefore, I pass over at this time.

CHAPTER XXXII

Of the goodness of the folk of the Isle of Bragman. Of King Alexander. And wherefore the Emperor of Ind is clept Prester John

AND beyond that isle is another isle, great and good and plenteous, where that be good folk and true, and of good living after their belief and of good faith. And albeit that they be not christened, ne have no perfect law, yet, natheles, of kindly law they be full of all virtue, and they eschew all vices and all malices and all sins. For they be not proud, ne covetous, ne envious, ne wrathful, ne gluttons, ne lecherous. Ne they do to any man otherwise than they would that other men did to them, and in this point they fulfil the ten commandments of God, and give no charge of avoir, ne of riches. And they lie not, ne they swear not for none occasion, but they say simply, yea and nay ; for they say, he that sweareth will deceive his neighbour, and therefore, all that they do, they do it without oath.

And men clepe that isle the Isle of Bragman, and some men clepe it the Land of Faith. And through that land runneth a great river that is clept Thebe. And, in general, all the men of those isles and of all the marches thereabout be more true than in any other countries thereabout, and more rightfull than others in all things. In that isle is no thief, ne murderer, ne common woman, ne poor beggar, ne never was man slain in that country. And they be so chaste, and lead so good life, as that they were religious men, and they fast all days. And because they be so true and so rightfull, and so full of all good conditions, they were never grieved with tempests, ne with thunder, ne with light, ne with hail, ne with pestilence, ne with war, ne with hunger, ne with none other tribulation, as we be, many times, amongst us, for our sins. Wherefore, it seemeth well, that God loveth them and is pleased with their creaunce for their good deeds. They believe well in God, that made all things, and him they worship. And they prize none earthly riches; and so they be all rightfull. And they live full ordinately, and so soberly in meat and drink, that they live right long. And the most part of them die without sickness, when nature faileth them, for eld.

And it befell in King Alexander's time, that he purposed him to conquer that isle and to make them to hold of him. And when they of the country heard it, they sent messengers to him with letters, that said thus; What may be enough to that man to whom all the world is insufficient? Thou shalt find nothing in us, that may cause thee to war against us. For we have no riches, ne none we covet, and all the goods of our country be in common. Our meat, that we sustain withal our bodies, is our riches. And, instead of treasure of gold and silver, we make our treasure of accord and peace, and for to love every man other. And for to apparel with our bodies we use a silly little clout for to wrap in our carrion. Our wives ne be not arrayed for to make no man pleasance, but only convenable array for to eschew folly. When men pain them to array the body for to make it seem fairer than God made it, they do great sin. For man should not devise ne ask greater beauty, than God hath ordained man to be at his birth. The earth ministereth to us two things,—our livelihood, that cometh of the earth that we live by, and our sepulture after our death. We have been in perpetual peace till now, that thou come to disinherit us. And also we have a king, not only for to do justice to every man, for he shall find no forfeit among us; but for to keep noblesse, and for to shew that we be obeissant, we have a king. For justice ne hath not among us no place, for we do to no man otherwise than we desire that men do to us. So that righteousness ne vengeance have nought to do among us. So that nothing thou may take from us, but our good peace, that always hath dured among us.

And when King Alexander had read these letters, he thought that he should do great sin, for to trouble them. And then he sent them sureties, that they should not be afeard of him, and that they should keep their good manners and their good peace, as they had used before, of custom. And so he let them alone.

Another isle there is, that men clepe Oxidrate, and another isle, that men clepe Gynosophe, where there is also good folk, and full of good faith. And they hold, for the most part, the good conditions and customs and good manners, as men of the country abovesaid; but they go all naked.

Into that isle entered King Alexander, to see the manner. And when he saw their great faith, and their truth that was amongst them, he said that he would not grieve them, and bade them ask of him what that they would have of him, riches or anything else, and they should have it, with good will. And they answered, that he was rich enough that had meat and drink to sustain the body with, for the riches of this world, that is transitory, is not worth; but if it were in his power to make them immortal, thereof would they pray him, and thank him. And Alexander answered them that it was not in his power to do it, because he was mortal, as they were. And then they asked him why he was so proud and so fierce, and so busy for to put all the world under his subjection, right as thou were a God, and hast no term of this life, neither day ne hour, and willest to have all the world at thy commandment, that shall leave thee without fail, or thou leave it. And right as it hath been to other men before thee, right so it shall be to other after thee. And from hence

shalt thou bear nothing; but as thou were born naked,
right so all naked shall thy body be turned into earth that
thou were made of. Wherefore thou shouldest think and
impress it in thy mind, that nothing is immortal, but only
God, that made all thing. By the which answer Alexander
was greatly astonished and abashed, and all confused
departed from them.

And albeit that these folk have not the articles of our
faith as we have, natheles, for their good faith natural,
and for their good intent, I trow fully, that God loveth
them, and that God take their service to gree, right as he
did of Job, that was a paynim, and held him for his true
servant. And therefore, albeit that there be many diverse
laws in the world, yet I trow, that God loveth always them
that love him, and serve him meekly in truth, and namely
them that despise the vain glory of this world, as this folk
do and as Job did also.

And therefore said our Lord by the mouth of Hosea
the prophet, *Ponam eis multiplices leges meas*; and also in
another place, *Qui totum orbem subdit suis legibus*. And
also our Lord saith in the Gospel, *Alias oves habeo, que non
sunt ex hoc ovili*, that is to say, that he had other servants
than those that be under Christian law. And to that
accordeth the avision that Saint Peter saw at Jaffa, how the
angel came from heaven, and brought before him diverse
beasts, as serpents and other creeping beasts of the earth,
and of other also, great plenty, and bade him take and
eat. And Saint Peter answered; I eat never, quoth he,
of unclean beasts. And then said the angel, *Non dicas
immunda, que Deus mundavit*. And that was in token that
no man should have in despite none earthly man for their
diverse laws, for we know not whom God loveth, ne
whom God hateth. And for that example, when men say,
De profundis, they say it in common and in general, with
the Christian, *Pro animabus omnium defunctorum, pro quibus
sit orandum*.

And therefore say I of this folk, that be so true and so
faithful, that God loveth them. For he hath amongst
them many of the prophets, and alway hath had. And

in those isles, they prophesied the Incarnation of our
Lord Jesu Christ, how he should be born of a maiden,
three thousand year or more or our Lord was born
of the Virgin Mary. And they believe well in the
Incarnation, and that full perfectly, but they know not
the manner, how he suffered his passion and death for
us.

And beyond these isles there is another isle that is clept
Pytan. The folk of that country ne till not, ne labour
not the earth, for they eat no manner thing. And they
be of good colour and of fair shape, after their greatness.
But the small be as dwarfs, but not so little as be the
Pigmies. These men live by the smell of wild apples.
And when they go any far way, they bear the apples with
them; for if they had lost the savour of the apples, they
should die anon. They ne be not full reasonable, but they
be simple and bestial.

After that is another isle, where the folk be all skinned
rough hair, as a rough beast, save only the face and the
palm of the hand. These folk go as well under the water
of the sea, as they do above the land all dry. And they
eat both flesh and fish all raw. In this isle is a great river
that is well a two mile and an half of breadth that is clept
Beaumare.

And from that river a fifteen journeys in length, going
by the deserts of the tother side of the river—whoso might
go it, for I was not there, but it was told us of them of
the country, that within those deserts were the trees of the
sun and of the moon, that spake to King Alexander, and
warned him of his death. And men say that the folk that
keep those trees, and eat of the fruit and of the balm that
groweth there, live well four hundred year or five hundred
year, by virtue of the fruit and of the balm. For men say
that balm groweth there in great plenty and nowhere else,
save only at Babylon, as I have told you before. We
would have gone toward the trees full gladly if we had
might. But I trow that 100,000 men of arms might not
pass those deserts safely, for the great multitude of wild
beasts and of great dragons and of great serpents that

there be, that slay and devour all that come anent them.
In that country be many white elephants without number,
and of unicorns and of lions of many manners, and many
of such beasts that I have told before, and of many other
hideous beasts without number.

Many other isles there be in the land of Prester John,
and many great marvels, that were too long to tell all, both
of his riches and of his noblesse and of the great plenty
also of precious stones that he hath.   I trow that ye know
well enough, and have heard say, wherefore this emperor
is clept Prester John.   But, natheles, for them that know
not, I shall say you the cause.

It was sometime an emperor there, that was a worthy
and a full noble prince, that had Christian knights in his
company, as he hath that is now.   So it befell, that he
had great list for to see the service in the church among
Christian men.   And then dured Christendom beyond
the sea, all Turkey, Syria, Tartary, Jerusalem, Palestine,
Arabia, Aleppo and all the land of Egypt.   And so it
befell that this emperor came with a Christian knight with
him into a church in Egypt.   And it was the Saturday in
Whitsun-week.   And the bishop made orders.   And he
beheld, and listened the service full tentively.   And he
asked the Christian knight what men of degree they
should be that the prelate had before him.   And the
knight answered and said that they should be priests.
And then the emperor said that he would no longer be
clept king ne emperor, but priest, and that he would have
the name of the first priest that went out of the church,
and his name was John.   And so ever-more sithens, he is
clept Prester John.

In his land be many Christian men of good faith and of
good law, and namely of them of the same country, and
have commonly their priests, that sing the Mass, and
make the sacrament of the altar, of bread, right as the
Greeks do; but they say not so many things at the Mass
as men do here.   For they say not but only that that the
apostles said, as our Lord taught them, right as Saint
Peter and Saint Thomas and the other apostles sung the

Mass, saying the *Pater Noster* and the words of the sacrament. But we have many more additions that divers popes have made, that they ne know not of.

CHAPTER XXXIII

Of the Hills of Gold that Pismires keep. And of the four Floods that come from Paradise Terrestrial

TOWARD the east part of Prester John's land is an isle good and great, that men clepe Taprobane, that is full noble and full fructuous. And the king thereof is full rich, and is under the obeissance of Prester John. And always there they make their king by election. In that isle be two summers and two winters, and men harvest the corn twice a year. And in all the seasons of the year be the gardens flourished. There dwell good folk and reasonable, and many Christian men amongst them, that be so rich that they wit not what to do with their goods. Of old time, when men passed from the land of Prester John unto that isle, men made ordinance for to pass by ship, twenty-three days, or more; but now men pass by ship in seven days. And men may see the bottom of the sea in many places, for it is not full deep.

Beside that isle, toward the east, be two other isles. And men clepe that one Orille, and that other Argyte, of the which all the land is mine of gold and silver. And those isles be right where that the Red Sea departeth from the sea ocean. And in those isles men see there no stars so clearly as in other places. For there appear no stars, but only one clear star that men clepe Canopos. And there is not the moon seen in all the lunation, save only the second quarter.

In the isle also of this Taprobane be great hills of gold, that pismires keep full diligently. And they fine the pured gold, and cast away the un-pured. And these

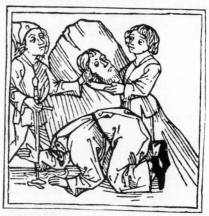

pismires be great as hounds, so that no man dare come to those hills, for the pismires would assail them and devour them anon. So that no man may get of that gold, but by great sleight. And therefore when it is great heat, the pismires rest them in the earth, from prime of the day into noon. And then the folk of the country take camels, dromedaries, and horses and other beasts, and go thither, and charge them in all haste that they may ; and after that, they flee away in all haste that the beasts may go, or the pismires come out of the earth. And in other times, when it is not so hot, and that the pismires ne rest them not in the earth, then they get gold by this subtlety. They take mares that have young colts or foals, and lay upon the mares void vessels made there-for ; and they be all open above, and hanging low to the earth. And then they send forth those mares for to pasture about those hills, and with-hold the foals with them at home. And when the pismires see those vessels, they leap in anon : and they have this kind that they let nothing be empty among them, but anon they fill it, be it what manner of thing that it be ; and so they fill those vessels with gold. And when that the folk suppose that the vessels be full, they put forth anon the young foals, and make them to neigh after their dams. And then anon the mares return towards their foals with their charges of gold. And then men discharge them, and get gold enough by this subtlety. For the pismires will suffer beasts to go and pasture amongst them, but no man in no wise.

And beyond the land and the isles and the deserts of Prester John's lordship, in going straight toward the east, men find nothing but mountains and rocks, full great. And there is the dark region, where no man may see, neither by day ne by night, as they of the country say. And that desert and that place of darkness dure from this coast unto Paradise terrestrial, where that Adam, our formest father, and Eve were put, that dwelled there but little while : and that is towards the east at the beginning of the earth. But that is not that east that we clepe our east, on this half, where the sun riseth to us. For when the sun is east in those parts towards Paradise terrestrial, it is then midnight in our parts on this half, for the roundness of the earth, of the which I have touched to you of before. For our Lord God made the earth all round in the mid place of the firmament. And there as mountains and hills be and valleys, that is not but only of Noah's flood, that wasted the soft ground and the tender, and fell down into valleys, and the hard earth and the rocks abide mountains, when the soft earth and tender waxed nesh through the water, and fell and became valleys.

Of Paradise ne can I not speak properly. For I was not there. It is far beyond. And that forthinketh me. And also I was not worthy. But as I have heard say of wise men beyond, I shall tell you with good will.

Paradise terrestrial, as wise men say, is the highest place of earth, that is in all the world. And it is so high that it toucheth nigh to the circle of the moon, there as the moon maketh her turn; for she is so high that the flood of Noah ne might not come to her, that would have covered all the earth of the world all about and above and beneath, save Paradise only alone. And this Paradise is enclosed all about with a wall, and men wit not whereof it is; for the walls be covered all over with moss, as it seemeth. And it seemeth not that the wall is stone of nature, ne of none other thing that the wall is. And that wall stretcheth from the south to the north, and it hath not but one entry that is closed with fire, burning; so that no man that is mortal ne dare not enter.

And in the most high place of Paradise, even in the middle place, is a well that casteth out the four floods that run by divers lands. Of the which, the first is clept Pison, or Ganges, that is all one; and it runneth throughout Ind or Emlak, in the which river be many precious stones, and much of lignum aloes and much gravel of gold. And that other river is clept Nilus or Gison, that goeth by Ethiopia and after by Egypt. And that other is clept Tigris, that runneth by Assyria and by Armenia the great. And that other is clept Euphrates, that runneth also by Media and Armenia and by Persia. And men there beyond say, that all the sweet waters of the world, above and beneath, take their beginning of the well of Paradise, and out of that well all waters come and go.

The first river is clept Pison, that is to say in their language, Assembly; for many other rivers meet them there, and go into that river. And some men clepe it Ganges, for a king that was in Ind, that hight Gangeres, and that it ran throughout his land. And that water [is] in some place clear, and in some place troubled, in some place hot, and in some place cold.

The second river is clept Nilus or Gison; for it is always trouble; and Gison, in the language of Ethiopia, is to say, trouble, and in the language of Egypt also.

The third river, that is clept Tigris, is as much for to say as, fast-running; for he runneth more fast than any of the tother; and also there is a beast, that is clept tigris, that is fast-running.

The fourth river is clept Euphrates, that is to say, well-bearing; for there grow many goods upon that river, as corns, fruits and other goods enough plenty.

And ye shall understand that no man that is mortal ne may not approach to that Paradise. For by land no man may go for wild beasts that be in the deserts, and for the high mountains and great huge rocks that no man may pass by, for the dark places that be there, and that many. And by the rivers may no man go. For the water runneth so rudely and so sharply, because that it cometh down so outrageously from the high places above, that it runneth in so great waves, that no ship may not row ne sail against it. And the water roareth so, and maketh so huge noise and so great tempest, that no man may hear other in the ship, though he cried with all the craft that he could in the highest voice that he might. Many great lords have assayed with great will, many times, for to pass by those rivers towards Paradise, with full great companies. But they might not speed in their voyage. And many died for weariness of rowing against those strong waves. And many of them became blind, and many deaf, for the noise of the water. And some were perished and lost within the waves. So that no mortal man may approach to that place, without special grace of God, so that of that place I can say you no more; and therefore, I shall hold me still, and return to that, that I have seen.

CHAPTER XXXIV

Of the Customs of Kings and other that dwell in the Isles coasting to Prester John's Land. And of the Worship that the Son doth to the Father when he is dead

FROM those isles that I have spoken of before, in the Land of Prester John, that be under earth as to us that be on this half, and of other isles that be more further beyond, whoso will, pursue them for to come again right to the parts that he came from, and so environ all earth. But what for the isles, what for the sea, and what for strong rowing, few folk assay for to pass that passage; albeit that men might do it well, that might be of power to dress them thereto, as I have said you before. And therefore men return from those isles abovesaid by other isles, coasting from the land of Prester John.

And then come men in returning to an isle that is clept Casson. And that isle hath well sixty journeys in length, and more than fifty in breadth. This is the best isle and the best kingdom that is in all those parts, out-taken Cathay. And if the merchants used as much that country as they do Cathay, it would be better than Cathay in a short while. This country is full well inhabited, and so full of cities and of good towns inhabited with people, that when a man goeth out of one city, men see another city even before them; and that is what part that a man go, in all that country. In that isle is great plenty of all goods for to live with, and of all manner of spices. And there be great forests of chestnuts. The king of that isle is full rich and full mighty, and, natheles, he holds his land of the great Chan, and is obeissant to him. For it is one of the twelve provinces that the great Chan hath under him, without his proper land, and without other less isles that he hath; for he hath full many.

From that kingdom come men, in returning, to another isle that is clept Rybothe, and it is also under the great Chan. That is a full good country, and full plenteous of all goods and of wines and fruit and all other riches. And the folk of that country have no houses, but they dwell and lie all under tents made of black fern, by all the country. And the principal city and the most royal is all walled with black stone and white. And all the streets also be pathed of the same stones. In that city is no man so hardy to shed blood of any man, ne of no beast, for the reverence of an idol that is worshipped there. And in that isle dwelleth the pope of their law, that they clepe Lobassy. This Lobassy giveth all the benefices, and all other dignities and all other things that belong to the idol. And all those that hold anything of their churches, religious and other, obey to him, as men do here to the Pope of Rome.

In that isle they have a custom by all the country, that when the father is dead of any man, and the son list to do great worship to his father, he sendeth to all his friends and to all his kin, and for religious men and priests, and for minstrels also, great plenty. And then men bear the dead body unto a great hill with great joy and solemnity. And when they have brought it thither, the chief prelate smiteth off the head, and layeth it upon a great platter of gold and of silver, if so [he] be a rich man. And then he taketh the head to the son. And then the son and his other kin sing and say many orisons. And then the priests and the religious men smite all the body of the dead man in pieces. And then they say certain orisons. And the fowls of ravine of all the country about know the custom of long time before, [and] come flying above in the air ; as eagles, gledes, ravens and other fowls of ravine, that eat flesh. And then the priests cast the gobbets of the flesh ;

and then the fowls, each of them, taketh that he may, and
goeth a little thence and eateth it ; and so they do whilst
any piece lasteth of the dead body.

And after that, as priests amongst us sing for the dead,
Subvenite Sancti Dei, etc., right so the priests sing with high
voice in their language ; Behold how so worthy a man and
how good a man this was, that the angels of God come for
to seek him and for to bring him into Paradise.   And then
seemeth it to the son, that he is highly worshipped, when
that many birds and fowls and ravens come and eat his
father ; and he that hath most number of fowls is most
worshipped.

And then the son bringeth home with him all his kin, and
his friends, and all the others to his house, and maketh
them a great feast.   And then all his friends make their
vaunt and their dalliance, how the fowls came thither, here
five, here six, here ten, and there twenty, and so forth ; and
they rejoice them hugely for to speak thereof.   And when
they be at meat, the son let bring forth the head of his
father, and thereof he giveth of the flesh to his most special
friends, instead of *entre messe*, or a *sukkarke*.   And of the
brain pan, he letteth make a cup, and thereof drinketh he
and his other friends also, with great devotion, in remembrance of the holy man, that the angels of God have eaten.
And that cup the son shall keep to drink of all his lifetime, in remembrance of his father.

From that land, in returning by ten journeys throughout the land of the great Chan, is another good isle
and a great kingdom, where the king is full rich and
mighty.

And amongst the rich men of his country is a passing
rich man, that is no prince, ne duke, ne earl, but he
hath more that hold of him lands and other lordships, for
he is more rich.   For he hath, every year, of annual rent
300,000 horses charged with corn of diverse grains and of
rice.   And so he leadeth a full noble life and a delicate,
after the custom of the country.   For he hath, every day,
fifty fair damosels, all maidens, that serve him evermore at
his meat, and for to lie by him o' night, and for to do

with them that is to his pleasance. And when he is at table, they bring him his meat at every time, five and five together; and in bringing their service they sing a song. And after that, they cut his meat, and put it in his mouth; for he toucheth nothing, ne handleth nought, but holdeth evermore his hands before him upon the table. For he hath so long nails, that he may take nothing, ne handle nothing. For the noblesse of that country is to have long nails, and to make them grow always to be as long as men may. And there be many in that country, that have their nails so long, that they environ all the hand. And that is a great noblesse. And the noblesse of the women is for to have small feet and little. And therefore anon as they be born, they let bind their feet so strait, that they may not grow half as nature would. And this is the nobleye of the women there to have small feet and little. And always these damosels, that I spake of before, sing all the time that this rich man eateth. And when that he eateth no more of his first course, then other five and five of fair damsels bring him his second course, always singing as they did before. And so they do continually every day to the end of his meat. And in this manner he leadeth his life. And so did they before him, that were his ancestors. And so shall they that come after him, without doing of any deeds of arms, but live evermore thus in ease, as a swine that is fed in sty for to be made fat. He hath a full fair palace and full rich, where that he dwelleth in, of the which the walls be, in circuit, two mile. And he hath within many fair gardens, and many fair halls and chambers; and the pavement of his halls and chambers be of gold and silver. And in the mid place of one of his gardens is a little mountain, where there is a little meadow. And in that meadow is a little toothill with towers and pinnacles, all of gold. And in that little toothill will he sit often-time, for to take the air and to disport him. For the place is made for nothing else, but only for his disport.

From that country men come by the land of the great Chan also, that I have spoken of before.

And ye shall understand, that of all these countries, and of all these isles, and of all the diverse folk, that I have spoken of before, and of diverse laws, and of diverse beliefs that they have, yet is there none of them all but that they have some reason within them and understanding, but if it be the fewer, and that have certain articles of our faith and some good points of our belief, and that they believe in God, that formed all things and made the world, and clepe him God of Nature ; after that the prophet saith, *Et metuent eum omnes fines terrae*, and also in another place, *Omnes gentes servient ei*, that is to say, 'All folk shall serve him.'

But yet they cannot speak perfectly (for there is no man to teach them), but only that they can devise by their natural wit. For they have no knowledge of the Son, ne of the Holy Ghost. But they can all speak of the Bible, and namely of Genesis, of the prophet's saws and of the books of Moses. And they say well, that the creatures that †they worship ne be no gods; but they worship them for the virtue that is in them, that may not be but only by the grace of God. And of simulacres and of idols, they say, that there be no folk, but that they have simulacres. And that they say, for we Christian men have images, as of our Lady and of other saints that we worship; not the images of tree or of stone, but the saints, in whose name they be made after. For right as the books and the scripture of them teach the clerks how and in what manner they shall believe, right so the images and the paintings teach the lewd folk to worship the saints and to have them in their mind, in whose names that the images be made after. They say also, that the angels of God speak to them in those idols, and that they do many great miracles. And they say sooth, that there is an angel within them. For there be two manner of angels, a good and an evil, as the Greeks say, Cacho and Calo. This Cacho is the wicked angel, and Calo is the good angel. But the tother is not the good angel, but the wicked angel that is within the idols to deceive them and for to maintain them in their error.

There be many other divers countries and many other marvels beyond, that I have not seen. Wherefore, of them I cannot speak properly to tell you the manner of them. And also in the countries where I have been, be many more diversities of many wonderful things than I make mention of; for it were too long thing to devise you the manner. And therefore, that that I have devised you of certain countries, that I have spoken of before, I beseech your worthy and excellent noblesse, that it suffice to you at this time. For if that I devised you all that is beyond the sea, another man, peradventure, that would pain him and travail his body for to go into those marches for to ensearch those countries, might be blamed by my words in rehearsing many strange things; for he might not say nothing of new, in the which the hearers might have either solace, or disport, or lust, or liking in the hearing. For men say always, that new things and new tidings be pleasant to hear. Wherefore I will hold me still, without any more rehearsing of diversities or of marvels that be beyond, to that intent and end, that whoso will go into those countries, he shall find enough to speak of, that I have not touched of in no wise.

And ye shall understand, if it like you, that at mine home-coming, I came to Rome, and shewed my life to our holy father the pope, and was assoiled of all that lay in my conscience, of many a diverse grievous point; as men must needs that be in company, dwelling amongst so many a diverse folk of diverse sect and of belief, as I have been.

And amongst all I shewed him this treatise, that I had made after information of men that knew of things that I had not seen myself, and also of marvels and customs that I had seen myself, as far as God would give me grace; and besought his holy fatherhood, that my book might be examined and corrected by advice of his wise and discreet council. And our holy father, of his special grace, remitted my book to be examined and proved by the advice of his said counsel. By the which my book was proved for true, insomuch, that they shewed me a book, that my book was examined by, that comprehended full much more, by an hundred part, by the which the *Mappa Mundi* was made after.   And so my book (albeit that many men ne list not to give credence to nothing, but to that that they see with their eye, ne be the author ne the person never so true) is affirmed and proved by our holy father, in manner and form as I have said.

And I, John Mandevile, knight, abovesaid (although I be unworthy), that departed from our countries and passed the sea, the year of grace a thousand three hundred and twenty two, that have passed many lands and many isles and countries, and searched many full strange places, and have been in many a full good honourable company, and at many a fair deed of arms (albeit that I did none myself, for mine unable insuffisance), now I am come home, maugre myself, to rest, for gouts artetykes that me distrain, that define the end of my labour ; against my will (God knoweth).

And thus, taking solace in my wretched rest, recording the time passed, I have fulfilled these things, and put them written in this book, as it would come into my mind, the year of grace a thousand three hundred and fifty six, in the thirty-fourth year, that I departed from our countries.

Wherefore, I pray to all the readers and hearers of this book, if it please them, that they would pray to God for me ; and I shall pray for them.   And all those that say for me a *Pater Noster*, with an *Ave Maria*, that God forgive me my sins, I make them partners, and grant them part of all the good pilgrimages and of all the good deeds that I have done, if any be to his pleasance ; and not only of those, but of all that ever I shall do unto my life's end.   And I beseech Almighty God, from whom all goodness and grace cometh from, that he vouchsafe of his excellent mercy and abundant grace, to fulfil their souls with inspiration of the Holy Ghost, in making defence of all their ghostly enemies here in earth, to their salvation both of body and soul ; to worship and thanking of him, that is three and one, without beginning and without ending ; that is without quality, good, without quantity, great ;

that in all places is present, and all things containing; the which that no goodness may amend, ne none evil impair; that in perfect Trinity liveth and reigneth God, by all worlds, and by all times!

Amen! Amen! Amen!

[Here Endeth the Book of
John Mandeville.]

THREE NARRATIVES ILLUSTRATIVE OF MANDEVILLE

I. THE VOYAGE OF JOHANNES DE PLANO CARPINI
II. THE JOURNAL OF FRIAR WILLIAM DE RUBRUQUIS
III. THE JOURNAL OF FRIAR ODORIC

Taken from the 1598-1600 *Edition of Richard Hakluyt's*
" Navigations, Voyages, and Discoveries "

THE VOYAGE OF
JOHANNES DE PLANO CARPINI

UNTO THE NORTHEAST PARTS OF THE WORLD IN THE YEAR OF OUR LORD, 1246

Of the first Sending of certain Friars Praedicants and Minorites unto the Tartars, taken out of the 32. Book of Vincentius Beluacensis, his Speculum Historiale: beginning at the second Chapter

ABOUT this time also, Pope Innocentius the fourth sent Friar Ascelline, being one of the order of the Praedicants, together with three other friars (of the same authority whereunto they were called) consorted with him out of divers convents of their order, with letters apostolical unto the Tartars' camp; wherein he exhorted them to give over their bloody slaughter of mankind, and to receive the Christian faith. And I, in very deed, received the relations concerning the deeds of the Tartars only (which, according to the congruence of times, I have above inserted into this my work) from a friar minorite, called Simon de Sanct Quintin, who lately returned from the same voyage. And at that very time also, there was a certain other friar minorite, namely, Friar John de Plano Carpini, sent with certain associates unto the Tartars, who likewise (as himself witnesseth) abode and conversed with them a year and three months at the least. For both he and one Friar Benedict, a Polonian, being of the same order, and a

213

partaker of all his misery and tribulation, received strait commandment from the Pope, that both of them should diligently search out all things that concerned the state of the Tartars.   And therefore this Friar John hath written a little History (which is come to our hands) of such things, as with his own eyes he saw among the Tartars, of which he heard from divers Christians worthy of credit, remaining there in captivity.   Out of which nistory I thought good by way of conclusion, to insert somewhat for the supply of those things which are wanting in the said Friar Simon.

CHAPTER III

Of the Situation and Quality of the Tartar's Land.
By Johannes de Plano Carpini

THERE is towards the east a land which is called Mongal or Tartaria, lying in that part of the world which is thought to be most north easterly.   On the east part it hath the country of Kythay and of the people called Solangi: on the south part the country of the Saracens: on the south-east the land of the Huini: and on the west the province of Naimani: but on the north side it is environed with the ocean sea.   In some part thereof it is full of mountains, and in other places plain and smooth ground, but everywhere sandy and barren, neither is the hundredth part thereof fruitful.   For it cannot bear fruit unless it be moistened with river waters, which be very rare in that country.   Whereupon they have neither villages, nor cities among them, except one which is called Cracurim, and is said to be a proper town.   We ourselves saw not this town, but were almost within half a day's journey thereof, when we remained at Syra Orda, which is the great court of their emperor.   And albeit the foresaid land is otherwise unfruitful, yet it is very commodious for

the bringing up of cattle. In certain places thereof are
some small store of trees growing, but otherwise it is
altogether destitute of woods. Therefore the emperor,
and his noble men and all other warm themselves, and
dress their meat with fires made of the dung of oxen, and
horses. The air also in that country is very intemperate.
For in the midst of summer there be great thunders and
lightnings, by the which many men are slain, and at the
same time there falleth great abundance of snow. There
be also such mighty tempests of cold winds, that sometimes men are not able to sit on horseback. Whereupon,
being near unto the Orda (for by this name they call the
habitations of their emperors and noble men), in regard of
the great wind we were constrained to lie groveling on
the earth, and could not see by reason of the dust. There
is never any rain in winter, but only in summer, albeit in
so little quantity, that sometimes it scarcely sufficeth to
allay the dust, or to moisten the roots of the grass. There
is often times great store of hail also. Insomuch that
when the emperor elect was to be placed in his imperial
throne (myself being then present) there fell such abundance of hail, that, upon the sudden melting thereof, more
than 160 persons were drowned in the same place ; there
were many tents and other things also carried away.
Likewise, in the summer season there is on the sudden
extreme heat, and suddenly again intolerable cold.

CHAPTER IV

Of their Form, Habit, and Manner of Living

THE Mongals or Tartars, in outward shape, are unlike to
all other people. For they are broader between the eyes,
and the balls of their cheeks, than men of other nations
be. They have flat and small noses, little eyes, and
eyelids standing straight upright, they are shaven on the

crowns like priests.   They wear their hair somewhat
longer about their ears, than upon their foreheads ; but
behind they let it grow long like woman's hair, whereof
they braid two locks, binding each of them behind either ear.
They have short feet also.   The garments, as well of their
men, as of their women are all of one fashion.   They use
neither cloaks, hats, nor capes.   But they wear jackets
framed after a strange manner, of buckram, scarlet, or
baldakins.   Their shoubes or gowns are hairy on the
outside, and open behind, with tails hanging down to their
hams.   They use not to wash their garments, neither will
in anywise suffer them to be washed, especially in the time
of thunder.   Their habitations be round and cunningly
made with wickers and staves in manner of a tent.   But
in the midst of the tops thereof, they have a window open
to convey the light in and the smoke out.   For their fire
is always in the midst.   Their walls be covered with felt.
Their doors are made of felt also.   Some of these
tabernacles may quickly be taken asunder, and set together
again, and are carried upon beasts' backs.   Other some
cannot be taken asunder, but are stowed upon carts.   And
whithersoever they go, be it either to war or to any
other place, they transport their tabernacles with them.
They are very rich in cattle, as in camels, oxen, sheep,
and goats.   And I think they have more horses and
mares than all the world besides.   But they have no kine
nor other beasts.   Their emperors, dukes, and other of
their nobles do abound with silk, gold, silver, and precious
stones.   Their victuals are all things that may be eaten ;
for we saw some of them eat lice.   They drink milk in
great quantity, but especially mares' milk, if they have it.
They seeth mill also in water, making it so thin, that they
may drink thereof.   Every one of them drinks off a cup-
full, or two, in a morning, and sometime they eat nought
else all the day long.   But in the evening each man hath
a little flesh given him to eat, and they drink the broth
thereof.   Howbeit in summer time, when they have mares'
milk enough, they seldom eat flesh, unless perhaps it be
given them, or they take some beast or bird in hunting.

CHAPTER V

Of their Manners both good and bad

THEIR manners are partly praiseworthy, and partly detestable; for they are more obedient unto their lords and masters, than any other either clergy or lay-people in the whole world. For they do highly reverence them, and will deceive them neither in words nor deeds. They seldom or never fall out among themselves, and, as for fightings or brawlings, wounds or manslaughters, they never happen among them. There are neither thieves nor robbers of great riches to be found, and therefore the tabernacles and carts of them that have any treasures are not strengthened with locks or bars. If any beast go astray, the finder thereof either lets it go, or driveth it to them that are put in office for the same purpose, at whose hands the owner of the said beast demandeth it, and without any difficulty receiveth it again. One of them honoureth another exceedingly, and bestoweth banquets very familiarly and liberally, notwithstanding that good victuals are dainty and scarce among them. They are also very hardy, and when they have fasted a day or two without any manner of sustenance, they sing and are merry as if they had eaten their bellies full. In riding, they endure much cold and extreme heat. There be, in a manner, no contentions among them, and although they use commonly to be drunken, yet do they not quarrel in their drunkenness. No one of them despiseth another but helpeth and furthereth him, as much as conveniently he can. Their women are chaste, neither is there so much as a word uttered concerning their dishonesty. Some of them will notwithstanding speak filthy and immodest words. But towards other people, the said Tartars be most insolent, and they scorn and set nought by all other noble and ignoble persons whatsoever. For we saw in the emperor's court the great Duke of Russia, the king's son of Georgia, and many great soldans receiving no due

honour and estimation among them. So that even the
very Tartars assigned to give attendance unto them, were
they never so base, would always go before them, and
take the upper hand of them, yea, and sometimes would
constrain them to sit behind their backs. Moreover they
are angry and of a disdainful nature unto other people, and
beyond all measure deceitful, and treacherous towards them.
They speak fair in the beginning, but in conclusion, they
sting like scorpions. For crafty they are, and full of falsehood, circumventing all men whom they are able, by their
sleights. Whatsoever mischief they intend to practise
against a man, they keep it wonderfully secret, so that he
may by no means provide for himself, nor find a remedy
against their conspiracies. They are unmannerly also and
uncleanly in taking their meat and their drink, and in other
actions. Drunkenness is honourable among them, and
when any of them hath taken more drink than his stomach
can well bear, he calleth it up and falls to drinking again.
They are most intolerable exactors, most covetous pos-
sessors, and most niggardly givers. The slaughter of other
people is accounted a matter of nothing with them.

CHAPTER VI

Of their Laws and Customs

MOREOVER, they have this law or custom, that whatsoever
man or woman be manifestly taken in adultery, they are
punished with death. A virgin likewise that hath committed fornication, they slay together with her mate.
Whosoever be taken in robbery or theft, is put to death
without all pity. Also, if any man disclose their secrets,
especially in time of war, he receiveth an hundred blows on
the back with a bastinado, laid on by a tall fellow. In
like sort when any inferiors offend in aught, they find no
favour at their superiors' hands, but are punished with

grievous stripes.   They are joined in matrimony to all in
general, yea, even to their near kinsfolks except their
mother, daughter and sister by the mother's side.   For
they use to marry their sister by the father's side only, and
also the wife of their father after his decease.   The younger
brother also, or some other of his kindred, is bound to
marry the wife of his elder brother deceased.   For, at the
time of our abode in the country, a certain duke of Russia
named Andreas, was accused before Duke Baty for conveying the Tartars' horses out of the land, and for selling
them to others; and although it could not be proved, yet
was he put to death.   His younger brother and the wife
of the party deceased hearing this, came and made their
supplication unto the forenamed duke, that the dukedom
of Russia might not be taken from them.   But he commanded the youth to marry his deceased brother's wife,
and the woman also to take him unto her husband, according to the custom of the Tartars.   She answered, that she
had rather die, than so heinously transgress the law.
Howbeit, he delivered her unto him, although they both
refused as much as they could.   Wherefore carrying them
to bed, they constrained the youth, lamenting and weeping,
to lie down and commit incest with his brother's wife.
To be short, after the death of their husbands, the Tartars'
wives use very seldom to marry the second time, unless
perhaps some man takes his brother's wife, or his step-
mother, in marriage.   They make no difference between
the son of their wife and of their concubine, but the father
gives what he pleaseth unto each one; for of late the king
of Georgia having two sons, one lawfully begotten called
Melich; but the other, David, born in adultery, at his
death left part of his land unto his base son.   Hereupon
Melich (unto whom the kingdom fell by right of his
mother, because it was governed beforetime by women)
went unto the Emperor of the Tartars, David also having
taken his journey unto him.   Now both of them coming
to the court and proffering large gifts, the son of the
harlot made suit, that he might have justice, according to
the custom of the Tartars.   Well, sentence passed against

Melich, that David, being his elder brother, should have superiority over him, and should quietly and peaceably possess the portion of land granted unto him by his father. Whensoever a Tartar hath many wives, each one of them hath her family and dwelling-place by herself. And sometime the Tartar eateth, drinketh and lieth with one, and sometime with another. One is accounted chief among the rest, with whom he is oftener conversant than with the other. And notwithstanding (as it hath been said) they are many, yet do they seldom fall out among themselves.

CHAPTER VII

Of their Superstitious Traditions

But by reason of certain traditions, which either they or their predecessors have devised, they account some things indifferent to be faults. One is to thrust a knife into the fire, or any way to touch the fire with a knife, or with their knife to take flesh out of the cauldron, or to hew with an hatchet near unto the fire. For they think by that means to take away the head or force from the fire. Another is to lean upon the whip, wherewith they beat their horses: for they ride not with spurs. Also to touch arrows with a whip, to take or kill young birds, to strike an horse with the rein of their bridle, and to break one bone against another. Also to pour out milk, meat, or any kind of drink upon the ground or to make water within their tabernacle: which whosoever doth willingly, he is slain, but otherwise he must pay a great sum of money to the enchanter to be purified. Who likewise must cause the tabernacle, with all things therein, to pass between two fires. Before it be on this wise purified no man dare once enter into it, nor convey anything thereout. Besides, if any man hath a morsel given him, which he is not able to swallow, and for that cause casteth it out of his mouth, there is an hole made under his tabernacle, by which he is drawn forth and slain without all compassion. Likewise, whosoever treads upon the threshold of any of their duke's tabernacles, he is put to death. Many other things there be, like unto these, which they take for heinous offences. But to slay men, to invade the dominions of other people, and to rifle their goods, to transgress the commandments and prohibitions of God, are with them no offences at all. They know nothing concerning eternal life, and everlasting damnation, and yet they think that after death they shall live in another world, that they shall multiply their cattle, that they shall eat and drink and do other things which living men perform here upon earth. At a new moon, or a full moon, they begin all enterprises that they take in hand, and they call the moon the Great Emperor, and worship it upon their knees. All men that abide in their tabernacles must be purified with fire : which purification is on this wise. They kindle two fires, and pitch two javelins into the ground near unto the said fires, bending a cord to the tops of the javelins. And about the cord they tie certain jags of buckram, under which cord, and between which fires, men, beasts, and tabernacles do pass. There stand two women also, one on the right side, and another on the left, casting water, and repeating certain charms. If any man be slain by lightning, all that dwell in the same tabernacle with him must pass by fire in manner aforesaid. For their tabernacles, beds, and carts, theirselves and garments, and whatsoever such things they have, are touched by no man, yea, and are abandoned by all men as things unclean. And to be short, they think that all things are to be purged by fire. Therefore, when any ambassadors, princes, or other personages whatsoever come unto them, they and their gifts must pass between two fires to be purified, lest peraventure they have practised some witchcraft, or have brought some poison or other mischief with them.

CHAPTER VIII

Of the beginning of their Empire or Government

THE east country, whereof we have entreated, which is
called Mongal, is reported to have had of old time four
forces of people. One of their companions was called
Yeka Mongal, that is, the Great Mongals. The second
company was called Sumongal, that is, the Water-Mongals,
who called themselves Tartars, of a certain river running
through their country named Tartar. The third was
called Merkat, and the fourth Metrit. All these people
had one and the same person, attire of body and language,
albeit they were divided by princes and provinces. In the
province of Yeka Mongal, there was a certain man called
Chingis. This man became a mighty hunter. For he
learned to steal men, and to take them for a prey. He
ranged into other countries taking as many captives as he
could, and joining them unto himself. Also he allured
the men of his own country unto him, who followed him
as their captain and ringleader to do mischief. Then
began he to make war upon the Sumongals or Tartars,
and slew their captain, and after many conflicts, subdued
them unto himself, and brought them all into bondage.
Afterward he used their help to fight against the Merkats,
dwelling by the Tartars, whom also he vanquished in
battle. Proceeding from thence, he fought against the
Metrites, and conquered them also. The Naimani hearing
that Chingis was thus exalted, greatly disdained thereat.
For they had a mighty and puissant emperor, unto whom
all the foresaid nations paid tribute. Whose sons, when
he was dead, succeeded him in his empire. Howbeit,
being young and foolish, they knew not how to govern
the people, but were divided, and fell at variance among
themselves. Now Chingis being exalted, as is aforesaid,
they nevertheless invaded the forenamed countries, put
the inhabitants to the sword, and carried away their goods

for a prey.   Which Chingis having intelligence of, gathered
all his subjects together.   The Naimani also and the people
called Karakitay assembled and banded themselves at a
certain strait valley, where, after a battle fought they were
vanquished by the Mongals.   And being thus vanquished,
they were, the greater part of them, slain; and others,
which could not escape, were carried into captivity.   In
the land of the foresaid Karakytayans, Occoday Cham, the
son of Chingis Cham, after he was created emperor, built
a certain city, which he called Chanyl.   Near unto which
city, on the south side, there is an huge desert, wherein
wild men are certainly reported to inhabit, which cannot
speak at all, and are destitute of joints in their legs, so
that if they fall, they cannot rise alone by themselves.
Howbeit, they are of discretion to make felts of camel's
hair, wherewith they clothe themselves, and which they
hold against the wind.   And if at any time, the Tartars
pursuing them, chance to wound them with their arrows,
they put herbs into their wounds, and fly strongly before
them.

CHAPTER IX

*Of the Mutual Victories between them, and the People of
Kythay*

BUT the Mongals returning home into their own country,
prepared themselves to battle against the Kythayans:
which their Emperor hearing, set forward against them
with his army, and they fought a cruel battle, wherein the
Mongals were overcome, and all their nobles in the army,
except seven, were slain.   And for this cause, when they,
purposing to invade any region, are threatened by the
inhabitants thereof to be slain, they do, to this day, answer:
In old time also our whole number besides being slain, we
remained but seven of us alive, and yet notwithstanding we
are now grown unto a great multitude; think not there-

fore to daunt us with such brags. But Chingis and the residue that remained alive, fled home into their country. And having breathed him a little, he prepared himself to war, and went forth against the people called Huyri. These men were Christians of the sect of Nestorius. And these also the Mongals overcame, and received letters or learning from them : for before that time they had not the art of writing, and now they call it the hand or letters of the Mongals. Immediately after, he marched against the country of Saruyur, and of the Karanites, and against the land of Hudirat ; all which he vanquished. Then returned he home into his own country, and breathed himself. Afterward, assembling his warlike troops, they marched with one accord against the Kythayans, and waging war with them a long time, they conquered a great part of their land, and shut up their emperor into his greatest city ; which city they had so long time besieged, that they began to want necessary provision for their army. And when they had no victuals to feed upon, Chingis Cham commanded his soldiers, that they should eat every tenth man of the company. But they of the city fought manfully against them, with engines, darts, and arrows, and when stones wanted they threw silver, and especially melted silver : for the same city abounded with great riches. Also, when the Mongals had fought a long time and could not prevail by war, they made a great trench underneath the ground from the army unto the midst of the city, and there issuing forth they fought against the citizens, and the remnant also without the walls fought in like manner. At last, breaking open the gates of the city, they entered, and putting the emperor, with many other to the sword, they took possession thereof and conveyed away the gold, silver, and all the riches therein. And having appointed certain deputies over the country, they returned home into their own land. This is the first time, when the Emperor of the Kythayans, being vanquished, Chingis Cham obtained the empire. But some part of the country, because it lieth within the sea, they could by no means conquer unto this day. The men of

Kytay are pagans, having a special kind of writing by themselves, and (as it is reported) the Scriptures of the Old and New Testament.   They have also recorded in histories the lives of their forefathers: and they have hermits, and certain houses made after the manner of our churches, which in those days they greatly resorted unto. They say that they have divers saints also, and they worship one God.   They adore and reverence Christ Jesus our Lord, and believe the article of eternal life, but are not baptized.   They do also honourably esteem and reverence our Scriptures.   They love Christians, and bestow much alms, and are a very courteous and gentle people.   They have no beards, and they agree partly with the Mongals in the disposition of their countenance.   In all occupations which men practise, there are not better artificers in the whole world.   Their country is exceeding rich, in corn, wine, gold, silk, and other commodities.

CHAPTER X

Of their War against India Major and Minor

AND when the Mongals with their Emperor Chingis Cham had awhile rested themselves after the foresaid victory, they divided their armies.   For the emperor sent one of his sons, named Thossut (whom also they called Can, that is to say emperor), with an army against the people of Comania, whom he vanquished with much war, and afterward returned into his own country.   But he sent his other son with an army against the Indians, who also subdued India Minor.   These Indians are the black Saracens, which are also called Aethiopians.   But here the army marched forward to fight against Christians dwelling in India Major. Which the king of the country hearing (who is commonly called Presbiter John) gathered his soldiers together, and came forth against them.   And making men's images of copper, he set each of them upon a saddle on horseback, and put fire within them, and placed a man with a pair of bellows on the horseback behind every image. And so with many horses and images in such sort furnished, they marched on to fight against the Mongals or Tartars. And coming near unto the place of the battle, they first of all sent those horses in order one after another. But the men that sat behind laid I wot not what upon the fire within the images, and blew strongly with their bellows. Whereupon it came to pass, that the men and the horses were burnt with wild fire, and the air was darkened with smoke. Then the Indians cast darts upon the Tartars, of whom many were wounded and slain. And so they expelled them out of their dominions with great confusion, neither did we hear, that ever they returned thither again.

CHAPTER XI

How being repelled by Monstrous Men shapen like Dogs, they overcame the People of Burithabeth

BUT returning through the deserts, they came into a certain country, wherein (as it was reported unto us in the emperor's court, by certain clergymen of Russia, and others, who were long time among them, and that by strong and steadfast affirmation) they found certain monsters resembling women: who being asked by many interpreters, where the men of that land were, they answered, that whatsoever women were borne there, were indued with the shape of mankind, but the males were like unto dogs. And delaying the time, in that country they met with the said dogs on the other side of the river. And in the midst of sharp winter, they cast themselves into the water: afterward they wallowed in the dust upon the main land, and so the dust being mingled with water, was frozen to their backs, and having often times so done,

the ice being strongly frozen upon them, with great fury
they came to fight against the Tartars.   And when the
Tartars threw their darts, or shot their arrows among them,
they rebounded back again, as if they had lighted upon
stones.   And the rest of their weapons could by no means
hurt them.   Howbeit, the dogs made an assault upon the
Tartars, and wounding some of them with their teeth, and
flaying others, at length they drove them out of their
countries.   And thereupon they have a proverb of the same
matter, as yet rife among them, which they speak in jesting
sort one to another : my father or my brother was slain of
dogs.   The women which they took, they brought into
their own country, who remained there till their dying
day.   And in travelling homewards, the said army of the
Mongals came unto the land of Burithabeth (the inhabitants
whereof are pagans) and conquered the people in battle.
These people have a strange or rather a miserable kind of
custom.   For when anyman's father deceaseth, he assembleth
all his kindred, and they eat him.   These men have no
beards at all, for we saw them carry a certain iron instrument in their hands, wherewith, if any hairs grow upon
their chin, they presently pluck them out.   They are also
very deformed.   From thence the Tartars army returned
to their own home.

CHAPTER XII

*How they had the Repulse at the Caspian Mountains, and
were driven back by Men dwelling in Caves*

MOREOVER, Chingis Cham, at the same time when he sent
other armies against the east, he himself marched with a
power into the land of Kergis, which notwithstanding, he
conquered not in that expedition, and as it was reported
unto us, he went on forward even to the Caspian mountains.   But the mountains on that part where they en-
camped themselves, were of adamant, and therefore they

drew unto them their arrows, and weapons of iron. And certain men contained within those Caspian mountains, hearing, as it was thought, the noise of the army, made a breach through, so that when the Tartars returned unto the same place ten years after, they found the mountain broken. And attempting to go unto them, they could not : for there stood a cloud before them, beyond which they were not able to pass, being deprived of their sight so soon as they approached thereunto. But they on the contrary side thinking that the Tartars durst not come nigh them, gave the assault, and when they came at the cloud, they could not proceed for the cause aforesaid. Also the Tartars, before they came unto the said mountains, passed for the space of a month and more through a vast wilderness, and departing thence towards the east, they were above a month travelling through another huge desert. At length, they came unto a land wherein they saw beaten ways, but could not find any people. Howbeit, at the last, diligently seeking, they found a man and his wife, whom they presented before Chingis Cham : and demanding of them where the people of that country were they answered, that the people inhabited under the ground in mountains. Then Chingis Cham keeping still the woman, sent her husband unto them, giving them charge to come at his command. And going unto them, he declared all things that Chingis Cham had commanded them. But they answered, that they would upon such a day visit him, to satisfy his desire. And in the mean season, by blind and hidden passages under the earth, assembling themselves, they came against the Tartars in warlike manner, and suddenly issuing forth, they slew a great number of them. This people were not able to endure the terrible noise, which in that place the sun made at his uprising : for at the time of the sunrising, they were enforced to lay one ear upon the ground, and to stop the other close, lest they should hear that dreadful sound. Neither could they so escape, for by this means many of them were destroyed. Chingis Cham, therefore, and his company, seeing that they prevailed not, but continually lost some of their

number, fled and departed out of that land.   But the man
and his wife aforesaid they carried along with them, who
all their lifetime continued in the Tartars' country.   Being
demanded why the men of their country do inhabit under
the ground, they said, that at a certain time of the year, when
the sun riseth, there is such an huge noise, that the people
cannot endure it.   Moreover, they use to play upon
cymbals, drums, and other musical instruments, to the
end they may not hear that sound.

CHAPTER XIII

Of the Statutes of Chingis Cham, of his Death, of his Sons, and of his Dukes

But as Chingis Cham returned out of that country, his
people wanted victuals, and suffered extreme famine.
Then by chance they found the fresh entrails of a beast:
which they took, and casting away the dung thereof,
caused it to be sodden, brought it before Chingis Cham,
and did eat thereof.   And hereupon Chingis Cham en-
acted : that neither the blood, nor the entrails, nor any
other part of a beast which might be eaten, should be
cast away, save only the dung.   Wherefore he returned
thence into his own land, and there he ordained laws and
statutes, which the Tartars do most strictly and inviolably
observe, of the which we have before spoken.   He was
afterward slain by a thunderclap.   He had four sons : the
first was called Occoday, the second Thossut Can, the
third Thiaday : the name of the fourth is unknown.
From these four descended all the dukes of the Mongals.
The first son of Occoday is Cuyne, who is now emperor,
his brothers be Cocten and Chyrinen.   The sons of
Thossut Can are Bathy, Ordu, Siba, and Bora.   Bathy
next unto the emperor, is richer and mightier than all the
rest.   But Ordu is the seignior of all the dukes.   The sons

of Thiaday be Hurin and Cadan.   The sons of Chingis
Cham his other son, whose name is unknown, are Mengu,
Bithat, and certain others.   The mother of Mengu was
named Seroctan, and of all others most honoured among
the Tartars, except the emperor's mother, and mightier
than any subject except Bathy.   These be the names of
the dukes : Ordu, who was in Poland, and in Hungary ;
Bathy also and Hurin and Cadan, and Siban, and Ouygat,
all which were in Hungary.   In like manner Cyrpodan,
who is as yet beyond the sea, making war against certain
soldans of the Saracens, and other inhabitants of far
countries.   Others remained in the land, as namely
Mengu, Chyrinen, Hubilai, Sinocur, Cara, Gay, Sybedey,
Bora, Berca, Corrensa.   There be many other of their
dukes, whose names are unknown unto us.

CHAPTER XIV

Of the Authority of the Emperor, and of his Dukes

MOREOVER, the Emperor of the Tartars hath a wonderful
dominion over all his subjects, for no man dare abide in
any place, unless he hath assigned him to be there.   Also
he himself appointeth to his dukes where they should inhabit.   Likewise the dukes assign places unto every
millenary, or conductor of a thousand soldiers, the millenaries unto each captain of an hundred, the captains unto
every corporal of ten.   Whatsoever is given them in
charge, whensoever, or wheresoever, be it to fight or to
lose their lives, or howsoever it be, they obey without any
gainsaying.   For if he demandeth any man's daughter, or
sister, being a virgin, they presently deliver her unto him
without all contradiction ; yea, often times he makes a
collection of virgins throughout all the Tartars dominions,
and those whom he means to keep, he retaineth unto himself, others he bestoweth unto his men.   Also, whatsoever

messenger he sendeth, or whithersoever, his subjects must
without delay find them horses and other necessaries.   In
like sort, from what country soever tribute-payers, or
ambassadors come unto him, they must have horses,
carriages, and expenses allowed them.   Notwithstanding,
ambassadors coming from other places do suffer great
misery, and are in much want both of victuals, and of
apparel : especially when they come to any of the dukes,
and there they are constrained to make some lingering
abode.   Then ten men are allowed so little sustenance,
that scarcely two could live thereon.   Likewise, if any
injuries be offered them, they cannot without danger make
complaint.   Many gifts also are demanded of them, both
by dukes and others, which if they do not bestow, they are
basely esteemed, and set at nought.   And hereupon, we
were of necessity enforced to bestow in gifts a great part
of those things which were given us by well disposed people,
to defray our charges.   To be short, all things are so in the
power and possession of the emperor, that no man dare
say, This is mine, or this is my neighbour's ; but all, both
goods, cattle and men are his own.   Concerning this matter
also he published a statute of late.   The very same authority
and jurisdiction, do the dukes in like sort exercise upon
their subjects.

CHAPTER XV

*Of the Election of Emperor Occoday, and of the Expedition of
Duke Bathy*

AFTER the death of Chingis Cham aforesaid, the dukes
assembled themselves and chose Occoday his son to be
their emperor.   And he, entering into consultation with
his nobles, divided his armies, and sent Duke Bathy his
nephew against the country of Altisoldan, and against the
people called Bisermini, who were Saracens, but spake the
language of Comania.   The Tartars invading their country,

fought with them and subdued them in battle. But a certain city called Barchin resisted them a long time. For the citizens had cast up many ditches and trenches about their city, in regard whereof the Tartars could not take it, till they had filled the said ditches. But the citizens of Sarguit hearing this, came forth to meet them, yielding themselves unto them of their own accord. Whereupon their city was not destroyed, but they slew many of them and others they carried away captive, and taking spoils, they filled the city with other inhabitants, and so marched forth against the city of Orna. This town was very populous and exceeding rich. For there were many Christians therein, as namely Gasarians, Russians, and Alanians, with others, and Saracens also. The government of the city was in the Saracens' hand. It standeth upon a mighty river, and is a kind of port town having a great mart exercised therein. And when the Tartars could not otherwise overcome it, they turned the said river, running through the city, out of his channel, and so drowned the city with the inhabitants and their goods. Which being done, they set forward against Russia, and made foul havoc there, destroying cities and cattles and murdering the people. They laid siege a long while unto Kiow, the chief city of Russia, and at length they took it and slew the citizens. Whereupon, travelling through that country, we found an innumerable multitude of dead men's skulls and bones lying upon the earth. For it was a very large and populous city, but it is now in a manner brought to nothing: for there do scarce remain 200 houses, the inhabitants whereof are kept in extreme bondage. Moreover, out of Russia and Comania, they proceeded forward against the Hungarians, and the Polonians, and there many of them were slain, as is aforesaid; and had the Hungarians manfully withstood them, the Tartars had been confounded and driven back. Returning from thence, they invaded the country of the Morduans, being pagans, and conquered them in battle. Then they marched against the people called Byleri, or Bulgaria magna, and utterly wasted the country. From thence they proceeded towards the north against the people called Bastarci, or Hungaria magna, and conquered them also.   And so going on further north, they came into the Parossitae, who having little stomachs and small mouths, eat not anything at all, but seeing flesh they stand or sit over the pot, and receiving the steam or smoke thereof, are therewith only nourished, and if they eat anything it is very little.   From thence they came to the Samogetae, who live only upon hunting, and use to dwell in tabernacles only, and to wear garments made of beasts' skins.   From thence they proceeded unto a country lying upon the ocean sea, where they found certain monsters, who in all things resembled the shape of men, saving that their feet were like the feet of an ox, and they had indeed men's heads but dogs' faces.   They spake, as it were, two words like men, but at the third they barked like dogs.   From hence they retired into Comania, and there some of them remain unto this day.

CHAPTER XVI

Of the Expedition of Duke Cyrpodan

At the same time Occoday Can sent Duke Cyrpodan with an army against Kergis, who also subdued them in battle. These men are pagans, having no beards at all.   They have a custom when any of their fathers die, for grief and in token of lamentation, to draw as it were, a leather thong overthwart their faces, from one ear to the other.   This nation being conquered, Duke Cyrpodan marched with his forces southward against the Armenians.   And travelling through certain desert places, they found monsters in the shape of men, which had each of them but one arm and one hand growing out of the midst of their breast, and but one foot.   Two of them used to shoot in one bow, and they ran so swiftly, that horses could not overtake them.   They ran also upon that one foot by hopping and leaping, and being weary of such walking they went upon their hand and their foot, turning themselves round, as it were in a circle. And being weary of so doing, they ran again according to their wonted manner. Isidore calleth them cyclopedes. And as it was told us in court, by the clergymen of Russia, who remain with the foresaid emperor, many ambassadors were sent from them unto the emperor's court, to obtain peace. From thence they proceeded forth into Armenia, which they conquered in battle, and part also of Georgia. And the other part is under their jurisdiction, paying as yet every year unto them for tribute, 20,000 pieces of coin called Yperpera. From thence they marched into the dominions of the puissant and mighty Soldan called Deurum, whom also they vanquished in fight. And to be short, they went on farther sacking and conquering, even unto the Soldan of Aleppo his dominions, and now they have subdued that land also, determining to invade other countries beyond it : neither returned they afterward into their own land unto this day. Likewise the same army marched forward against the Caliph of Baldach his country, which they subdued also, and exacted at his hands the daily tribute of 400 byzantines,[1] besides baldakines and other gifts. Also every year they send messengers unto the caliph moving him to come unto them. Who sending back great gifts together with his tribute beseecheth them to be favourable unto him. Howbeit the Tartarian Emperor receiveth all his gifts, and yet nevertheless sends for him, to have him come.

CHAPTER XVII

How the Tartars behave themselves in War

CHINGIS CHAM divided his Tartars by captains of ten, captains of an hundred, and captains of a thousand, and over

[1] *i.e.* Bezants.

ten millenaries or captains of a thousand, he placed as it
were, one colonel, and yet notwithstanding over one whole
army he authorized two or three dukes, but yet so that all
should have especial regard unto one of the said dukes.
And when they join battle against any other nation, unless
they do all with one consent give back, every man that
flies is put to death.   And if one or two, or more of ten
proceed manfully to the battle, but the residue of those ten
draw back and follow not the company, they are in like
manner slain.   Also, if one among ten or more be taken,
their fellows, if they rescue them not, are punished with
death.   Moreover they are enjoined to have these weapons
following.   Two long bows or one good one at the least,
three quivers full of arrows, and one axe, and ropes to draw
engines withal.   But the richer sort have single-edged
swords, with sharp points, and somewhat crooked.   They
have also armed horses, with their shoulders and breasts
defenced; they have helmets and brigandines.   Some of
them have jackets, and caparisons for their horses made
of leather artificially doubled or trebled upon their bodies.
The upper part of their helmet is of iron or steel, but that
part which compasseth about the neck and the throat is of
leather.   Howbeit some of them have all their foresaid
furniture of iron framed in manner following.   They beat
out many thin plates a finger broad, and a handful long,
and making in every one of them eight little holes, they
put thereunto three strong and straight leather thongs.
So they join the plates one to another, as it were, ascending by degrees.   Then they tie the plates unto the said
thongs, with other small and slender thongs, drawn through
the holes aforesaid, and in the upper part, on each side
thereof, they fasten one small doubled thong unto another,
that the plates may firmly be knit together.   These they
make, as well for their horses' caparisons, as for the armour
of their men: and they scour them so bright that a man
may behold his face in them.   Some of them upon the
neck of their lance have an hook, wherewithal they attempt
to pull men out of their saddles.   The heads of their
arrows are exceedingly sharp, cutting both ways like a

two-edged sword, and they always carry a file in their quivers to whet their arrowheads. They have targets made of wickers, or of small rods. Howbeit they do not (as we suppose) accustom to carry them, but only about the tents, or in the emperor's or duke's guards, and that only in the night season. They are most politic in wars, having been exercised therein with other nations for the space of these forty-two years. When they come at any rivers, the chief men of the company have a round and light piece of leather, about the borders whereof making many loops, they put a rope into them to draw it together like a purse, and so bring it into the round form of a ball, which leather they fill with their garments and other necessaries, trussing it up most strongly. But upon the midst of the upper part thereof, they lay their saddles and other hard things ; there also do the men themselves sit. This their boat they tie unto an horse tail, causing a man to swim before, and to guide over the horse, or sometime they have two oars to row themselves over. The first horse, therefore, being driven into the water, all the others' horses of the company follow him, and so they pass through the river. But the poorer sort of common soldiers have every man his leather bag or satchel well sewn together, wherein he packs up all his trinkets, and strongly trussing it up hangs it at his horse's tail, and so passeth over, in manner aforesaid.

CHAPTER XVIII

How they may be Resisted

I DEEM not any one kingdom or province able to resist them : because they use to take up soldiers out of every country of their dominions. And if so be the neighbour province which they invade, will not aid them, utterly wasting it, with the inhabitants thereof, whom they take from thence with them, they proceed on to fight against another country.   And placing their captives in the forefront of the battle, if they fight not courageously they put them to the sword.   Wherefore, if Christians would withstand them, it is expedient, that the provinces and governors of countries should agree in one, and so by common counsel, should give them resistance.   Their soldiers also must be furnished with strong hand-bows and cross-bows, which they greatly dread, and with sufficient arrows, with maces also of good iron, or an axe with a long handle or staff.   When they make their arrowheads, they must (according to the Tartars' custom) dip them red-hot into water mingled with salt, that they may be strong to pierce the enemies' armour.   They that will may have swords also and lances with hooks at the ends, to pull them from their saddles, out of which they are easily removed. They must have helmets likewise and other armour to defend themselves and their horses from the Tartars' weapons and arrows, and they that are unarmed, must (according to the Tartars' custom) march behind their fellows, and discharge at the enemy with long-bows and cross-bows.   And (as it is above said of the Tartars) they must orderly dispose their bands and troops, and ordain laws for their soldiers.   Whosoever runneth to the prey or spoil, before the victory be achieved, must undergo a most severe punishment.   For such a fellow is put to death among the Tartars without all pity or mercy.   The place of battle must be chosen, if it be possible, in a plain field, where they may see round about ; neither must all be in one company, but in many and several bands, not very far distant one from another. They which give the first encounter must send one band before, and must have another in a readiness to relieve and second the former in time convenient. They must have spies, also, on every side, to give them notice when the rest of the enemy's bands approach. For therefore ought they always to send forth band against band and troop against troop, because the Tartar ever practiseth to get his enemy in the midst and so to environ him. Let our bands take this caveat also, if the enemy retire, not to make any long pursuit after him, lest peradventure (according to his custom) he might draw them into some secret ambush : for the Tartar fights more by policy than by main force.   And again, lest our horses be tired : for we are not so well stored with horses as they.   Those horses which the Tartars use one day, they ride not upon three or four days after.   Moreover, if the Tartars draw homeward, our men must not therefore depart and cashier their bands, or separate themselves asunder : because they do this upon policy, namely to have our army divided, that they may more securely invade and waste the country.   And in very deed, our captains ought both day and night to keep their army in a readiness : and not to lie out of their armour, but at all assays, to be provided for battle.   For the Tartars like devils are always watching and devising how to practise mischief.   Furthermore, if in battle any of the Tartars be cast off their horsebacks, they must presently be laid hold on and taken, for being on foot they shoot strongly, wounding and killing both horses and men.

CHAPTER XIX

*Of the Journey of Friar John unto the First Guard of the
Tartars*

WE therefore by the commandment of the See Apostolic setting forth towards the nations of the East, chose first to travel unto the Tartars, because we feared that there might be great danger imminent upon the Church of God next unto them, by their invasions.   Proceeding on therefore, we came to the King of Bohemia, who being of our familiar acquaintance, advised us to take our journey through Polonia and Russia.   For we had kinsfolks in Polonia, by whose assistance, we might enter Russia. Having given us his letters, he caused our charges also to

be defrayed, in all his chief houses and cities, till we came
unto his nephew Boleslaus, Duke of Slesia, who also was
familiar and well known unto us.   The like favour he
shewed us also, till we came unto Conradus, Duke of
Lautiscia, unto whom then (by God's especial favour
towards us) Lord Wasilico, Duke of Russia, was come,
from whose mouth we heard more at large concerning the
deeds of the Tartars : for he had sent ambassadors thither,
who were returned back unto him.   Wherefore, it being
given us to understand, that we must bestow gifts upon
them, we caused certain skins of beavers and other beasts
to be bought with part of that money, which was given
upon alms to succour us by the way.   Which thing Duke
Conradus and the dukes of Cracow, and a bishop, and
certain soldiers being advertised of, gave us likewise more
of the same skins.   And to be short, Duke Wasilico being
earnestly requested by the Duke of Cracow, and by the
bishop and barons, on our behalf, conducted us with him,
unto his own land, and there for certain days, entertained
us at his own charges, to the end that we might refresh
ourselves awhile.   And when, being requested by us, he
had caused his bishops to consort unto him, we read before
them the Pope's letters, admonishing them to return unto
the unity of the church.   To the same purpose also, we
ourselves admonished them, and to our ability, induced as
well the duke as the bishops and others thereunto.   Howbeit, because Duke Daniel the brother of Wasilico
aforesaid (having as then taken his journey unto Baty)
was absent, they could not at that time make a final
answer.   After these things Duke Wasilico sent us forward
with one of his servants as far as Kiow, the chief city of
Russia.   Howbeit we were always in danger of our lives
by reason of the Lituanians, who did often invade the
borders of Russia, even in those very places by which we
were to pass.   But in regard of the foresaid servant,
we were out of the Russians' danger, the greatest part of
whom were either slain, or carried into captivity by the
Tartars.   Moreover, at Danilon we were feeble even unto
the death.   (Notwithstanding we caused ourselves to be

carried in a waggon through the snow and extreme cold.)
And being come unto Kiow, we consulted with the
millenary, and other noble men there concerning our
journey. They told us, that if we carried those horses,
which we then had, unto the Tartars, great store of snow
lying upon the ground, they would all die : because they
knew now how to dig up the grass under the snow, as the
Tartarian horses do, neither could there be aught found
for them to eat, the Tartars having neither hay nor straw,
nor any other fodder. We determined therefore to leave
them behind at Kiow with two servants appointed to keep
them. And we were constrained to bestow gifts upon the
millenary, that we might obtain his favour to allow us post
horses and a guide. Wherefore beginning our journey the
second day after the feast of the purification, we arrived at
the town of Canow, which was immediately under the
dominion of the Tartars. The governor whereof allowed
us horses and a guide unto another town, wherein we
found one Michaeas to be governor, a man full of malice
and despite, who notwithstanding, having received gifts
at our hands, according to his manner conducted us to the
first guard of the Tartars.

CHAPTER XX

*How he and his Company were at the first received of
the Tartars*

WHEREFORE the first Saturday next after Ashwednesday,
having about the sun's going down taken up our place of
rest, the armed Tartars came rushing upon us in uncivil
and horrible manner, being very inquisitive of us what
manner of persons, or of what condition we were : and
when we had answered them that we were the Pope's
Legates, receiving some victuals at our hands, they immediately departed. Moreover in the morning rising and

proceeding on our journey, the chief of them which were in the guard met with us, demanding why, or for what intent and purpose we came thither ; and what business we had with them : unto whom we answered, We are the legates of our lord the Pope, who is the father and lord of the Christians. He hath sent us as well unto your emperor, as to your princes, and all other Tartars for this purpose, because it is his pleasure, that all Christians should be in league with the Tartars, and should have peace with them. It is his desire also that they should become great or in favour with God in heaven, therefore he admonisheth them as well by us, as by his own letters, to become Christians, and to embrace the faith of our Lord Jesus Christ, because they could not otherwise be saved. Moreover, he gives them to understand that he much marvelleth at their monstrous slaughters and massacres of mankind, and especially of Christians, but most of all of Hungarians, mountaineers, and Polonians, being all his subjects, having not injured them in aught, nor attempted to do them injury. And because the Lord God is grievously offended thereat, he adviseth them from henceforth to beware of such dealing, and to repent them of that which they had done. He requesteth also, that they would write an answer unto him, what they purpose to do hereafter, and what their intention is. All which things being heard and understood, the Tartars said that they would appoint us post horses and a guide unto Corrensa. And immediately demanding gifts at our hands they obtained them. Then receiving the same horses, from which they dismounted, together with a guide we took our journey into Corrensa. But they riding a swift pace, sent a messenger before unto the said Duke Corrensa, to signify the message which we had delivered unto them. This duke is governor of all them which lie in guard against the nations of the west, lest some enemy might on the sudden and at unawares break in upon them. And he is said to have 60,000 men under him.

CHAPTER XXI

How they were received at the Court of Corrensa

BEING come therefore unto his court, he caused our tent to be placed far from him, and sent his agents to demand of us with what we would incline upon him, that is to say, what gifts we would offer, in doing our obeisance unto him. Unto whom we answered, that our lord the Pope had not sent any gifts at all, because he was not certain that we should ever be able to come at them: for we passed through most dangerous places. Notwithstanding, to our ability, we will honour him with some part of those things, which have been, by the goodness of God, and the favour of the Pope, bestowed upon us for our sustenance. Having received our gifts, they conducted us unto the orda or tent of the duke, and we were instructed to bow thrice with our left knee before the door of the tent, and in any case to beware, lest we set our foot upon the threshold of the said door. And that after we were entered, we should rehearse before the duke and all his nobles, the same words, which we had before said, kneeling upon our knees. Then presented we the letters of our lord the Pope: but our interpreter whom we had hired and brought with us from Kiow was not sufficiently able to interpret them, neither was there any other esteemed to be meet for the same purpose. Here certain post horses and three Tartars were appointed for us to conduct us from hence with all speed unto Duke Bathy. This Bathy is the mightiest prince among them except the emperor, and they are bound to obey him before all other princes. We began our journey towards his court the first Tuesday in Lent, and riding as fast as our horses could trot (for we had fresh horses almost thrice or four times a day) we posted from morning till night, yea very often in the night season also, and yet could we not come at him before Maundy Thursday. All this journey we went through the land of Comania, which is all plain ground, and hath four mighty rivers running through it : the first is called Neper, on the side whereof towards Russia, Duke Corrensa and Montij marched up and down, which Montij on the other side upon the plains is greater than he. The second is called Don, upon the bank whereof marcheth a certain prince having in marriage the sister of Bathy, his name is Tirbon. The third is called Volga, which is an exceeding great river, upon the banks whereof Duke Bathy marcheth. The fourth is called Iace, upon which two millenaries do march, on each side of the river one. All these, in the winter time, descend down to the sea, and in summer ascend back by the banks of the said rivers up to the mountains. The sea last named is the Great Sea, out of which the arm of S. George proceedeth, which runneth by Constantinople. These rivers do abound with plenty of fishes, but especially Volga, and they exonerate themselves into the Grecian Sea, which is called Mare Major. Over Neper we went many days upon the ice. Along the shore also of the Grecian Sea we went very dangerously upon the ice in sundry places, and that for many days together. For about the shore the waters are frozen three leagues into the sea. But before we came unto Bathy, two of our Tartars rode afore, to give him intelligence of all the sayings which we had uttered in the presence of Corrensa.

CHAPTER XXII

How we were received at the Court of the great Prince Bathy

MOREOVER, when we came unto Bathy in the land of Comania, we were seated a good league distant from his tabernacles. And when we should be conducted unto his court, it was told us that we must pass between two fires. But we would by no means be induced thereunto. Howbeit, they said unto us; you may pass through without all danger: for we would have you to do it for none other cause, but only that if you intend any mischief against our lord, or bring any poison with you, fire may take away all evil. Unto whom we answered, that to the end we might clear ourselves from all suspicion of any such matter, we were contented to pass through. When therefore we were come unto the orda, being demanded by his agent Eldegay with what present or gift we would do our obeisance: we gave the same answer which we did at the court of Corrensa. The gifts being given and received, the causes of our journey also being heard, they brought us into the tabernacle of the prince, first bowing ourselves at the door, and being admonished, as before, not to tread upon the threshold. And being entered, we spake unto him kneeling upon our knees, and delivered him our letters, and requested him to have interpreters to translate them. Who accordingly on Good Friday were sent unto us, and we together with them, diligently translated our said letters into the Russian, Tartarian, and Saracen languages. This interpretation was presented unto Bathy, which he read, and attentively noted. At length we were conducted home again unto our own lodging, howbeit no victuals were given unto us, except it were once a little millet in a dish, the first night of our coming. This Bathy carries himself very stately and magnificently, having porters and all officers after the manner of the emperor, and sits in a lofty seat or throne together with one of his wives. The rest, namely, as well his brethren and sons, as other great personages, sit underneath him in the midst upon a bench, and others sit down upon the ground, behind him, but the men on the right hand and the women on the left. He hath very fair and large tents of linen cloth also, which were once the king's of Hungaria. Neither dare any man come into his tent (besides them of his own family) unless he be called, be he never so mighty and great, except perhaps it be known that it is his pleasure. We also, for the same cause, sat on the left hand; for so do all ambassadors in going: but in returning from the emperor, we were always placed on the right hand. In the midst stands his table, near unto the door of the tent, upon the which there is drink filled in golden and silver vessels. Neither doth Bathy at any time drink, nor any other of the Tartarian princes, especially being in a public place, but they have singing and minstrelsy before them. And always, when he rides, there is a canopy or small tent carried over his head upon the point of a javelin. And so do all the great princes of the Tartars, and their wives also. The said Bathy is courteous enough unto his own men, and yet is he had in great awe by them. He is most cruel in fight: he is exceedingly prudent and politic in war, because he hath now continued a long time in martial affairs.

CHAPTER XXIII

How departing from Bathy, they passed through the Land of Comania and of the Kangittae

MOREOVER, upon Easter eve we were called unto the tent, and there came forth to meet us the foresaid agent of Bathy, saying on his master's behalf, that we should go into their land, unto the Emperor Cuyne, detaining certain of our company with this pretence, that they would send them back unto the pope, to whom we gave letters of all our affairs to deliver unto him. But being come as far as Duke Montij aforesaid, there they were kept until our return. Upon Easter day, having said our prayers, and taken a slender breakfast, in the company of two Tartars which were assigned unto us by Corensa, we departed with many tears, not knowing whether we went to death or to life. And we were so feeble in body, that we were scarce able to ride. For all that Lent through, our meat was millet only with a little water and salt. And so likewise upon other fasting days. Neither had we aught to drink, but snow melted in a skillet. And passing through Comania we rode most earnestly, having change of horses five times or oftener in a day, except when we went through deserts, for then we were allowed better and stronger horses, which could undergo the whole labour. And thus far had we travelled from the beginning of Lent until eight days after Easter. The land of Comania on the north side immediately after Russia hath the people called Morduyni Byleri, that is Bulgaria magna, the Bastarci, that is, Hungaria magna, next unto the Bastarci, the Parositae and the Samogetae. Next unto the Samogetae are those people which are said to have dogs' faces, inhabiting upon the desert shores of the occan. On the south side it hath the Alani, the Circassi, the Gazari, Greece and Constantinople ; also the land of Iberia, the Cathes, the Brutaches who are said to be Jews shaving their heads all over, the lands also of Scythia, of Georgia, of Armenia, of Turkey. On the west side it hath Hungaria and Russia. Also Comania is a most large and long country. The inhabitants whereof called Comani the Tartars slew, some notwithstanding fled from them, and the rest were subdued under their bondage. The most of them that fled are returned again. Afterward we entered the land of the Kangittae, which in many places hath great scarcity of waters, wherein there are but few inhabitants by reason of the foresaid defect of water. For this cause divers of the servants of Jeroslaus, Duke of Russia, as they were travelling towards him into the land of Tartaria, died for thirst in that desert. As before in Comania, so likewise in this country, we found many skulls and bones of dead men lying upon the earth like a dunghill. Through this country we were travelling from the eight day after Easter until Ascension day. The inhabitants thereof were pagans, and neither they nor the Comanians used to till the ground, but lived only upon cattle, neither built they any houses but dwelt in tents. These men also have the Tartars rooted out, and do possess and inhabit their country, howbeit, those that remained are reduced into their bondage.

CHAPTER XXIV

How they came unto the first Court of the new Emperor

MOREOVER, out of the land of the Kangittae, we entered into the country of the Bisermini, who speak the language of Comania, but observe the law of the Saracens.   In this country we found innumerable cities with castles ruined, and many towns left desolate.   The lord of this country was called Soldan Alti, who with all his progeny was destroyed by the Tartars.   This country hath most huge mountains.   On the south side it hath Jerusalem and Baldach, and all the whole country of the Saracens.   In the next territories adjoining do inhabit two carnal brothers, dukes of the Tartars, namely Burin and Cadan, the sons of Thyaday, who was the son of Chingis Can.   On the north side thereof it hath the land of the black Kythayans, and the ocean.   In the same country Sybon the brother of Bathy remaineth.   Through this country we were travelling from the Feast of Ascension, until eight days before the Feast of Saint John Baptist.   And then we entered into the land of the black Kythayans, in which the emperor built an house, where we were called in to drink. Also the emperor's deputy in that place caused the chief men of the city and his two sons to dance before us. Departing from hence, we found a certain small sea, upon the shore whereof stands a little mountain.   In which mountain is reported to be a hole, from whence, in winter time such vehement tempests of winds do issue that travellers can scarcely and with great danger pass by the same way.   In summer time, the noise indeed of the wind is heard there, but it proceedeth gently out of the hole. Along the shores of the foresaid sea we travelled for the space of many days, which although it be not very great, yet hath it many islands, and we passed by leaving it on our left hand.   In this land dwelleth Ordu, whom we said to be ancient unto all the Tartarian dukes.   And it is the orda or court of his father which he inhabiteth, and one of his wives beareth rule there. For it is a custom among the Tartars, that the courts of princes or of noble men are not dissolved, but always some women are appointed to keep and govern them, upon whom certain gifts are bestowed, in like sort as they are given unto their lords. And so at length we arrived at the first court of the emperor, wherein one of his wives dwelt.

CHAPTER XXV

How they came unto Cuyne himself, who was forthwith to be chosen Emperor

But because we had not as yet seen the emperor, they would not invite us nor admit us into his orda, but caused good attendance and entertainment, after the Tartars' fashion, to be given unto us in our own tent, and they caused us to stay there, and to refresh ourselves with them one day. Departing from thence upon the even of Saint Peter and Saint Paul, we entered into the land of Naymani, who are pagans. But upon the very feast day of the said apostles, there fell a mighty snow in that place, and we had extreme cold weather. This land is full of mountains, and cold beyond measure, and there is little plain ground to be seen. These two nations last mentioned used not to till their ground, but, like unto the Tartars, dwelt in tents, which the said Tartars had destroyed. Through this country we were travelling many days. Then entered we into the land of the Mongals, whom we call Tartars. Through the Tartars' land we continued our travel (as we suppose) for the space of some three weeks, riding always hastily and with speed, and upon the day of Mary Magdalene we arrived at the court of Cuyne the emperor elect. But therefore did we make great haste all this way, because our Tartarian guides were straitly commanded to bring us unto the court imperial with all speed, which court had been these many years, ordained for the election of the emperor. Wherefore rising early, we travelled until night without eating of anything, and oftentimes we came so late unto our lodging, that we had no time to eat the same night, but that which we should have eaten over night was given us in the morning. And often changing our horses, we spared no horse flesh, but rode swiftly and without intermission, as fast as our horses could trot.

CHAPTER XXVI

How Cuyne entertained the Minorite Friars

BUT when we were come unto the court of Cuyne, he caused (after the Tartars' manner) a tent and all expenses necessary to be provided for us. And his people treated us with more regard and courtesy, than they did any other ambassadors. Howbeit we were not called before his presence, because he was not as yet elected, nor admitted unto his empire. Notwithstanding, the interpretation of the pope's letters, and the message which we delivered, were sent unto him by the foresaid Bathy. And having stayed there five or six days, he sent us unto his mother, under whom there was maintained a very solemn and royal court. And being come thither, we saw an huge tent of fine white cloth pitched, which was, to our judgement, of so great quantity that more than two thousand men might stand within it, and round about it there was a wall of planks set up, painted with divers images. We therefore with our Tartars assigned to attend upon us, took our journey thither, and there were all the dukes assembled, each one of them riding up and down with his train over the hills and dales. The first day they were all clad in white, but the second in scarlet robes. Then came Cuyne unto the said tent. Moreover, the third day they were all in blue robes, and the fourth in most rich robes of baldakin cloth.   In the wall of boards, about the tent aforesaid, were two great gates, by one of the which gates, the emperor only was to enter, and at that gate there was no guard of men appointed to stand, although it stood continually open, because none durst go in or come out the same way : all that were admitted, entered by another gate, at which there stood watchmen, with bows, swords, and arrows.   And whosoever approached unto the tent beyond the bounds and limit assigned, being caught, was beaten, but if he fled, he was shot at with arrows or iron.   There were many that to our judgement, had upon their bridles, trappings, saddles, and such like furniture, to the value of twenty marks in pure gold.   The foresaid dukes (as we think) communed together within the tent, and consulted about the election of their emperor.   But all the residue of the people were placed far away without the walls of board, and in this manner they stayed almost till noon.   Then began they to drink mares' milk, and so continued drinking till even tide, and that in so great quantity, as it was wonderful.   And they called us in unto them, and gave us of their ale, because we could not drink their mares' milk.   And this they did unto us in token of great honour.   But they compelled us to drink so much, that in regard of our customary diet, we could by no means endure it.   Whereupon, giving them to understand that it was hurtful unto us, they ceased to compel us any more. Without the door stood Duke Jeroslaus of Susdal, in Russia, and a great many dukes of the Kythayans, and of the Solangi.   The two sons also of the King of Georgia, the ligier of the Caliph of Baldach, who was a soldan, and (as we think) above ten soldans of the Saracens beside. And, as it was told us by the agents, there were more than four thousand ambassadors, partly of such as paid tributes, and such as presented gifts, and other soldans, and dukes, which came to yield themselves, and such as the Tartars had sent for, and such as were governors of lands.   All these were placed withouts the lists, and had drink given unto them. But almost continually they all of them gave us and Duke Jeroslaus the upper hand, when we were abroad in their company.

CHAPTER XXVII

How he was exalted to his Empire

AND to our remembrance, we remained there, about the space of four weeks. The election was to our thinking there celebrated, but it was not published and proclaimed there. And it was greatly suspected so to be, because always when Cuyne came forth out of the tent, he had a noise of music, and was bowed unto, or honoured with fair wands, having purple wool upon the tops of them, and that, so long as he remained abroad, which service was performed to none of the other dukes. The foresaid tent or court is called by them Syra orda. Departing thence, we all with one accord rode three or four leagues unto another place, where, in a goodly plain by a river's side, between certain mountains, there was another tent erected, which was called the golden orda. For there was Cuyne to be placed in the throne imperial, upon the day of the Assumption of Our Lady. But, for the abundance of hail which fell at the same time, as is above said, the matter was deferred. There was also a tent erected upon pillars, which were covered with plates of gold, and were joined unto other timber with golden nails. It was covered above with baldakin cloth, but there was other cloth spread over that, next unto the air. We abode there unto the feast of Saint Bartholomew, what time there was assembled an huge multitude standing with their faces towards the south. And a certain number of them being a stone's cast distant from the residue, making continual prayers, and kneeling upon their knees, proceeded farther and farther towards the south. Howbeit we, not knowing whether they used enchantments, or whether they bowed their knees to God or to some other, would not kneel upon the ground with them. And having done so a long time, they returned to the tent, and placed Cuyne in his throne imperial, and his dukes bowed their knees before him. Afterward the whole multitude knelt down in like manner, except ourselves, for we were none of his subjects.

CHAPTER XXVIII

Of his Age and Demeanour, and of his Seal

THIS emperor, when he was exalted unto his government, seemed to be about the age of forty or forty-five years. He was of a mean stature, very wise and politic, and passing serious and grave in all his demeanour. A rare thing it was, for a man to see him laugh or behave himself lightly, as those Christians report, which abode continually with him. Certain Christians of his family earnestly and strongly affirmed unto us, that he himself was about to become a Christian. A token and argument whereof was, that he received divers clergymen of the Christians. He had likewise at all times a chapel of Christians, near unto his great tent, where the clerks (like unto other Christians, and according to the custom of the Graecians) do sing publicly and openly, and ring bells at certain hours, be there never so great a multitude of Tartars, or of other people in presence. And yet none of their dukes do the like. It is the manner of the emperor never to talk his own self with a stranger, though he be never so great, but heareth and answereth by a speaker. And when any of his subjects (how great so ever they be) are in propounding any matter of importance unto him, or in hearing his answer, they continue kneeling upon their knees unto the end of their conference. Neither is it lawful for any man to speak of any affairs, after they have been determined of by the emperor. The said emperor, hath in his affairs both public and private, an agent, and secretary of estate, with scribes and all other officials, except advocates. For, without the noise of pleading, or sentence giving, all things are done according to the emperor's will and pleasure. Other Tartarian princes do the like in those things which belong unto them. But, be it known unto all men, that whilst we remained at the said emperor's court, which hath been ordained and kept for these many years, the said Cuyne being emperor new elect, together with all his princes, erected a flag of defiance against the Church of God, and the Roman empire, and against all Christian kingdoms and nations of the west, unless peradventure (which God forbid) they will condescend unto those things, which he hath injoined unto our lord the Pope, and to all potentates and people of the Christians, namely, that they will become obedient unto him. For, except Christendom, there is no land under heaven, which they stand in fear of, and for that cause they prepare themselves to battle against us. This emperor's father, namely Occoday, was poisoned to death, which is the cause why they have for a short space abstained from war. But their intent and purpose is (as I have above said) to subdue the whole world unto themselves, as they were commanded by Chingis Can. Hence it is that the emperor in his letters writeth after this manner : The power of God, and emperor of all men. Also upon his seal, there is this posy engraved : God in heaven, and Cuyne Can upon earth, the power of God : the seal of the emperor of all men.

CHAPTER XXIX

Of the Admission of the Friars and Ambassadors unto the Emperor

In the same place where the emperor was established into his throne, we were summoned before him. And Chingay his chief secretary having written down our names, and the names of them that sent us, with the name of the Duke of Solangi, and of others, cried out with a loud voice, rehearsing the said names before the emperor, and the assembly of his dukes. Which being done, each one of us bowed his left knee four times, and they gave us warning not to touch the threshold. And after they had searched us most diligently for knives, and could not find any about us, we entered in at the door upon the east side; because no man dare presume to enter at the west door, but the emperor only. In like manner, every Tartarian duke entereth on the west side into his tent. Howbeit the inferior sort do not greatly regard such ceremonies. This therefore was the first time, when we entered into the emperor's tent in his presence, after he was created emperor. Likewise all other ambassadors were there received by him, but very few were admitted into his tent. And there were presented unto him such abundance of gifts by the said ambassadors, that they seemed to be infinite, namely in samites, robes of purple, and of baldakin cloth, silk girdles wrought with gold, and costly skins, with other gifts also. Likewise there was a certain sun canopy, or small tent (which was to be carried over the emperor's head), presented unto him, being set full of precious stones. And a governor of one province brought unto him a company of camels covered with baldakins. They had saddles also upon their backs, with certain other instruments, within the which were places for men to sit upon. Also they brought many horses and mules unto him furnished with trappings and caparisons, some being made of leather, and some of iron. And we were demanded whether we would bestow any gifts upon him or not: but we were not of ability so to do, having in a manner spent all our provision. There were also upon an hill standing a good distance from the tents, more than five hundred carts, which were all full of silver and of gold, and silk garments. And they were all divided between the emperor and his dukes, and every duke bestowed upon his own followers what pleased him.

CHAPTER XXX

Of the Place where the Emperor and his Mother took their Leaves one of another, and of Jeroslaus, Duke of Russia

DEPARTING thence, we came unto another place, where a wonderful brave tent, all of red purple, given by the Kythayans, was pitched.   We were admitted into that also, and always when we entered, there was given unto us ale and wine to drink, and sodden flesh (when we would) to eat.   There was also a lofty stage built of boards, where the emperor's throne was placed, being very curiously wrought out of ivory, wherein also there was gold and precious stones, and (as we remember) there were certain degrees or stairs to ascend unto it.   And it was round upon the top.   There were benches placed about the said throne, whereon the ladies sat toward the left hand of the emperor upon stools (but none sat aloft on the right hand), and the dukes sat upon benches below, the said throne being in the midst.   Certain others sat behind the dukes, and every day there resorted great company of ladies thither.   The three tents whereof we spake before, were very large, but the emperor his wives had other great and fair tents made of white felt.   This was the place where the emperor parted company with his mother: for she went into one part of the land, and the emperor into another to execute justice.   For there was taken a certain concubine of this emperor, which had poisoned his father to death, at the same time when the Tartar's army was in Hungary, which, for the same cause returned home.   Moreover, upon the foresaid concubine, and many other of her confederates sentence of judgment was pronounced, and they were put to death.   At the same time Jeroslaus the great Duke of Soldal, which is a part of Russia, deceased.   For being (as it were for honour's sake) invited to eat and drink with the emperor's mother, and immediately after the banquet, returning into his lodging, he fell sick, and within seven days, died. And after his death, his body was of a strange blue colour, and it was commonly reported, that the said duke was poisoned, to the end that the Tartars might freely and totally possess his dukedom.

CHAPTER XXXI

How the Friars coming at length unto the Emperor gave, and received Letters

To be short, the Tartars brought us unto their emperor, who when he had heard of them, that we were come unto him, commanded that we should return, unto his mother. For he was determined the next day (as it is above said) to set up a flag of defiance against all the countries of the west, which he would have us in no case to know. Wherefore returning, we stayed some few days with his mother, and so returned back again unto him. With whom we continued for the space of one whole month in such extreme hunger and thirst, that we could scarce hold life and soul together. For the provision allowed us for four days, was scantly sufficient for one day. Neither could we buy us any sustenance, because the market was too far off. Howbeit, the Lord provided for us a Russian goldsmith, named Cosmas, who being greatly in the emperor's favour, procured us some sustenance. This man shewed unto us the throne of the emperor, which he had made, before it was set in the proper place, and his seal, which he also had framed. Afterward the emperor sent for us, giving us to understand by Chingay his chief secretary, that we should write down our messages and affairs, and should deliver them unto him. Which thing we performed accordingly. After many days he called for us again, demanding whether there were any with our lord the pope, which understood the Russian, the Saracen, or the Tartarian languages : to whom we answered, that we had none of those letters or languages.   Howbeit, that there were certain Saracens in the land, but inhabiting a great distance from our lord the Pope.   And we said, that we thought it most expedient, that when they had written their minds in the Tartarian language, and had interpreted the meaning thereof unto us, we should diligently translate it into our own tongue, and so deliver both the letter and the translation thereof unto our lord the Pope.   Then departed they from us, and went unto the emperor.   And after the day of S. Martin, we were called for again. Then Kadac, principal agent for the whole empire, and Chingay, and Bala, with divers other scribes, came unto us, and interpreted the letter word for word.   And having written it in Latin, they caused us to interprete unto them each sentence, to wit if we had erred in any word.   And when both letters were written, they made us to read them over twice more, lest we should have mistaken aught.   For they said unto us : Take heed that ye understand all thing throughly, for if ye should not understand the whole matter aright, it might breed some inconvenience.   They wrote the said letters also in the Saracen tongue, that there might be some found in our dominions which could read and interprete them, if need should require.

CHAPTER XXXII

How they were licensed to depart

AND (as our Tartars told us) the emperor was purposed to send his ambassadors with us.   Howbeit, he was desirous (as we thought) that we ourselves should crave that favour at his hands.   And when one of our Tartars, being an ancient man, exhorted us to make the said petition, we thought it not good for us, that the emperor should send his ambassadors.   Wherefore we gave him answer, that it was not for us to make any such petition, but if it pleased the emperor of his own accord to send them, we would diligently (by God's assistance) see them conducted in safety.   Howbeit, we thought it expedient for us, that they should not go, and that for divers causes.   First, because we feared, lest they, seeing the dissensions and wars which are among us, should be the more encouraged to make war against us.   Secondly, we feared, that they would be instead of spies and intelligencers in our dominions. Thirdly, we misdoubted that they would be slain by the way.   For our nations be arrogant and proud.   For when as those servants (which at the request of the cardinal, attended upon us, namely the legates of Almaine) returned unto him in the Tartars' attire, they were almost stoned in the way, by the Dutch, and were compelled to put off those garments.   And it is the Tartars' custom, never to be reconciled unto such as have slain their ambassadors, till they have revenged themselves.   Fourthly, lest they should be taken from us by main force.   Fifthly, because there could come no good by their ambassade, for they were to have none other commission, or authority, but only to deliver their emperor's letter unto the Pope, and to the Princes of Christendom, which very same letters we ourselves had, and we knew right well, that much harm might ensue thereof.   Wherefore, the third day after this, namely, upon the Feast of Saint Brice, they gave us our pass-port and a letter sealed with the emperor's own seal, sending us unto the emperor's mother, who gave unto each of us a gown made of fox skins, with the fur on the outside, and a piece of purple.   And our Tartars stole a yard out of every one of them.   And out of that which was given unto our servant, they stole the better half, which false dealing of theirs, we knew well enough, but would make no words thereof.

CHAPTER XXXIII

How they returned Homewards

THEN taking our journey to return, we travelled all winter long, lying in the deserts oftentimes upon the snow, except with out feet we made a piece of ground bare to lie upon. For there were no trees, but the plain champion field. And oftentimes in the morning, we found ourselves all covered with snow driven over us by the wind. And so travelling till the feast of our Lord's Ascension, we arrived at the court of Bathy. Of whom when we had inquired, what answer he would send unto our lord the Pope, he said that he had nothing to give us in charge, but only that we would diligently deliver that which the emperor had written. And, having received letters for our safe conduct, the thirteenth day after Pentecost, being Saturday, we were proceeded as far as Montij, with whom our foresaid associates and servants remained, which were withheld from us, and we caused them to be delivered unto us. From hence we travelled unto Corrensa, to whom, requiring gifts the second time at our hands, we gave none, because we had not wherewithal. And he appointed us two Comanians, which lived among the common people of the Tartars, to be our guides unto the city of Kiow in Russia. Howbeit, one of our Tartars parted not from us, till we were passed the utmost guard of the Tartars. But the other guides, namely the Comanians, which were given us by Corrensa, brought us from the last guard unto the city of Kiow, in the space of six days. And there we arrived fifteen days before the feast of Saint John Baptist. Moreover, the citizens of Kiow having intelligence of our approach, came forth all of them to meet us, with great joy. For they rejoiced over us, as over men that had been risen from death to life. So likewise they did unto us throughout all Russia, Polonia, and Bohemia. Daniel and his brother Wasilico made us a royal feast, and entertained us with them against our wills for the space of eight days. In the meantime, they with their bishops, and other men of account, being in consultation together about those matters which we had propounded unto them in our journey towards the Tartars, answered us with common consent, saying that they would hold the pope for their special lord and father, and the Church of Rome for their lady and mistress, confirming likewise all things which they had sent concerning this matter, before our coming, by their abbot. And for the same purpose, they sent their ambassadors and letters by us also, unto our lord the Pope.

THE JOURNAL OF
FRIAR WILLIAM DE RUBRUQUIS

a Frenchman of the Order of the Minorite Friars, unto the East Parts of the World.   An. Dom. 1253

To his most sovereign, and most Christian Lord Lewis, by God's grace the renowned king of France, Friar William de Rubruk, the meanest of the Minorites' order, wisheth health and continual triumph in Christ.   It is written in the book of Ecclesiasticus concerning the wise man: He shall travel into foreign countries, and good and evil shall he try in all things.   The very same action (my lord and king) have I achieved: howbeit I wish that I have done it like a wise man, and not like a fool.   For many there be, that perform the same action which a wise man doth, not wisely but more undiscreetly: of which number I fear myself to be one.   Notwithstanding howsoever I have done it, because you commanded me, when I departed from your highness, to write all things unto you, which I should see among the Tartars, and you wished me also that I should not fear to write long letters: I have done as your majesty enjoined me, yet with fear and reverence, because I want words and eloquence sufficient to write unto so great a majesty.   Be it known therefore unto your sacred majesty, that in the year of our Lord 1253, about the nones of May, we entered into the sea of Pontus, which the Bulgarians call the Great Sea.   It containeth in length (as I learned of certain merchants) 1008 miles, and

is in a manner, divided into two parts. About the midst
thereof are two provinces, one towards the north, and
another towards the south. The south province is called
Synopolis, and it is the castle and port of the Soldan of
Turkey; but the north province is called of the Latins,
Gasaria: of the Greeks, which inhabit upon the sea shore
thereof, it is called Cassaria, that is to say Caesaria. And
there are certain headlands stretching forth into the sea
towards Synopolis. Also there are three hundred miles
of distance between Synopolis and Cassaria. Insomuch
that the distance from those points or places to Constantinople, in length and breadth is about seven hundred
miles: and seven hundred miles also from thence to
the east, namely to the country of Hiberia which is
a province of Georgia. At the province of Gasaria or
Cassaria we arrived, which province is, in a manner,
three square, having a city on the west part thereof
called Kersova, wherein S. Clement suffered martyrdom. And sailing before the said city, we saw an
island, in which a church is said to be built by the hands
of angels. But about the midst of the said province
toward the south, as it were, upon a sharp angle or point,
standeth a city called Soldaia, directly over against
Synopolis. And there do all the Turkey merchants,
which traffic into the north countries, in their journey
outward, arrive, and as they return homeward also from
Russia, and the said northern regions, into Turkey. The
foresaid merchants transport thither ermines and gray furs,
with other rich and costly skins. Others carry clothes
made of cotton or bombast, and silk, and divers kinds of
spices. But upon the east part of the said province
standeth a city called Matriga, where the river Tanais
dischargeth his streams into the sea of Pontus, the mouth
whereof is twelve miles in breadth. For this river, before
it entereth into the sea of Pontus, maketh a little sea,
which hath in breadth and length seven hundred miles,
and it is no place there of above six paces deep, whereupon
great vessels cannot sail over it. Howbeit the merchants
of Constantinople, arriving at the foresaid city of Materta,

send their barques unto the river of Tanais to buy dried
fishes, sturgeons, thosses, barbels, and an infinite number of
other fishes.   The foresaid province of Cassaria is compassed in with the sea on three sides thereof: namely on
the west side, where Kersova the city of Saint Clement is
situate : on the south side the city of Soldaia whereat we
arrived : on the east side Maricandis, and there stands the
city of Matriga upon the mouth of the river Tanais.
Beyond the said mouth standeth Zikia, which is not in
subjection unto the Tartars : also the people called Suevi
and Hiberi towards the east, who likewise are not under
the Tartars' dominion.   Moreover towards the south,
standeth the city of Trapesunda, which hath a governour
proper to itself, named Guido, being of the lineage of
the emperors of Constantinople, and is subject unto the
Tartars.   Next unto that is Synopolis the city of the
Soldan of Turkey, who likewise is in subjection unto
them.   Next unto these lieth the country of Vastacius,
whose son is called Astar, of his grandfather by the
mother's side, who is not in subjection.   All the land from
the mouth of Tanais westward as far as Danubius is
under their subjection.   Yea, beyond Danubius also, towards
Constantinople, Valakia, which is the land of Assanus, and
Bulgaria minor as far as Solonia, do all pay tribute unto
them.   And besides the tribute imposed, they have also of
late years exacted of every household an axe, and all such
corn as they found lying on heaps.

We arrived therefore at Soldaia the twelfth of the kalends
of June.   And divers merchants of Constantinople, which
were arrived there before us, reported that certain
messengers were coming thither from the holy land, who
were desirous to travel unto Sartach.   Notwithstanding I
myself had publicly given out upon Palm Sunday, within
the Church of St. Sophia, that I was not your nor any other
man's messenger, but that I travelled unto those infidels
according to the rule of our order.   And being arrived, the
said merchants admonished me to take diligent heed what I
spake : because they having reported me to be a messenger,
if I should say the contrary, that I were no messenger, I

could not have free passage granted unto me. Then I
spake after this manner unto the governours of the city, or
rather unto their lieutenants, because the governours themselves were gone to pay tribute unto Baatu, and were not as
yet returned. We heard of your lord Sartach (quoth I)
in the holy land, that he was become a Christian: and the
Christians were exceeding glad thereof, and especially the
most Christian King of France, who is there now in
pilgrimage, and fighteth against the Saracens to redeem the
holy places out of their hands: wherefore I am determined
to go unto Sartach, and to deliver unto him the letters
of my lord the king, wherein he admonisheth him concerning the good and commodity of all Christendom.
And they received us with gladness, and gave us entertainment in the cathedral church. The bishop of which church
was with Sartach, who told me many good things concerning
the said Sartach, which after I found to be nothing so.

Then put they us to our choice, whether we would
have carts and oxen, or packhorses to transport our
carriages. And the merchants of Constantinople advised
me, not to take carts of the citizens of Soldaia but to buy
covered carts of mine own (such as the Russians carry
their skins in), and to put all our carriages, which I would
daily take out, into them: because, if I should use horses,
I must be constrained at every bait to take down my
carriages, and to lift them up again on sundry horses'
backs: and besides, that I should ride a more gentle pace
by the oxen drawing the carts. Wherefore contenting
myself with their evil counsel, I was travelling unto Sartach
two months which I could have done in one, if I had gone
by horse. I brought with me from Constantinople (being
by the merchants advised so to do) pleasant fruits, muscadel
wine, and delicate biscuit bread to present unto the governours
of Soldaia, to the end I might obtain free passage: because
they look favourably upon no man which cometh with an
empty hand. All of which things I bestowed in one of my
carts (not finding the governours of the city at home), for
they told me, if I could carry them to Sartach, that they
would be most acceptable unto him. We took our journey

therefore about the kalends of June, with four covered
carts of our own, and with two other which we borrowed
of them, wherein we carried our bedding to rest upon in
the night, and they allowed us five horses to ride upon.
For there were just five persons in our company: namely,
I myself and mine associate Friar Bartholomew of Cremona,
and Goset the bearer of these presents, the man of God
Turgemannus, and Nicolas, my servant, whom I bought at
Constantinople with some part of the alms bestowed upon
me.   Moreover, they allowed us two men, which drove
our carts and gave attendance unto our oxen and horses.

There be high promontories on the sea shore from
Kersova unto the mouth of Tanais.   Also there are
forty castles between Kersova and Soldaia, every one of
which almost have their proper languages: amongst whom
there were many Goths, who spake the Dutch tongue.
Beyond the said mountains towards the north there is a
most beautiful wood growing on a plain full of fountains
and freshets.   And beyond the wood there is a mighty
plain champion, continuing five days' journey unto the very
extremity and borders of the said province northward, and
there it is a narrow isthmus or neck land, having sea on the
east and west sides thereof, insomuch that there is a ditch
made from one sea unto the other.   In the same plain
(before the Tartars sprang up) were the Comanians wont
to inhabit, who compelled the foresaid cities and castles to
pay tribute unto them.   But when the Tartars came upon
them, the multitude of the Comanians entered into the
foresaid province, and fled all of them, even unto the sea
shore, being in such extreme famine, that they which were
alive, were constrained to eat up those which were dead;
and (as a merchant reported unto me who saw it with his
own eyes) that the living men devoured and tore with their
teeth the raw flesh of the dead, as dogs would gnaw upon
carrion.   Towards the border of the said province there be
many great lakes: upon the banks whereof are salt pits or
fountains, the water of which so soon as it entereth into
the lake, becometh hard salt like unto ice.   And out of
those salt pits Baatu and Sartach have great revenues: for

they repair thither out of all Russia for salt; and for each cart-load they give two webs of cotton amounting to the value of half an yperpera. There come by sea also many ships for salt, which pay tribute every one of them according to their burden. The third day after we were departed out of the precincts of Soldaia, we found the Tartars. Amongst whom being entered, methought I was come into a new world. Whose life and manners I will describe unto your highness as well as I can.

CHAPTER II

Of the Tartars, and of their Houses

THEY have in no place any settled city to abide in, neither know they of the celestial city to come. They have divided all Scythia among themselves, which stretcheth from the river Danubius even unto the rising of the sun. And every of their captains, according to the great or small number of his people, knoweth the bound of his pastures, and where he ought to feed his cattle, winter and summer, spring and autumn. For in the winter they descend unto the warme regions southward. And in the summer they ascend unto the cold regions northward. In winter when snow lieth upon the ground, they feed their cattle upon pastures without water, because then they use snow instead of water. Their houses wherein they sleep, they ground upon a round foundation of wickers artificially wrought and compacted together : the roof whereof consisteth (in like sort) of wickers, meeting above into one little roundell, out of which roundell ascendeth a neck like unto a chimney, which they cover with white felt, and oftentimes they lay mortar or white earth upon the said felt, with the powder of bones, that it may shine white. And sometimes also they cover it with black felt. The said felt on the neck of their house, they do garnish over with beautiful variety of pictures.

Before the door likewise they hang a felt curiously
painted over. For they spend all their coloured felt in
painting vines, trees, birds, and beasts thereupon. The
said houses they make so large, that they contain thirty
foot in breadth. For measuring once the breadth between
the wheel-ruts of one of their carts, I found it to be twenty
feet over: and when the house was upon the cart, it
stretched over the wheels on each side five feet at the least.
I told twenty-two oxen in one team, drawing an house
upon a cart, eleven in one order according to the breadth
of the cart, and eleven more before them : the axletree of
the cart was of an huge bigness, like unto the mast of a ship.
And a fellow stood in the door of the house, upon the
forestall of the cart, driving forth the oxen. Moreover,
they make certain foursquare baskets of small slender
wickers as big as great chests : and afterward, from one
side to another, they frame an hollow lid or cover of such
like wickers, and make a door in the fore side thereof.
And then they cover the said chest or little house with
black felt rubbed over with tallow or sheep's milk to keep
the rain from soaking through, which they deck likewise
with painting or with feathers. And in such chests they
put their whole household stuff and treasure. Also the
same chests they do strongly bind upon other carts, which
are drawn with camels, to the end they may wade through
rivers. Neither do they at any time take down the said
chests from off their carts. When they take down their
dwelling houses, they turn the doors always to the south :
and next of all they place the carts laden with their chests,
here and there, within half a stone's cast of the house :
insomuch that the house standeth between two ranks
of carts, as it were, between two walls. The matrons
make for themselves most beautiful carts, which I am not
able to describe unto your majesty but by pictures only :
for I would right willingly have painted all things for you,
had my skill been aught in that art. One rich Moal or
Tartar hath two hundred or one hundred such carts with
chests. Duke Baatu hath sixteen wives, every one of which
hath one great house, besides other little houses, which they

place behind the great one, being as it were chambers for their maidens to dwell in. And unto every of the said houses do belong two hundred carts. When they take their houses from off the carts, the principal wife placeth her court on the west frontier, and so all the rest in their order: so that the last wife dwelleth upon the east frontier: and one of the said ladies' courts is distant from another about a stone's cast. Whereupon the court of one rich Moal or Tartar will appear like unto a great village, very few men abiding in the same. One woman will guide twenty or thirty carts at once, for their countries are very plain, and they bind the carts with camels or oxen, one behind another. And there sits a wench in the foremost cart driving the oxen, and all the residue follow on a like pace. When they chance to come at any bad passage, they let them loose, and guide them over one by one: for they go a slow pace, as fast as a lamb or an ox can walk.

CHAPTER III

Of their Beds, and of their Drinking Pots

HAVING taken down their houses from off their carts, and turning the doors southward, they place the bed of the master of the house, at the north part thereof. The women's place is always on the east side, namely on the left hand of the good man of the house, sitting upon his bed with his face southwards; but the men's place is upon the west side, namely at the right hand of their master. Men when they enter into the house, will not in any case hang their quivers on the women's side. Over the master's head is always an image, like a puppet, made of felt, which they call the master's brother: and another over the head of the good wife or mistress, which they call her brother being fastened to the wall: and above between both of them, there is a little lean one, which is as it were the keeper of the whole house. The good wife or mistress of the house placeth aloft at her bed's feet, on the right hand, the skin of a kid stuffed with wool or some other matter, and near unto that a little image or puppet looking towards the maidens and women. Next unto the door also on the women's side, there is another image with a cow's udder, for the women that milk the kine. For it is the duty of their women to milk kine. On the other side of the door next unto the men, there is another image with the udder of a mare, for the men which milk mares. And when they come together to drink and make merry, they sprinkle part of their drink upon the image which is above the master's head : afterward upon other images in order : then goeth a servant out of the house with a cup full of drink sprinkling it thrice towards the south, and bowing his knee at every time : and this is done for the honour of the fire. Then performeth he the like superstitious idolatry towards the east, for the honour of the air : and then to the west for the honour of the water : and lastly to the north in the behalf of the dead. When the master holdeth a cup in his hand to drink, before he tasteth thereof, he poureth his part upon the ground. If he drinketh sitting on horse-back, he poureth out part thereof upon the neck or mane of his horse before he himself drinketh. After the servant aforesaid hath so discharged his cups to the four quarters of the world, he returneth into the house : and two other servants stand ready with two cups, and two basins, to carry drink unto their master and his wife, sitting together upon a bed. And if he hath more wives than one, she with whom he slept the night before, sitteth by his side the day following : and all his other wives must that day resort unto the same house to drink : and there is the court holden for that day : the gifts also which are presented that day are laid up in the chests of the said wife. And upon a bench stands a vessel of milk or of other drink and drinking cups.

CHAPTER IV

*Of their Drinks, and how they provoke one another
to Drinking*

In winter time they make excellent drink of rice, of mill, and of honey, being well and highly coloured like wine. Also they have wine brought unto them from far countries. In summer time they care not for any drink but cosmos. And it standeth always within the entrance of his door, and next unto it stands a minstrel with his fiddle. I saw there no such citherns and viols as ours commonly be, but many other musical instruments which are not used among us. And when the master of the house begins to drink, one of his servants crieth out with a loud voice, Ha! and the minstrel plays upon his fiddle. And when they make any great solemn feast, they all of them clap their hands and dance to the noise of music, the men before their master and the women before their mistress. And when the master hath drunk, then cries out his servant as before, and the minstrel stayeth his music. Then drink they all around both men and women: and sometimes they carouse for the victory very filthily and drunkenly. Also when they will provoke any man, they pull him by the ears to the drink, and so lug and draw him strongly to stretch out his throat, clapping their hands and dancing before him. Moreover when some of them will make great feasting and rejoicing, one of the company takes a full cup, and two other stand, one on his right hand and another on his left, and so they three come singing to the man who is to have the cup reached unto him, still singing and dancing before him: and when he stretcheth forth his hand to receive the cup, they leap suddenly back, returning again as they did before, and so having deluded him thrice or four times by drawing back the cup until he be merry, and hath gotten a good appetite, then they give him the cup, singing and dancing and stamping with their feet, until he hath done drinking.

CHAPTER V

Of their Food and Victuals

CONCERNING their food and victuals, be it known unto your highness that they do, without all difference or exception, eat all their dead carrions. And amongst so many droves it cannot be, but some cattle must needs die. Howbeit in summer, so long as their cosmos, that is, their mares' milk lasteth, they care not for any food. And if they chance to have an ox or an horse die, they dry the flesh thereof: for cutting it into thin slices and hanging it up against the sun and the wind, it is presently dried without salt, and also without stench or corruption. They make better puddings of their horses than of their hogs, which they eat being new made: the rest of the flesh they reserve until winter. They make of their ox skins great bladders or bags, which they do wonderfully dry in the smoke. Of the hinder part of their horse hides they make very fine sandals and pantofles. They give unto fifty or an hundred men the flesh of one ram to eat. For they mince it in a bowl with salt and water (other sauce they have none) and then with the point of a knife, or a little fork which they make for the same purpose (such as we use to take roasted pears or apples out of wine withall), they reach unto every one of the company a morsel or twain, according to the multitude of guests. The master of the house, before the ram's flesh be distributed, first of all himself taketh thereof, what he pleaseth. Also, if he giveth unto any of the company a special part, the receiver thereof must eat it alone, and must not impart ought thereof unto any other. Not being able to eat it up all, he carries it with him, or delivers it unto his boy, if he be present, to keep it: if not, he puts it up into his saptargat, that is to say, his four-square budget, which they use to carry about with them for the saving of all such provision, and wherein they lay up their bones, when they have not time to gnaw them thoroughly, that they may burnish them afterward, to the end that no whit of their food may come to nought.

CHAPTER VI

How they make their Drink called Cosmos

THEIR drink called cosmos, which is mares' milk, is prepared after this manner. They fasten a long line unto two posts standing firmly in the ground, and unto the same line they tie the young foals of those mares which they mean to milk. Then come the dams to stand by their foals, gently suffering themselves to be milked. And if any of them be too unruly, then one takes her foal and puts it under her, letting it suck a while, and presently carrying it away again, there comes another man to milk the said mare. And having gotten a good quantity of this milk together (being as sweet as cow's milk), while it is new they pour it into a great bladder or bag, and they beat the said bag with a piece of wood made for the purpose, having a club at the lower end like a man's head, which is hollow within : and so soon as they beat upon it, it begins to boil like new wine, and to be sour and sharp of taste, and they beat it in that manner 'till butter come thereof. Then taste they thereof, and being indifferently sharp they drink it : for it biteth a man's tongue like the wine of raspes, when it is drunk. After a man hath taken a draught thereof, it leaveth behind it a taste like the taste of almond milk, and goeth down very pleasantly, intoxicating weak brains : also it causeth wine to be avoided in great measure. Likewise caracosmos, that is to say black cosmos, for great lords to drink, they make on this manner. First they beat the said milk so long till the thickest part thereof descend right down to the bottom like the lees of white wine, and that which is thin and pure remaineth above, being like unto whey or white must. The said lees or dregs being very white, are given to servants, and will cause them to sleep exceedingly. That which is thin and clear their masters drink: and in very deed it is marvellous sweet and wholesome liquor. Duke Baatu hath thirty cottages or granges within a day's journey of his abiding place: every one of which serveth him daily with the caracosmos of an hundred mares' milk, and so all of them together every day with the milk of three thousand mares, besides white milk which other of his subjects bring. For even as the husbandmen of Syria bestow the third part of their fruits and carry it unto the courts of their lords, even so do they their mares' milk every third day. Out of their cows' milk they first churn butter, boiling the which butter unto a perfect decoction, they put it into rams' skins, which they reserve for the same purpose. Neither do they salt their butter: and yet by reason of the long seething it putrefieth not: and they keep it in store for winter. The churnmilk which remaineth of the butter, they let alone till it be as sour as possibly it may be, then they boil it and in boiling, it is turned all into curds, which curds they dry in the sun, making them as hard as the dross of iron: and this kind of food also they store up in satchels against winter. In the winter season when milk faileth them, they put the foresaid curds (which they call gry-ut) into a bladder, and pouring hot water thereinto, they beat it lustily till they have resolved it into the said water, which is thereby made exceedingly sour, and that they drink instead of milk. They are very scrupulous, and take diligent heed that they drink not fair water by itself.

CHAPTER VII

Of the Beasts which they Eat, of their Garments, and of their Manner of Hunting

GREAT lords have cottages or granges towards the south, from whence their tenants bring them millet and meal against winter. The poorer sort provide themselves of such necessaries, for the exchange of rams, and of other beasts' skins. The Tartars' slaves fill their bellies with thick water, and are therewithall contented. They will neither eat mice with long tails, nor any kind of mice with short tails. They have also certain little beasts called by them sogur, which lie in a cave twenty or thirty of them together, all the whole winter sleeping there for the space of six months: and these they take in great abundance. There are also a kind of conies having long tails like unto cats: and on the outside of their tails grow black and white hairs. They have many other small beasts good to eat, which they know and discern right well. I saw no deer there, and but a few hares, but a great number of roes. I saw wild asses in great abundance, which be like unto mules. Also I saw another kind of beast called artak, having in all resemblance the body of a ram, and crooked horns, which are of such bigness, that I could scarce lift up a pair of them with one hand; and of these horns they make great drinking cups. They have falcons, gerfalcons, and other hawks in great plenty: all which they carry upon their right hands: and they put always about their falcons' necks a string of leather, which hangeth down to the midst of their gorges, by the which string, when they cast them off the fist at their game, with their left hand they bow down the heads and breasts of the said hawks, lest they should be tossed up and down, and beaten with the wind, or lest they should soar too high. Wherefore they get a great part of their victuals by hunting and hawking. Concerning their garments and attire be it

known unto your majesty, that out of Cataya and other
regions of the east, out of Persia also and other countries
of the south, there are brought unto them stuffs of silk,
cloth of gold, and cotton cloth, which they wear in time of
summer.   But out of Russia, Moxel, Bulgaria the greater,
and Pascatir, that is Hungaria the greater, and out of
Kersis (all which are northern regions and full of woods)
and also out of many other countries of the north, which
are subject unto them, the inhabitants bring them rich and
costly skins of divers sorts (which I never saw in our
countries) wherewithal they are clad in winter.   And
always against winter they make themselves two gowns,
one with the fur inward to their skin, and another with
the fur outward, to defend them from wind and snow,
which for the most part are made of wolves' skins, or fox
skins, or else of papions.   And when they sit within the
house, they have a finer gown to wear.   The poorer sort
make their upper gown of dogs' or of goats' skins.
When they go to hunt for wild beasts, there meets a great
company together, and environing the place round about,
where they are sure to find some game, by little and little
they approach on all sides, till they have gotten the wild
beasts into the midst, as it were into a circle, and then
they discharge their arrows at them.   Also they make
themselves breeches of skins.   The rich Tartars sometimes fur their gowns with pelluce or silk shag, which is
exceeding soft, light and warm.   The poorer sort do line
their clothes with cotton cloth which is made of the finest
wool they can pick out, and of the coarser part of the said
wool, they make felt to cover their houses and their
chests, and for their bedding also.   Of the same wool,
being mixed with one third part of horse hair, they make all
their cordage.   They make also of the said felt coverings
for their stools, and caps to defend their heads from the
weather: for all which purposes they spend a great
quantity of their wool.   And thus much concerning the
attire of the men.

CHAPTER VIII

Of the Fashion which the Tartars use in Cutting their Hair, and of the Attire of their Women

THE men shave a plot four square upon the crowns of their heads, and from the two foremost corners they shave, as it were, two seams down to their temples : they shave also their temples and the hinder part of their head even unto the nape of the neck : likewise they shave the fore part of their scalp down to their foreheads, and upon their foreheads they leave a lock of hair reaching down unto their eyebrows : upon the two hindermost corners of their heads, they have two locks also, which they twine and braid into knots and so bind and knit them under each ear one. Moreover their women's garments differ not from their men's, saving that they are somewhat longer. But on the morrow after one of their women is married, she shaves her scalp from the midst of her head down to her forehead, and wears a wide garment like unto the hood of a nun, yea larger and longer in all parts than a nun's hood, being open before and girt unto them under the right side. For herein do the Tartars differ from the Turks, because the Turks fasten their garments to their bodies on the left side : but the Tartars always on the right side. They have also an ornament for their heads which they call botta, being made of the bark of a tree, or of some such other lighter matter as they can find, which by reason of the thickness and roundness thereof cannot be holden but in both hands together : and it hath a square sharp spire rising from the top thereof, being more than a cubit in length, and fashioned like unto a pinnacle. The said botta they cover all over with a piece of rich silk : and it is hollow within : and upon the midst of the said spire or square top, they put a bunch of quills or of slender canes a cubit long and more : and the said bunch, on the top thereof, they beautify with peacocks' feathers, and round about all the length thereof, with the feathers of a mallard's tail, and with precious stones also. Great ladies wear this kind of ornament upon their heads, binding it strongly with a certain hat or coif, which hath an hole in the crown, fit for the spire to come through it : and under the foresaid ornament they cover the hairs of their heads, which they gather up round together from the hinder part thereof to the crown, and so lap them up in a knot or bundle within the said botta, which afterward they bind strongly under their throats. Hereupon when a great company of such gentlewomen ride together, and are beheld afar off, they seem to be soldiers with helmets on their heads carrying their lances upright : for the said botta appeareth like an helmet with a lance over it. All their women sit on horseback bestriding their horses like men : and they bind their hoods or gowns about their waists with a sky-coloured silk scarf, and with another scarf they gird it above their breasts : and they bind also a piece of white silk like a muffler or mask under their eyes, reaching down unto their breast. These gentlewomen are exceeding fat, and the lesser their noses be, the fairer are they esteemed : they daub over their sweet faces with grease too shamefully : and they never lie in bed for their travail of child-birth.

CHAPTER IX

Of the Duties enjoined unto the Tartarian Women, and of their Labours, and also of their Marriages

THE duties of women are, to drive carts : to lay their houses upon carts and to take them down again : to milk kine : to make butter and gry-ut : to dress skins and to sew them, which they usually sew with thread made of sinews, for they divide sinews into slender threads, and then twine them into one long thread. They make sandals and socks and other garments. Howbeit they never wash any apparel: for they say that God is then angry, and that dreadful thunder will ensue, if washed garments be hanged forth to dry: yea, they beat such as wash, and take their garments from them. They are wonderfully afraid of thunder: for in the time of thunder they thrust all strangers out of their houses, and then wrapping themselves in black felt, they lie hidden therein, till the thunder be overpast. They never wash their dishes or bowls: yea, when their flesh is sodden, they wash the platter wherein it must be put, with scalding hot broth out of the pot, and then pour the said broth into the pot again. They make felt also, and cover their houses therewith. The duties of the men are to make bows and arrows, stirrups, bridles, and saddles: to build houses and carts, to keep horses: to milk mares: to churn cosmos and mares' milk, and to make bags wherein to put it: they keep camels also and lay burdens upon them. As for sheep and goats they tend and milk them, as well the men as the women. With sheep's milk thickened and salted they dress and tan their hides. When they will wash their hands or their heads, they fill their mouths full of water, and spouting it into their hands by little and little, they sprinkle their hair and wash their heads therewith. As touching marriages, your highness is to understand, that no man can have a wife among them till he hath bought her: whereupon sometimes their maids are very stale before they be married, for their parents always keep them 'till they can sell them. They keep the first and second degrees of consanguinity inviolable, as we do: but they have no regard of the degrees of affinity: for they will marry together, or by succession, two sisters. Their widows marry not at all, for this reason: because they believe that all who have served them in this life, shall do them service in the life to come also. Whereupon they are persuaded, that every widow after death shall return unto her own husband. And herehence ariseth an abominable and filthy custom among them, namely that the son marrieth sometimes all his father's wives except his own mother: for the court or house of the father or

mother falleth by inheritance always to the younger son.
Whereupon he is to provide for all his father's wives,
because they are part of his inheritance as well as his
father's possessions.   And then if he will he useth them
for his own wives: for he thinks it no injury or disparage-
ment unto himself, although they return unto his father
after death.   Therefore when any man hath bargained
with another for a maid, the father of the said damosel
makes him a feast: in the mean while she fleeth unto some
of her kinsfolk to hide herself.   Then saith her father unto
the bridegroom: Lo, my daughter is yours, take her wheresoever you can find her.   Then he and his friends seek for
her till they can find her, and having found her he must
take her by force and carry her, as it were, violently unto
his own house.

CHAPTER X

Of their Execution of Justice and Judgement: and of their Deaths and Burials

CONCERNING their laws or their execution of justice, your
majesty is to be advertised, that when two men fight, no
third man dare intrude himself to part them.   Yea, the
father dare not help his own son.   But he that goes by the
worst must appeal unto the court of his lord.   And whosoever else offereth him any violence after appeal, is put to
death.   But he must go presently without all delay: and
he that hath suffered the injury, carrieth him, as it were
captive.   They punish no man with sentence of death,
unless he be taken in the deed doing, or confesseth the
same.   But being accused by the multitude, they put him
into extreme torture to make him confess the truth.   They
punish murder with death, and carnal copulation also with
any other besides his own.   By his own I mean his wife or
his maid-servant, for he may use his slave as he listeth
himself.   Heinous theft also or felony they punish with

death.   For a light theft, as namely for stealing of a ram,
the party (not being apprehended in the deed doing, but
otherwise detected) is cruelly beaten.   And if the execu-
tioner lays on an hundred strokes, he must have an hundred
staves, namely for such as are beaten upon sentence given
in the court.   Also counterfeit messengers, because they
feign themselves to be messengers, whenas indeed they
are none at all, they punish with death.   Sacrilegious
persons they use in like manner (of which kind of male-
factors your majesty shall understand more fully hereafter)
because they esteem such to be witches.   When any man
dieth, they lament and howl most pitifully for him: and
the said mourners are free from paying any tribute for one
whole year after.   Also whosoever is present at the house
where any one grown to man's estate lieth dead, he must
not enter into the court of Mangu-Can till one whole
year be expired.   If it were a child deceased he must not
enter into the said court till the next month after.   Near
unto the grave of the party deceased they always leave one
cottage.   If any of their nobles (being of the stock of
Chingis, who was their first lord and father) deceaseth, his
sepulchre is unknown.   And always about those places
where they inter their nobles, there is one house of men to
keep the sepulchres.   I could not learn that they use to
hide treasures in the graves of their dead.   The Comanians
build a great tomb over their dead, and erect the image of
the dead party thereupon, with his face towards the east,
holding a drinking cup in his hand, before his navel.   They
erect also upon the monuments of rich men, pyramids,
that is to say little sharp houses or pinnacles: and in some
places I saw mighty towers made of brick, in other places
pyramids made of stones, albeit there are no stones to be
found thereabout.   I saw one newly buried, in whose behalf
they hanged up sixteen horse hides, unto each quarter of
the world four, between certain high posts: and they set
beside his grave cosmos for him to drink, and flesh to eat:
and yet they said that he was baptized.   I beheld other
kinds of sepulchres also towards the east: namely large
flowers or pavements made of stone, some round and some

square, and then four long stones pitched upright, about
the said pavement towards the four regions of the world.
When any man is sick, he lieth in his bed, and causeth a
sign to be set upon his house, to signify that there lieth
a sick person there, to the end that no man may enter into
the said house: whereupon none at all visit any sick party
but his servant only.   Moreover, when any one is sick in
their great courts, they appoint watchmen to stand round
about the said court, who will not suffer any person to
enter within the precincts thereof.   For they fear lest evil
spirits or winds should come together with the parties that
enter in.   They esteem of soothsayers as of their priests.

CHAPTER XI

Of our first Entrance among the Tartars, and of
their Ingratitude

AND being come amongst those barbarous people, methought (as I said before) that I was entered into a new
world: for they came flocking about us on horseback,
after they had made us a long time to await for them,
sitting in the shadow under their black carts.   The first
question which they demanded was whether we had ever
been with them heretofore, or no?   And giving them
answer that we had not, they began impudently to beg our
victuals from us.   And we gave them some of our biscuit
and wine, which we had brought with us from the town of
Soldaia.   And having drunk off one flagon of our wine
they demanded another, saying, that a man goeth not into
the house with one foot.   Howbeit we gave them no
more, excusing ourselves that we had but a little.   Then
they asked us, whence we came, and whither we were
bound?   I answered them with the words above-mentioned:
that we had heard concerning Duke Sartach that he was
become a Christian, and that unto him our determination

was to travel, having your majesty's letters to deliver unto
him. They were very inquisitive to know whether I came
of mine own accord, or whether I were sent? I answered
that no man compelled me to come, neither had I come,
unless I myself had been willing: and that therefore I was
come according to mine own will, and to the will of my
superior. I took diligent heed never to say that I was
your majesty's ambassador. Then they asked what I had
in my carts; whether it were gold or silver, or rich garments to carry unto Sartach? I answered that Sartach should
see what we had brought, when we were once come unto
him, and that they had nothing to do to ask such questions,
but rather ought to conduct me unto their captain, and
that he, if he thought good, should cause me to be directed
unto Sartach: if not, that I would return. For there was
in the same province one of Baatu his kinsmen called
Scacati, unto whom my lord the Emperor of Constantinople had written letters of request to suffer me to pass
through his territory. With this answer of ours they
were satisfied, giving us horses and oxen, and two men to
conduct us. Howbeit before they would allow us the
foresaid necessaries for our journey, they made us to await
a long while, begging our bread for their young brats,
wondering at all things which they saw about our servants,
as their knives, gloves, purses, and points, and desiring to
have them. I excused myself that we had a long way to
travel, and that we must in no wise so soon deprive ourselves of things necessary to finish so long a journey.
Then they said that I was a very varlet. True it is that
they took nothing by force from me: howbeit they will
beg that which they see very importunately and shamelessly. And if a man bestow ought upon them, it is but
cost lost, for they are thankless wretches. They esteem
themselves lords and think that nothing should be denied
them by any man. If a man gives them nought, and
afterwards stands in need of their service, they will do
right nought for him. They gave us of their cows' milk
to drink after the butter was churned out of it, being
very sour, which they call apram. And so we departed

from them.   And in very deed it seemed to me that we
were escaped out of the hands of devils.   On the morrow
we were come unto the captain.   From the time wherein
we departed from Soldaia till we arrived at the court of
Sartach, which was the space of two months, we never lay
in house or tent, but always under the starry canopy, and
in the open air, or under our carts.   Neither yet saw we
any village, nor any mention of building where a village
had been, but the graves of the Comanians in great
abundance.   The same evening our guide which had conducted us gave us some cosmos.   After I had drunk
thereof I sweat most extremely for the novelty and
strangeness, because I never dranke of it before.   Notwithstanding methought it was very savoury, as indeed
it was.

CHAPTER XII

Of the Court of Scacatai: and how the Christians drink no
Cosmos

ON the morrow after we met with the carts of Scacatai
laden with houses, and methought that a mighty city came
to meet me.   I wondered also at the great multitude of
huge droves of oxen, and horses, and at the flocks of sheep.
I could see but a few men that guided all these matters :
whereupon I enquired how many men he had under him,
and they told me that he had not above 500 in all, the
one half of which number we were come past, as they lay
in another lodging.   Then the servant which was our
guide told me, that I must present somewhat unto Scacatay:
and so he caused us to stay, going himself before to
give notice of our coming.   By this time it was past
three of the clock, and they unladed their houses near
unto a certain water : and there came unto us his interpreter, who being advertised by us that we were never
there before, demanded some of our victuals, and we yielded

unto his request.   Also he required of us some garment
for a reward, because he was to interpret our sayings unto
his master.   Howbeit we excused ourselves as well as we
could.   Then he asked us, what we would present unto
his lord?   And we tooke a flagon of wine, and filled a
maund with biscuit, and a platter with apples and other
fruits.   But he was not contented therewith, because we
brought him not some rich garment.   Notwithstanding we
entered so into his presence with fear and bashfulness.   He
sat upon his bed holding a citron in his hand, and his wife
sat by him : who (as I verily think) had cut and pared her
nose between the eyes, that she might seem to be more flat
and saddle-nosed : for she had left herself no nose at all in
that place, having anointed the very same place with a
black ointment, and her eyebrows also : which sight seemed
most ugly in our eyes.   Then I rehearsed unto him the
same words, which I had spoken in other places before.
For it stood us in hand to use one and the same speech in
all places.   For we were well forewarned of this circum-
stance by some which had been amongst the Tartars, that
we should never vary in our tale.   Then I besought him,
that he would vouchsafe to accept that small gift at our
hands, excusing myself that I was a monk, and that it was
against our profession to possess gold, or silver, or precious
garments, and therefore that I had not any such thing to
give him, howbeit he should receive some part of our
victuals instead of a blessing.   Hereupon he caused our
present to be received, and immediately distributed the
same among his men, who were met together for the same
purpose, to drink and make merry.   I delivered also unto
him the Emperor of Constantinople his letters (this was
eight days after the feast of Ascension), who sent them
forthwith to Soldaia to have them interpreted there : for
they were written in Greek, and he had none about him
that was skilfull in the Greek tongue.   He asked us also
whether we would drink any cosmos, that is to say mares'
milk ?   (For those that are Christians among them, as
namely the Russians, Grecians, and Alanians, who keep
their own law very strictly, will in no case drink thereof,

yea, they account themselves no Christians after they have once drunk of it, and their priests reconcile them unto the church as if they had renounced the Christian faith.) I gave him answer, that we had as yet sufficient of our own to drink, and that when our drink failed us, we must be constrained to drink such as should be given unto us. He enquired also what was contained in our letters, which your majesty sent unto Sartach? I answered: that they were sealed up, and that there was nothing contained in them, but good and friendly words. And he asked what words we would deliver unto Sartach? I answered: the words of Christian faith. He asked again what these words were? For he was very desirous to hear them. Then I expounded unto him as well as I could, by mine interpreter (who had no wit nor any utterance of speech), the Apostles' creed. Which after he had heard, holding his peace, he shook his head. Then he assigned unto us two men, who should give attendance upon ourselves, upon our horses, and upon our oxen. And he caused us to ride in his company, till the messenger whom he had sent for the interpretation of the emperor's letters, was returned. And so we travelled in his company till the morrow after Pentecost.

CHAPTER XIII

How the Alanians came unto us on Pentecost or Whitsun Even

UPON the even of Pentecost, there came unto us certain Alanians, who are called Acias, being Christians after the manner of the Grecians, using Greek books and Grecian priests: howbeit they are not schismatics as the Grecians are, but without exception of persons, they honour all Christians. And they brought unto us sodden flesh, requesting us to eat of their meat, and to pray for one of their company being dead. Then I said, because it was the eve of so great and so solemn a feast day, that we would not eat any flesh for that time. And I expounded unto them the solemnity of the said feast, whereat they greatly rejoiced: for they were ignorant of all things appertaining to Christian religion, except only the name of Christ. They and many other Christians, both Russians and Hungarians, demanded of us, whether they might be saved or no, because they were constrained to drink cosmos, and to eat the dead carcases of such things as were slain by the Saracens and other infidels? Which even the Greek and Russian priests themselves also esteem as things strangled or offered unto idols: because they were ignorant of the times of fasting, neither could they have observed them albeit they had known them. Then instructed I them as well as I could and strengthened them in the faith. As for the flesh which they had brought we reserved it until the feast day. For there was nothing to be sold among the Tartars for gold and silver, but only for cloth and garments of the which kind of merchandise we had none at all. When our servants offered them any coin called yperpera, they rubbed it with their fingers, and put it unto their noses, to try by the smell whether it were copper or no. Neither did they allow us any food but cows' milk only, which was very sour and filthy. There was one thing most necessary greatly wanting unto us. For the water was so foul and muddy by reason of their horses, that it was not meet to be drunk. And but for certain biscuit, which was by the goodness of God remaining unto us, we had undoubtedly perished.

CHAPTER XIV

*Of a Saracen which said that he would be baptised:
and of certain Men which seemed to be Lepers*

UPON the day of Pentecost there came unto us a certain Saracen, unto whom, as he talked with us, we expounded the Christian faith. Who (hearing of God's benefits exhibited unto mankind by the incarnation of our Saviour Christ, and the resurrection of the dead, and the judgement to come, and that in baptism was a washing away of sins) said that he would be baptised. But when we prepared ourselves to the baptising of him, he suddenly mounted on horseback, saying that he would go home and consult with his wife what were best to be done. And on the morrow after he told us that he durst in no case receive baptism, because then he should drink no more cosmos. For the Christians of that place affirm that no true Christians ought to drink thereof : and that without the said liquor he could not live in that desert. From which opinion I could not for my life remove him. Wherefore be it known of a certainty unto your highness, that they are much estranged from the Christian faith by reason of that opinion, which hath been broached and confirmed among them by the Russians, of whom there is a great multitude in that place. The same day Scacatay the captain aforesaid gave us one man to conduct us to Sartach, and two other to guide us unto the next lodging, which was distant from that place five days' journey for oxen to travell. They gave unto us also a goat for victuals, and a great many bladders of cows' milk, and but a little cosmos, because it is of so great estimation among them. And so taking our journey directly toward the north, methought that we had passed through one of hell gates. The servants which conducted us began to play the bold thieves with us, seeing us take so little heed unto ourselves. At length having lost much by their thievery, harm taught us wisdom. And then we came unto the extremity of that province, which is fortified with a ditch from one sea unto another : without the bounds whereof their lodging was situate. Into the which, so soon as we had entered, all the inhabitants there seemed unto us to be infected with leprosy : for certain base fellows were placed there to receive tribute of all such as took salt out of the salt pits aforesaid. From that place they told us that we must travel fifteen days' journey, before we should find

any other people. With them we drank cosmos, and
gave unto them a basket full of fruits and of biscuit. And
they gave unto us eight oxen and one goat, to sustain us
in so great a journey, and I know not how many bladders
of milk. And so changing our oxen, we took our journey
which we finished in ten days, arriving at another lodging:
neither found we any water all that way, but only in
certain ditches made in the valleys, except two small rivers.

And from the time wherein we departed out of the foresaid
province of Gasaria, we travelled directly eastward, having
a sea on the south side of us, and a waste desert on the
north, which desert, in some places reacheth twenty days'
journey in breadth, and there is neither tree, mountain,
nor stone therein. And it is most excellent pasture.
Here the Comanians, which were called Capthac, were
wont to feed their cattle. Howbeit by the Dutchmen
they are called Valani, and the province itself Valania.
But Isidore calleth all that tract of land stretching from
the river of Tanais to the lake of Maeotis, and so long as
far as Danubius, the country of Alania. And the same
land continueth in length from Danubius unto Tanais
(which divideth Asia from Europe) for the space of two
months' journey, albeit a man should ride post as fast as
the Tartars use to ride : and it was all over inhabited by
the Comanians, called Capthac : yea and beyond Tanais as
far as the river of Edil or Volga : the space between the
two which rivers is a great and long journey to be travelled
in ten days. To the north of the same province lieth
Russia, which is full of wood in all places, and stretcheth
from Polonia and Hungaria, even to the river of Tanais :
and it hath been wasted all over by the Tartars, and as yet
is daily wasted by them. They prefer the Saracens before
the Russians, because they are Christians, and when they
are able to give them no more gold or silver, they drive
them and their children like flocks of sheep into the
wilderness, constraining them to keep their cattle there.
Beyond Russia lieth the country of Prussia, which the
Dutch knights of the order of Saint Mary's hospital of
Jerusalem have of late wholly conquered and subdued.

And in very deed they might easily win Russia, if they would put to their helping hand. For if the Tartars should but once know, that the great priest, that is to say the Pope, did cause the ensign of the cross to be displayed against them, they would flee all into their desert and solitary places.

CHAPTER XV

Of our Afflictions which we sustained: and of the Comanians'
Manner of Burial

WE therefore went on towards the east, seeing nothing but heaven and earth, and sometimes the sea on our right hand, called the sea of Tanais, and the sepulchres of the Comanians, which appeared unto us two leagues off, in which places they were wont to bury their kindred all together.   So long as we were travelling through the desert it went reasonably well with us.   For I cannot sufficiently express in words the irksome and tedious troubles which I sustained, when I came at any of their places of abode.   For our guide would have us go in unto every captain with a present, and our expenses would not extend so far.   For we were every day eight persons of us spending our wayfaring provision, for the Tartars' servants would all of them eat of our victuals.   We ourselves were five in number, and the servants our guides were three, two to drive our carts, and one to conduct us unto Sartach.   The flesh which they gave us was not sufficient for us: neither could we find anything to be bought for our money.   And as we sat under our carts in the cool shadow, by reason of the extreme and vehement heat which was there at that time, they did so importunately and shamelessly intrude themselves into our company, that they would even tread upon us to see whatsoever things we had.   Having list at any time to ease themselves, the filthy lozels had not the manners to withdraw

themselves farther from us than a bean can be cast. Yea,
like vile slovens they would lay their tails in our presence
while they were yet talking with us : many other things
they committed which were most tedious and loathsome
unto us. But above all things it grieved me to the very
heart, that when I would utter ought unto them which
might tend to their edification, my foolish interpreter
would say : You shall not make me become a preacher
now : I tell you I cannot, nor I will not, rehearse any such
words. And true it was which he said, For I perceived
afterward, when I began to have a little smattering in the
language, that when I spake one thing he would say quite
another, whatsoever came next unto his witless tongue's
end. Then seeing the danger I might incur in speaking
by such an interpreter, I resolved much rather to hold my
peace, and thus we travelled with great toil from lodging
to lodging, till at the length, a few days before the feast
of Saint Mary Magdalene, we arrived at the bank of the
mighty river Tanais which divideth Asia from Europe,
even as the river Nilus of Egypt disjoineth Asia from
Africa. At the same place where we arrived, Baatu and
Sartach did cause a certain cottage to be built upon the
eastern bank of the river, for a company of Russians to
dwell in, to the end they might transport ambassadors and
merchants in ferry boats over that part of the river. First
they ferried us over, and then our carts, putting one wheel
into one lighter and the other wheel into another lighter,
having bound both the lighters together, and so they row
them over.

In this place our guide played the fool most extremely.
For he, imagining that the said Russians, dwelling
in the cottage, should have provided us horses, sent
home the beasts which we brought with us, in another
cart, that they might return unto their own masters. And
when we demanded to have some beasts of them, they
answered that they had a privilege from Baatu, whereby
they were bound to none other service but only to ferry
over goers and comers : and that they received great
tribute of merchants in regard thereof. We stayed there-

fore by the said river's side three days. The first day
they gave unto us a great fresh turbot: the second day
they bestowed rye bread and a little flesh upon us, which
the purveyor of the village had taken up at every house
for us: and the third day dried fishes, which they have
there in great abundance. The said river was even as
broad in that place as the river of the Seine is at Paris.
And before we came there we passed over many goodly
waters, and full of fish: howbeit the barbarous and
rude Tartars know not how to take them: neither do
they make any reckoning of any fish, except it be so great
that they may prey upon the flesh thereof as upon the
flesh of a ram. The river is the limit of the east part
of Russia, and it springeth out of the fens of Maeotis,
which fens stretch unto the North Ocean. And it runneth
southward into a certain great sea 700 miles about before
it falleth into the sea called Pontus Euxinus. And all the
rivers which we passed over, ran with full stream into
those quarters. The foresaid river hath great store of
wood also growing upon the west side thereof. Beyond
this place the Tartars ascend no farther unto the north:
for at that season of the year, about the first of August,
they begin to return back unto the south. And therefore
there is another cottage somewhat lower, where passengers
are ferried over in winter time. And in this place we were
driven to great extremity, by reason that we could get
neither horses nor oxen for any money. At length, after
I had declared unto them that my coming was to labour for
the common good of all Christians, they sent us oxen and
men; howbeit we ourselves were fain to travel on foot. At
this time they were reaping their rye. Wheat prospereth
not well in that soil. They have the seed of millium in
great abundance. The Russian women attire their heads
like unto our women. They embroider their safeguards or
gowns on the outside, from their feet unto their knees,
with particoloured or grey stuff. The Russian men wear
caps like unto the Dutchmen. Also they wear upon their
heads certain sharp and high-crowned hats made of felt,
much like unto a sugar loaf.

Then travelled we three days together not finding any people. And when ourselves and our oxen were exceeding weary and faint, not knowing how far off we should find any Tartars, on the sudden there came two horses running towards us, which we took with great joy, and our guide and interpreter mounted upon their backs, to see how far off they could descry any people. At length upon the fourth day of our journey, having found some inhabitants, we rejoiced like seafaring men which had escaped out of a dangerous tempest, and had newly recovered the haven. Then having taken fresh horses and oxen, we passed on from lodging to lodging, till at the last, upon the second of the kalends of August, we arrived at the habitation of Duke Sartach himself.

CHAPTER XVI

Of the Dominion of Sartach and of his Subjects

THE region lying beyond Tanais is a very goodly country, having store of rivers and woods toward the north part thereof. There be mighty huge woods which two sorts of people do inhabit. One of them is called Moxel, being mere pagans and without law. They have neither towns nor cities, but only cottages in the woods. Their lord and a great part of themselves were put to the sword in high Germany. Whereupon they highly commend the brave courage of the Almans, hoping as yet to be delivered out of the bondage of the Tartars by their means. If any merchant come unto them, he must provide things necessary for him, with whom he is first of all entertained, all the time of his abode among them. If any lieth with another man's wife, her husband, unless he be an eye-witness thereof, regardeth it not : for they are not jealous over their wives. They have abundance of hogs, and great store of honey and wax, and divers sorts of rich and costly skins, and plenty of falcons. Next unto them

are other people called Merclas, which the Latins call
Merdui, and they are Saracens.   Beyond them is the river
of Etilia or Volga, which is the mightiest river that ever I
saw.   And it issueth from the north part of Bulgaria the
greater, and so trending along southward, disimboqueth
into a certain lake containing in circuit the space of
four months' travel, whereof I will speak hereafter.   The
two foresaid rivers, namely Tanais and Etilia, otherwise
called Volga, towards the northern regions through the
which we travelled, are not distant asunder above ten days'
journey, but southward they are divided a great space one
from another.   For Tanais descendeth into the sea of
Pontus : Etilia maketh the foresaid sea or lake, with the
help of many other rivers which fall thereinto out of Persia.
And we had to the south of us huge high mountains, upon
the sides whereof towards the said desert do the people
called Cergis, and the Alani or Acas inhabit, who are as
yet Christians and wage war against the Tartars.   Beyond
them, next unto the sea or lake of Etilia, there are certain
Saracens called Lesgi, who are in subjection unto the Tartars.
Beyond these is Porta Ferrea, or the iron gate, now called
Derbent, which Alexander built to exclude the barbarous
nations out of Persia.   Concerning the situation whereof,
your majesty shall understand more about the end of this
treatise : for I travelled in my return by the very same
place.   Between the two foresaid rivers, in the regions
through the which we passed did Comanians of old time
inhabit, before they were overrun by the Tartars.

CHAPTER XVII

Of the Court of Sartach, and of the Magnificence thereof

AND we found Sartach lying within three days' journey of
the river Etilia : whose court seemed unto us to be very
great.   For he himself had six wives, and his eldest son

also had three wives: every one of which women hath a great house, and they have each one of them about two hundred carts. Our guide went unto a certain Nestorian named Coiat, who is a man of great authority in Sartach's court. He made us to go very far unto the lord's gate. For so they call him who hath the office of entertaining ambassadors. In the evening Coiac commanded us to come unto him. Then our guide began to enquire what we would present him withall, and was exceedingly offended when he saw that we had nothing ready to present. We stood before him, and he sat majestically, having music and dancing in his presence. Then I spake unto him in the words before recited, telling him for what purpose I was come unto his lord, and requesting so much favour at his hands as to bring our letters unto the sight of his lord. I excused myself also, that I was a monk, not having, nor receiving, nor using any gold or silver, or any other precious thing, save only our books and the vestments wherein we served God: and that this was the cause why I brought no present unto him nor unto his lord. For I that had abandoned mine own goods, could not be a transporter of things for other men. Then he answered very courteously, that being a monk and so doing, I did well: for so I should observe my vow: neither did himself stand in need of ought that we had, but rather was ready to bestow upon us such thing as we ourselves stood in need of: and he caused us to sit down, and to drink of his milk. And presently after he requested us to say our devotions for him: and we did so. He enquired also who was the greatest prince among the Franks? And I said the emperor, if he could enjoy his own dominions in quiet. No (quoth he) but the King of France. For he had heard of your highness by Lord Baldwin of Henault. I found there also one of the Knights of the Temple, who had been in Cyprus, and had made report of all things which he saw there. Then returned we unto our lodging. And on the morrow we sent him a flagon of muscadel wine (which had lasted very well in so long a journey) and a box full of biscuit, which was most acceptable unto him. And he kept our servants with him for that evening. The next morning he commanded me to come unto the court, and to bring the king's letters and my vestments and books with me; because his lord was desirous to see them. Which we did accordingly, lading one cart with our books and vestments, and another with biscuit, wine and fruit. Then he caused all our books and vestments to be laid forth. And there stood round about us many Tartars, Christians and Saracens on horseback. At the sight whereof he demanded whether I would bestow all those things upon his lord or no? Which saying made me to tremble, and grieved me full sore. Howbeit, dissembling our grief as well as we could, we shaped him this answer: Sir, our humble request is, that our lord your master would vouchsafe to accept our bread, wine, and fruits, not as a present, because it is too mean, but as a benediction, lest we should come with an empty hand before him. And he shall see the letters of my sovereign lord the king, and by them he shall understand for what cause we are come unto him, and then both ourselves and all that we have shall stand to his courtesy: for our vestments be holy, and it is unlawful for any but priests to touch them.

Then he commanded us to invest ourselves in the said garments, that we might go before his lord: and we did so. Then I myself putting on our most precious ornaments, took in mine arms a very fair cushion, and the Bible which your majesty gave me, and a most beautiful psalter, which the queen's grace bestowed upon me, wherein there were goodly pictures. Mine associate took a missal and a cross: and the clerk having put on his surplice, took a censer in his hand. And so we came unto the presence of his lord: and they lifted up the felt hanging before his door, that he might behold us. Then they caused the clerk and the interpreter thrice to bow the knee: but of us they required no such submission. And they diligently admonished us to take heed that in going in, and in coming out, we touched not the threshold of the house, and requested us to sing a benediction for him. Then we entered in, singing *Salve Regina*. And within the entrance of the door stood a bench with cosmos and drinking cups thereupon. And all his wives were there assembled. Also the Moals, or rich Tartars, thrusting in with us pressed us sore. Then Coiat carried unto his lord the censer with incense, which he beheld very diligently, holding it in his hand. Afterward he carried the psalter unto him, which he looked earnestly upon, and his wife also that sat beside him. After that he carried the Bible : then Sartach asked if the Gospel were contained therein ? Yea (said I) and all the holy scriptures besides. He took the cross also in his hand, and demanded concerning the image whether it were the image of Christ or no ? I said it was. The Nestorians and the Armenians do never make the figure of Christ upon their crosses. Wherefore either they seem not to think well of his passion, or else they are ashamed of it. Then he caused them that stood about us to stand aside, that he might more fully behold our ornaments. Afterward I delivered unto him your majesty's letters, with translation thereof into the Arabic and Syriac languages. For I caused them to be translated at Acon into the character and dialect of both the said tongues. And there were certain Armenian priests which had skill in the Turkish and Arabian languages. The aforesaid knight also of the Order of the Temple had knowledge in the Syriac, Turkish, and Arabian tongues. Then we departed forth, and put off our vestments, and there came unto us certain scribes together with the foresaid Coiat, and caused our letters to be interpreted. Which letters being heard, he caused our bread, wine and fruits to be received. And he permitted us also to carry our vestments and books unto our own lodging. This was done upon the feast of St. Peter ad vincula.

CHAPTER XVIII

How they were given in charge to go unto Baatu the Father of Sartach

THE next morning betimes came unto us a certain priest who was brother unto Coiat, requesting to have our box of chrism, because Sartach (as he said) was desirous to see it : and so we gave it him.   About eventide Coiat sent for us, saying : My lord your king wrote good words unto my lord and master Sartach.   Howbeit there are certain matters of difficulty in them, concerning which he dare not determine aught, without the advice and counsel of his father.   And therefore of necessity you must depart unto his father, leaving behind you the two carts, which you brought hither yesterday with vestments and books, in my custody : because my lord is desirous to take more diligent view thereof.   I presently suspecting what mischief might ensue by his covetousness, said unto him ; Sir, we will not only leave those with you, but the two other carts also, which we have in our possession, will we commit unto your custody.   You shall not (quoth he) leave those behind you, but for the other two carts first named we will satisfy your request.   I said that this could not conveniently be done : but needs we must leave all with him.   Then he asked whether we meant to tarry in the land ?   I answered : If you thoroughly understand the letters of my lord the king, you know that we are even so determined.   Then he replied, that we ought to be patient and lowly : and so we departed from him that evening.   On the morrow after he sent a Nestorian priest for the carts, and we caused all the four carts to be delivered.   Then came the foresaid brother of Coiat to meet us, and separated all those things which we had brought the day before unto the court, from the rest, namely the books and vestments, and took them away with him.   Howbeit Coiat had commanded that we should carry those vestments with us which we wore in the presence of Sartach, that we might put them on before Baatu, if need should require: but the said priest took them from us by violence, saying: Thou hast brought them unto Sartach, and wouldst thou carry them unto Baatu? And when I would have rendered a reason he answered: Be not too talkative, but go your ways. Then I saw that there was no remedy but patience: for we could have no access unto Sartach himself, neither was there any other that would do us justice. I was afraid also in regard of the interpreter, lest he had spoken other things than I said unto him: for his will was good that we should have given away all that we had. There was yet one comfort remaining unto me: for when I once perceived their covetous intent, I conveyed from among our books the Bible, and the Sentences, and certain other books which I made special account of. Howbeit I durst not take away the psalter of my sovereign lady the queen, because it was too well known by reason of the golden pictures therein. And so we returned with the two other carts unto our lodging. Then came he that was appointed to be our guide unto the court of Baatu, willing us to take our journey in all post-haste: unto whom I said that I would in no case have the carts to go with me. Which thing he declared unto Coiat. Then Coiat commanded that we should leave them and our servant with him: and we did as he commanded. And so travelling directly eastward towards Baatu, the third day we came to Etilia or Volga: the streams whereof when I beheld, I wondered from what regions of the north such huge and mighty waters should descend. Before we were departed from Sartach, the foresaid Coiat, with many other scribes of the court said unto us: do not make report that our lord is a Christian, but a Moal. Because the name of a Christian seemeth unto them to be the name of some nation. So great is their pride, that albeit they believe perhaps some things concerning Christ, yet will they not be called Christians, being desirous that their own name, that is to say Moal, should be exalted above all other names. Neither will they be called by the name of Tartars. For

the Tartars were another nation, as I was informed by
them.

CHAPTER XIX

How Sartach, and Mangu-Can, and Ken-Can do Reverence unto Christians

At the same time when the French-men took Antioch,
a certain man named Con Can had dominion over the
northern regions, lying thereabouts.   Con is a proper
name : Can is a name of authority or dignity, which
signifieth a diviner or soothsayer.   All diviners are called
Can amongst them.   Whereupon their princes are called
Can, because that unto them belongeth the government of
the people by divination.   We do read also in the history
of Antiochia, that the Turks sent for aid against the
French-men unto the kingdom of Con Can.   For out
of those parts the whole nation of the Turks first came.
The said Con was of the nation of Kara-Catay.   Kara
signifieth black, and Katay is the name of a country.
So that Kara-Catay signifieth the black Catay.   This name
was given to make a difference between the foresaid people
and the people of Catay, inhabiting eastward over against
the ocean sea : concerning whom your majesty shall understand more hereafter.   These Catayans dwelt upon certain
Alps, by the which I travelled.   And in a certain plain
country within those Alps, there inhabited a Nestorian
shepherd, being a mighty governor over the people called
Yaymen, which were Christians, following the sect of
Nestorius.   After the death of Con Can, the said Nestorian
exalted himself to the kingdom, and they called him King
John, reporting ten times more of him than was true.   For
so the Nestorians which come out of those parts use to do.
For they blaze abroad great rumours and reports upon just
nothing.   Whereupon they gave out concerning Sartach
that he was become a Christian, and the like also they

reported concerning Mangu Can and Ken Can : namely
because these Tartars make more account of Christians
than they do of other people, and yet in very deed themselves are no Christians. So likewise there went forth
a great report concerning the said King John. Howbeit,
when I travelled along by his territories, there was no man
that knew anything of him, but only a few Nestorians. In
his pastures or territories dwelleth Ken Can, at whose
court Friar Andrew was. And I myself passed by it at
my return. This John had a brother, being a mighty
man also, and a shepherd like himself, called Vut, and he
inhabited beyond the Alps of Kara-Catay, being distant
from his brother John the space of three weeks' journey.
He was lord over a certain village called Cara Carum,
having people also for his subjects named Crit or Merkit,
who were Christians of the sect of Nestorius. But their
lord, abandoning the worship of Christ, followed after
idols, retaining with him priests of the said idols, who all
of them are worshippers of devils and sorcerers. Beyond
his pastures, some ten or fifteen days' journey, were the
pasture of Moal, who were a poor and beggarly nation,
without governor and without law, except their sooth-
sayings and their divinations, unto the which detestable
studies all in those parts do apply their minds. Near unto
Moal were other poor people called Tartars. The foresaid King John died without issue male, and thereupon his
brother Vut was greatly enriched, and caused himself to be
named Can ; and his droves and flocks ranged even unto
the borders of Moal. About the same time there was one
Cyngis, a blacksmith among the people of Moal. This
Cyngis stole as many cattle from Vut Can as he could
possibly get : insomuch that the shepherds of Vut com-
plained unto their lord. Then provided he an army, and
marched up into the country of Moal to seek for the said
Cyngis. But Cyngis fled among the Tartars, and hid
himself amongst them. And Vut having taken some
spoils both from Moal and also from the Tartars, returned
home. Then spake Cyngis unto the Tartars and unto the
people of Moal, saying : Sirs, because we are destitute of a

governor and captain, you see how our neighbours do oppress us.   And the Tartars and Moals appointed him to be their chieftain.   Then having secretly gathered together an army, he brake in suddenly upon Vut and overcame him, and Vut fled into Cataya.   At the same time was the daughter of Vut taken, which Cyngis married unto one of his sons, by whom she conceived and brought forth the great Can which now reigneth, called Mangu-Can.   Then Cyngis sent the Tartars before him in all places where he came : and thereupon was their name published and spread abroad : for in all places the people would cry out : Lo, the Tartars come, the Tartars come. Howbeit, through continual wars they are now, all of them in a manner, consumed and brought to nought.   Where-upon the Moals endeavour what they can to extinguish the name of the Tartars, that they may exalt their own name.   The country wherein they first inhabited, and where the court of Cyngis Can as yet remaineth, is called Mancherule.   But because Tartaria is the region about which they have obtained their conquests, they esteem that as their royal and chief city, and there for the most part do they elect their great Can.

CHAPTER XX

Of the Russians, Hungarians, and Alanians: and of the Caspian Sea

Now, as concerneth Sartach, whether he believes in Christ or no I know not.   This I am sure of, that he will not be called a Christian.   Yea rather he seemeth unto me to deride and scoff at Christians.   He lieth in the way of the Christians, as namely of the Russians, the Valachians, the Bulgarians of Bulgaria the lesser, the Soldaians, the Kerkis, and the Alanians : who all of them pass by him as they are going to the court of his father Baatu to carry gifts :

whereupon he is more in league with them. Howbeit if the Saracens come, and bring greater gifts than they, they are dispatched sooner. He hath about him certain Nestorian priests, who pray upon their beads and sing their devotions. Also there is another under Baatu, called Berta, who feedeth his cattle toward Porta Ferrea or Derbent, where lieth the passage of all those Saracens which come out of Persia and out of Turkey to go unto Baatu, and passing by they give rewards unto him. And he professeth himself to be a Saracen, and will not permit swine's flesh to be eaten in his dominions. Howbeit, at the time of our return Baatu commanded him to remove himself from that place, and to inhabit upon the east side of Volga: for he was unwilling that the Saracens' messengers should pass by the said Berta, because he saw it was not for his profit.

For the space of four days while we remained in the court of Sartach, we had not any victuals at all allowed us, but once only a little cosmos. And in our journey between him and his father we travelled in great fear. For certain Russians, Hungarians, and Alanians being servants unto the Tartars (of whom they have great multitudes among them) assemble themselves twenty or thirty in a company, and so secretly in the night conveying themselves from home, they take bows and arrows with them, and whomsoever they find in the night season they put him to death, hiding themselves in the day time. And having tired their horses, they go in the night unto a company of other horses feeding in some pasture, and change them for new, taking with them also one or two horses besides, to eat them when they stand in need. Our guide therefore was sore afraid lest we should have met with such companions. In this journey we had died for famine, had we not carried some of our biscuit with us. At length we came unto the mighty river of Etilia or Volga. For it is four times greater than the river of Seine, and of a wonderful depth: and issuing forth of Bulgaria the greater, it runneth into a certain lake or sea, which of late they call the Hircan Sea, according to the name of a certain city in Persia, standing upon the shore

thereof. Howbeit Isidore calleth it the Caspian Sea. For
it hath the Caspian mountains and the land of Persia
situate on the south side thereof: and the mountains of
Musihet, that is to say of the people called Assassini,
towards the east, which mountains are cojoined unto the
Caspian mountains: but on the north side thereof lieth
the same desert wherein the Tartars do now inhabit.
Howbeit heretofore there dwelt certain people called
Changlae. And on that side it receiveth the streams of
Etilia; which river increaseth in summer time, like unto
the river Nilus in Egypt. Upon the west part thereof it
hath the mountains of Alani, and Lesgi, and Porta Ferrea,
or Derbent, and the mountains of Georgia. This sea
therefore is compassed in on three sides with the mountains, but on the north side by plain ground. Friar
Andrew in his journey travelled round about two sides
thereof, namely, the south and the east sides: and I
myself about other two, that is to say the north side in
going from Baatu to Mangu-Can, and in returning likewise: and the west side in coming home from Baatu into
Syria. A man may travel round about it in four months.
And it is not true what Isidore reporteth, namely that this
sea is a bay or gulf coming forth of the ocean: for it
doth in no part thereof join with the ocean, but is environed
on all sides with land.

CHAPTER XXI

Of the Court of Baatu; and how we were entertained by him

ALL the region extending from the west shore of the foresaid sea, where Alexander's iron gate, otherwise called the
city of Derbent, is situate, and from the mountains of
Alaria, all along by the fens of Meotis, whereinto the
river of Tanais falleth, and so forth, to the North Ocean,
was wont to be called Albania. Of which country Isidore
reporteth, that there be dogs of such an huge stature, and

so fierce, that they are able in fight to match bulls, and to master lions. Which is true, as I understand by divers, who told me, that there towards the North Ocean they make their dogs to draw in carts like oxen, by reason of their bigness and strength. Moreover, upon that part of Etilia where we arrived, there is a new cottage built, wherein they have placed Tartars and Russians both together, to ferry over, and transport messengers going and coming to and fro the court of Baatu. For Baatu remaineth upon the farther side towards the east. Neither ascendeth he in summer time more northward than the foresaid place where we arrived, but was even then descending to the south. From January until August both he and all other Tartars ascend by the banks of rivers towards cold and northerly regions, and in August they begin to return back again. We passed down the stream therefore in a barque, from the foresaid cottage unto his court.

From the same place unto the villages of Bulgaria the greater, standing toward the north, it is five days' journey. I wonder what devil carried the religion of Mahomet thither. For, from Derbent, which is upon the extreme borders of Persia, it is about thirty days' journey to pass overthwart the desert, and so to ascend by the bank of Etilia, into the foresaid country of Bulgaria. All which way there is no city, but only certain cottages near unto that place where Etilia falleth into the sea. Those Bulgarians are most wicked Saracens, more earnestly professing the damnable religion of Mahomet, than any other nation whatsoever. Moreover, when I first beheld the court of Baatu, I was astonished at the sight there of : for his houses or tents seemed as though they had been some huge and mighty city, stretching out a great way in length, the people ranging up and down about it for the space of some three or four leagues. And even as the people of Israel knew every man, on which side of the tabernacle to pitch his tent : even so every one of them knoweth right well, towards which side of the court he ought to place his house when he takes it from off the cart. Whereupon the court is called in their language Horda, which signi-

fieth, the midst: because the governor or chieftain among
them dwells always in the midst of his people: except
only that towards the south no subject or inferior person
placeth himself, because towards that region the court
gates are set open: but unto the right hand, and the left
hand they extend themselves as far as they will, according
to the conveniency of places, so that they place not their
houses directly opposite against the court.   At our arrival
we were conducted unto a Saracen, who provided not
for us any victuals at all.   The day following, we were
brought unto the court: and Baatu had caused a great
tent to be erected, because his house or ordinary tent
could not contain so many men and women as were
assembled.   Our guide admonished us not to speak, till
Baatu had given us commandment so to do, and that then
we should speak our minds briefly.   Then Baatu demanded
whether your majesty had sent ambassadors unto him or
not; I answered, that your majesty had sent messengers to
Ken-Can: and that you would not have sent messengers
unto him, or letters unto Sartach, had not your highness
been persuaded that they were become Christians: because
you sent not unto them for any fear, but only for con-
gratulation, and courtesy's sake, in regard that you heard
they were converted to Christianity.   Then led he us unto
his pavilion: and we were charged not to touch the cords
of the tent, which they account in stead of the threshold of
the house.   There we stood in our habit bare-footed, and
bare-headed, and were a great and strange spectacle in
their eyes.   For indeed Friar John de Plano Carpini had
been there before my coming: howbeit, because he was
the pope's messenger, he changed his habit that he might
not be condemned.   Then we were brought into the very
midst of the tent, neither required they of us to do any
reverence by bowing our knees, as they use to do of other
messengers.   We stood therefore before him for the space
wherein a man might have rehearsed the psalm, Miserere
mei Deus: and there was great silence kept of all men.
Baatu himself sat upon a seat long and broad like unto
a bed, gilt all over, with three stairs to ascend thereunto,

and one of his ladies sat beside him. The men there assembled, sat down scattering, some on the right hand of the said lady, and some on the left. Those places on the one side which the women filled not up (for there were only the wives of Baatu) were supplied by the men. Also, at the very entrance of the tent, stood a bench furnished with cosmos, and with stately great cups of silver, and gold, being richly set with precious stones. Baatu beheld us earnestly, and we him : and he seemed to me to resemble in personage, Monsieur John de Beaumont, whose soul resteth in peace. And he had a fresh ruddy colour in his countenance. At length he commanded us to speak.

Then our guide gave us direction, that we should bow our knees and speak. Whereupon I bowed one knee as unto a man : then he signified that I should kneel upon both knees : and I did so, being loath to contend about such circumstances. And again he commanded me to speak. Then I thinking of prayer unto God, because I kneeled on both my knees, began to pray on this wise: Sir, we beseech the Lord, from whom all good things do proceed, and who hath given you these earthly benefits, that it would please him hereafter to make you partaker of his heavenly blessings : because the former without these are but vain and unprofitable. And I added further, Be it known unto you of a certainty, that you shall not obtain the joys of heaven, unless you become a Christian : for God saith, Whosoever believeth and is baptized, shall be saved ; but he that believeth not, shall be condemned. At this word he modestly smiled ; but the other Moals began to clap their hands, and to deride us. And my silly interpreter, of whom especially I should have received comfort in time of need, was himself abashed and utterly dashed out of countenance. Then after silence made, I said unto him, I came unto your son, because we heard that he was become a Christian : and I brought unto him letters on the behalf of my sovereign lord the King of France : and your son sent me hither unto you. The cause of my coming therefore is best known unto yourself. Then he caused me to rise up, and he inquired your majesty's name, and my name, and the name of my associate and interpreter, and caused them all to be put down in writing. He demanded likewise (because he had been informed, that you were departed out of your own country with an army) against whom you waged war. I answered : Against the Saracens, who had defiled the house of God at Jerusalem. He asked also, whether your highness had ever before that time sent any messengers unto him, or not. To you sir ? (said I). Never. Then caused he us to sit down, and gave us of his milk to drink, which they account to be a great favour, especially when any man is admitted to drink cosmos with him in his own house. And as I sat looking down upon the ground, he commanded me to lift up my countenance, being desirous as yet to take more diligent view of us, or else perhaps for a kind of superstitious observation. For they esteem it a sign of ill luck, or a prognostication of evil unto them, when any man sits in their presence, holding down his head, as if he were sad : especially when he leans his cheek or chin upon his hand. Then we departed forth, and immediately after came our guide unto us, and conducting us unto our lodging, said unto me : Your master the king requesteth that you may remain in this land, which request Baatu cannot satisfy without the knowledge and consent of Mangu-Can. Wherefore you, and your interpreter must of necessity go unto Mangu-Can. Howbeit your associate, and the other man shall return unto the court of Sartach, staying there for you, till you come back. Then began the man of God mine interpreter to lament, esteeming himself but a dead man. Mine associate also protested, that they should sooner chop off his head, than withdraw him out of my company. Moreover I myself said, that without mine associate I could not go ; and that we stood in need of two servants at the least, to attend upon us, because, if one should chance to fall sick, we could not be without another. Then returning unto the court, he told these sayings unto Baatu. And Baatu commanded saying : Let the two priests and the interpreter go together, but let the clerk return unto Sartach. And coming again unto us, he told us even so. And when I would have spoken for the clerk to have had him with us, he said: No more words, for Baatu hath resolved, that so it shall be, and therefore I dare not go unto the court any more. Goset the clerk had remaining of the alms money bestowed unto him, twenty-six yperperas, and no more: ten whereof he kept for himself and for the lad, and sixteen he gave unto the man of God for us. And thus were we parted asunder with tears: he returning unto the court of Sartach, and ourselves remaining still in the same place.

CHAPTER XXII

Of our Journey towards the Court of Mangu-Can

Upon Assumption even our clerk arrived at the court of Sartach. And on the morrow after, the Nestorian priests were adorned with our vestments in the presence of the said Sartach. Then we ourselves were conducted unto another host, who was appointed to provide us houseroom, victuals, and horses. But because we had not aught to bestow upon him, he did all things untowardly for us. Then we rode on forward with Baatu, descending along by the bank of Etilia, for the space of five weeks together: sometimes mine associate was so extremely hungry, that he would tell me in a manner weeping, that it fared with him as though he had never eaten any thing in all his life before. There is a fair or market following the court of Baatu at all times; but it was so far distant from us that we could not have recourse thereunto. For we were constrained to walk on foot for want of horses. At length certain Hungarians (who had some time been after a sort clergymen) found us out: and one of them could as yet sing many songs without book, and was accounted of other Hungarians as a priest, and was sent for unto the funerals of his deceased country men. There was another of them also prettily well instructed in his grammar: for he could understand the meaning of anything that we spake, but could not answer us. These Hungarians were a great comfort unto us, bringing us cosmos to drink, yea, and sometimes flesh for to eat also : who, when they requested to have some books of us, and I had not any to give them (for indeed we had none, but only a Bible, and a breviary) it grieved me exceedingly. And I said unto them : Bring me some ink and paper, and I will write for you so long as we shall remain here; and they did so. And I copied out for them Horas beatae Virginis, and Officium defunctorum. Moreover, upon a certain day, there was a Comanian that accompanied us, saluting us in Latin, and saying : Saluite Domini. Wondering thereat, and saluting him again, I demanded of him, who had taught him that kind of salutation. He said that he was baptized in Hungaria by our friars, and that of them he had learned it. He said, moreover, that Baatu had inquired many things of him concerning us, and that he told him the estate of our order. Afterward I saw Baatu riding with his company, and all his subjects that were householders or masters of families riding with him, and (in my estimation) they were not five hundred persons in all.

At length about the end of Holy rood, there came a certain rich Moal unto us (whose father was a millenary, which is a great office among them) saying : I am the man that must conduct you unto Mangu-Can, and we have thither a journey of four months long to travel; and there is such extreme cold in those parts, that stones and trees do even rive asunder in regard thereof. Therefore I would wish you throughly to advise yourselves, whether you be able to endure it or no. Unto whom I answered : I hope by God's help that we shall be able to brook that which other men can endure. Then he said : If you cannot endure it, I will forsake you by the way. And I answered him : It were not just dealing for you so to do : for we go not thither upon any business of our own, but by reason that we are sent by your lord. Wherefore since we are committed unto your charge, you ought in no wise to forsake us. Then he said : All shall be well. Afterward he

caused us to show him all our garments: and whatsoever
he deemed to be less needful for us, he willed us to leave
it behind in the custody of our host.   On the morrow
they brought unto each of us a furred gown, made all of
ram's skins, with the wool still upon them, and breeches
of the same, and boots also of buskins according to their
fashion, and shoes made of felt, and hoods also made of
skins after their manner.   The second day after Holy
rood, we began to set forward on our journey, having
three guides to direct us : and we rode continually eastward, till the feast of All Saints.   Throughout all that
region, and beyond also did the people of Changle inhabit,
who were by parentage descended from the Romans.
Upon the north side of us, we had Bulgaria the greater,
and on the south, the foresaid Caspian Sea.

CHAPTER XXIII

Of the River of Jagac: and of divers Regions or Nations

HAVING travelled twelve days' journey from Etilia, we
found a mighty river called Jagac: which river issuing out
of the north, from the land of Pascatir, descendeth into
the foresaid sea.   The language of Pascatir, and of the
Hungarians is all one, and they are all of them shepherds,
not having any cities.   And their country bordereth upon
Bulgaria the greater, on the west frontier thereof.   From
the north-east part of the said country, there is no city at
all.   For Bulgaria the greater is the farthest country that
way, that hath any city therein.   Out of the forenamed
region of Pascatir, proceeded the Hunnes of old time, who
afterward were called Hungarians.   Next unto it is Bulgaria
the greater.   Isidore reporteth concerning the people of
this nation, that with swift horses they traversed the im-
pregnable walls and bounds of Alexander (which, together
with the rocks of Caucasus, served to restrain those barbarous

and blood-thirsty people from invading the regions of the south), insomuch that they had tribute paid unto them, as far as Egypt. Likewise they wasted all countries even unto France. Whereupon they were more mighty than the Tartars as yet are. And unto them the Blacians, the Bulgarians, and the Vandals joined themselves. For out of Bulgaria the greater, came those Bulgarians. Moreover, they which inhabit beyond Danubius, near unto Constantinople, and not far from Pascatir, are called Ilac, which (saving the pronunciation) is all one with Blac (for the Tartars cannot pronounce the letter B), from whom also descended the people which inhabit the land of Assani. For they are both of them called Ilac (both these, and the other) in the languages of the Russians, the Polonians, and the Bohemians. The Sclavonians speak all one language with the Vandals, all which banded themselves with the Hunnes: and now for the most part, they unite themselves unto the Tartars: whom God hath raised up from the utmost parts of the earth, according to that which the Lord saith: I will provoke them to envy (namely such as keep not his law) by a people, which is no people, and by a foolish nation will I anger them. This prophecy is fulfilled, according to the literal sense thereof, upon all nations which observe not the law of God. All this which I have written concerning the land of Pascatir, was told me by certain friars Praedicants, which travelled thither before ever the Tartars came abroad. And from that time they were subdued unto their neighbours the Bulgarians, being Saracens, whereupon many of them proved Saracens also. Other matters concerning this people, may be known out of chronicles. For it is manifest, that those provinces beyond Constantinople, which are now called Bulgaria, Valachia, and Sclavonia, were of old time provinces belonging to the Greeks. Also Hungaria was heretofore called Pannonia. And we were riding over the land of Cangle, from the feast of Holy rood, until the feast of All Saints: travelling almost every day (according to mine estimation) as far as from Paris to Orleans, and sometimes farther, as we were provided of post horses: for some days we had change of horses twice or thrice in a day. Sometimes we travelled two or three days together, not finding any people, and then we were constrained not to ride so fast. Of twenty or thirty horses we had always the worst, because we were strangers. For every one took their choice of the best horses before us. They provided me always of a strong horse, because I was very corpulent and heavy: but whether he ambled a gentle pace or no, I durst not make any question. Neither yet durst I complain, although he trotted full sore. But every man must be contented with his lot as it fell. Whereupon we were exceedingly troubled for oftentimes our horses were tired before we could come at any people. And then we were constrained to beat and whip on our horses, and to lay our garments upon other empty horses: yea and sometimes two of us to ride upon one horse.

CHAPTER XXIV

Of the Hunger and Thirst, and other Miseries, which we sustained in our Journey

OF hunger and thirst, cold and weariness, there was no end. For they gave us no victuals, but only in the evening. In the morning they used to give us a little drink, or some sodden millet to sup off. In the evening they bestowed flesh upon us, as namely, a shoulder and breast of ram's mutton, and every man a measured quantity of broth to drink. When we had sufficient of the flesh broth, we were marvellously well refreshed. And it seemed to me most pleasant, and most nourishing drink. Every Saturday I remained fasting until night, without eating or drinking of aught. And when night came I was constrained, to my great grief and sorrow, to eat flesh. Sometimes we were fain to eat flesh half sodden, or almost raw, and all for want of fuel to seethe it withal; especially when we lay in the

fields, or were benighted before we came at our journey's
end: because we could not then conveniently gather
together the dung of horses or oxen: for other fuel
we found but seldom, except perhaps a few thorns in
some places.   Likewise upon the banks of some rivers,
there are woods growing here and there.   Howbeit they
are very rare.   In the beginning our guide highly disdained us, and it was tedious unto him to conduct such
base fellows.   Afterward, when he began to know us
somewhat better, he directed us on our way by the
courts of rich Moals, and we were requested to pray
for them.   Wherefore, had I carried a good interpreter
with me, I should have had opportunity to have done
much good.   The foresaid Chingis, who was the first
great Can or Emperor of the Tartars, had four sons,
of whom proceeded by natural descent many children,
every one of which doth at this day enjoy great
possessions: and they are daily multiplied and dispersed
over that huge and waste desert, which is, in dimensions,
like unto the ocean sea.   Our guide therefore directed
us, as we were going on our journey, unto many of
their habitation.   And they marvelled exceedingly, that
we would receive neither gold, nor silver, nor precious
and costly garments at their hands.   They inquired also,
concerning the great Pope, whether he was of so lasting
an age as they had heard.   For there had gone a report
among them, that he was five hundred years old.   They
inquired likewise of our countries, whether there were
abundance of sheep, oxen, and horses or no: concerning the Ocean sea, they could not conceive of it, because
it was without limits or banks.

Upon the even of the feast of All Saints, we forsook
the way leading towards the east (because the people were
now descended very much south), and we went on our
journey by certain alps, or mountains, directly southward,
for the space of eight days together.   In the foresaid desert
I saw many asses (which they call colan) being rather like
unto mules; these did our guide and his companions
chase very eagerly; howbeit, they did but lose their

labour ; for the beasts were too swift for them.   Upon the seventh day there appeared to the south of us huge high mountains, and we entered into a place which was well watered, and fresh as a garden, and found land tilled and manured.   The eighth day after the feast of All Saints, we arrived at a certain town of the Saracens, named Kenchat, the governor whereof met our guide at the town's end with ale and cups.   For it is their manner at all towns and villages, subject unto them, to meet the messengers of Baatu and Mangu-Can with meat and drink.   At the same time of the year, they went upon the ice in that country.   And before the feast of S. Michael, we had frost in the desert.   I inquired the name of that province : but being now in a strange territory, they could not tell me the name thereof, but only the name of a very small city in the same province.   And there descended a great river down from the mountains, which watered the whole region, according as the inhabitants would give it passage, by making divers channels and sluices : neither did this river exonerate itself into any sea, but was swallowed up by an hideous gulf into the bowels of the earth : and it caused many fens or lakes.   Also I saw many vines, and drank of the wine thereof.

CHAPTER XXV

How Ban was put to Death : and concerning the Habitation of the Dutch Men

THE day following, we came unto another cottage near unto the mountains.   And I inquired what mountains they were, which I understood to be the mountains of Caucasus, which are stretched forth, and continued on both parts to the sea, from the west unto the east; and on the west part they are conjoined unto the foresaid Caspian Sea, whereinto the river of Volga dischargeth his streams.   I inquired also of the city of Talas, wherein were certain Dutchmen, servants unto one Buri, of whom Friar Andrew made mention.   Concerning whom also I inquired very diligently in the courts of Sartach and Baatu.   Howbeit, I could have no intelligence of them, but only that their lord and master Ban was put to death upon the occasion following.   This Ban was not placed in good and fertile pastures.   And upon a certain day being drunken, he spake on this wise unto his men.   Am not I of the stock and kindred of Chingis Can, as well as Baatu ? (for in very deed he was brother or nephew unto Baatu).   Why then do I not pass and repass upon the bank of Etilia, to feed my cattle there, as freely as Baatu himself doeth ?   Which speeches of his were reported unto Baatu.   Whereupon Baatu wrote unto his servants to bring their lord bound unto him.   And they did so.   Then Baatu demanded of him whether he had spoken any such words.   And he confessed that he had.   Howbeit (because it is the Tartars' manner to pardon drunken men), he excused himself that he was drunken at the same time.   How durst thou (quoth Baatu) once name me in thy drunkenness ?   And with that he caused his head to be chopped off.   Concerning the foresaid Dutchmen, I could not understand aught, till I was come unto the court of Mangu-Can.   And there I was informed that Mangu-Can had removed them out of the jurisdiction of Baatu, for the space of a month's journey from Talas, eastward, unto a certain village, called Bolac: where they are set to dig gold, and to make armour.   Whereupon I could neither go nor come by them.   I passed very near the said city in going forth, as namely, within three days' journey thereof: but I was ignorant that I did so : neither could I have turned out of my way, albeit I had known so much.

From the foresaid cottage we went directly eastward, by the mountains aforesaid.   And from that time we travelled among the people of Mangu-Can, who in all places sang and danced before our guide, because he was the messenger of Baatu.   For this courtesy they do afford each to other ; namely, the people of Mangu-Can receiving the messengers of Baatu in manner aforesaid : and so likewise the people of Baatu entertaining the messengers of Mangu-Can. Notwithstanding the people of Baatu are more surly and stout, and show not so much courtesey unto the subjects of Mangu-Can, as they do unto them. A few days after, we entered upon those alps where the Cara Catayans were wont to inhabit. And there we found a mighty river : insomuch that we were constrained to imbarque ourselves, and to sail over it. Afterward we came into a certain valley, where I saw a castle destroyed, the walls whereof were only of mud : and in that place the ground was tilled also. And there we found a certain village, named Equius, wherein were Saracens, speaking the Persian language : howbeit they dwelt an huge distance from Persia. The day following, having passed over the foresaid alps, which descended from the great mountains southward, we entered into a most beautiful plain, having high mountains on our right hand, and on the left hand of us a certain sea or lake, which containeth fifteen days' journey in circuit. All the foresaid plain is most commodiously watered with certain freshets distilling from the said mountains, all which do fall into the lake. In summer time we returned by the north shore of the said lake, and there were great mountains on that side also. Upon the forenamed plain there were wont to be great store of villages : but for the most part they were all wasted, in regard of the fertile pastures, that the Tartars might feed their cattle there. We found one great city there named Cailac, wherein was a mart, and great store of merchants frequenting it. In this city we remained fifteen days, staying for a certain scribe or secretary of Baatu, who ought to have accompanied our guide for the despatching of certain affairs in the court of Mangu. All this country was wont to be called Organum ; and the people thereof had their proper language, and their peculiar kind of writing. But it was altogether inhabited of the people called Contomanni.

The Nestorians likewise in those parts used the very same kind of language and writing. They are called Organa, because they were wont to be most skilful in playing upon the organs or cithern, as it was reported unto me. Here first did I see worshippers of idols, concerning whom, be it known unto your majesty, that there be many sects of them in the east countries.

CHAPTER XXVI

How the Nestorians, Saracens, and Idolaters are joined together

THE first sort of these idolaters are called Jugures: whose land bordered upon the foresaid land of Organum, within the said mountains eastward: and in all their cities Nestorians do inhabit together, and they are dispersed likewise towards Persia in the cities of the Saracens. The citizens of the foresaid city of Cailac had three idol temples; and I entered into two of them, to behold their foolish superstitions. In the first of which I found a man having a cross painted with ink upon his hand, whereupon I supposed him to be a Christian: for he answered like a Christian unto all questions which I demanded of him. And I asked him, why therefore have you not the cross with the image of Jesu Christ thereupon? And he answered; We have no such custom. Whereupon I conjectured that they were indeed Christians; but, that for lack of instruction they omitted the foresaid ceremony. For I saw there behind a certain chest (which was unto them instead of an altar, whereupon they set candles and oblations) an image having wings like unto the image of Saint Michael, and other images also, holding their fingers, as if they would bless some body. That evening I could not find anything else. For the Saracens do only invite men thither, but they will not have them speak of their religion. And therefore, when I inquired of the Saracens concerning such ceremonies, they were offended thereat. On the morrow after were the Kalends, and the Saracens' feast of Passover. And changing mine inn or lodging the same day, I took up mine abode near unto another idol-temple. For the citizens of the said city of Cailac do courteously invite, and lovingly entertain all messengers, every man of them according to his ability and portion. And entering into the foresaid idol-temple, I found the priests of the said idols there. For always at the Kalends they set open their temples, and the priests adorn themselves, and offer up the people's oblation of bread and fruits. First therefore I will describe unto you those rites and ceremonies, which are common unto all their idol-temples: and then the superstitions of the foresaid Jugures, which be, as it were, a sect distinguished from the rest. They do all of them worship towards the north, clapping their hands together, and prostrating themselves on their knees upon the earth, holding also their foreheads in their hands. Whereupon the Nestorians of those parts will in no case join their hands together in time of prayer: but they pray, displaying their hands before their breasts. They extend their temples in length east and west; and upon the north side they build a chamber, in manner of a vestry, for themselves to go forth into. Or sometimes it is otherwise. If it be a four square temple, in the midst of the temple, towards the north side thereof, they take in one chamber in that place where the choir should stand. And within the said chamber they place a chest long and broad like unto a table: and behind the said chest towards the south stands their principal idol: which I saw at Caracarum, and it was as big as the idol of Saint Christopher. Also a certain Nestorian priest, which had been in Catay, said that in that country there is an idol of so huge a bigness, that it may be seen two days' journey before a man come at it. And so they place other idols round about the foresaid principal idol, being all of them finely gilt over with pure gold: and upon the said chest, which is in manner of a table,

they set candles and oblations.   The doors of their temples
are always opened towards the south, contrary to the
custom of the Saracens.   They have also great bells like
unto us.   And that is the cause (as I think) why the
Christians of the east will in no case use great bells.
Notwithstanding they are common among the Russians,
and Grecians of Gasaria.

CHAPTER XXVII

*Of their Temples and Idols: and how they behave them-
selves in Worshipping their False Gods*

ALL their priests had their heads and beards shaven quite
over: and they are clad in saffron coloured garments: and
being once shaven, they lead an unmarried life from that
time forward: and they live an hundred or two hundred
of them together in one cloister or convent.   Upon those
days when they enter into their temples, they place two
long forms therein: and so sitting upon the said forms like
singing men in a choir, namely the one half of them directly
over against the other, they have certain books in their
hands, which sometimes they lay down by them upon the
forms: and their heads are bare so long as they remain in
the temple.   And there they read softly unto themselves,
not uttering any voice at all.   Whereupon coming in
amongst them, at the time of their superstitious devotions,
and finding them all sitting mute in manner aforesaid, I
attempted divers ways to provoke them unto speech, and
yet could not by any means possible.   They have with
them also whithersoever they go, a certain string with an
hundred or two hundred nutshells thereupon, much like to
our bead-roll which we carry about with us.   And they do
always utter these words: Ou mam Hactani, God thou
knowest; as one of them expounded it unto me.   And so
often do they expect a reward at God's hands, as they

pronounce these words in remembrance of God. Round about their temple they do always make a fair court, like unto a churchyard, which they environ with a good wall: and upon the south part thereof they build a great portal, wherein they sit and confer together. And upon the top of the said portal they pitch a long pole right up, exalting it, if they can, above all the whole town besides. And by the same pole all men may know, that there stands the temple of their idols. These rites and ceremonies aforesaid be common unto all idolaters in those parts.

Going upon a time towards the foresaid idol-temple, I found certain priests sitting in the outward portal. And those which I saw, seemed unto me, by their shaven beards, as if they had been Frenchmen. They wore certain ornaments upon their heads made of paper. The priests of the foresaid Jugures do use such attire whithersoever they go. They are always in their saffron coloured jackets, which be very straight being laced or buttoned from the bosom right down, after the French fashion. And they have a cloak upon their left shoulder descending before and behind under their right arm, like unto a deacon carrying the housel-box in time of Lent. Their letters or kind of writing the Tartars did receive. They begin to write at the top of their paper drawing their lines right down: and so they read and multiply their lines from the left hand to the right. They do use certain papers and characters in their magical practices. Whereupon their temples are full of such short scrolls hung round about them. Also Mangu-Can hath sent letters unto your majesty written in the language of the Moals or Tartars, and in the foresaid hand or letter of the Jugures. They burn their dead according to the ancient custom, and lay up the ashes in the top of a pyramis. Now, after I had sat a while by the foresaid priests, and entered into their temple and seen many of their images both great and small, I demanded of them what they believed concerning God: and they answered: We believe that there is only one God. And I demanded further: Whether do you believe that he is a spirit or some bodily substance? They said: We believe that he is a spirit. Then said I: Do you believe

that God ever took man's nature upon him? They
answered: No.   And again I said: Since ye believe that
he is a spirit, to what end do you make so many bodily
images to represent him?   Since also you believe not that
he was made man: Why do you resemble him rather unto
the image of a man than of any other creature?   Then they
answered saying: We frame not those images whereby to
represent God.   But when any rich man amongst us, or
his son, or his wife, or any of his friends deceaseth, he
causeth the image of the dead party to be made, and to be
placed here: and we in remembrance of him do reverence
thereunto.   Then I replied: You do these things only for
the friendship and flattery of men.   No (said they) but
for their memory.   Then they demanded of me, as it
were in scoffing wise: Where is God?   To whom I
answered: Where is your soul.   They said, in our bodies.
Then said I, Is it not in every part of your body, ruling
and guiding the whole body, and yet notwithstanding is
not seen or perceived?   Even so God is everywhere and
ruleth all things, and yet is he invisible, being understanding and wisdom itself.   Then being desirous to have had
some more conference with them, by reason, that mine
interpreter was weary, and not able to express my meaning,
I was constrained to keep silence.

The Moals or Tartars are in this regard of their sect:
namely they believe that there is but one God: howbeit
they make images of felt, in remembrance of their deceased
friends, covering them with five most rich and costly garments, and putting them into one or two carts, which carts
no man dare once touch: and they are in the custody of
their soothsayers, who are their priests, concerning whom
I will give your highness more at large to understand
hereafter.   These soothsayers or diviners do always attend
upon the court of Mangu and of other great personages.
As for the poorer or meaner sort, they have them not, but
such only as are of the stock and kindred of Chingis.   And
when they are to remove or to take any journey, the said
diviners go before them, even as the cloudy pillar went before
the children of Israel.   And they appoint ground where

the tents must be pitched, and first of all they take down their own houses : and after them the whole court doth the like. Also upon their festival days or kalends they take forth the foresaid images, and place them in order round, or circle wise within the house. Then come the Moals or Tartars, and enter into the same house, bowing themselves before the said images and worship them. Moreover, it is not lawful for any stranger to enter into that house. For upon a certain time I myself would have gone in, but I was chidden full well for my labour.

CHAPTER XXVIII

Of Divers and Sundry Nations: and of certain People which were wont to eat their own Parents

BUT the foresaid Jugures (who live among the Christians, and the Saracens) by their sundry disputations, as I suppose, have been brought unto this, to believe, that there is but one only God. And they dwell in certain cities, which afterward were brought in subjection unto Chingis Can : whereupon he gave his daughter in marriage unto their king. Also the city of Caracarum itself is in a manner within their territory : and the whole country of king or Presbyter John, and of his brother Vut lieth near unto their dominions : saying that they inhabit in certain pastures northward, and the said Jugures between the mountains towards the south. Whereupon it came to pass, that the Moals received letters from them. And they are the Tartars' principal scribes : and all the Nestorians almost can skill of their letters. Next unto them, between the foresaid mountains eastward, inhabiteth the nation of Tangur, who are a most valiant people, and took Chingis in battle. But after the conclusion of a league he was set at liberty by them, and afterwards subdued them. These people of Tangut have oxen of great strength, with tails like unto horses, and with long shaggy hair upon their backs and bellies.   They have legs greater than other oxen have, and they are exceedingly fierce. These oxen draw the great houses of the Moals : and their horns are slender, long, straight, and most sharp pointed : insomuch that their owners are fain to cut off the ends of them.   A cow will not suffer herself to be coupled unto one of them, unless they whistle or sing unto her.   They have also the qualities of a buffe, for if they see a man clothed in red, they run upon him immediately to kill him.

Next unto them are the people of Teber, men which were wont to eat the carcases of their deceased parents ; that for pities' sake, they might make no other sepulchre for them, than their own bowels.   Howbeit, of late they have left off this custom, because that thereby they became abominable and odious unto all other nations.   Notwithstanding unto this day they make fine cups of the skulls of their parents, to the end that when they drink out of them, they may amidst all their jollities and delights call their dead parents to remembrance.   This was told me by one that saw it.   The said people of Teber have great plenty of gold in their land.   Whosoever therefore wanteth gold, diggeth till he hath found some quantity, and then taking so much thereof as will serve his turn, he layeth up the residue within the earth : because, if he should put it into his chest or storehouse he is of opinion that God would withhold from him all other gold within the earth.   I saw some of those people, being very deformed creatures.   In Tangut I saw lusty tall men, but brown and swart in colour.   The Jugures are of a middle stature like unto our Frenchmen.   Amongst the Jugures is the original and root of the Turkish, and Comanian languages.   Next unto Teber are the people of Langa and Solanga, whose messengers I saw in the Tartars' court.   And they had brought more than ten great carts with them, every one of which was drawn with six oxen.   They be little brown men like unto Spaniards.   Also they have jackets, like unto the upper vestment of a deacon, saving that the sleeves are somewhat straighter.   And they have mitres

upon their heads like bishops. But the fore part of their
mitre is not so hollow within as the hinder part: neither is
it sharp pointed or cornered at the top: but there hang
down certain square flaps compacted of a kind of straw
which is made rough and rugged with extreme heat, and is
so trimmed, that it glittereth in the sun beams, like unto a
glass, or an helmet well burnished. And about their
temples they have long bands of the foresaid matter
fastened unto their mitres, which hover in the wind as if
two long horns grew out of their heads. And when the
wind tosseth them up and down too much, they tie them
over the midst of their mitre from one temple to another:
and so they lie circle wise overthwart their heads. Moreover their principal messenger coming into the Tartars'
court had a table of elephant's tooth about him of a cubit
in length, and a handful in breadth, being very smooth.
And whensoever he spake unto the emperor himself, or
unto any other great personage, he always beheld that
table, as if he had found therein those things which he
spake: neither did he cast his eyes to the right hand, nor
to the left, nor upon his face, with whom he talked. Yea,
going to and fro before his lord, he looketh nowhere but
only upon his table.

Beyond them (as I understand of a certainty) there
are other people called Muc, having villages, but no
one particular man of them appropriating any cattle unto
himself. Notwithstanding there are many flocks and
droves of cattle in their country, and no man appointed
to keep them. But when any one of them standeth
in need of any beast, he ascendeth up unto an hill, and
there maketh a shout, and all the cattle which are
within hearing of the noise, come flocking about him, and
suffer themselves to be handled and taken, as if they were
tame. And when any messenger or stranger cometh into
their country, they shut him up into an house, ministering
there things necessary unto him, until his business be
dispatched. For if any stranger should travel through
that country, the cattle would flee away at the very scent
of him, and so would become wild. Beyond Muc is great

Cathaya, the inhabitants whereof (as I suppose) were of old time, called Seres. For from them are brought most excellent stuffs of silk. And this people is called Seres of a certain town in the same country. I was credibly informed, that in the said country, there is one town having walls of silver, and bulwarks or towers of gold. There be many provinces in that land, the greater part whereof are not as yet subdued unto the Tartars.

⁎ The copy of the Latin narrative of William de Rubruquis to which Hakluyt had access ended here, and he was therefore unable to translate the remaining chapters. These contain very few illustrations of the Travels of Mandeville.

THE JOURNAL OF FRIAR ODORIC

*Here beginneth the Journal of Friar Odoricus, of the Order of
the Minorites, concerning Strange Things which he saw
among the Tartars of the East*

ALBEIT many and sundry things are reported by divers
authors concerning the fashions and conditions of this
world : notwithstanding I Friar Odoricus of Friuli, de
portu Vahonis, being desirous to travel unto the foreign
and remote nations of infidels, saw and heard great and
miraculous things, which I am able truly to avouch. First of
all therefore sailing from Pera by Constantinople, I arrived
at Trapesunda. This place is right commodiously situate,
as being an haven for the Persians and Medes, and other
countries beyond the sea. In this land I beheld with great
delight a very strange spectacle, namely a certain man
leading about with him more than four thousand partridges.
The man himself walked upon the ground, and the partridges flew in the air, which he led unto a certain castle
called Zauena, being three days' journey distant from
Trapesunda. The said partridges were so tame, that when
the man was desirous to lie down and rest they would all
come flocking about him like chickens. And so he led
them unto Trapesunda, and unto the palace of the emperor,
who took as many of them as he pleased, and the rest the
said man carried unto the place from whence he came. In
this city lyeth the body of Athanasius upon the gate of the
city. And then I passed on further unto Armenia major,

326

to a certain city called Azaron, which had been very rich in old time, but now the Tartars have almost laid it waste. In the said city there was abundance of bread and flesh, and of all other victuals except wine and fruits. This city also is very cold, and is reported to be higher situated, than any other city in the world. It hath most wholesome and sweet waters about it ; for the veins of the said waters seem to spring and flow from the mighty river of Euphrates, which is but a day's journey from the said city. Also, the said city stands directly in the way to Tauris. And I passed on unto a certain mountain called Sobissacalo. In the foresaid country there is the very same mountain whereupon the Ark of Noah rested: unto the which I would willingly have ascended, if my company would have stayed for me. Howbeit, the people of that country report, that no man could ever ascend the said mountain, because (say they) it pleaseth not the highest God. And I travelled on further unto Tauris that great and royal city, which was in old time called Susis. This city is accounted for traffic of merchandise the chief city of the world : for there is no kind of victuals, nor anything else belonging unto merchandise, which is not to be had there in great abundance. This city stands very commodiously, for unto it all the nations of the whole world in a manner may resort for traffic. Concerning the said city, the Christians in those parts are of opinion, that the Persian Emperor receives more tribute out of it, than the King of France out of all his dominions. Near unto the said city there is a salt-hill yielding salt unto the city : and of that salt each man may take what pleaseth him, not paying aught to any man therefore. In this city many Christians of all nations do inhabit, over whom the Saracens bear rule in all things.

Then I travelled on further unto a city called Soldania, wherein the Persian Emperor lieth all summer time : but in winter he takes his progress unto another city standing upon the sea called Baku. Also the foresaid city is very great and cold, having good and wholesome waters therein, unto the which also store of merchandise is brought. Moreover I travelled with a certain company of caravans toward upper India : and in the way, after many days' journey, I came unto the city of the three Wise Men called Cassan, which is a noble and renowned city, saving that the Tartars have destroyed a great part thereof : and it aboundeth with bread, wine, and many other commodities. From this city unto Jerusalem (whither the three foresaid Wise Men were miraculously led) it is fifty days' journey. There be many wonders in this city also, which, for brevity's sake, I omit. From thence I departed unto a certain city called Geste, whence the Sea of Sand is distant, one day's journey, which is a most wonderful and dangerous thing. In this city there is abundance of all kinds of victuals, and especially of figs, raisins, and grapes : more (as I suppose) than in any part of the whole world besides. This is one of the three principal cities in all the Persian Empire. Of this city the Saracens report, that no Christian can by any means live therein above a year. Then passing many days' journey on forward, I came unto a certain city called Comum, which was an huge and mighty city in old time, containing well nigh fifty miles in circuit, and hath done in times past great damage unto the Romans. In it there are stately palaces altogether destitute of inhabitants, notwithstanding it aboundeth with great store of victuals. From hence travelling through many countries, at length I came unto the land of Job named Hus, which is full of all kind of victuals, and very pleasantly situated. Thereabouts are certain mountains having good pastures for cattle upon them. Here also manna is found in great abundance. Four partridges are here sold for less than a groat. In this country there are most comely old men. Here also the men spin and card, and not the women. This land bordereth upon the north part of Chaldea.

CHAPTER II

Of the Manners of the Chaldaeans, and of India

FROM thence I travelled into Chaldea, which is a great
kingdom, and I passed by the tower of Babel. This
region hath a language peculiar unto itself, and there are
beautiful men, and deformed women. The men of the
same country use to have their hair kempt and trimmed
like unto women: and they wear golden turbans upon
their heads richly set with pearl, and precious stones.
The women are clad in a coarse smock only reaching to
their knees, and having long sleeves hanging down to the
ground. And they go bare-footed, wearing breeches
which reach to the ground also. They wear no attire
upon their heads, but their hair hang disheveled about
their ears; and there be many other strange things also.
From thence I came into the lower India, which the
Tartars overran and wasted. And in this country the
people eat dates for the most part, whereof forty-two lb.
are there sold for less than a groat. I passed further also
many days' journey unto the Ocean sea, and the first land
where I arrived, is called Ormes, being well fortified, and
having great store of merchandise and treasure therein.
Such and so extreme is the heat in that country, that the
privities of men come out of their bodies and hang down
even unto their mid-legs. And therefore the inhabitants
of the same place, to preserve their own lives, do make a
certain ointment, and anointing their privy members therewith, do lap them up in certain bags fastened unto their
bodies, for otherwise they must needs die. Here also
they use a kind of barque or ship called Iase being com-
pact together only with hemp. And I went on board into
one of them, wherein I could not find any iron at all,
and in the space of twenty-eight days I arrived at the city
of Thana, wherein four of our friars were martyred for
the faith of Christ. This country is well situate, having

abundance of bread and wine, and of other victuals therein.   This kingdom in old time was very large and under the dominion of King Porus, who fought a great battle with Alexander the Great.   The people of this country are idolaters worshipping fire, serpents and trees. And over all this land the Saracens do bear rule, who took it by main force, and they themselves are in subjection unto King Daldilus.   There be divers kinds of beasts, as namely black lions in great abundance, and apes also, and monkeys, and bats as big as doves.   Also there are mice as big as our country dogs, and therefore they are hunted with dogs, because cats are not able to encounter them. Moreover, in the same country every man hath a bundle of great boughs standing in a water-pot before his door, which bundle is as great as a pillar, and it will not wither, so long as water is applied thereunto : with many other novelties and strange things, the relation whereof would breed great delight.

CHAPTER III

How Pepper is had : and where it groweth

MOREOVER, that it may be manifest how pepper is had, it is to be understood that it groweth in a certain kingdom whereat I myself arrived, being called Minibar, and it is not so plentiful in any other part of the world as it is there.   For the wood wherein it grows containeth in circuit eighteen days' journey.   And in the said wood or forest there are two cities, one called Flandrina, and the other Cyncilim.   In Flandrina both Jews and Christians do inhabit, between whom there is often contention and war : howbeit the Christians overcome the Jews at all times.   In the foresaid wood pepper is had after this manner : first it groweth in leaves like unto pot-herbs, which they plant near unto great trees as we do our vines, and they bring forth pepper in clusters, as our vines do yield grapes, but being ripe, they are of a green colour, and are gathered as we gather grapes, and then the grains are laid in the sun to be dried, and being dried are put into earthen vessels : and thus is pepper made and kept. Now, in the same wood there be many rivers, wherein are great store of crocodiles, and of other serpents, which the inhabitants thereabout do burn up with straw and with other dry fuel, and so they go to gather their pepper without danger. At the south end of the said forests stands the city of Polumbrum, which aboundeth with merchandise of all kinds. All the inhabitants of that country do worship a living ox, as their god, whom they put to labour for six years, and in the seventh year they cause him to rest from all his work, placing him in a solemn and public place, and calling him an holy beast. Moreover they use this foolish ceremony : every morning they take two basins, either of silver, or of gold, and with one they receive the urine of the ox, and with the other his dung. With the urine they wash their face, their eyes, and all their five senses. Of the dung they put into both their eyes, then they anoint the balls of their cheeks therewith, and thirdly their breast : and then they say that they are sanctified for all that day. And as the people do, even so do their king and queen.

This people worshippeth also a dead idol, which, from the navel upward, resembleth a man, and from the navel downward an ox. The very same idol delivers oracles unto them, and sometimes requireth the blood of forty virgins for his hire. And therefore the men of that region do consecrate their daughters and their sons unto their idols, even as Christians do their children unto some religion or saint in heaven. Likewise they sacrifice their sons and their daughters, and so, much people is put to death before the said idol by reason of that accursed ceremony. Also many other heinous and abominable villainies doth that brutish beastly people commit : and I saw many more strange things among them which I mean not here to insert. Another most vile custom the foresaid nation doth retain : for when any man dieth they burn his dead corpse to ashes : and if his wife surviveth him, her they burn quick, because (say they) she shall accompany her husband in his tilthe and husbandry, when he is come into a new world. Howbeit the said wife having children by her husband, may if she will, remain still alive with them, without shame or reproach : notwithstanding, for the most part, they all of them make choice to be burnt with their husbands. Now, albeit the wife dieth before her husband, that law bindeth not the husband to such inconvenience, but he may marry another wife also. Likewise, the said nation hath another strange custon, in that their women drink wine, but their men do not. Also the women have the lids and brows of their eyes and beards shaven, but their men have not : with many other base and filthy fashions which the said women do use contrary to the nature of their sex. From that kingdom I travelled ten days' journey unto another kingdom called Mobar, which containeth many cities. Within a certain church of the same country, the body of Saint Thomas the apostle is interred, the very same church being full of idols : and in fifteen houses round about the said church, there dwell certain priests who are Nestorians, that is to say, false, and bad Christians, and schismatics.

CHAPTER IV

Of a Strange and Uncouth Idol : and of certain Customs and Ceremonies

In the said kingdom of Mobar there is a wonderful strange idol, being made after the shape and resemblance of a man, as big as the image of our Christopher, and consisting all of most pure and glittering gold. And about the neck thereof hangeth a silk ribbon, full of most rich and precious stones, some one of which is of more value than a whole kingdom. The house of this idol is all of beaten gold, namely the roof, the pavement, and the ceiling of the wall within and without. Unto this idol the Indians go on pilgrimage, as we do unto S. Peter. Some go with halters about their necks, some with their hands bound behind them, some other with knives sticking on their arms or legs: and if after their peregrination, the flesh of their wounded arm festereth or corrupteth, they esteem their limb to be holy, and think that their god is well pleased with them.

Near unto the temple of that idol is a lake made by the hands of men in an open and common place, whereinto the pilgrims cast gold, silver, and precious stones, for the honour of the idol and the repairing of his temple. And therefore when anything is to be adorned or mended, they go unto this lake taking up the treasure which was cast in. Moreover at every yearly feast of the making or repairing of the said idol, the king and queen, with the whole multitude of the people, and all the pilgrims assemble themselves, and placing the said idol in a most stately and rich chariot, they carry him out of their temple with songs, and with all kind of musical harmony, and a great company of virgins go procession-wise two and two in a rank singing before him. Many pilgrims also put themselves under the chariot wheels, to the end that their false god may go over them: and all they over whom the chariot runneth are crushed in pieces, and divided in sunder in the midst, and slain right out. Yea, and in doing this, they think themselves to die most holily and securely, in the service of their god. And by this means every year, there die under the said filthy idol more than 500 persons, whose carcasses are burned, and their ashes are kept for relics, because they died in that sort for their god.

Moreover they have another detestable ceremony. For when any man offers to die in the service of his false god, his parents, and all his friends assemble themselves together with a consort of musicians, making him a great and solemn feast: which feast being ended, they hang five sharp knives about his neck carrying him before the idol, and so soon as he is come thither, he taketh one of his knives crying with a loud voice, For the worship of my god do I cut this my flesh, and then he casteth the morsel which is cut, at the face of his idol: but at the very last wound wherewith he murdereth himself, he uttereth these words: Now do I yield myself to death in the behalf of my god, and being dead, his body is burned, and is esteemed by all men to be holy. The king of the said region is most rich in gold, silver and precious stones, and there be the fairest unions in all the world.

Travelling from thence by the Ocean sea fifty days' journey southward, I came unto a certain land named Lammori, where, in regard of extreme heat, the people both men and women go stark-naked from top to toe: who seeing me apparelled scoffed at me, saying, that God made Adam and Eve naked. In this country all women are common, so that no man can say, this is my wife. Also when any of the said women beareth a son or a daughter, she bestoweth it upon anyone that hath lien with her, whom she pleaseth. Likewise all the land of that region is possessed in common, so that there is not mine and thine, or any propriety of possession in the division of lands: howbeit every man hath his own house peculiar unto himself. Man's flesh, if it be fat, is eaten as ordinarily there, as beef in our country. And albeit the people are most lewd, yet the country is exceeding good, abounding with all commodities, as flesh, corn, rice, silver, gold, wood of aloes, camphor, and many other things. Merchants coming unto this region for traffic do usually bring with them fat men, selling them unto the inhabitants as we sell hogs, who immediately kill and eat them. In this island towards the south there is another kingdom called Simoltra, where both men and women mark themselves with red-hot iron in twelve sundry spots of their faces; and this nation is at continual war with certain naked people in another region. Then I travelled further unto another island called Java, the compass whereof by sea is 3000 miles. The king of this island hath seven other crowned kings under his jurisdiction. The said island is throughly inhabited, and is thought to be one of the principal islands of the whole world. In the same island there groweth great plenty of cloves, cubebs, and nutmegs, and in a word all kinds of spices are there to be had, and great abundance of all victuals except wine. The king of the said land of Java hath a most brave and sumptuous palace, the most loftily built, that ever I saw any, and it hath most high greeses and stairs to ascend up to the rooms therein contained, one stair being of silver, and another of gold, throughout the whole building. Also the lower rooms were paved all over with one square plate of silver, and another of gold. All the walls upon the inner side were seeled over with plates of beaten gold, whereupon were engraven the pictures of knights, having about their temples, each of them, a wreath of gold, adorned with precious stones. The roof of the palace was of pure gold. With this king of Java the great Can of Catay hath had many conflicts in war; whom notwithstanding the said king hath always overcome and vanquished.

CHAPTER V

Of certain Trees yielding Meal, Honey, and Poison

NEAR unto the said island is another country called Panten, or Tathalamasin. And the king of the same country hath many islands under his dominion. In this land there are trees yielding meal, honey, and wine, and the most deadly poison in all the whole world: for against it there is but one only remedy : and that is this : if any man hath taken of the poison, and would be delivered of the danger thereof, let him temper the dung of a man in water, and so drink a good quantity thereof, and it expels the poison immediately, making it to avoid at the fundament. Meal is produced out of the said trees after this manner. They be mighty huge trees, and when they are cut with an axe by the ground, there issueth out of the stock a certain liquor like unto gum, which they take and put into bags made of leaves, laying them for fifteen days together abroad in the sun, and at the end of those fifteen days, when the said liquor is throughly parched, it becometh meal. Then they steep it first in sea water, washing it afterward with fresh water, and so it is made very good and savoury paste, whereof they make either meat or bread, as they think good. Of which bread I myself did eat, and it is fairer without and somewhat brown within.

By this country is the sea called Mare mortuum, which runneth continually southward, into the which whosoever falleth is never seen after. In this country also are found canes of an incredible length, namely of sixty paces high or more, and they are as big as trees. Other canes there be also called Cassan, which overspread the earth like grass, and out of every knot of them spring forth certain branches, which are continued upon the ground almost for the space of a mile. In the said canes there are found certain stones, one of which stones, whosoever carryeth about with him, cannot be wounded with any iron: and therefore the men of that country for the most part, carry such stones with them, whithersoever they go. Many also cause one of the arms of their children, while they are young, to be lanced, putting one of the said stones into the wound, healing also, and closing up the said wound with the powder of a certain fish (the name whereof I do not know), which powder doth immediately consolidate and cure the said wound. And by the virtue of these stones, the people aforesaid do for the most part triumph both on sea and land. Howbeit there is one kind of stratagem, which the enemies of this nation, knowing the virtue of the said stones, do practise against them: namely, they provide themselves armour of iron or steel against their arrows, and weapons also poisoned with the poison of trees, and they carry in their hands wooden stakes most sharp and hard-pointed, as if they were iron: likewise they shoot arrows without iron heads, and so they confound and slay some of their unarmed foes trusting too securely unto the virtue of their stones. Also of the foresaid canes called cassan they make sails for their ships, and little houses, and many other necessaries. From thence after

many days' travel, I arrived at another kingdom called
Campa, a most beautiful and rich country, and abounding
with all kinds of victuals: the king thereof, at my being
there, had so many wives and concubines, that he had
three hundred sons and daughters by them. This king
hath 10,004 tame elephants, which are kept even as we
keep droves of oxen, or flocks of sheep in pasture.

CHAPTER VI

*Of the Abundance of Fishes, which cast themselves upon
the Shore*

IN this country there is one strange thing to be observed,
the every several kind of fishes in those seas come swimming towards the said country in such abundance, that, for
a great distance into the sea, nothing can be seen but the
backs of fishes ; which casting themselves upon the shore
when they come near unto it, do suffer men, for the space
of three days, to come and to take as many of them as
they please, and then they return again unto the sea.
After that kind of fishes comes another kind, offering
itself after the same manner, and so in like sort all other
kinds whatsoever : notwithstanding they do this but once in
a year. And I demanded of the inhabitants there, how,
or by what means this strange accident could come to pass.
They answered, that fishes were taught, even by nature, to
come and to do homage unto their emperor. There be
tortoises also as big as an oven. Many other thing I saw
which are incredible, unless a man should see them with
his own eyes. In this country also dead men are burned,
and their wives are burned alive with them, as in the city of
Polumbrum above mentioned : for the men of the country
say that she goeth to accompany him in another world,
that he should take none other wife in marriage. Moreover I travelled on further by the Ocean-sea towards the

south, and passed through many countries and islands, whereof one is called Moumoran, and it containeth in compass 2000 miles, wherein men and women have dogs' faces, and worship an ox for their god : and therefore every one of them carry the image of an ox of gold or silver upon their foreheads.   The men and women of this country go all naked, saving that they hang a linen cloth before their privities.   The men of that country are very tall and mighty, and by reason that they go naked, when they are to make battle, they carry iron or steel targets before them, which do cover and defend their bodies, from top to toe : and whomsoever of their foes they take in battle not being able to ransom himself for money, they presently devour him : but if he be able to redeem himself for money, they let him go free.   Their king weareth about his neck three hundred great and most beautiful unions, and saith every day three hundred prayers unto his god.   He weareth upon his finger also a stone of a span long, which seemed to be a flame of fire, and therefore when be weareth it, no man dare once approach him: and they say that there is not any stone in the whole world of more value than it.   Neither could at any time the great Tartarian Emperor of Katay either by force, money, or policy obtain it at his hands : notwithstanding that he hath done the utmost of his endeavour for this purpose.

CHAPTER VII

Of the Island of Sylan : and of the Mountain where Adam mourned for his son Abel

I PASSED also by another island called Sylan, which containeth in compass above 2000 miles : wherein are an infinite number of serpents, and great store of lions, bears, and all kinds of ravening and wild beasts, and especially of elephants. In the said country there is an huge mountain, where upon the inhabitants of that region do report that Adam mourned for his son Abel the space of five hundred years. In the midst of this mountain there is a most beautiful plain, wherein is a little lake containing great plenty of water, which water the inhabitants report to have proceeded from the tears of Adam and Eve : howbeit I proved that to be false, because I saw the water flow in the lake. This water is full of horse-leeches, and blood suckers, and of precious stones also : which precious stones the king taketh not unto his own use, but once or twice every year he permitteth certain poor people to dive under the water for the said stones, and all that they can get, he bestoweth upon them, to the end that they may pray for his soul. But that they may with less danger dive under the water, they take lemons which they peel, anointing themselves throughly with the juice thereof, and so they may dive naked under the water, the horse-leeches not being able to hurt them. From this lake the water runneth even unto the sea, and at a low ebb, the inhabitants dig rubies, diamonds, pearls and other precious stones out of the shore : whereupon it is thought, that the king of this island hath greater abundance of precious stones, than any other monarch in the whole earth besides.

In the said country there be all kinds of beasts and fowls, and the people told me, that those beasts would not invade nor hurt any stranger, but only the natural inhabitants. I saw in this island fowls as big as our country geese, having two heads, and other miraculous things, which I will not here write of. Travelling on further toward the south, I arrived at a certain island called Bodin, which signifieth in our language unclean. In this island there do inhabit most wicked persons, who devour and eat raw flesh, committing all kinds of uncleanness and abominations in such sort, as it is incredible. For the father eateth his son, and the son his father, the husband his own wife, and the wife her husband : and that after this manner. If any man's father be sick, the son straight goes unto the sooth-saying or prognosticating priest, requesting him to demand of his god, whether his father shall recover of that infirmity or not. Then both of them go unto an idol of gold or of silver, making their prayers unto it in manner following: Lord, thou art our god, and thee we do adore, beseeching thee to resolve us, whether such a man must die, or recover of such an infirmity or no. Then the devil answereth out of the foresaid idol: if he saith (he shall live) then returneth his son and ministreth things necessary unto him, till he hath attained unto his former health: but if he saith (he shall die) then goes the priest unto him, and putting a cloth into his mouth doth strangle him therewith: which being done, he cuts his dead body into morsels, and all his friends and kinsfolks are invited unto the eating thereof, with music and all kinds of mirth: howbeit his bones are solemnly buried. And when I found fault with that custom demanding a reason thereof, one of them gave me this answer: This we do, lest the worms should eat his flesh, for then his soul should suffer great torments, neither could I by any means remove them from that error. Many other novelties and strange things there be in this country, which no man would credit, unless he saw them with his own eyes. Howbeit, I (before almighty God) do here make relation of nothing but of that only, whereof I am as sure, as a man may be sure. Concerning the foresaid islands I inquired of divers well-experienced persons, who all of them, as it were with one consent, answered me, saying, That this India contained 4400 islands under it, or within it, in which islands there are sixty and four crowned kings: and they say moreover, that the greater part of those islands are well inhabited. And here I conclude concerning that part of India.

CHAPTER VIII

Of the Upper India : and of the Province of Mancy

FIRST of all, therefore, having travelled many days' journey upon the Ocean-sea toward the east, at length I arrived at a certain great province called Mancy, being in Latin named India. Concerning this India I inquired of Christians, of Saracens, and of idolaters, and of all such as bear any office under the great Can. Who all of them with one consent answered, that this province of Mancy hath more than 2000 great cities within the precincts thereof, and that it aboundeth with all plenty of victuals, as namely with bread, wine, rice, flesh, and fish. All the men of this province be artificers and merchants, who, though they be in never so extreme penury, so long as they can help themselves by the labour of their hands, will never beg alms of any man. The men of this province are of a fair and comely personage, but somewhat pale, having their heads shaven but a little : but the women are the most beautiful under the sun. The first city of the said India which I came unto, is called Ceuskalon, which being a day's journey distant from the sea, stands upon a river, the water whereof, near unto the mouth, where it exonerateth itself into the sea, doth overflow the land for the space of twelve days' journey. All the inhabitants of this India are worshippers of idols. The foresaid city of Ceuskalon hath such an huge navy belonging thereunto, that no man would believe it unless he should see it. In this city I saw 300 lb. of good and new ginger sold for less than a groat. There are the greatest and the fairest geese, and most plenty of them to be sold in all the whole world, as I suppose. They are as white as milk, and have a bone upon the crown of their heads as big as an egg, being of the colour of blood : under their throat they have a skin or bag hanging down half a foot. They are exceeding fat and well sold.

Also they have ducks and hens in that country, one as big as two of ours. There be monstrous great serpents likewise, which are taken by the inhabitants and eaten: whereupon a solemn feast among them without serpents is nought set by: and to be brief, in this city there are all kind of victuals in great abundance. From thence I passed by many cities, and at length I came unto a city named Caitan, wherein the Friars Minorites have two places of abode, unto the which I transported the bones of the dead friars, which suffered martyrdom for the faith of Christ, as it is above mentioned. In this city there is abundance of all kind of victuals very cheap. The said city is as big as two of Bononia, and in it are many monasteries of religious persons, all which do worship idols. I myself was in one of those monasteries, and it was told me, that there were in it 3000 religious men, having 11,000 idols: and one of the said idols, which seemed unto me but little in regard of the rest, was as big as our Christopher. These religious men every day do feed their idol gods: whereupon at a certain time I went to behold the banquet: and indeed those things which they brought unto them were good to eat, and fuming hot, insomuch that the stream of the smoke thereof ascended up unto their idols, and they said that their gods were refreshed with the smoke: howbeit, all the meat they conveyed away, eating it up their own selves, and so they fed their dumb gods with the smoke only.

CHAPTER IX

Of the City Fuco

TRAVELLING more eastward, I came unto a city named Fuco, which containeth thirty miles in circuit, wherein be exceeding great and fair cocks, and all their hens are as white as the very snow, having wool instead of feathers,

like unto sheep. It is a most stately and beautiful city
and standeth upon the sea. Then I went eighteen days'
journey on further, and passed by many provinces and
cities, and in the way I went over a certain great mountain,
upon the one side whereof I beheld all living creatures to
be as black as a coal, and the men and women on that side
differed somewhat in manner of living from others ; howbeit, on the other side of the said hill every living thing
was snow-white, and the inhabitants in their manner of
living, were altogether unlike unto others. There, all
married women carry in token that they have husbands, a
great trunk of horn upon their heads. From thence I
travelled eighteen days' journey further, and came unto a
certain great river, and entered also into a city, whereunto
belongeth a mighty bridge to pass the said river. And
mine host with whom I sojourned, being desirous to
show me some sport, said unto me : Sir, if you will see
any fish taken, go with me. Then he led me unto the
foresaid bridge, carrying in his arms with him certain dive-
doppers or water fowls, bound unto a company of poles,
and about every one of their necks he tied a thread, lest
they should eat the fish as fast as they took them : and he
carried three great baskets with him also. Then loosed he
the dive-doppers from the poles, which presently went into
the water, and within less than the space of one hour,
caught as many fishes as filled the three baskets: which
being full, mine host untied the threads from about their
necks, and entering the second time into the river they fed
themselves with fish, and being satisfied they returned and
suffered themselves to be bound unto the said poles as
they were before. And when I did eat of those fishes, me
thought they were exceeding good. Travelling thence
many days' journey, at length I arrived at another city
called Canasia, which signifieth in our language, the city of
heaven. Never in my life did I see so great a city : for it
containeth in circuit an hundred miles : neither saw I any
plot thereof, which was not throughly inhabited : yea, I
saw many houses of ten or twelve stories high, one above
another. It hath mighty large suburbs containing more

people than the city itself.   Also it hath twelve principal
gates: and about the distance of eight miles, in the highway unto every one of the said gates standeth a city as big
by estimation as Venice, and Padua.   The foresaid city of
Canasia is situated in waters or marshes, which always
stand still, neither ebbing nor flowing: howbeit, it hath a
defence for the wind like unto Venice.   In this city there
are more than 11,000 bridges, many whereof I numbered
and passed over them : and upon every of those bridges
stand certain watchmen of the city, keeping continual
watch and ward about the said city, for the great Can the
Emperor of Catay.   The people of this country say, that
they have one duty enjoined unto them by their lord ; for
every fire payeth one balis in regard of tribute : and a
balis is five papers or pieces of silk, which are worth one
florin and an half of our coin.   Ten or twelve households
are accounted for one fire, and so pay tribute but for one
fire only.   All those tributary fires amount unto the
number of eighty-five thuman, with other four thuman of
the Saracens, which make eighty-nine in all : and one
thuman consisteth of 10,000 fires.   The residue of the
people of the city are some of them Christians, some
merchants, and some travellers through the country,
whereupon I marvelled much how such an infinite number
of persons could inhabit and live together.   There is great
abundance of victuals in this city, as namely of bread and
wine, and especially of hogs' flesh, with other necessaries.

CHAPTER X

*Of a Monastery where many strange beasts of divers kinds
do live upon an hill*

In the foresaid city four of our friars had converted a
mighty and rich man unto the faith of Christ, at whose
house I continually abode, for so long time as I remained

in the city.   Who upon a certain time said unto me : Ara,
that is to say, father, will you go and behold the city.
And I said, Yea.   Then embarqued we ourselves, and
directed our course unto a certain great monastery : where
being arrived, he called a religious person with whom he
was acquainted, saying unto him concerning me : this
Raban Francus, that is to say, this religious Frenchman,
cometh from the western parts of the world, and is now
going to the city of Cambaleth to pray for the life of the
great Can, and therefore you must show him some rare
thing, that when he returns into his own country, he may
say, this strange sight or novelty have I seen in the city of
Canasia.   Then the said religious man took two great
baskets full of broken relics which remained of the table,
and led me unto a little walled park, the door whereof he
unlocked with his key, and there appeared unto us a
pleasant fair green plot, into the which we entered.   In
the said green stands a little mount in form of a
steeple, replenished with fragrant herbs, and fine shady
trees.   And while we stood there, he took a cymbal or
bell, and rang therewith, as they use to ring to dinner or
bevoir in cloisters, at the sound whereof many creatures of
divers kinds came down from the mount, some like apes,
some like cats, some like monkeys : and some having faces
like men.   And while I stood beholding of them, they
gathered themselves together about him, to the number of
4200 of those creatures, putting themselves in good order,
before whom he set a platter, and gave them the said
fragments to eat.   And when they had eaten he rang upon
his cymbal the second time, and they all returned unto
their former places.   Then, wondering greatly at the
matter, I demanded what kind of creatures those might
be.   They are (quoth he) the souls of noble men which we
do here feed, for the love of God who governeth the
world : and as a man was honourable or noble in this life,
so his soul after death, entereth into the body of some
excellent beast or other, but the souls of simple and
rustical people do possess the bodies of more vile and
brutish creatures.   Then I began to refute that foul error :

howbeit my speech did nothing at all prevail with him: for he could not be persuaded that any soul might remain without a body.

From thence I departed unto a certain city named Chilenso, the walls whereof contained forty miles in circuit. In this city there are 360 bridges of stone, the fairest that ever I saw: and it is well inhabited, having a great navy belonging thereunto, and abounding with all kind of victuals and other commodities. And thence I went unto a certain river called Thalay, which, where it is most narrow, is seven miles broad: and it runneth through the midst of the land of Pygmaei, whose chief city is called Cakam, and is one of the goodliest cities in the world. These Pigmaeans are three of my spans high, and they make larger and better cloth of cotton and silk, than any other nation under the sun. And coasting along by the said river, I came unto a certain city named Janzu, in which city there is one receptacle for the friars of our order, and there be also three churches of the Nestorians.

This Janzu is a noble and great city, containing forty-eight thuman of tributary fires, and in it are all kinds of victuals, and great plenty of such beasts, owls and fishes, as Christians do usually live upon. The lord of the same city hath in yearly revenues for salt only, fifty thuman of balis, and one balis is worth a florin and a half of our coin: insomuch that one thuman of balis amounteth unto the value of fifteen thousand florins. Howbeit the said lord favoureth his people in one respect, for sometimes he forgiveth them freely two hundred thuman, lest there should be any scarcity or dearth among them. There is a custom in this city, that when any man is determined to banquet his friends, going about unto certain taverns or cooks' houses appointed for the same purpose, he saith unto every particular host, you shall have such, and such of my friends, whom you must entertain in my name, for so much I will bestow upon the banquet. And by that means his friends are better feasted at diverse places, than they should have been at one. Ten miles from the said city, about the head of the foresaid river of Thalay, there is a certain other city called Montu, which hath the greatest navy that I saw in the whole world. All their ships are as white as snow, and they have banqueting houses in them, and many other rare things also, which no man would believe, unless he had seen them with his own eyes.

CHAPTER XI

Of the City of Cambaleth

TRAVELLING eight days' journey further by divers territories and cities, at length I came by fresh water unto a certain city named Lencyn, standing upon the river of Karauoran, which runneth through the midst of Cataie, and doth great harm in the country when it overfloweth the banks, or breaketh forth of the channel. From thence passing along the river eastward, after many days' travel, and the sight of divers cities, I arrived at a city called Sumakoto, which aboundeth more with silk than any other city of the world : for when there is great scarcity of silk, forty pound is sold for less than eight groats. In this city there is abundance of merchandise, and of all kinds of victuals also, as of bread, wine, flesh, fish, with all choice and delicate spices. Then travelling on still towards the east by many cities, I came unto the noble and renowned city of Cambaleth, which is of great antiquity, being situate in the province of Cataie. This city the Tartars took, and near unto it within the space of half a mile, they built another city called Caido. The city of Caido hath twelve gates, being each of them two miles distant from another. Also the space lying in the midst between the two foresaid cities is very well and throughly inhabited, so that they make as it were but one city between them both. The whole compass or circuit of both cities together, is forty miles. In this city the great emperor Can hath his principal seat, and his imperial palace, the

walls of which palace contain four miles in circuit : and
near unto this his palace are many other palaces and houses
of his nobles which belong unto his court. Within the
precincts of the said palace imperial, there is a most
beautiful mount, set and replenished with trees, for which
cause it is called the Green Mount, having a most royal
and sumptuous palace standing thereupon, in which, for
the most part, the great Can is resident. Upon the one
side of the said mount there is a great lake, whereupon a
most stately bridge is built, in which lake is great abundance of geese, ducks, and all kinds of water-fowls : and in
the wood growing upon the mount there is great store of
all birds, and wild beasts. And therefore when the great
Can will solace himself with hunting or hawking, he needs
not so much as once to step forth of his palace. Moreover, the principal palace, wherein he maketh his abode, is
very large, having within it fourteen pillars of gold, and
all the walls thereof are hung with red skins, which are said
to be the most costly skins in all the world. In the midst
of the palace stands a cistern of two yards high, which
consisteth of a precious stone called Merdochas, and is
wreathed about with gold, and at each corner thereof is
the golden image of a serpent, as it were, furiously shaking
and casting forth his head. This cistern also hath a kind
of network of pearl wrought about it. Likewise by the
said cistern there is drink conveyed through certain pipes
and conducts, such as useth to be drunk in the emperor's
court, upon the which also there hang many vessels of
gold, wherein, whosoever will make drink of the said
liquor. In the foresaid palace there are many peacocks of
gold : and when any Tartar maketh a banquet unto his
lord, if the guests chance to clap their hands for joy and
mirth, the said golden peacocks also will spread abroad
their wings, and lift up their trains, seeming as if they
danced : and this I suppose to be done by art magic or
by some secret engine under the ground.

CHAPTER XII

Of the glory and magnificence of the great Can

MOREOVER, when the great Emperor Can sitteth in his imperial throne of estate, on his left side sitteth his queen or empress, and upon another inferior seat there sit two other women, which are to accompany the emperor, when his spouse is absent, but in the lowest place of all, there sit all the ladies of his kindred. All the married women wear upon their heads a kind of ornament in shape like unto a man's foot, of a cubit and a half in length, and the lower part of the said foot is adorned with cranes' feathers, and is all over thick set with great and orient pearls. Upon the right hand of the great Can sitteth his first begotten son and heir apparent unto his empire, and under him sit all the nobles of the blood royal. There be also four secretaries, which put all things in writing that the emperor speaketh. In whose presence likewise stand his barons and divers others of his nobility, with great trains of followers after them, of whom none dare speak so much as one word, unless they have obtained licence of the emperor so to do, except his jesters and stage-players, who are appointed of purpose to solace their lord. Neither yet dare they attempt to do aught, but only according to the pleasure of their emperor, and as he enjoineth them by law. About the palace gate stand certain barons to keep all men from treading upon the threshold of the said gate. When it pleaseth the great Can to solemnize a feast, he hath about him 14,000 barons, carrying wreaths and little crowns upon their heads, and giving attendance upon their lord, and every one of them weareth a garment of gold and precious stones, which is worth ten thousand florins. His court is kept in very good order, by governors of tens, governors of hundreds, and governors of thousands, insomuch that every one in his place performeth his duty committed unto him, neither is there any defect to be

found.   I Friar Odoricus was there present in person for
the space of three years, and was often at the said banquets: for we Friars Minorites have a place of abode
appointed out for us in the emperor's court, and are
enjoined to go and bestow our blessing upon him.   And
I inquired of certain courtiers concerning the number of
persons pertaining to the emperor's court.   And they
answered me, that of stage-players, musicians, and such
like, there were eighteen thuman at the least, and that the
keepers of dogs, beasts and fowls were fifteen thuman,
and the physicians for the emperor's body, were four
hundred: the Christians also were eight in number,
together with one Saracen.   At my being there, all the
foresaid number of persons had all kinds of necessaries
both for apparel and victuals out of the emperor's court.

Moreover, when he will make his progress from one
country to another, he hath four troops of horsemen, one
being appointed to go a day's journey before, and another
to come a day's journey after him, the third to march on
his right hand, and the fourth on his left, in the manner of
a cross, he himself being in the midst, and so every
particular troop have their daily journeys limited unto
them, to the end they may provide sufficient victuals without defect.   Now the great Can himself is carried in
manner following: he rideth in a chariot with two wheels,
upon which a majestical throne is built of the wood of aloe,
being adorned with gold and great pearls, and precious
stones, and four elephants bravely furnished do draw the
said chariot, before which elephants four great horses richly
trapped and covered do lead the way.   Hard by the chariot
on both sides thereof, are four barons laying hold and
attending thereupon, to keep all persons from approaching
near unto their emperor.   Upon the chariot also two milk-
white ger-falcons do sit, and seeing any game which he
would take, he letteth them fly, and so they take it, and
after this manner doth he solace himself as he rideth.
Moreover, no man dare come within a stone's cast of the
chariot, but such as are appointed.   The number of his
own followers, of his wives' attendants, and of the train of

his first begotten son and heir apparent, would seem incredible unto any man, unless he had seen it with his own eyes. The foresaid great Can hath divided his empire into twelve parts or provinces, and one of the said provinces hath two thousand great cities within the precincts thereof. Whereupon his empire is of that length and breadth, that unto whatsoever part thereof he intendeth his journey, he hath space enough for six months' continual progress, except his islands which are at the least 5000.

CHAPTER XIII

Of certain inns or hospitals appointed for travellers throughout the whole Empire

The foresaid emperor (to the end that travellers may have all things necessary throughout his whole empire) hath caused certain inns to be provided in sundry places upon the highways, where all things pertaining unto victuals are in a continual readiness. And when any alteration or news happen in any part of his empire, if he chance to be far absent from that part, his ambassadors upon horses or dromedaries ride post unto him ; and when themselves and their beasts are weary, they blow their horn, at the noise whereof, the next inn likewise provideth a horse and a man who takes the letter of him that is weary, and runneth unto another inn : and so by divers inns, and divers posts, the report, which ordinarily could scarce come in thirty days, is in one natural day brought unto the emperor : and therefore no matter of any moment can be done in his empire, but straightway he hath intelligence thereof. Moreover, when the great Can himself will go on hunting, he useth this custom. Some twenty days' journey from the city of Kambaleth there is a forest containing six days' journey in circuit, in which forest there are so many kinds of beasts and birds, as it is incredible to report. Unto this forest, at the end of every third or fourth year, himself with his whole train resorteth, and they all of them together environ the said forest, sending dogs into the same, which by hunting do bring forth the beasts: namely, lions and stags, and other creatures, unto a most beautiful plain in the midst of the forest, because all the beasts of the forest do tremble, especially at the cry of the hounds. Then cometh the great Can himself, being carried upon three elephants, and shooteth five arrows into the whole herd of beasts, and after him all his barons, and after them the rest of his courtiers and family do all in like manner discharge their arrows also, and every man's arrow hath a sundry mark. Then they all go unto the beasts which are slain (suffering the living beasts to return into the wood that they may have more sport with them another time) and every man enjoyeth that beast as his own, wherein he findeth his arrow sticking.

CHAPTER XIV

Of the four feasts which the great Can solemnizeth every year in his Court

FOUR great feasts in a year doeth the Emperor Can celebrate: namely, the feast of his birth, the feast of his circumcision, the feast of his coronation, and the feast of his marriage. And unto these feasts he inviteth all his barons, his stage-players, and all such as are of his kindred. Then the great Can sitting in his throne, all his barons present themselves before him, with wreaths and crowns upon their heads, being diversly attired, for some of them are in green, namely, the principal; the second are in red, and the third in yellow, and they hold each man in his hand a little ivory table of elephant's tooth, and they are girt with golden girdles of half a foot broad, and they

stand upon their feet keeping silence. About them stand
the stage-players or musicians with their instruments. And
in one of the corners of a certain great palace, all the
philosophers or magicians remain for certain hours, and do
attend upon points or characters : and when the point and
hour which the said philosophers expected for, is come, a
certain crier crieth out with a loud voice, saying, Incline or
bow yourselves before your Emperor ; with that all the
barons fall flat upon the earth. Then he crieth out again :
Arise all, and immediately they all arise. Likewise the
philosophers attend upon a point or character the second
time, and when it is fulfilled, the crier crieth out amain :
Put your fingers in your ears ; and forthwith again he
sayeth : Pluck them out. Again, at the third point he
crieth, Bolt this meal. Many other circumstances also do
they perform, all which they say have some certain significa-
tion ; howbeit, neither would I write them, nor give any
heed unto them, because they are vain and ridiculous.
And when the musicians' hour is come, then the philosophers say, Solemnize a feast unto your lord : with that
all of them sound their instruments, making a great and
melodious noise. And immediately another crieth, Peace,
peace, and they are all whist. Then come the women
musicians and sing sweetly before the Emperor, which
music was more delightful unto me. After them come in
the lions and do their obeisance unto the great Can. Then
the jugglers cause golden cups full of wine to fly up and
down in the air, and to apply themselves unto men's
mouths that they may drink of them. These and many
other strange things I saw in the court of the great Can,
which no man would believe unless he had seen them with
his own eyes, and therefore I omit to speak of them. I
was informed also by certain credible persons, of another
miraculous thing, namely that in a certain kingdom of the
said Can, wherein stand the mountains called Kapsei (the
kingdom's name is Kalor) there grow great gourds or
pompions, which being ripe, do open at the tops, and
within them is found a little beast like unto a young lamb,
even as I myself have heard reported, that there stand

certain trees upon the shore of the Irish Sea, bearing fruit like unto a gourd, which, at a certain time of the year do fall into the water, and become birds called bernacles, and this is most true.

CHAPTER XV

Of divers Provinces and Cities

AND after three years I departed out of the empire of Cataie, travelling fifty days' journey towards the West. And at length I came unto the empire of Pretegoani, whose principal city is Kosan, which hath many other cities under it. From thence passing many days' travel, I came unto a province called Casan, which is for good commodities, one of the only provinces under the sun, and is very well inhabited, insomuch that when we depart out of the gates of one city we may behold the gates of another city, as I myself saw in divers of them. The breadth of the said province is fifty days' journey, and the length about sixty. In it there is great plenty of all victuals, and especially of chestnuts, and it is one of the twelve provinces of the great Can. Going on further, I came unto a certain kingdom called Tebek, which is in subjection unto the great Can also, wherein I think there is more plenty of bread and wine than in any other part of the world besides. The people of the said country do, for the most part, inhabit in tents made of black felt. Their principal city is environed with fair and beautiful walls, being built of most white and black stones, which are disposed chequerwise one by another, and curiously compiled together: likewise all the highways in this country are exceedingly well paved. In the said country none dare shed the blood of a man, or of any beast, for the reverence of a certain idol. In the foresaid city their Abassi, that is to say, their Pope is resident, being the head and prince of all idolaters (upon whom he bestoweth and distributeth gifts after his manner) even as

our Pope of Rome accounts himself to be the head of all
Christians. The women of this country wear above an
hundred tricks and trifles about them, and they have two
teeth in their mouths as long as the tusks of a boar.
When any man's father deceaseth among them, his son
assembleth together all the priests and musicians that he
can get, saying that he is determined to honour his father :
then causeth he him to be carried into the field (all his
kinsfolks, friends, and neighbours accompanying him in
the said action), where the priests with great solemnity cut
off the father's head, giving it unto his son, which being
done, they divide the whole body into morsels, and so
leave it behind them, returning home with prayers in the
company of the said son. So soon as they are departed,
certain vultures, which are accustomed to such banquets,
come flying from the mountains, and carry away all the
said morsels of flesh : and from thenceforth a fame is
spread abroad, that the said party deceased was holy,
because the angels of God carried him into paradise. And
this is the greatest and highest honour, that the son can
devise to perform unto his deceased father. Then the said
son taketh his father's head seething it and eating the flesh
thereof, but of the skull he makes a drinking cup, wherein
himself with all his family and kindred do drink with great
solemnity and mirth, in the remembrance of his dead and devoured father. Many other vile and abominable things doth
the said nation commit, which I mean not to write, because
men neither can nor will believe, except they should have
the sight of them.

CHAPTER XVI

Of a certain rich man, who is fed and nourished
by fifty virgins

WHILE I was in the province of Mancy, I passed by the
palace of a certain famous man, which hath fifty virgin

damsels continually attending upon him, feeding him every meal, as a bird feeds her young ones. Also he hath sundry kinds of meat served in at his table, and three dishes of each kind : and when the said virgins feed him, they sing most sweetly. This man hath in yearly revenues thirty thuman of tagars of rice, every of which thuman yieldeth ten thousand tagars, and one tagar is the burden of an ass. His palace is two miles in circuit, the pavement whereof is one place of gold, and another of silver. Near unto the wall of the said palace there is a mount artificially wrought with gold and silver, whereupon stand turrets and steeples and other delectable things for the solace and recreation of the foresaid great man. And it was told me that there were four such men in the said kingdom. It is accounted a great grace for the men of that country to have long nails upon their fingers, and especially upon their thumbs, which nails they may fold about their hands: but the grace and beauty of their women is to have small and slender feet; and therefore the mothers when their daughters are young, do bind up their feet, that they may not grow great.

Travelling on further towards the South, I arrived at a certain country called Melistorte, which is a very pleasant and fertile place. And in this country there was a certain aged man called Senex de monte, who round about two mountains had built a wall to enclose the said mountains. Within this wall there were the fairest and most crystal fountains in the whole world : and about the said fountains there were most beautiful virgins in great number, and goodly horses also, and in a word, everything that could be devised for bodily solace and delight, and therefore the inhabitants of the country call the same place by the name of Paradise. The said old Senex, when he saw any proper and valiant young man, he would admit him into his paradise. Moreover by certain conduits he makes wine and milk to flow abundantly. This Senex, when he hath a mind to revenge himself or to slay any king or baron, commandeth him that is governor of the said paradise, to bring thereunto some of the acquaintance

of the said king or baron, permitting him a while to take
his pleasure therein, and then to give him a certain potion
being of force to cast him into such a slumber as should
make him quite void of all sense, and so being in a pro-
found sleep to convey him out of his paradise : who being
awaked, and seeing himself thrust out of the paradise
would become so sorrowful, that he could not in the world
devise what to do, or whither to turn him.   Then would
he go unto the foresaid old man, beseeching him that he
might be admitted again into his paradise : who saith unto
him, You cannot be admitted thither, unless you will slay
such or such a man for my sake, and if you will give the
attempt only, whether you kill him or no, I will place you
again in paradise, that there you may remain always; then
would the party without fail put the same in execution,
endeavouring to murder all those against whom the said
old man had conceived any hatred.   And therefore all the
kings of the East stood in awe of the said old man, and
gave unto him great tribute.

CHAPTER XVII

Of the Death of Senex de monte

AND when the Tartars had subdued a great part of the
world, they came unto the said old man, and took from
him the custody of his paradise : who being incensed
thereat, sent abroad divers desperate and resolute persons
out of his forenamed paradise, and caused many of the
Tartarian nobles to be slain.   The Tartars seeing this,
went and besieged the city wherein the said old man was,
took him, and put him to a most cruel and ignominious
death.   The friars in that place have this special gift and
prerogative : namely, that by the virtue of the name of
Christ Jesu, and in the virtue of his precious blood, which
he shed upon the cross for the salvation of mankind, they
do cast forth devils out of them that are possessed.   And

because there are many possessed men in those parts, they are bound and brought ten days' journey unto the said friars, who being dispossessed of the unclean spirits, do presently believe in Christ who delivered them, accounting him for their God, and being baptized in his name, and also delivering immediately unto the friars all their idols, and the idols of their cattle, which are commonly made of felt or of women's hair. Then the said friars kindle a fire in a public place (whereunto the people resort, that they may see the false gods of their neighbours burnt) and cast the said idols thereunto ; howbeit at the first those idols came out of the fire again. Then the friars sprinkled the said fire with holy water, casting the idols into it the second time, and with that the devils fled in the likeness of black smoke, and the idols still remained till they were consumed unto ashes. Afterward, this noise and outcry was heard in the air : Behold and see how I am expelled out of my habitation. And by these means the friars do baptize great multitudes, who presently revolt again unto their idols : insomuch that the said friars must eftsoons, as it were, underprop them, and inform them anew.

There was another terrible thing which I saw there : for passing by a certain valley, which is situate beside a pleasant river, I saw many dead bodies, and in the said valley also I heard divers sweet sounds and harmonies of music, especially the noise of citherns, whereat I was greatly amazed. This valley containeth in length seven or eight miles at the least, into the which whosoever entereth, dieth presently, and can by no means pass alive through the midst thereof : for which cause all the inhabitants there about decline unto the one side. Moreover, I was tempted to go in, and to see what it was. At length making my prayers, and recommending myself to God in the name of Jesu, I entered, and saw such swarms of dead bodies there, as no man would believe unless he were an eye-witness thereof. At the one side of the foresaid valley upon a certain stone, I saw the visage of a man, which beheld me with such a terrible aspect, that I thought verily I should have died in the same place. But always this sentence, The Word became flesh, and dwelt amongst us, I ceased not to pronounce, signing myself with the sign of the cross, and nearer than seven or eight paces I durst not approach unto the said head: but I departed and fled unto another place in the said valley, ascending up into a little sandy mountain, where looking round about, I saw nothing but the said citherns, which methought I heard miraculously sounding and playing by themselves without the help of musicians. And being upon the top of the mountain, I found silver there like the scales of fishes in great abundance: and I gathered some part thereof into my bosom to show for a wonder, but my conscience rebuking me, I cast it up the earth, reserving no whit at all unto myself, and so, by God's grace, I departed without danger. And when the men of the country knew that I was returned out of the valley alive, they reverenced me much, saying that I was baptized and holy, and that the foresaid bodies were men subject unto the devils infernal, who used to play upon citherns, to the end they might allure people to enter, and so murder them. Thus much concerning those things which I beheld most certainly with mine eyes, I friar Odoricus have here written: many strange things also I have of purpose omitted, because men will not believe them unless they should see them.

CHAPTER XVIII

Of the honour and reverence done unto the great Can

I WILL report one thing more, which I saw, concerning the great Can. It is an usual custom in those parts, that when the foresaid Can travelleth through any country, his subjects kindle fires before their doors, casting spices therein to make a perfume, that their lord passing by may smell the sweet and delectable odours thereof, and much people come forth to meet him. And upon a certain time

when he was coming towards Cambaleth, the fame of his
approach being published, a bishop of ours, with certain of
our Minorite Friars and myself, went two days' journey to
meet him : and being come nigh unto him, we put a cross
upon wood, I myself having a censer in my hand, and
began to sing with a loud voice: Veni creator spirituis.
And as we were singing on this wise, he caused us to be
called, commanding us to come unto him: notwithstanding (as it is above mentioned) that no man dare
approach within a stone's cast of his chariot, unless he be
called, but such only as keep his chariot.   And when we
came near unto him, he vailed his hat or bonnet being of
an inestimable price, doing reverence unto the cross.   And
immediately I put incense into the censer, and our bishop
taking the censer perfumed him, and gave him his benediction.   Moreover, they that come before the said Can
do always bring some oblation to present unto him,
observing the ancient law: Thou shalt not appear in my
presence with an empty hand.   And for that cause we
carried apples with us, and offered them in a platter with
reverence unto him : and taking out two of them he did
eat some part of one.   And then he signified unto us, that
we should go apart, lest the horse coming on might in
aught offend us.   With that we departed from him, and
turned aside, going unto certain of his barons, which had
been converted to the faith by certain friars of our order,
being at the same time in his army: and we offered unto
them the foresaid apples, who received them at our hands
with great joy, seeming unto us to be as glad as if we had
given them some great gift.

All the premises above written friar William de Solanga
hath put down in writing even as the foresaid friar
Odoricus uttered them by word of mouth, in the year of
our Lord 1330, in the month of May, and in the place of
S. Anthony of Padua.   Neither did he regard to write
them in difficult Latin or in an eloquent style, but even as
Odoricus himself rehearsed them, to the end that men
might the more easily understand the things reported.
I Friar Odoricus of Friuli, of a certain territory called

Portuis Vahonis, and of the order of the Minorites, do testify and bear witness unto the reverend father Guidotus, minister of the province of S. Anthony, in the marquisate of Treuiso (being by him required upon my obedience so to do) that all the premises above written, either I saw with mine own eyes, or heard the same reported by credible and substantial persons. The common report also of the countries where I was, testifieth those things, which I saw, to be true. Many other things I have omitted, because I beheld them not with mine own eyes. Howbeit from day to day I purpose with myself to travel countries or lands, in which action I dispose myself to die or to live, as it shall please my God.

CHAPTER XIX

Of the Death of Friar Odoricus

In the year therefore of our Lord 1331 the foresaid friar Odoricus preparing himself for the performance of his intended journey, that his travel and labour might be to greater purpose, he determined to present himself unto Pope John the two and twentieth, whose benediction and obedience being received, he, with a certain number of friars willing to bear him company, might convey himself unto all the countries of infidels. And as he was travelling towards the Pope, and not far distant from the city of Pisa, there meets him by the way a certain old man, in the habit and attire of a pilgrim, saluting him by name, and saying: All hail friar Odoricus. And when the friar demanded how he had knowledge of him, he answered: Whilst you were in India I knew you full well, yea, and I knew your holy purpose also: but see that you return immediately unto the convent from whence you came, for ten days hence you shall depart out of this present world. Wherefore being astonished and amazed at these words (especially the old man vanishing out of his sight, presently after he had spoken them) he determined to return. And so he returned in perfect health, feeling no crazedness nor infirmity of body. And being in his convent at Udene in the province of Padua, the tenth day after the foresaid vision, having received the communion, and preparing himself unto God, yea, being strong and sound of body, he happily rested in the Lord: whose sacred departure was signified unto the Pope aforesaid, under the hand of the public notary in these words following :

In the year of our Lord 1331, the 14 day of January, Beatus Odoricus a Friar Minorite, deceased in Christ, at whose prayers God showed many and sundry miracles, which I Guetelus public notary of Utina, son of M. Damianus de Porto Gruaro, at the commandment and direction of the honourable Conradus of the Borough of Gastaldion, and one of the Council of Utina, have written as faithfully as I could, and have delivered a copy thereof unto the Friars Minorites: howbeit not of all, because they are innumerable, and too difficult for me to write.

INDEX AND GLOSSARY

[THIS index is mainly a finding-list, such geographical information as it contains is for the most part borrowed from Mr. Warner's edition referred to in the Bibliographical Note. A. W. P.]

Abassi, name for Pope of Tibet, 354.

Abbana, River, 85.

Abbot of Mt. Sinai, miraculous election of, 41.

Abchaz (Abkhasia), kingdom of, between the Caucasus and the Black Sea, 169, 171.

Abdon, prophet, S. John Baptist buried near, 71.

Abebissam, name for fruit of balm, 34.

Abednego, one of the Three Children, 23.

Abraham, leaves Haran, 29; dwells at Beersheba, 44; his house at Hebron, 45; offered his sacrifice at Golgotha, 51; his garden, 66; Mahommedan belief as to, 92; his birth, 103.

Absalom, image of stone made by, 62.

Abzor, Mt. (Mt. Elbruz), in Georgia, 170.

Aceldama, the field of, 62.

Achelleke (? Atteleke, Et-Tih), wilderness of, 23.

Acias, Alanians called, 285, 293.

Acre, see Akon.

Adam, sends Seth for the oil of mercy, 9; wept a century for

Abel, 44; lake from his tears in Isle of Sylan (Ceylon), 131, 339; dwells at Hebron, 45; his head found at Golgotha, 51.

Adamants, rocks of, attract ships, 109 sq., 178; mountains of, attract arrows, 227 sq.

Adder, issuing from a tomb, 19; adders eaten as a delicacy, 135. *See also* Serpents.

Admirals, governors of cities, 26, 55, 152.

Adread, afraid, 186.

Adrian, Emperor, 56.

Adultery, punishment of, 218; children born of, 219.

Advertised, informed, 239.

Aelia, Adrian's name for Jerusalem, 56.

Again-bought, redeemed, 4.

Agenor, father of Dido, 21.

Aghast, terrify, 186.

Ai (Hayla), city of, 70.

Akon, Acre, city of, 21; taken by the Soldan, 25.

Alabrandines, alabandines, precious stones found at Alabanda in Caria, 143.

Alamo, or Alania, country, near the Caucasus, called, 171.

Barbara, S., shrine of, at Babylon, 23.

Barbarines, sweet (? white) thorns, 11.

Barchin, city of, resists Tartars, 232.

Barnabas, S., town in Cyprus, 20.

Barnacle Geese, see Bernakes.

Barrets, frauds, 179.

Bartholomew, Friar, of Cremona, Rubruk's associate, 265, 307 sq.

Basilisk, women with its power of slaying, 188.

Bastarci, of Hungaria Magna, conquered by Tartars, 233, 246.

Bastards, bitten by serpents in Sicily, 37.

Bathsheba, or Bersabe, Uriah's wife, 44.

Beads, of pearl, 130.

Beards, not shaved in Greek Church, 15; people of Burithabeth have none, 227.

Beasts, people transformed into, 137, 344 sq.

Beaumare, or Buemare, river, in land of Ichthyophagi, 196.

Beaumont, Jean de, Baatu's resemblance to, 306.

Beauvais, Vincent de, 213.

Beclippe, curdle, 35.

Bedouin, described, 43.

Beersheba, founded by Bathsheba, 44; placed at eight miles from Jerusalem, 49.

Begging, unknown in Manzi, 341.

Behight, promised, 4.

Behote, promise, 165, 166.

Beirout, 21, 83.

Beleth (Belbeis), town at end of kingdom of Aleppo (? confused with Baalbak), 23.

Belian, Mount (the desert Baldjuna to the east of Lake Baikal), 148.

Belinas, see Dan.

Bells, reason why Eastern Christians dislike, 319.

Beluacensis, Vincentius, Vincent de Beauvais, 213.

Bendochdare, Soldan, 25.

Benedict, Friar, a Polonian, 213.

Benefices, sale of, 14.

Bernakes, barnacle geese, 174, 354.

Bersabee, town of Beersheba, founded by Bathsheba, 44.

Berta, subject of Baatu, 302.

Beruch (Beirout), 21, 83.

Betemga, isle of, 125.

Bethany, S. John Chrysostom buried at, 12; described, 64 sq.

Bethe or Gethe (Yezd, or perhaps Isfahán), city of, 101.

Bethel, Mt. Moriah, called, 57.

Bethesda, pool of, 59.

Bethlehem, described, 46; placed at two miles from Jerusalem, 49.

Bethphage, 64.

Bethsaida, 73.

Bethshan, Saul's head hanged there, 75.

Betook, gave, 93.

Betron (Buzrah), land of, 69.

Bevoir, a lunch or collation, 345.

Bezaleel, or Dozeleel, the Shadow of God, 40.

Bezanzon, Bysantium, 7.

Bible, relics of S. Jerome's translation of, 47.

Bigged, built, 65.

Bigon, wine of Cassay, 136.

Bills, written documents, 115.

Bisermini, Tartar expedition against, 231, 247.

Bithal, grandson of Chinghis Can, 230.

Blacians, Wallachians, 311.

Blood-drinking, 129 sq.

Bochar (El Bukaca), vale of, 82.

Bodin, isle of, cannibalism in, 339.

Bohemia, King of, aids Carpini, 238.

Bolac, village of, 315.

Boleslaus, Duke of Slesia, helps Carpini, 239.

Boleyne, Godfrey de, see Bouillon.

Farde, or Faro (of Messina), passage, 37.

Farfar or Farphar (Orontes), bridge and water of, 86 : *see also* Ferne.

Fasting, in Greek church, 14 sq.

Feasts, made at inns, 139, 346 ; of the Great Chan, 151 sq., 352 sq.

Feet, women with small, 205, 356.

Ferne (Orontes), River, 85 ; city of (Ilgun), 86 : *see also* Farfar.

Fertre, bier, palanquin, 40, 147.

Fiends, lie with women, 145.

Figs, of Pharaoh, 33.

Fire, purification by, 163, 220 sq.; fires perfumed when Can passes, 359 ; taxes on, 344.

Firmament, division of the, 124.

Fish, caught by loirs, 136 ; in the Gravelly Sea, 180; who come to be caught, 128 sq., 337 ; caught by dive-doppers, 343.

Fladriene (Flandrina), city of, 112, 330.

Flagram, land of, in Syria, 86.

Flaxon (? Naxos), isle of, 12.

Flom, river, 66.

Florach, castle of, in Asia Minor, 85.

Floridus, field of, at Bethlehem, 46.

Folily, foolishly, 91.

Food, notes of, 164, 216, 271, 312 ; *see also* Cannibalism.

Foot, folk with only one, 105; counterfeit of, worn by wives as a headdress, 142, 349.

Forcelets, strongholds, 31.

Forme father, first father, 4.

Former, matter, 4.

Formest, earliest, 199.

Fornication, Greek view of, 14 ; miracle of maiden condemned for, 46 ; punishment of, 218.

Forthinketh, repents, 200.

Foss, or ditch, of Mennon, 22.

Found with, supplied, 39.

Fox, that shall shew Jews of Caspian Mountains a way to escape, 176.

France, relics of Christ preserved in, 10.

Friars, in Janzu, 346 ; able to cast out devils, 357 sq.

Friars Minorite, Franciscans, 213 ; at Great Chan's court, 350.

Friars Praedicant, Dominicans.

Friuli, Odoric born there, 326.

Froteth, rubs, 40.

Fructuous, fruitful, 4.

Fruit, given to Great Chan, 160, 360 ; of faerie, 180 ; bearing a little beast like a lamb, 174, 353.

Frussch, rush, 155.

Fulfille, black pepper, 113.

Funeral customs and rites, 112, 114, 118, 129, 132, 166, 203, 227, 233, 280, 321, 323, 355.

Fynepape (Philippolis), city of, 7.

Gabbers, cheats.

Gabriel, speaks with Mahomet, 95; well of, at Nazareth, 75.

Gadrige (Kadija), Mahomet's wife, 95.

Gaius, *see* Caesar, Julius.

Galilee, Mount, 65 ; province of, 73.

Galiot, helmet, 160.

Gallamelle, Mohammedan drink, 96.

Ganges, river, *see* Pison.

Garantez, some dark-coloured gem, 143.

Gardens in Egypt, bear fruit seven times a year, 33.

Garners of Joseph, 35.

Gasarians, in the city of Orna, 232.

Gascony, miles of, 78 sq.

Gate of Hell, city called by mistranslation, *see* Hell.

Gatholonabes (Senex de Monte), his mock Paradise, 183.

Gaydo, residence of Great Chan, *see* Caido.

Gaza, city of the Philistines, 22.

Gebel (Djiblé), city of, 86.

Geen, *see* Genoa.

Necromancy, divination by means of the dead, 153.

Neigh, neighen, draw near, 186, 143.

Nemroth, see Nimrod.

Neople, see Sichem.

Neper (Dnieper), River, 243.

Nestorians, 81, 224, 308, 317, 332, 346.

Nicholas, S., born at Patera, 17; church of, at Bethlehem, 47.

Nicholas, servant of Rubruk, 265.

Nicosea, Archbishop of, in Cyprus, 19.

Nile, the river, 29 sq., 200 sq.

Nimrod or Nemroth, king, 27, 145.

Nine, the number held in reverence by the Tartars, 149.

Ninus, founder of Nineveh, 103.

Noah or Noe, his dove, 9; founded Dain, 100; began Nineveh, 103, legend of the ark, 100, 327.

Nones of May, May 7th, 261.

Norway, stopping point of circumnavigation of the world, 123; not included in Mandeville's reckoning of the earth's surface, 124.

Noses, Tartar views as to, 277, 284.

Notre Dame la grande, Notre Dame de Latine, churches at Jerusalem, 54.

Nubia, people of, 31; Nubian Christians, 81.

Nuns cordelers, made by mistranslation into ' Nuns of an hundred orders,' 72.

Nye (Nisch, in Servia), city of, 7.

Nyfland (Livonia), 7, 87.

Nyke (Nicaea), city of, 16; described, 85.

Nyse (Nisa), Prester John's capital, 178, 182.

Occoday Can, son of Chingis, 223, 229; election as Can, 231 sq.; poisoned, 253.

Odenthos, beasts called, 191.

Odoric, Friar, his Journal, 326 sqq.; scoffed at by Lammori, 334; eats bread made from meal or trees (sago), 336; sees fishes offering themselves to be caught, 337; argues against cannibal rites, 340; sees idols feasted, 342; fish caught by dive-doppers; park where men in guise of beasts are fed, 345; inquires as to numbers in Great Chan's court, 350; stays three years in Cathay, 354; passes the palace of the man with the long nails, 355; enters the Valley of Dead Bodies, 358; dictates his travels, 359; desires to present himself to the Pope, 361; dies, 362.

Oertige, isle of, see Critige.

Oft-sithes, often times.

Oil made from branches of olive brought by birds to Mt. Sinai, 40; dropped from image of the B. Virgin at Sardenak, 82.

Oil of mercy, 9.

Olivet, Mount, 64.

Olympus, Mount, 12.

Orafles (giraffes), beasts called, 191.

Orda, tent, court, 244, 248, 304.

Orda, city of, 87.

Ordinatly, orderly, in good array, 117.

Ordu, grandson of Chingis Can, 229 sq.; 247.

Orfrayed, embroidered with gold, 152.

Organum, country once called, 316.

Orille (Chryse), isle of, 198.

Ormanx, town of, in Asia Minor, 85.

Ormes, land of, 329.

Orna, city of, besieged by Tartars, 232.

Orped, brave, 104.

Out-take, except, 161, 202.

Overthwart, cross, across, 9, 137.

Rubies, found by seaside, 20 ; gigantic specimen of, 131 ; one belonging to Great Chan, 157 (cp. 338).

Rubruquis, William de, his Journal, 261 sqq.; gives out that he is not travelling as messenger of King of France, 263, 282 ; importuned by Tartars for food and presents, 281 sqq.; received by Scacatai, 283 ; expounds the solemnity of Pentecost, 286 ; his Saracen convert, 287 ; sent on to Sartach, 287 sqq.; received by him, 293 sqq.; made to surrender his vestments, 297; received by Baatu, 305 sqq.; sent on to Mangu Can, 308 sq.; talks with Jugures priests, 320 sq.

Ruffynell, castle of, in Asia Minor, 85.

Russia, held by King of Hungary, 7 ; Tartar expedition against, 232 ; country described, 291 ; Russian bishops answer to Pope's letters, 260,

Ryboth (Tibet), " isle " of, 203.

Saba, city of, in Ethiopia, 105.

Sabatory, river, only runs on Saturdays, 83.

Sabissacole, hill of, in Armenia, 100, 327.

Sachala (Satalia), city of, in Asia Minor, 173.

Sadonia (Soldonia), city of, in Persia, 101, 327.

Saduz (Shangtu), summer residence of the Great Chan, 157.

Safra (Shefa 'Amr), castle of, birthplace of SS. James and John, 22, 77.

Sahythe (Said), province of Egypt, 31.

Saints, Indian, compared with Christian, 118.

Sakers, sakrets, falcons, 156.

Saladin, soldan of Egypt, 24.

Salem, name for Jerusalem, 49.

Salt-hill, 101, 327 ; salt-pits, 265, 287.

Samar, county of, on the Euphrates, 27.

Samaria, 71.

Samaritan woman, well at which Christ spake with her, 71.

Samaritans, their religion, dress, etc., 74 sq.

Samites, satin robes, 254.

Samogetae, Tartar invasion of, 233, 246.

Samson, at Gaza, 22.

Samuel, the prophet, 63, 70.

Sanct Quintin, Simon de, 213 sq.

Saphor, castle of, near Capernaum, 78.

Sapphires, diamonds counterfeited from, 107 sq.; preservatives from lechery, 182.

Saracens, have destroyed Tyre, 20; counterfeit balm, 34 ; whitewash painted portraits, 38 ; drink no wine and eat no pork, 48 ; reverence the Temple at Jerusalem, 56 ; wickedness of at Nazareth, 75 ; of their customs and law, 88 sqq.; descent of, 95 ; object to questions on their religion, 317 sq.: see also Mahommedans.

Sarak (Sarai), chief city of Comania, 169.

Sarche (Baroch), city of, in India, 112.

Sardenare, or Sardenak (Sardenaya), five miles from Damascus, 21 ; Church of Our Lady at, 82.

Sarepta (Sûrafend), 21.

Sarguit, city of, surrendered to Tartars, 232.

Sarmassan, in Persia, 170.

Sarmois, language, 70,

Sarphen, city of, in Sarepta, 21.

Sarras, city of Media, Saracens in, 170.

CATALOG OF DOVER BOOKS

Books Explaining Science and Mathematics

WHAT IS SCIENCE?, N. Campbell. The role of experiment and measurement, the function of mathematics, the nature of scientific laws, the difference between laws and theories, the limitations of science, and many similarly provocative topics are treated clearly and without technicalities by an eminent scientist. "Still an excellent introduction to scientific philosophy," H. Margenau in PHYSICS TODAY. "A first-rate primer . . . deserves a wide audience," SCIENTIFIC AMERICAN. 192pp. 5⅜ x 8.   S43 Paperbound **$1.25**

THE NATURE OF PHYSICAL THEORY, P. W. Bridgman. A Nobel Laureate's clear, non-technical lectures on difficulties and paradoxes connected with frontier research on the physical sciences. Concerned with such central concepts as thought, logic, mathematics, relativity, probability, wave mechanics, etc. he analyzes the contributions of such men as Newton, Einstein, Bohr, Heisenberg, and many others. "Lucid and entertaining . . . recommended to anyone who wants to get some insight into current philosophies of science," THE NEW PHILOSOPHY. Index. xi + 138pp. 5⅜ x 8.   S33 Paperbound **$1.25**

EXPERIMENT AND THEORY IN PHYSICS, Max Born. A Nobel Laureate examines the nature of experiment and theory in theoretical physics and analyzes the advances made by the great physicists of our day: Heisenberg, Einstein, Bohr, Planck, Dirac, and others. The actual process of creation is detailed step-by-step by one who participated. A fine examination of the scientific method at work. 44pp. 5⅜ x 8.   S308 Paperbound **75¢**

THE PSYCHOLOGY OF INVENTION IN THE MATHEMATICAL FIELD, J. Hadamard. The reports of such men as Descartes, Pascal, Einstein, Poincaré, and others are considered in this investigation of the method of idea-creation in mathematics and other sciences and the thinking process in general. How do ideas originate? What is the role of the unconscious? What is Poincaré's forgetting hypothesis? are some of the fascinating questions treated. A penetrating analysis of Einstein's thought processes concludes the book. xiii + 145pp. 5⅜ x 8.   T107 Paperbound **$1.25**

THE NATURE OF LIGHT AND COLOUR IN THE OPEN AIR, M. Minnaert. Why are shadows sometimes blue, sometimes green, or other colors depending on the light and surroundings? What causes mirages? Why do multiple suns and moons appear in the sky? Professor Minnaert explains these unusual phenomena and hundreds of others in simple, easy-to-understand terms based on optical laws and the properties of light and color. No mathematics is required but artists, scientists, students, and everyone fascinated by these "tricks" of nature will find thousands of useful and amazing pieces of information. Hundreds of observational experiments are suggested which require no special equipment. 200 illustrations; 42 photos. xvi + 362pp. 5⅜ x 8.   T196 Paperbound **$1.95**

THE UNIVERSE OF LIGHT, W. Bragg. Sir William Bragg, Nobel Laureate and great modern physicist, is also well known for his powers of clear exposition. Here he analyzes all aspects of light for the layman: lenses, reflection, refraction, the optics of vision, x-rays, the photoelectric effect, etc. He tells you what causes the color of spectra, rainbows, and soap bubbles, how magic mirrors work, and much more. Dozens of simple experiments are described. Preface. Index. 199 line drawings and photographs, including 2 full-page color plates. x + 283pp. 5⅜ x 8.   T538 Paperbound **$1.85**

SOAP-BUBBLES: THEIR COLOURS AND THE FORCES THAT MOULD THEM, C. V. Boys. For continuing popularity and validity as scientific primer, few books can match this volume of easily-followed experiments, explanations. Lucid exposition of complexities of liquid films, surface tension and related phenomena, bubbles' reaction to heat, motion, music, magnetic fields. Experiments with capillary attraction, soap bubbles on frames, composite bubbles, liquid cylinders and jets, bubbles other than soap, etc. Wonderful introduction to scientific method, natural laws that have many ramifications in areas of modern physics. Only complete edition in print. New Introduction by S. Z. Lewin, New York University. 83 illustrations; 1 full-page color plate. xii + 190pp. 5⅜ x 8½.   T542 Paperbound **95¢**

CATALOGUE OF DOVER BOOKS

THE STORY OF X-RAYS FROM RONTGEN TO ISOTOPES, A. R. Bleich, M.D. This book, by a member of the American College of Radiology, gives the scientific explanation of x-rays, their applications in medicine, industry and art, and their danger (and that of atmospheric radiation) to the individual and the species. You learn how radiation therapy is applied against cancer, how x-rays diagnose heart disease and other ailments, how they are used to examine mummies for information on diseases of early societies, and industrial materials for hidden weaknesses. 54 illustrations show x-rays of flowers, bones, stomach, gears with flaws, etc. 1st publication. Index. xix + 186pp. 5⅜ x 8. **T622 Paperbound $1.35**

SPINNING TOPS AND GYROSCOPIC MOTION, John Perry. A classic elementary text of the dynamics of rotation — the behavior and use of rotating bodies such as gyroscopes and tops. In simple, everyday English you are shown how quasi-rigidity is induced in discs of paper, smoke rings, chains, etc., by rapid motions; why a gyrostat falls and why a top rises; precession; how the earth's motion affects climate; and many other phenomena. Appendix on practical use of gyroscopes. 62 figures. 128pp. 5⅜ x 8. **T416 Paperbound $1.00**

SNOW CRYSTALS, W. A. Bentley, M. J. Humphreys. For almost 50 years W. A. Bentley photographed snow flakes in his laboratory in Jericho, Vermont; in 1931 the American Meteorological Society gathered together the best of his work, some 2400 photographs of snow flakes, plus a few ice flowers, windowpane frosts, dew, frozen rain, and other ice formations. Pictures were selected for beauty and scientific value. A very valuable work to anyone in meteorology, cryology; most interesting to layman; extremely useful for artist who wants beautiful, crystalline designs. All copyright free. Unabridged reprint of 1931 edition. 2453 illustrations. 227pp. 8 x 10½. **T287 Paperbound $2.95**

A DOVER SCIENCE SAMPLER, edited by George Barkin. A collection of brief, non-technical passages from 44 Dover Books Explaining Science for the enjoyment of the science-minded browser. Includes work of Bertrand Russell, Poincaré, Laplace, Max Born, Galileo, Newton; material on physics, mathematics, metallurgy, anatomy, astronomy, chemistry, etc. You will be fascinated by Martin Gardner's analysis of the sincere pseudo-scientist, Moritz's account of Newton's absentmindedness, Bernard's examples of human vivisection, etc. Illustrations from the Diderot Pictorial Encyclopedia and De Re Metallica. 64 pages. **FREE**

THE STORY OF ATOMIC THEORY AND ATOMIC ENERGY, J. G. Feinberg. A broader approach to subject of nuclear energy and its cultural implications than any other similar source. Very readable, informal, completely non-technical text. Begins with first atomic theory, 600 B.C. and carries you through the work of Mendelejeff, Röntgen, Madame Curie, to Einstein's equation and the A-bomb. New chapter goes through thermonuclear fission, binding energy, other events up to 1959. Radioactive decay and radiation hazards, future benefits, work of Bohr, moderns, hundreds more topics. "Deserves special mention . . . not only authoritative but thoroughly popular in the best sense of the word," Saturday Review. Formerly, "The Atom Story." Expanded with new chapter. Three appendixes. Index. 34 illustrations. vii + 243pp. 5⅜ x 8. **T625 Paperbound $1.45**

THE STRANGE STORY OF THE QUANTUM, AN ACCOUNT FOR THE GENERAL READER OF THE GROWTH OF IDEAS UNDERLYING OUR PRESENT ATOMIC KNOWLEDGE, B. Hoffmann. Presents lucidly and expertly, with barest amount of mathematics, the problems and theories which led to modern quantum physics. Dr. Hoffmann begins with the closing years of the 19th century, when certain trifling discrepancies were noticed, and with illuminating analogies and examples takes you through the brilliant concepts of Planck, Einstein, Pauli, Broglie, Bohr, Schroedinger, Heisenberg, Dirac, Sommerfeld, Feynman, etc. This edition includes a new, long postscript carrying the story through 1958. "Of the books attempting an account of the history and contents of our modern atomic physics which have come to my attention, this is the best," H. Margenau, Yale University, in "American Journal of Physics." 32 tables and line illustrations. Index. 275pp. 5⅜ x 8. **T518 Paperbound $1.45**

SPACE AND TIME, E. Borel. Written by a versatile mathematician of world renown with his customary lucidity and precision, this introduction to relativity for the layman presents scores of examples, analogies, and illustrations that open up new ways of thinking about space and time. It covers abstract geometry and geographical maps, continuity and topology, the propagation of light, the special theory of relativity, the general theory of relativity, theoretical researches, and much more. Mathematical notes. 2 Indexes. 4 Appendices. 15 figures. xvi + 243pp. 5⅜ x 8. **T592 Paperbound $1.45**

FROM EUCLID TO EDDINGTON: A STUDY OF THE CONCEPTIONS OF THE EXTERNAL WORLD, Sir Edmund Whittaker. A foremost British scientist traces the development of theories of natural philosophy from the western rediscovery of Euclid to Eddington, Einstein, Dirac, etc. The inadequacy of classical physics is contrasted with present day attempts to understand the physical world through relativity, non-Euclidean geometry, space curvature, wave mechanics, etc. 5 major divisions of examination: Space; Time and Movement; the Concepts of Classical Physics; the Concepts of Quantum Mechanics; the Eddington Universe. 212pp. 5⅜ x 8. **T491 Paperbound $1.35**

Nature, Biology

NATURE RECREATION: Group Guidance for the Out-of-doors, William Gould Vinal. Intended for both the uninitiated nature instructor and the education student on the college level, this complete "how-to" program surveys the entire area of nature education for the young. Philosophy of nature recreation; requirements, responsibilities, important information for group leaders; nature games; suggested group projects; conducting meetings and getting discussions started; etc. Scores of immediately applicable teaching aids, plus completely updated sources of information, pamphlets, field guides, recordings, etc. Bibliography. 74 photographs. + 310pp. 5⅜ x 8½.　　　　　　　　　　　　　　　　T1015 Paperbound **$1.75**

HOW TO KNOW THE WILD FLOWERS, Mrs. William Starr Dana. Classic nature book that has introduced thousands to wonders of American wild flowers. Color-season principle of organization is easy to use, even by those with no botanical training, and the genial, refreshing discussions of history, folklore, uses of over 1,000 native and escape flowers, foliage plants are informative as well as fun to read. Over 170 full-page plates, collected from several editions, may be colored in to make permanent records of finds. Revised to conform with 1950 edition of Gray's Manual of Botany. xlii + 438pp. 5⅜ x 8½.　　T332 Paperbound **$1.85**

HOW TO KNOW THE FERNS, F. T. Parsons. Ferns, among our most lovely native plants, are all too little known. This classic of nature lore will enable the layman to identify almost any American fern he may come across. After an introduction on the structure and life of ferns, the 57 most important ferns are fully pictured and described (arranged upon a simple identification key). Index of Latin and English names. 61 illustrations and 42 full-page plates. xiv + 215pp. 5⅜ x 8.　　　　　　　　　　　　　　　　　　　　　T740 Paperbound **$1.25**

MANUAL OF THE TREES OF NORTH AMERICA, Charles Sprague Sargent. Still unsurpassed as most comprehensive, reliable study of North American tree characteristics, precise locations and distribution. By dean of American dendrologists. Every tree native to U.S., Canada, Alaska, 185 genera, 717 species, described in detail—leaves, flowers, fruit, winterbuds, bark, wood, growth habits etc. plus discussion of varieties and local variants, immaturity variations. Over 100 keys, including unusual 11-page analytical key to genera, aid in identification. 783 clear illustrations of flowers, fruit, leaves. An unmatched permanent reference work for all nature lovers. Second enlarged (1926) edition. Synopsis of families. Analytical key to genera. Glossary of technical terms. Index. 783 illustrations, 1 map. Two volumes. Total of 982pp. 5⅜ x 8.　　　　　　　　　　　T277 Vol. I Paperbound **$2.00**
　　　　　　　　　　　　　　　　　　　　　　T278 Vol. II Paperbound **$2.00**
　　　　　　　　　　　　　　　　　　　　　　The set **$4.00**

TREES OF THE EASTERN AND CENTRAL UNITED STATES AND CANADA, W. M. Harlow. A revised edition of a standard middle-level guide to native trees and important escapes. More than 140 trees are described in detail, and illustrated with more than 600 drawings and photographs. Supplementary keys will enable the careful reader to identify almost any tree he might encounter. xiii + 288pp. 5⅜ x 8.　　　　　　　　　　T395 Paperbound **$1.35**

GUIDE TO SOUTHERN TREES, Ellwood S. Harrar and J. George Harrar. All the essential information about trees indigenous to the South, in an extremely handy format. Introductory essay on methods of tree classification and study, nomenclature, chief divisions of Southern trees, etc. Approximately 100 keys and synopses allow for swift, accurate identification of trees. Numerous excellent illustrations, non-technical text make this a useful book for teachers of biology or natural science, nature lovers, amateur naturalists. Revised 1962 edition. Index. Bibliography. Glossary of technical terms. 920 illustrations; 201 full-page plates. ix + 709pp. 4⅝ x 6⅜.　　　　　　　　　　　　　　T945 Paperbound **$2.25**

FRUIT KEY AND TWIG KEY TO TREES AND SHRUBS, W. M. Harlow. Bound together in one volume for the first time, these handy and accurate keys to fruit and twig identification are the only guides of their sort with photographs (up to 3 times natural size). "Fruit Key": Key to over 120 different deciduous and evergreen fruits. 139 photographs and 11 line drawings. Synoptic summary of fruit types. Bibliography. 2 Indexes (common and scientific names). "Twig Key": Key to over 160 different twigs and buds. 173 photographs. Glossary of technical terms. Bibliography. 2 Indexes (common and scientific names). Two volumes bound as one. Total of xvii + 126pp. 5⅝ x 8⅜.　　　　　　　　　　　　　　　　　T511 Paperbound **$1.25**

INSECT LIFE AND INSECT NATURAL HISTORY, S. W. Frost. A work emphasizing habits, social life, and ecological relations of insects, rather than more academic aspects of classification and morphology. Prof. Frost's enthusiasm and knowledge are everywhere evident as he discusses insect associations and specialized habits like leaf-rolling, leaf-mining, and case-making, the gall insects, the boring insects, aquatic insects, etc. He examines all sorts of matters not usually covered in general works, such as: insects as human food, insect music and musicians, insect response to electric and radio waves, use of insects in art and literature. The admirably executed purpose of this book, which covers the middle ground between elementary treatment and scholarly monographs, is to excite the reader to observe for himself. Over 700 illustrations. Extensive bibliography. x + 524pp. 5⅜ x 8.　　T517 Paperbound **$2.45**

CATALOGUE OF DOVER BOOKS

COMMON SPIDERS OF THE UNITED STATES, J. H. Emerton. Here is a nature hobby you can pursue right in your own cellar! Only non-technical, but thorough, reliable guide to spiders for the layman. Over 200 spiders from all parts of the country, arranged by scientific classification, are identified by shape and color, number of eyes, habitat and range, habits, etc. Full text, 501 line drawings and photographs, and valuable introduction explain webs, poisons, threads, capturing and preserving spiders, etc. Index. New synoptic key by S. W. Frost. xxiv + 225pp. 5⅜ x 8.   T223 Paperbound **$1.35**

THE LIFE STORY OF THE FISH: HIS MANNERS AND MORALS, Brian Curtis. A comprehensive, non-technical survey of just about everything worth knowing about fish. Written for the aquarist, the angler, and the layman with an inquisitive mind, the text covers such topics as evolution, external covering and protective coloration, physics and physiology of vision, maintenance of equilibrium, function of the lateral line canal for auditory and temperature senses, nervous system, function of the air bladder, reproductive system and methods—courtship, mating, spawning, care of young—and many more. Also sections on game fish, the problems of conservation and a fascinating chapter on fish curiosities. "Clear, simple language . . . excellent judgment in choice of subjects . . . delightful sense of humor," New York Times. Revised (1949) edition. Index. Bibliography of 72 items. 6 full-page photographic plates. xii + 284pp. 5⅜ x 8.   T929 Paperbound **$1.50**

BATS, Glover Morrill Allen. The most comprehensive study of bats as a life-form by the world's foremost authority. A thorough summary of just about everything known about this fascinating and mysterious flying mammal, including its unique location sense, hibernation and cycles, its habitats and distribution, its wing structure and flying habits, and its relationship to man in the long history of folklore and superstition. Written on a middle-level, the book can be profitably studied by a trained zoologist and thoroughly enjoyed by the layman. "An absorbing text with excellent illustrations. Bats should have more friends and fewer thoughtless detractors as a result of the publication of this volume," William Beebe, Books. Extensive bibliography. 57 photographs and illustrations. x + 368pp. 5⅜ x 8½.
T984 Paperbound **$2.00**

BIRDS AND THEIR ATTRIBUTES, Glover Morrill Allen. A fine general introduction to birds as living organisms, especially valuable because of emphasis on structure, physiology, habits, behavior. Discusses relationship of bird to man, early attempts at scientific ornithology, feathers and coloration, skeletal structure including bills, legs and feet, wings. Also food habits, evolution and present distribution, feeding and nest-building, still unsolved questions of migrations and location sense, many more similar topics. Final chapter on classification, nomenclature. A good popular-level summary for the biologist; a first-rate introduction for the layman. Reprint of 1925 edition. References and index. 51 illustrations. viii + 338pp. 5⅜ x 8½.   T957 Paperbound **$1.85**

LIFE HISTORIES OF NORTH AMERICAN BIRDS, Arthur Cleveland Bent. Bent's monumental series of books on North American birds, prepared and published under auspices of Smithsonian Institute, is the definitive coverage of the subject, the most-used single source of information. Now the entire set is to be made available by Dover in inexpensive editions. This encyclopedic collection of detailed, specific observations utilizes reports of hundreds of contemporary observers, writings of such naturalists as Audubon, Burroughs, William Brewster, as well as author's own extensive investigations. Contains literally everything known about life history of each bird considered: nesting, eggs, plumage, distribution and migration, voice, enemies, courtship, etc. These not over-technical works are musts for ornithologists, conservationists, amateur naturalists, anyone seriously interested in American birds.

BIRDS OF PREY. More than 100 subspecies of hawks, falcons, eagles, buzzards, condors and owls, from the common barn owl to the extinct caracara of Guadaloupe Island. 400 photographs. Two volume set. Index for each volume. Bibliographies of 403, 520 items. 197 full-page plates. Total of 907pp. 5⅜ x 8½.   Vol. I T931 Paperbound **$2.35**
                                                     Vol. II T932 Paperbound **$2.35**

WILD FOWL. Ducks, geese, swans, and tree ducks—73 different subspecies. Two volume set. Index for each volume. Bibliographies of 124, 144 items. 106 full-page plates. Total of 685pp. 5⅜ x 8½.   Vol. I T285 Paperbound **$2.35**
                                                     Vol. II T286 Paperbound **$2.35**

SHORE BIRDS. 81 varieties (sandpipers, woodcocks, plovers, snipes, phalaropes, curlews, oyster catchers, etc.). More than 200 photographs of eggs, nesting sites, adult and young of important species. Two volume set. Index for each volume. Bibliographies of 261, 188 items. 121 full-page plates. Total of 860pp. 5⅜ x 8½.   Vol. I T933 Paperbound **$2.35**
                                                     Vol. II T934 Paperbound **$2.35**

THE LIFE OF PASTEUR, R. Vallery-Radot. 13th edition of this definitive biography, cited in Encyclopaedia Britannica. Authoritative, scholarly, well-documented with contemporary quotes, observations; gives complete picture of Pasteur's personal life; especially thorough presentation of scientific activities with silkworms, fermentation, hydrophobia, inoculation, etc. Introduction by Sir William Osler. Index. 505pp. 5⅜ x 8.   T632 Paperbound **$2.00**

Puzzles, Mathematical Recreations

SYMBOLIC LOGIC and THE GAME OF LOGIC, Lewis Carroll. "Symbolic Logic" is not concerned with modern symbolic logic, but is instead a collection of over 380 problems posed with charm and imagination, using the syllogism, and a fascinating diagrammatic method of drawing conclusions. In "The Game of Logic" Carroll's whimsical imagination devises a logical game played with 2 diagrams and counters (included) to manipulate hundreds of tricky syllogisms. The final section, "Hit or Miss" is a lagniappe of 101 additional puzzles in the delightful Carroll manner. Until this reprint edition, both of these books were rarities costing up to $15 each. Symbolic Logic: Index. xxxi + 199pp. The Game of Logic: 96pp. 2 vols. bound as one. 5⅜ x 8.   **T492 Paperbound $1.50**

PILLOW PROBLEMS and A TANGLED TALE, Lewis Carroll. One of the rarest of all Carroll's works, "Pillow Problems" contains 72 original math puzzles, all typically ingenious. Particularly fascinating are Carroll's answers which remain exactly as he thought them out, reflecting his actual mental process. The problems in "A Tangled Tale" are in story form, originally appearing as a monthly magazine serial. Carroll not only gives the solutions, but uses answers sent in by readers to discuss wrong approaches and misleading paths, and grades them for insight. Both of these books were rarities until this edition, "Pillow Problems" costing up to $25, and "A Tangled Tale" $15. Pillow Problems: Preface and Introduction by Lewis Carroll. xx + 109pp. A Tangled Tale: 6 illustrations. 152pp. Two vols. bound as one. 5⅜ x 8.   **T493 Paperbound $1.50**

AMUSEMENTS IN MATHEMATICS, Henry Ernest Dudeney. The foremost British originator of mathematical puzzles is always intriguing, witty, and paradoxical in this classic, one of the largest collections of mathematical amusements. More than 430 puzzles, problems, and paradoxes. Mazes and games, problems on number manipulation, unicursal and other route problems, puzzles on measuring, weighing, packing, age, kinship, chessboards, joiners', crossing river, plane figure dissection, and many others. Solutions. More than 450 illustrations. vii + 258pp. 5⅜ x 8.   **T473 Paperbound $1.25**

THE CANTERBURY PUZZLES, Henry Dudeney. Chaucer's pilgrims set one another problems in story form. Also Adventures of the Puzzle Club, the Strange Escape of the King's Jester, the Monks of Riddlewell, the Squire's Christmas Puzzle Party, and others. All puzzles are original, based on dissecting plane figures, arithmetic, algebra, elementary calculus and other branches of mathematics, and purely logical ingenuity. "The limit of ingenuity and intricacy," The Observer. Over 110 puzzles. Full Solutions. 150 illustrations. vii + 225pp. 5⅜ x 8.   **T474 Paperbound $1.25**

MATHEMATICAL EXCURSIONS, H. A. Merrill. Even if you hardly remember your high school math, you'll enjoy the 90 stimulating problems contained in this book and you will come to understand a great many mathematical principles with surprisingly little effort. Many useful shortcuts and diversions not generally known are included: division by inspection, Russian peasant multiplication, memory systems for pi, building odd and even magic squares, square roots by geometry, dyadic systems, and many more. Solutions to difficult problems. 50 illustrations. 145pp. 5⅜ x 8.   **T350 Paperbound $1.00**

MAGIC SQUARES AND CUBES, W. S. Andrews. Only book-length treatment in English, a thorough non-technical description and analysis. Here are nasik, overlapping, pandiagonal, serrated squares; magic circles, cubes, spheres, rhombuses. Try your hand at 4-dimensional magical figures! Much unusual folklore and tradition included. High school algebra is sufficient. 754 diagrams and illustrations. viii + 419pp. 5⅜ x 8.   **T658 Paperbound $1.85**

CALIBAN'S PROBLEM BOOK: MATHEMATICAL, INFERENTIAL AND CRYPTOGRAPHIC PUZZLES, H. Phillips (Caliban), S. T. Shovelton, G. S. Marshall. 105 ingenious problems by the greatest living creator of puzzles based on logic and inference. Rigorous, modern, piquant; reflecting their author's unusual personality, these intermediate and advanced puzzles all involve the ability to reason clearly through complex situations; some call for mathematical knowledge, ranging from algebra to number theory. Solutions. xi + 180pp. 5⅜ x 8.   **T736 Paperbound $1.25**

MATHEMATICAL PUZZLES FOR BEGINNERS AND ENTHUSIASTS, G. Mott-Smith. 188 mathematical puzzles based on algebra, dissection of plane figures, permutations, and probability, that will test and improve your powers of inference and interpretation. The Odic Force, The Spider's Cousin, Ellipse Drawing, theory and strategy of card and board games like tit-tat-toe, go moku, salvo, and many others. 100 pages of detailed mathematical explanations. Appendix of primes, square roots, etc. 135 illustrations. 2nd revised edition. 248pp. 5⅜ x 8.   **T198 Paperbound $1.00**

MATHEMAGIC, MAGIC PUZZLES, AND GAMES WITH NUMBERS, R. V. Heath. More than 60 new puzzles and stunts based on the properties of numbers. Easy techniques for multiplying large numbers mentally, revealing hidden numbers magically, finding the date of any day in any year, and dozens more. Over 30 pages devoted to magic squares, triangles, cubes, circles, etc. Edited by J. S. Meyer. 76 illustrations. 128pp. 5⅜ x 8.   **T110 Paperbound $1.00**

THE BOOK OF MODERN PUZZLES, G. L. Kaufman. A completely new series of puzzles as fascinating as crossword and deduction puzzles but based upon different principles and techniques. Simple 2-minute teasers, word labyrinths, design and pattern puzzles, logic and observation puzzles — over 150 braincrackers. Answers to all problems. 116 illustrations. 192pp. 5⅜ x 8.
T143 Paperbound **$1.00**

NEW WORD PUZZLES, G. L. Kaufman. 100 ENTIRELY NEW puzzles based on words and their combinations that will delight crossword puzzle, Scrabble and Jotto fans. Chess words, based on the moves of the chess king; design-onyms, symmetrical designs made of synonyms; rhymed double-crostics; syllable sentences; addle letter anagrams; alphagrams; linkograms; and many others all brand new. Full solutions. Space to work problems. 196 figures. vi + 122pp. 5⅜ x 8.
T344 Paperbound **$1.00**

MAZES AND LABYRINTHS: A BOOK OF PUZZLES, W. Shepherd. Mazes, formerly associated with mystery and ritual, are still among the most intriguing of intellectual puzzles. This is a novel and different collection of 50 amusements that embody the principle of the maze: mazes in the classical tradition; 3-dimensional, ribbon, and Möbius-strip mazes; hidden messages; spatial arrangements; etc.—almost all built on amusing story situations. 84 illustrations. Essay on maze psychology. Solutions. xv + 122pp. 5⅜ x 8.
T731 Paperbound **$1.00**

MAGIC TRICKS & CARD TRICKS, W. Jonson. Two books bound as one. 52 tricks with cards, 37 tricks with coins, bills, eggs, smoke, ribbons, slates, etc. Details on presentation, misdirection, and routining will help you master such famous tricks as the Changing Card, Card in the Pocket, Four Aces, Coin Through the Hand, Bill in the Egg, Afghan Bands, and over 75 others. If you follow the lucid exposition and key diagrams carefully, you will finish these two books with an astonishing mastery of magic. 106 figures. 224pp. 5⅜ x 8. T909 Paperbound **$1.00**

PANORAMA OF MAGIC, Milbourne Christopher. A profusely illustrated history of stage magic, a unique selection of prints and engravings from the author's private collection of magic memorabilia, the largest of its kind. Apparatus, stage settings and costumes; ingenious ads distributed by the performers and satiric broadsides passed around in the streets ridiculing pompous showmen; programs; decorative souvenirs. The lively text, by one of America's foremost professional magicians, is full of anecdotes about almost legendary wizards: Dede, the Egyptian; Philadelphia, the wonder-worker; Robert-Houdin, "the father of modern magic;" Harry Houdini; scores more. Altogether a pleasure package for anyone interested in magic, stage setting and design, ethnology, psychology, or simply in unusual people. A Dover original. 295 illustrations; 8 in full color. Index. viii + 216pp. 8⅜ x 11¼.
T774 Paperbound **$2.25**

HOUDINI ON MAGIC, Harry Houdini. One of the greatest magicians of modern times explains his most prized secrets. How locks are picked, with illustrated picks and skeleton keys; how a girl is sawed into twins; how to walk through a brick wall — Houdini's explanations of 44 stage tricks with many diagrams. Also included is a fascinating discussion of great magicians of the past and the story of his fight against fraudulent mediums and spiritualists. Edited by W.B. Gibson and M.N. Young. Bibliography. 155 figures, photos. xv + 280pp. 5⅜ x 8.
T384 Paperbound **$1.25**

MATHEMATICS, MAGIC AND MYSTERY, Martin Gardner. Why do card tricks work? How do magicians perform astonishing mathematical feats? How is stage mind-reading possible? This is the first book length study explaining the application of probability, set theory, theory of numbers, topology, etc., to achieve many startling tricks. Non-technical, accurate, detailed! 115 sections discuss tricks with cards, dice, coins, knots, geometrical vanishing illusions, how a Curry square "demonstrates" that the sum of the parts may be greater than the whole, and dozens of others. No sleight of hand necessary! 135 illustrations. xii + 174pp. 5⅜ x 8.
T335 Paperbound **$1.00**

EASY-TO-DO ENTERTAINMENTS AND DIVERSIONS WITH COINS, CARDS, STRING, PAPER AND MATCHES, R. M. Abraham. Over 300 tricks, games and puzzles will provide young readers with absorbing fun. Sections on card games; paper-folding; tricks with coins, matches and pieces of string; games for the agile; toy-making from common household objects; mathematical recreations; and 50 miscellaneous pastimes. Anyone in charge of groups of youngsters, including hard-pressed parents, and in need of suggestions on how to keep children sensibly amused and quietly content will find this book indispensable. Clear, simple text, copious number of delightful line drawings and illustrative diagrams. Originally titled "Winter Nights Entertainments." Introduction by Lord Baden Powell. 329 illustrations. v + 186pp. 5⅜ x 8½.
T921 Paperbound **$1.00**

STRING FIGURES AND HOW TO MAKE THEM, Caroline Furness Jayne. 107 string figures plus variations selected from the best primitive and modern examples developed by Navajo, Apache, pygmies of Africa, Eskimo, in Europe, Australia, China, etc. The most readily understandable, easy-to-follow book in English on perennially popular recreation. Crystal-clear exposition; step-by-step diagrams. Everyone from kindergarten children to adults looking for unusual diversion will be endlessly amused. Index. Bibliography. Introduction by A. C. Haddon. 17 full-page plates. 960 illustrations. xxiii + 401pp. 5⅜ x 8½.
T152 Paperbound **$2.00**

Entertainments, Humor

ODDITIES AND CURIOSITIES OF WORDS AND LITERATURE, C. Bombaugh, edited by M. Gardner. The largest collection of idiosyncratic prose and poetry techniques in English, a legendary work in the curious and amusing bypaths of literary recreations and the play technique in literature—so important in modern works. Contains alphabetic poetry, acrostics, palindromes, scissors verse, centos, emblematic poetry, famous literary puns, hoaxes, notorious slips of the press, hilarious mistranslations, and much more. Revised and enlarged with modern material by Martin Gardner. 368pp. 5⅜ x 8. T759 Paperbound **$1.50**

A NONSENSE ANTHOLOGY, collected by Carolyn Wells. 245 of the best nonsense verses ever written, including nonsense puns, absurd arguments, mock epics and sagas, nonsense ballads, odes, "sick" verses, dog-Latin verses, French nonsense verses, songs. By Edward Lear, Lewis Carroll, Gelett Burgess, W. S. Gilbert, Hilaire Belloc, Peter Newell, Oliver Herford, etc., 83 writers in all plus over four score anonymous nonsense verses. A special section of limericks, plus famous nonsense such as Carroll's "Jabberwocky" and Lear's "The Jumblies" and much excellent verse virtually impossible to locate elsewhere. For 50 years considered the best anthology available. Index of first lines specially prepared for this edition. Introduction by Carolyn Wells. 3 indexes: Title, Author, First lines. xxxiii + 279pp. T499 Paperbound **$1.25**

THE BAD CHILD'S BOOK OF BEASTS, MORE BEASTS FOR WORSE CHILDREN, and A MORAL ALPHABET, H. Belloc. Hardly an anthology of humorous verse has appeared in the last 50 years without at least a couple of these famous nonsense verses. But one must see the entire volumes—with all the delightful original illustrations by Sir Basil Blackwood—to appreciate fully Belloc's charming and witty verses that play so subacidly on the platitudes of life and morals that beset his day—and ours. A great humor classic. Three books in one. Total of 157pp. 5⅜ x 8. T749 Paperbound **$1.00**

THE DEVIL'S DICTIONARY, Ambrose Bierce. Sardonic and irreverent barbs puncturing the pomposities and absurdities of American politics, business, religion, literature, and arts, by the country's greatest satirist in the classic tradition. Epigrammatic as Shaw, piercing as Swift, American as Mark Twain, Will Rogers, and Fred Allen, Bierce will always remain the favorite of a small coterie of enthusiasts, and of writers and speakers whom he supplies with "some of the most gorgeous witticisms of the English language" (H. L. Mencken). Over 1000 entries in alphabetical order. 144pp. 5⅜ x 8. T487 Paperbound **$1.00**

THE PURPLE COW AND OTHER NONSENSE, Gelett Burgess. The best of Burgess's early nonsense, selected from the first edition of the "Burgess Nonsense Book." Contains many of his most unusual and truly awe-inspiring pieces: 36 nonsense quatrains, the Poems of Patagonia, Alphabet of Famous Goops, and the other hilarious (and rare) adult nonsense that place him in the forefront of American humorists. All pieces are accompanied by the original Burgess illustrations. 123 illustrations. xiii + 113pp. 5⅜ x 8. T772 Paperbound **$1.00**

MY PIOUS FRIENDS AND DRUNKEN COMPANIONS and MORE PIOUS FRIENDS AND DRUNKEN COMPANIONS, Frank Shay. Folksingers, amateur and professional, and everyone who loves singing: here, available for the first time in 30 years, is this valued collection of 132 ballads, blues, vaudeville numbers, drinking songs, sea chanties, comedy songs. Songs of pre-Beatnik Bohemia; songs from all over America, England, France, Australia; the great songs of the Naughty Nineties and early twentieth-century America. Over a third with music. Woodcuts by John Held, Jr. convey perfectly the brash insouciance of an era of rollicking unabashed song. 12 illustrations by John Held, Jr. Two indexes (Titles and First lines and Choruses). Introductions by the author. Two volumes bound as one. Total of xvi + 235pp. 5⅜ x 8½. T946 Paperbound **$1.00**

HOW TO TELL THE BIRDS FROM THE FLOWERS, R. W. Wood. How not to confuse a carrot with a parrot, a grape with an ape, a puffin with nuffin. Delightful drawings, clever puns, absurd little poems point out far-fetched resemblances in nature. The author was a leading physicist. Introduction by Margaret Wood White. 106 illus. 60pp. 5⅜ x 8. T523 Paperbound **75¢**

PECK'S BAD BOY AND HIS PA, George W. Peck. The complete edition, containing both volumes, of one of the most widely read American humor books. The endless ingenious pranks played by bad boy "Hennery" on his pa and the grocery man, the outraged pomposity of Pa, the perpetual ridiculing of middle class institutions, are as entertaining today as they were in 1883. No pale sophistications or subtleties, but rather humor vigorous, raw, earthy, imaginative, and, as folk humor often is, sadistic. This peculiarly fascinating book is also valuable to historians and students of American culture as a portrait of an age. 100 original illustrations by True Williams. Introduction by E. F. Bleiler. 347pp. 5⅜ x 8. T497 Paperbound **$1.35**

THE HUMOROUS VERSE OF LEWIS CARROLL. Almost every poem Carroll ever wrote, the largest collection ever published, including much never published elsewhere: 150 parodies, burlesques, riddles, ballads, acrostics, etc., with 130 original illustrations by Tenniel, Carroll, and others. "Addicts will be grateful . . . there is nothing for the faithful to do but sit down and fall to the banquet," N. Y. Times. Index to first lines. xiv + 446pp. 5⅜ x 8.
T654 Paperbound **$1.85**

DIVERSIONS AND DIGRESSIONS OF LEWIS CARROLL. A major new treasure for Carroll fans! Rare privately published humor, fantasy, puzzles, and games by Carroll at his whimsical best, with a new vein of frank satire. Includes many new mathematical amusements and recreations, among them the fragmentary Part III of "Curiosa Mathematica." Contains "The Rectory Umbrella," "The New Belfry," "The Vision of the Three T's," and much more. New 32-page supplement of rare photographs taken by Carroll. x + 375pp. 5⅜ x 8.
T732 Paperbound **$1.65**

THE COMPLETE NONSENSE OF EDWARD LEAR. This is the only complete edition of this master of gentle madness available at a popular price. A BOOK OF NONSENSE, NONSENSE SONGS, MORE NONSENSE SONGS AND STORIES in their entirety with all the old favorites that have delighted children and adults for years. The Dong With A Luminous Nose, The Jumblies, The Owl and the Pussycat, and hundreds of other bits of wonderful nonsense. 214 limericks, 3 sets of Nonsense Botany, 5 Nonsense Alphabets, 546 drawings by Lear himself, and much more. 320pp. 5⅜ x 8.
T167 Paperbound **$1.00**

THE MELANCHOLY LUTE, The Humorous Verse of Franklin P. Adams ("FPA"). The author's own selection of light verse, drawn from thirty years of FPA's column, "The Conning Tower," syndicated all over the English-speaking world. Witty, perceptive, literate, these ninety-six poems range from parodies of other poets, Millay, Longfellow, Edgar Guest, Kipling, Masefield, etc., and free and hilarious translations of Horace and other Latin poets, to satiric comments on fabled American institutions—the New York Subways, preposterous ads, suburbanites, sensational journalism, etc. They reveal with vigor and clarity the humor, integrity and restraint of a wise and gentle American satirist. Introduction by Robert Hutchinson. vi + 122pp. 5⅜ x 8½.
T108 Paperbound **$1.00**

SINGULAR TRAVELS, CAMPAIGNS, AND ADVENTURES OF BARON MUNCHAUSEN, R. E. Raspe, with 90 illustrations by Gustave Doré. The first edition in over 150 years to reestablish the deeds of the Prince of Liars exactly as Raspe first recorded them in 1785—the genuine Baron Munchausen, one of the most popular personalities in English literature. Included also are the best of the many sequels, written by other hands. Introduction on Raspe by J. Carswell. Bibliography of early editions. xliv + 192pp. 5⅜ x 8.
T698 Paperbound **$1.00**

THE WIT AND HUMOR OF OSCAR WILDE, ed. by Alvin Redman. Wilde at his most brilliant, in 1000 epigrams exposing weaknesses and hypocrisies of "civilized" society. Divided into 49 categories—sin, wealth, women, America, etc.—to aid writers, speakers. Includes excerpts from his trials, books, plays, criticism. Formerly "The Epigrams of Oscar Wilde." Introduction by Vyvyan Holland, Wilde's only living son. Introductory essay by editor. 260pp. 5⅜ x 8.
T602 Paperbound **$1.00**

MAX AND MORITZ, Wilhelm Busch. Busch is one of the great humorists of all time, as well as the father of the modern comic strip. This volume, translated by H. A. Klein and other hands, contains the perennial favorite "Max and Moritz" (translated by C. T. Brooks), Plisch and Plum, Das Rabennest, Eispeter, and seven other whimsical, sardonic, jovial, diabolical cartoon and verse stories. Lively English translations parallel the original German. This work has delighted millions, since it first appeared in the 19th century, and is guaranteed to please almost anyone. Edited by H. A. Klein, with an afterword. x + 205pp. 5⅝ x 8½.
T181 Paperbound **$1.00**

HYPOCRITICAL HELENA, Wilhelm Busch. A companion volume to "Max and Moritz," with the title piece (Die Fromme Helena) and 10 other highly amusing cartoon and verse stories, all newly translated by H. A. Klein and M. C. Klein: Adventure on New Year's Eve (Abenteuer in der Neujahrsnacht), Hangover on the Morning after New Year's Eve (Der Katzenjammer am Neujahrsmorgen), etc. English and German in parallel columns. Hours of pleasure, also a fine language aid. x + 205pp. 5⅝ x 8½.
T184 Paperbound **$1.00**

THE BEAR THAT WASN'T, Frank Tashlin. What does it mean? Is it simply delightful wry humor, or a charming story of a bear who wakes up in the midst of a factory, or a satire on Big Business, or an existential cartoon-story of the human condition, or a symbolization of the struggle between conformity and the individual? New York Herald Tribune said of the first edition: ". . . a fable for grownups that will be fun for children. Sit down with the book and get your own bearings." Long an underground favorite with readers of all ages and opinions. v + 51pp. Illustrated. 5⅜ x 8½.
T939 Paperbound **75¢**

RUTHLESS RHYMES FOR HEARTLESS HOMES and MORE RUTHLESS RHYMES FOR HEARTLESS HOMES, Harry Graham ("Col. D. Streamer"). Two volumes of Little Willy and 48 other poetic disasters. A bright, new reprint of oft-quoted, never forgotten, devastating humor by a precursor of today's "sick" joke school. For connoisseurs of wicked, wacky humor and all who delight in the comedy of manners. Original drawings are a perfect complement. 61 illustrations. Index. vi + 69pp. Two vols. bound as one. 5⅜ x 8½.
T930 Paperbound **75¢**

CATALOGUE OF DOVER BOOKS

Say It language phrase books

These handy phrase books (128 to 196 pages each) make grammatical drills unnecessary for an elementary knowledge of a spoken foreign language. Covering most matters of travel and everyday life each volume contains:

> Over 1000 phrases and sentences in immediately useful forms — foreign language plus English.

> Modern usage designed for Americans. Specific phrases like, "Give me small change," and "Please call a taxi."

> Simplified phonetic transcription you will be able to read at sight.

> The only completely indexed phrase books on the market.

> Covers scores of important situations: — Greetings, restaurants, sightseeing, useful expressions, etc.

These books are prepared by native linguists who are professors at Columbia, N.Y.U., Fordham and other great universities. Use them independently or with any other book or record course. They provide a supplementary living element that most other courses lack. Individual volumes in:

Russian 75¢	Italian 75¢	Spanish 75¢	German 75¢
Hebrew 75¢	Danish 75¢	Japanese 75¢	Swedish 75¢
Dutch 75¢	Esperanto 75¢	Modern Greek 75¢	Portuguese 75¢
Norwegian 75¢	Polish 75¢	French 75¢	Yiddish 75¢
Turkish 75¢		English for German-speaking people 75¢	
English for Italian-speaking people 75¢		English for Spanish-speaking people 75¢	

Large clear type. 128-196 pages each. 3½ x 5¼. Sturdy paper binding.

Listen and Learn language records

LISTEN & LEARN is the only language record course designed especially to meet your travel and everyday needs. It is available in separate sets for FRENCH, SPANISH, GERMAN, JAPANESE, RUSSIAN, MODERN GREEK, PORTUGUESE, ITALIAN and HEBREW, and each set contains three 33⅓ rpm long-playing records—1½ hours of recorded speech by eminent native speakers who are professors at Columbia, New York University, Queens College.

Check the following special features found only in LISTEN & LEARN:

- **Dual-language recording.** 812 selected phrases and sentences, over 3200 words, spoken first in English, then in their foreign language equivalents. A suitable pause follows each foreign phrase, allowing you time to repeat the expression. You learn by unconscious assimilation.

- **128 to 206-page manual** contains everything on the records, plus a simple phonetic pronunciation guide.

- **Indexed for convenience.** The only set on the market that is completely indexed. No more puzzling over where to find the phrase you need. Just look in the rear of the manual.

- **Practical.** No time wasted on material you can find in any grammar. LISTEN & LEARN covers central core material with phrase approach. Ideal for the person with limited learning time.

- **Living, modern expressions,** not found in other courses. Hygienic products, modern equipment, shopping—expressions used every day, like "nylon" and "air-conditioned."

- **Limited objective.** Everything you learn, no matter where you stop, is immediately useful. You have to finish other courses, wade through grammar and vocabulary drill, before they help you.

- **High-fidelity recording.** LISTEN & LEARN records equal in clarity and surface-silence any record on the market costing up to $6.

"Excellent . . . the spoken records . . . impress me as being among the very best on the market," **Prof. Mario Pei,** Dept. of Romance Languages, Columbia University. "Inexpensive and well-done . . . it would make an ideal present," CHICAGO SUNDAY TRIBUNE. "More genuinely helpful than anything of its kind which I have previously encountered," **Sidney Clark,** well-known author of "ALL THE BEST" travel books.

UNCONDITIONAL GUARANTEE. Try LISTEN & LEARN, then return it within 10 days for full refund if you are not satisfied.

Each set contains three twelve-inch 33⅓ records, manual, and album.

SPANISH	the set $5.95	GERMAN	the set $5.95
FRENCH	the set $5.95	ITALIAN	the set $5.95
RUSSIAN	the set $5.95	JAPANESE	the set $5.95
PORTUGUESE	the set $5.95	MODERN GREEK	the set $5.95
MODERN HEBREW	the set $5.95		

Americana

THE EYES OF DISCOVERY, J. Bakeless. A vivid reconstruction of how unspoiled America appeared to the first white men. Authentic and enlightening accounts of Hudson's landing in New York, Coronado's trek through the Southwest; scores of explorers, settlers, trappers, soldiers. America's pristine flora, fauna, and Indians in every region and state in fresh and unusual new aspects. "A fascinating view of what the land was like before the first highway went through," Time. 68 contemporary illustrations, 39 newly added in this edition. Index. Bibliography. x + 500pp. 5⅜ x 8. **T761 Paperbound $2.00**

AUDUBON AND HIS JOURNALS, J. J. Audubon. A collection of fascinating accounts of Europe and America in the early 1800's through Audubon's own eyes. Includes the Missouri River Journals —an eventful trip through America's untouched heartland, the Labrador Journals, the European Journals, the famous "Episodes", and other rare Audubon material, including the descriptive chapters from the original letterpress edition of the "Ornithological Studies", omitted in all later editions. Indispensable for ornithologists, naturalists, and all lovers of Americana and adventure. 70-page biography by Audubon's granddaughter. 38 illustrations. Index. Total of 1106pp. 5⅜ x 8.

T675 Vol I Paperbound **$2.00**
T676 Vol II Paperbound **$2.00**
The set **$4.00**

TRAVELS OF WILLIAM BARTRAM, edited by Mark Van Doren. The first inexpensive illustrated edition of one of the 18th century's most delightful books is an excellent source of first-hand material on American geography, anthropology, and natural history. Many descriptions of early Indian tribes are our only source of information on them prior to the infiltration of the white man. "The mind of a scientist with the soul of a poet," John Livingston Lowes. 13 original illustrations and maps. Edited with an introduction by Mark Van Doren. 448pp. 5⅜ x 8. **T13 Paperbound $2.00**

GARRETS AND PRETENDERS: A HISTORY OF BOHEMIANISM IN AMERICA, A. Parry. The colorful and fantastic history of American Bohemianism from Poe to Kerouac. This is the only complete record of hoboes, cranks, starving poets, and suicides. Here are Pfaff, Whitman, Crane, Bierce, Pound, and many others. New chapters by the author and by H. T. Moore bring this thorough and well-documented history down to the Beatniks. "An excellent account," N. Y. Times. Scores of cartoons, drawings, and caricatures. Bibliography. Index. xxviii + 421pp. 5⅝ x 8⅜. **T708 Paperbound $1.95**

THE EXPLORATION OF THE COLORADO RIVER AND ITS CANYONS, J. W. Powell. The thrilling first-hand account of the expedition that filled in the last white space on the map of the United States. Rapids, famine, hostile Indians, and mutiny are among the perils encountered as the unknown Colorado Valley reveals its secrets. This is the only uncut version of Major Powell's classic of exploration that has been printed in the last 60 years. Includes later reflections and subsequent expedition. 250 illustrations, new map. 400pp. 5⅝ x 8⅜.
T94 Paperbound $2.00

THE JOURNAL OF HENRY D. THOREAU, Edited by Bradford Torrey and Francis H. Allen. Henry Thoreau is not only one of the most important figures in American literature and social thought; his voluminous journals (from which his books emerged as selections and crystallizations) constitute both the longest, most sensitive record of personal internal development and a most penetrating description of a historical moment in American culture. This present set, which was first issued in fourteen volumes, contains Thoreau's entire journals from 1837 to 1862, with the exception of the lost years which were found only recently. We are reissuing it, complete and unabridged, with a new introduction by Walter Harding, Secretary of the Thoreau Society. Fourteen volumes reissued in two volumes. Foreword by Henry Seidel Canby. Total of 1888pp. 8⅜ x 12¼. **T312-3 Two volume set, Clothbound $20.00**

GAMES AND SONGS OF AMERICAN CHILDREN, collected by William Wells Newell. A remarkable collection of 190 games with songs that accompany many of them; cross references to show similarities, differences among them; variations; musical notation for 38 songs. Textual discussions show relations with folk-drama and other aspects of folk tradition. Grouped into categories for ready comparative study: Love-games, histories, playing at work, human life, bird and beast, mythology, guessing-games, etc. New introduction covers relations of songs and dances to timeless heritage of folklore, biographical sketch of Newell, other pertinent data. A good source of inspiration for those in charge of groups of children and a valuable reference for anthropologists, sociologists, psychiatrists. Introduction by Carl Withers. New indexes of first lines, games. 5⅜ x 8½. xii + 242pp. **T354 Paperbound $1.65**

Art, History of Art, Antiques, Graphic Arts, Handcrafts

ART STUDENTS' ANATOMY, E. J. Farris. Outstanding art anatomy that uses chiefly living objects for its illustrations. 71 photos of undraped men, women, children are accompanied by carefully labeled matching sketches to illustrate the skeletal system, articulations and movements, bony landmarks, the muscular system, skin, fasciae, fat, etc. 9 x-ray photos show movement of joints. Undraped models are shown in such actions as serving in tennis, drawing a bow in archery, playing football, dancing, preparing to spring and to dive. Also discussed and illustrated are proportions, age and sex differences, the anatomy of the smile, etc. 8 plates by the great early 18th century anatomic illustrator Siegfried Albinus are also included. Glossary. 158 figures, 7 in color. x + 159pp. 5⅝ x 8⅜.   T744 Paperbound **$1.45**

AN ATLAS OF ANATOMY FOR ARTISTS, F Schider. A new 3rd edition of this standard text enlarged by 52 new illustrations of hands, anatomical studies by Cloquet, and expressive life studies of the body by Barcsay. 189 clear, detailed plates offer you precise information of impeccable accuracy. 29 plates show all aspects of the skeleton, with closeups of special areas, while 54 full-page plates, mostly in two colors, give human musculature as seen from four different points of view, with cutaways for important portions of the body. 14 full-page plates provide photographs of hand forms, eyelids, female breasts, and indicate the location of muscles upon models. 59 additional plates show how great artists of the past utilized human anatomy. They reproduce sketches and finished work by such artists as Michelangelo, Leonardo da Vinci, Goya, and 15 others. This is a lifetime reference work which will be one of the most important books in any artist's library. "The standard reference tool," AMERICAN LIBRARY ASSOCIATION. "Excellent," AMERICAN ARTIST. Third enlarged edition. 189 plates, 647 illustrations. xxvi + 192pp. 7⅞ x 10⅝.   T241 Clothbound **$6.00**

AN ATLAS OF ANIMAL ANATOMY FOR ARTISTS, W. Ellenberger, H. Baum, H. Dittrich. The largest, richest animal anatomy for artists available in English. 99 detailed anatomical plates of such animals as the horse, dog, cat, lion, deer, seal, kangaroo, flying squirrel, cow, bull, goat, monkey, hare, and bat. Surface features are clearly indicated, while progressive beneath-the-skin pictures show musculature, tendons, and bone structure. Rest and action are exhibited in terms of musculature and skeletal structure and detailed cross-sections are given for heads and important features. The animals chosen are representative of specific families so that a study of these anatomies will provide knowledge of hundreds of related species. "Highly recommended as one of the very few books on the subject worthy of being used as an authoritative guide," DESIGN. "Gives a fundamental knowledge," AMERICAN ARTIST. Second revised, enlarged edition with new plates from Cuvier, Stubbs, etc. 288 illustrations. 153pp. 11⅜ x 9.   T82 Clothbound **$6.00**

THE HUMAN FIGURE IN MOTION, Eadweard Muybridge. The largest selection in print of Muybridge's famous high-speed action photos of the human figure in motion. 4789 photographs illustrate 162 different actions: men, women, children—mostly undraped—are shown walking, running, carrying various objects, sitting, lying down, climbing, throwing, arising, and performing over 150 other actions. Some actions are shown in as many as 150 photographs each. All in all there are more than 500 action strips in this enormous volume, series shots taken at shutter speeds of as high as 1/6000th of a second! These are not posed shots, but true stopped motion. They show bone and muscle in situations that the human eye is not fast enough to capture. Earlier, smaller editions of these prints have brought $40 and more on the out-of-print market. "A must for artists," ART IN FOCUS. "An unparalleled dictionary of action for all artists," AMERICAN ARTIST. 390 full-page plates, with 4789 photographs. Printed on heavy glossy stock. Reinforced binding with headbands. xxi + 390pp. 7⅞ x 10⅝.   T204 Clothbound **$10.00**

ANIMALS IN MOTION, Eadweard Muybridge. This is the largest collection of animal action photos in print. 34 different animals (horses, mules, oxen, goats, camels, pigs, cats, guanacos, lions, gnus, deer, monkeys, eagles—and 21 others) in 132 characteristic actions. The horse alone is shown in more than 40 different actions. All 3919 photographs are taken in series at speeds up to 1/6000th of a second. The secrets of leg motion, spinal patterns, head movements, strains and contortions shown nowhere else are captured. You will see exactly how a lion sets his foot down; how an elephant's knees are like a human's—and how they differ; the position of a kangaroo's legs in mid-leap; how an ostrich's head bobs; details of the flight of birds—and thousands of facets of motion only the fastest cameras can catch. Photographed from domestic animals and animals in the Philadelphia zoo, it contains neither semiposed artificial shots nor distorted telephoto shots taken under adverse conditions. Artists, biologists, decorators, cartoonists, will find this book indispensable for understanding animals in motion. "A really marvelous series of plates," NATURE (London). "The dry plate's most spectacular early use was by Eadweard Muybridge," LIFE. 3919 photographs; 380 full pages of plates. 440pp. Printed on heavy glossy paper. Deluxe binding with headbands. 7⅞ x 10⅝.   T203 Clothbound **$10.00**

THE AUTOBIOGRAPHY OF AN IDEA, Louis Sullivan. The pioneer architect whom Frank Lloyd Wright called "the master" reveals an acute sensitivity to social forces and values in this passionately honest account. He records the crystallization of his opinions and theories, the growth of his organic theory of architecture that still influences American designers and architects, contemporary ideas, etc. This volume contains the first appearance of 34 full-page plates of his finest architecture. Unabridged reissue of 1924 edition. New introduction by R. M. Line. Index. xiv + 335pp. 5⅜ x 8.   T281 Paperbound **$2.00**

THE DRAWINGS OF HEINRICH KLEY. The first uncut republication of both of Kley's devastating sketchbooks, which first appeared in pre-World War I Germany. One of the greatest cartoonists and social satirists of modern times, his exuberant and iconoclastic fantasy and his extra-ordinary technique place him in the great tradition of Bosch, Breughel, and Goya, while his subject matter has all the immediacy and tension of our century. 200 drawings. viii + 128pp. 7¾ x 10¾.   T24 Paperbound **$1.85**

MORE DRAWINGS BY HEINRICH KLEY. All the sketches from Leut' Und Viecher (1912) and Sammel-Album (1923) not included in the previous Dover edition of Drawings. More of the bizarre, mercilessly iconoclastic sketches that shocked and amused on their original publica-tion. Nothing was too sacred, no one too eminent for satirization by this imaginative, in-dividual and accomplished master cartoonist. A total of 158 illustrations. lv + 104pp. 7¾ x 10¾.   T41 Paperbound **$1.85**

PINE FURNITURE OF EARLY NEW ENGLAND, R. H. Kettell. A rich understanding of one of America's most original folk arts that collectors of antiques, interior decorators, craftsmen, woodworkers, and everyone interested in American history and art will find fascinating and immensely useful. 413 illustrations of more than 300 chairs, benches, racks, beds, cupboards, mirrors, shelves, tables, and other furniture will show all the simple beauty and character of early New England furniture. 55 detailed drawings carefully analyze outstanding pieces. "With its rich store of illustrations, this book emphasizes the individuality and varied design of early American pine furniture. It should be welcomed," ANTIQUES. 413 illustrations and 55 working drawings. 475. 8 x 10¾.   T145 Clothbound **$10.00**

THE HUMAN FIGURE, J. H. Vanderpoel. Every important artistic element of the human figure is pointed out in minutely detailed word descriptions in this classic text and illustrated as well in 430 pencil and charcoal drawings. Thus the text of this book directs your attention to all the characteristic features and subtle differences of the male and female (adults, children, and aged persons), as though a master artist were telling you what to look for at each stage. 2nd edition, revised and enlarged by George Bridgman. Foreword. 430 illustrations. 143pp. 6⅛ x 9¼.   T432 Paperbound **$1.50**

LETTERING AND ALPHABETS, J. A. Cavanagh. This unabridged reissue of LETTERING offers a full discussion, analysis, illustration of 89 basic hand lettering styles — styles derived from Caslons, Bodonis, Garamonds, Gothic, Black Letter, Oriental, and many others. Upper and lower cases, numerals and common signs pictured. Hundreds of technical hints on make-up, construction, artistic validity, strokes, pens, brushes, white areas, etc. May be reproduced without permission! 89 complete alphabets; 72 lettered specimens. 121pp. 9¾ x 8. T53 Paperbound **$1.25**

STICKS AND STONES, Lewis Mumford. A survey of the forces that have conditioned American architecture and altered its forms. The author discusses the medieval tradition in early New England villages; the Renaissance influence which developed with the rise of the merchant class; the classical influence of Jefferson's time; the "Mechanicsvilles" of Poe's generation; the Brown Decades; the philosophy of the Imperial facade; and finally the modern machine age. "A truly remarkable book," SAT. REV. OF LITERATURE. 2nd revised edition. 21 illustra-tions. xvii + 228pp. 5⅜ x 8.   T202 Paperbound **$1.60**

THE STANDARD BOOK OF QUILT MAKING AND COLLECTING, Marguerite Ickis. A complete easy-to-follow guide with all the information you need to make beautiful, useful quilts. How to plan, design, cut, sew, appliqué, avoid sewing problems, use rag bag, make borders, tuft, every other aspect. Over 100 traditional quilts shown, including over 40 full-size patterns. At-home hobby for fun, profit. Index. 483 illus. 1 color plate. 287pp. 6¾ x 9½. T582 Paperbound **$2.00**

THE BOOK OF SIGNS, Rudolf Koch. Formerly $20 to $25 on the out-of-print market, now only $1.00 in this unabridged new edition! 493 symbols from ancient manuscripts, medieval cathe-drals, coins, catacombs, pottery, etc. Crosses, monograms of Roman emperors, astrological, chemical, botanical, runes, housemarks, and 7 other categories. Invaluable for handicraft workers, illustrators, scholars, etc., this material may be reproduced without permission. 493 illustrations by Fritz Kredel. 104pp. 6½ x 9¼.   T162 Paperbound **$1.00**

PRIMITIVE ART, Franz Boas. This authoritative and exhaustive work by a great American anthropologist covers the entire gamut of primitive art. Pottery, leatherwork, metal work, stone work, wood, basketry, are treated in detail. Theories of primitive art, historical depth in art history, technical virtuosity, unconscious levels of patterning, symbolism, styles, litera-ture, music, dance, etc. A must book for the interested layman, the anthropologist, artist, handicrafter (hundreds of unusual motifs), and the historian. Over 900 illustrations (50 ceramic vessels, 12 totem poles, etc.). 376pp. 5⅜ x 8.   T25 Paperbound **$1.95**

Fiction

FLATLAND, E. A. Abbott. A science-fiction classic of life in a 2-dimensional world that is also a first-rate introduction to such aspects of modern science as relativity and hyperspace. Political, moral, satirical, and humorous overtones have made FLATLAND fascinating reading for thousands. 7th edition. New introduction by Banesh Hoffmann. 16 illustrations. 128pp. 5⅜ x 8. T1 Paperbound **$1.00**

THE WONDERFUL WIZARD OF OZ, L. F. Baum. Only edition in print with all the original W. W. Denslow illustrations in full color—as much a part of "The Wizard" as Tenniel's drawings are of "Alice in Wonderland." "The Wizard" is still America's best-loved fairy tale, in which, as the author expresses it, "The wonderment and joy are retained and the heartaches and nightmares left out." Now today's young readers can enjoy every word and wonderful picture of the original book. New introduction by Martin Gardner. A Baum bibliography. 23 full-page color plates. viii + 268pp. 5⅜ x 8. T691 Paperbound **$1.45**

THE MARVELOUS LAND OF OZ, L. F. Baum. This is the equally enchanting sequel to the "Wizard," continuing the adventures of the Scarecrow and the Tin Woodman. The hero this time is a little boy named Tip, and all the delightful Oz magic is still present. This is the Oz book with the Animated Saw-Horse, the Woggle-Bug, and Jack Pumpkinhead. All the original John R. Neill illustrations, 10 in full color. 287 pp. 5⅜ x 8. T692 Paperbound **$1.45**

FIVE GREAT DOG NOVELS, edited by Blanche Cirker. The complete original texts of five classic dog novels that have delighted and thrilled millions of children and adults throughout the world with their stories of loyalty, adventure, and courage. Full texts of Jack London's "The Call of the Wild"; John Brown's "Rab and His Friends"; Alfred Ollivant's "Bob, Son of Battle"; Marshall Saunders's "Beautiful Joe"; and Ouida's "A Dog of Flanders." 21 Illustrations from the original editions. 495pp. 5⅜ x 8. T777 Paperbound **$1.50**

TO THE SUN? and OFF ON A COMET!, Jules Verne. Complete texts of two of the most imaginative flights into fancy in world literature display the high adventure that have kept Verne's novels read for nearly a century. Only unabridged edition of the best translation, by Edward Roth. Large, easily readable type. 50 illustrations selected from first editions. 462pp. 5⅜ x 8. T634 Paperbound **$1.75**

FROM THE EARTH TO THE MOON and ALL AROUND THE MOON, Jules Verne. Complete editions of 2 of Verne's most successful novels, in finest Edward Roth translations, now available after many years out of print. Verne's visions of submarines, airplanes, television, rockets, interplanetary travel; of scientific and not-so-scientific beliefs; of peculiarities of Americans; all delight and engross us today as much as when they first appeared. Large, easily readable type. 42 illus. from first French edition. 476pp. 5⅜ x 8. T633 Paperbound **$1.75**

THE CRUISE OF THE CACHALOT, Frank T. Bullen. Out of the experiences of many years on the high-seas, First Mate Bullen created this novel of adventure aboard an American whaler, shipping out of New Bedford, Mass., when American whaling was at the height of its splendor. Originally published in 1899, the story of the round-the-world cruise of the "Cachalot" in pursuit of the sperm whale has thrilled generations of readers. A maritime classic that will fascinate anyone interested in reading about the sea or looking for a solid old-fashioned yarn, while the vivid recreation of a brief but important chapter of Americana and the British author's often biting commentary on nineteenth-century Yankee mores offer insights into the colorful era of America's coming of age. 8 plates. xiii + 271pp. 5⅜ x 8½. T774 Paperbound **$1.00**

28 SCIENCE FICTION STORIES OF H. G. WELLS. Two full unabridged novels, MEN LIKE GODS and STAR BEGOTTEN, plus 26 short stories by the master science-fiction writer of all time! Stories of space, time, invention, exploration, future adventure—an indispensable part of the library of everyone interested in science and adventure. PARTIAL CONTENTS: Men Like Gods, The Country of the Blind, In the Abyss, The Crystal Egg, The Man Who Could Work Miracles, A Story of the Days to Come, The Valley of Spiders, and 21 more! 928pp. 5⅜ x 8. T265 Clothbound **$3.95**

DAVID HARUM, E. N. Westcott. This novel of one of the most lovable, humorous characters in American literature is a prime example of regional humor. It continues to delight people who like their humor dry, their characters quaint, and their plots ingenuous. First book edition to contain complete novel plus chapter found after author's death. Illustrations from first illustrated edition. 192pp. 5⅜ x 8. T580 Paperbound **$1.15**

GESTA ROMANORUM, trans. by Charles Swan, ed. by Wynnard Hooper. 181 tales of Greeks, Romans, Britons, Biblical characters, comprise one of greatest medieval story collections, source of plots for writers including Shakespeare, Chaucer, Gower, etc. Imaginative tales of wars, incest, thwarted love, magic, fantasy, allegory, humor, tell about kings, prostitutes, philosophers, fair damsels, knights, Noah, pirates, all walks, stations of life. Introduction. Notes. 500pp. 5⅜ x 8. T535 Paperbound **$1.85**

Music

A GENERAL HISTORY OF MUSIC, Charles Burney. A detailed coverage of music from the Greeks up to 1789, with full information on all types of music: sacred and secular, vocal and instrumental, operatic and symphonic. Theory, notation, forms, instruments, innovators, composers, performers, typical and important works, and much more in an easy, entertaining style. Burney covered much of Europe and spoke with hundreds of authorities and composers so that this work is more than a compilation of records . . . it is a living work of careful and first-hand scholarship. Its account of thoroughbass (18th century) Italian music is probably still the best introduction on the subject. A recent NEW YORK TIMES review said, "Surprisingly few of Burney's statements have been invalidated by modern research . . . still of great value." Edited and corrected by Frank Mercer. 35 figures. Indices. 1915pp. 5⅜ x 8. 2 volumes.   T36 The Set, Clothbound **$12.50**

A DICTIONARY OF HYMNOLOGY, John Julian. This exhaustive and scholarly work has become known as an invaluable source of hundreds of thousands of important and often difficult to obtain facts on the history and use of hymns in the western world. Everyone interested in hymns will be fascinated by the accounts of famous hymns and hymn writers and amazed by the amount of practical information he will find. More than 30,000 entries on individual hymns, giving authorship, date and circumstances of composition, publication, textual variations, translations, denominational and ritual usage, etc. Biographies of more than 9,000 hymn writers, and essays on important topics such as Christmas carols and children's hymns, and much other unusual and valuable information. A 200 page double-columned index of first lines — the largest in print. Total of 1786 pages in two reinforced clothbound volumes. 6¼ x 9¼.
The set, T333 Clothbound **$15.00**

MUSIC IN MEDIEVAL BRITAIN, F. Ll. Harrison. The most thorough, up-to-date, and accurate treatment of the subject ever published, beautifully illustrated. Complete account of institutions and choirs; carols, masses, and motets; liturgy and plainsong; and polyphonic music from the Norman Conquest to the Reformation. Discusses the various schools of music and their reciprocal influences; the origin and development of new ritual forms; development and use of instruments; and new evidence on many problems of the period. Reproductions of scores, over 200 excerpts from medieval melodies. Rules of harmony and dissonance; influence of Continental styles; great composers (Dunstable, Cornysh, Fairfax, etc.); and much more. Register and index of more than 400 musicians. Index of titles. General Index. 225-item bibliography. 6 Appendices. xix + 491pp. 5⅝ x 8¾.   T705 Clothbound **$10.00**

THE MUSIC OF SPAIN, Gilbert Chase. Only book in English to give concise, comprehensive account of Iberian music; new Chapter covers music since 1941. Victoria, Albéniz, Cabezón, Pedrell, Turina, hundreds of other composers; popular and folk music; the Gypsies; the guitar; dance, theatre, opera, with only extensive discussion in English of the Zarzuela; virtuosi such as Casals; much more. "Distinguished . . . readable," Saturday Review. 400-item bibliography. Index. 27 photos. 383pp. 5⅜ x 8.   T549 Paperbound **$2.00**

ON STUDYING SINGING, Sergius Kagen. An intelligent method of voice-training, which leads you around pitfalls that waste your time, money, and effort. Exposes rigid, mechanical systems, baseless theories, deleterious exercises. "Logical, clear, convincing . . . dead right," Virgil Thomson, N.Y. Herald Tribune. "I recommend this volume highly," Maggie Teyte, Saturday Review. 119pp. 5⅜ x 8.   T622 Paperbound **$1.25**

Dover publishes books on art, music, philosophy, literature, languages, history, social sciences, psychology, handcrafts, orientalia, puzzles and entertainments, chess, pets and gardens, books explaining science, intermediate and higher mathematics mathematical physics, engineering, biological sciences, earth sciences, classics of science, etc. Write to:

Dept. catrr.
Dover Publications, Inc.
180 Varick Street, N. Y. 14, N. Y.